**KEEP MUSIC EVIL
THE BRIAN JONESTOWN
MASSACRE STORY
JESSE VALENCIA**

**KEEP MUSIC EVIL
THE BRIAN JONESTOWN
MASSACRE STORY
JESSE VALENCIA**

A Jawbone book
First edition 2019
Published in the UK and the USA by
Jawbone Press
Office G1
141–157 Acre Lane
London SW2 5UA
England
www.jawbonepress.com

ISBN 978-1-911036-47-0

JACKET DESIGN Paul Palmer-Edwards,
www.paulpalmer-edwards.com

Printed in China

1 2 3 4 5 23 22 21 20 19

INTROESQUE

'*You*. Right *there*,' the man says as he points into the audience from the stage, teardrop guitar at his waist, blue eyes piercing through red stage lights. I thought he was looking at me, but he's pointing to someone just past me who had his phone up above everyone's heads with the flash on. 'You fuckin' hold that light in my eyes *one* more time, I will have you bounced on your fuckin' head. That was annoying as shit. How would you like it if *I* came to Taco Bell, where *you* work, and shined a light in *your* fuckin' eye?'

There is a mixture of cheers and groans from the crowd, as one might expect at a Brian Jonestown Massacre show, but what a way to close a song like 'Anemone.' Around the musician's neck is a wreath of holy beads. Sweat stains them against his white tunic, and he's dressed from head to toe in white, like an old desert prophet. A shaggy haircut and impressive sideburns frame his expression, which is quickly losing patience.

This man is Anton Newcombe, multi-instrumentalist, singer-songwriter, and leader of the psychedelic rock band known as The Brian Jonestown Massacre, though *band* may not be the right word. *Rogues gallery* might be more fitting.

They play on for another hour and a half. Then, at the close of 'Yeah, Yeah,' a drunk throws his half-empty beer can directly at Anton. It hits him in the back, leaking beer all over the stage and the people up front. Anton snaps angrily to the crowd and points in the general direction of this second assailant.

'Don't throw your fuckin' beer at me, you piece of shit. Why don't you come up here like a fuckin' man, you dickhead? Yeah, I asked you. Why don't you fuckin' come up here like a man? Don't throw your fuckin' beer can at me with my back turned to you, like a fuckin' pussy, but not even a pussy that does something good, like give birth to a nation. You're a fuckin' piece of shit. Don't throw your shit at me, you piece of shit. Have some respect for yourself, you fuckin' monkey. Thank you. There's ladies right in front of you, you know. You could hit them in the head. I don't care if you don't care about yourself, you fuckin' idiot. Have some respect for women, 'cause I can defend myself, you fuckin' asshole.'

There is applause as a minute or two passes, and then Anton addresses the audience at large. 'So, the guy who threw the beer can, you can thank him,' he says. 'We're just gonna wrap this show up.' Now there are boos and hollers. 'That's how people get beat up, basically,' Anton continues. 'By random mob violence.'

The show seems like it's about to end up in a riot, and for the better part of the twenty-five years leading up to this moment, that's exactly what would have happened.[*]

* * *

I witnessed my first Anton heckler at the band's show seven years earlier at the Clubhouse in Tempe. It was my first BJM show; Flavor Crystals opened. After they were finished, Anton and guitarist Ricky Maymi ran a Chang Fo Ji—a small plastic box with a speaker inside looping Buddhist prayers, given to them by Flavor Crystals' Josh Richardson—directly through the pedal board.

A half hour later, the BJM emerge from the green room. Anton is first on, tampering with quarter-inches and wires, sporting a denim jacket with the words 'The Kingdom Of God Is In' painted on the back—made for him by Icelandic multimedia artist Jón Sæmundur Auðarson, his collaborator for much of the album he's just put out, *My Bloody Underground*. The others walk around him as they make way to their places: organist/guitarist Rob 'The Cop' Campanella (so named for his constant wearing of aviator shades), then Ricky, then guitarist and former bassist Matt 'Good Times' Hollywood,[†] guitarist Frankie 'Teardrop' Emerson, bassist Collin Hegna, drummer Daniel Allaire, and, lastly, 'Spokesman For The Revolution,' percussionist

---

* A complete audio recording of this show, at the Crescent Ballroom in Phoenix, Arizona, on June 1, 2016, can be found on YouTube.

† 'I never have fun,' he says in *Dig!* 'That's why [they] call me Good Times.'

Joel Gion. The band fiddle around with cords, knobs, instruments, and mic placements for another three minutes or so. Once they start playing, everyone loses their minds because they are just fuckin' ripping through these songs. I make my way to almost the front of the stage when, after one song, the band are apparently taking too long to tune for one fan. He shouts '*Fuck you, Anton!*' and throws a water bottle in the singer's direction, but because there's nothing in it, it just flops through the air. A last few drops of water sprinkle over the crowd like a trail of comet dust.

Security make their way toward the perpetrator. All the real fans—the ones here for the music—single out the asshole trying to escape. The band ignore the incident until whatever song they're playing is over, at which point Anton reaches over to pick up the bottle.

'What is *this*?' he says. 'This is pathetic. Throwing shit at me?' he continues, not caring whether anyone can hear him or not. He scoffs and tosses aside the crunched-up plastic bottle as two beefy security guards drag the man away and throw him out the door. The band carry on into the next tune like nothing has happened, expressionless, except for maybe a 'here we go again' collective eye-roll, now that Anton's stopped the show.

Anton would not address the crowd again. He wouldn't even face us, but instead stood far off to the side, facing the band like a conductor. Another riot dodged, but throughout the set, he looked like he was pining for energy. Prior to this tour, he reportedly drank a liter of vodka a day before quitting drinking cold turkey, right before the first show. The next day, the band played Coachella.

I left that night feeling for the first time that I'd been a part of something greater than what my small mountain hometown of Show Low, Arizona, could offer. As everyone walked out of the venue, dazed and starry-eyed, I staggered into the parking lot to wait for my ride. My legs hurt a little, as I'd been standing too long, but at the same time I could feel every cell in my heart, mind, and soul bursting with sound, and it helped things hurt a little less.

* * *

Former guitarist Jeff Davies once described Anton as the 'father' of the band—he is both itself and its master. There is a general consensus that if there's anyone who truly knows the band's story from start to finish, Anton would be that person, because he *is* The Brian Jonestown Massacre, and the only consistent member throughout their decades-long history. One would therefore naturally assume that as such he is the only one who can really tell it from start to finish, and maybe one day he will. Until then, here we are.

Anton is not present in this narrative to any personal degree, beyond the few brushes I've had with him at BJM shows. Most of his quotes are from personal interactions I've had with him online; quotes from interviews across different media; or secondhand accounts by his bandmates and associates. Where relevant, I've drawn quotes from Ondi Timoner's 2004 documentary about the band, *Dig!*, but I must stress that Anton's absence in terms of participation should not be misread as a book incomplete, because at the same time it has opened up the possibility for other individuals in the band's history to express themselves freely. Some of them passed away before I could talk to them, and others passed away after I talked to them. Most are still here, at time of writing.

That's why this is not an unauthorized biography so much as it is a portrait. If Anton is sitting in a dark room, each voice is a different light on the subject, coming from a different angle. With enough of these lights, once you place them in the room a certain way, the picture becomes clearer and the portrait takes form.

I decided to write a book about the band because I fell in love with their music, and Anton's abrasive but charismatic personality, after seeing *Dig!* ten years ago, as I realized that all the bands I loved as a teenager in the early 2000s were in one way or another directly influenced by what the BJM and their friends The Dandy Warhols were doing the decade before. I also wanted to study Anton, learn from his craft, and apply what I took from the band's story to my own band and recording process, and then share what I learned with others.

I identify more as a musician than a writer, but writing this book has made me better at both. There is no point to art if it doesn't share with the world the roots of its inspiration, and that's something I feel Anton has achieved, greatly and consistently. In that way, its become a sort of duty to pass on what I've learned from this experience, as best as possible.

Dig! is now a cult classic, and it remains helpful with regards to the band's continued appeal. Anton's presence in the film has intrigued the public ever

7

since it was released. In it, he has fistfights with his band, tours the world, and pumps out record after record while enduring tragedies and struggles with heroin and alcohol. The film's narrative makes for good entertainment, but what isn't emphasized is who Anton really is: an artist bursting with creativity, shooting off ideas left and right with insatiable revolutionary fervor. He can also be very thoughtful, considerate, and helpful—all important aspects of his personality that are regrettably missing from the film. By now, we are well aware of his flaws.

Even so, his genius shines through. It's been fifteen years now since it came out, and writers still mention it in articles on the BJM or in interviews with Anton, but for all the good PR *Dig!* has generated for the group, an alternate narrative is long past due.

Since I started following them a year after first seeing it, the BJM have sold out venues around the world, and they are championed as prime movers in the contemporary psychedelic music scene.* I have had the privilege of riding this wave as a fan, and seeing the band's influence on American popular culture especially has been an endearing experience.

Sadly, because of 'fans' like the drunk hurling the beer can, it is still the case that some people go to BJM shows not to experience their music but to attempt to incite confrontation or violence by provoking Anton. They want to see an outburst—to experience the Anton of *Dig!* for themselves—and journalists have for years focused on these moments in ways that, from a PR perspective, has become the bane of the band's existence.†

Twenty years ago, during the filming of *Dig!*, Dave Deresinski, the band's old manager, would point directly into Ondi's camera as she sat next to him and prophesy that Anton will be put 'on trial' by the public as a result of the film. This book is, in some ways, an argument against their verdict.

* * *

---

* The word 'psychedelic' is derived from the Greek words *psihi* ('psyche' or 'soul') and *dilosi* ('manifest'), translating to 'a manifestation of the soul.' What better description could there be for the act of making music, whether premeditated or spontaneous? The soul manifests itself as sound and becomes music, existing as an object *in the world* so that others may make meaning through it for themselves.

† See, for example, Patrick James's 'The 20 Most Overrated Live Acts In Music' for *LA Weekly*, January 21, 2015.

The very first time I heard the BJM, I was frying on four hits of LSD. It was my first time using the drug; I'd been eager to try it as I was fascinated with its influence over the Western cultural renaissance of 1967. For me at that time, if this was the only chance I had to turn on, tune in, and drop out, as goes Dr. Leary's righteous maxim, I wanted my brain to explode.* It was a cold night in February 2008, and I was hanging out with my friends Jackson, Cody, and Tarryn in my hometown of Show Low. I was in the army at the time.

Jackson soaked four pieces of Honeycombs cereal from the dropper in his vial for me, and down the rabbit hole I went. Once the drug settled in, I remember, through an invisible wall of reverb and vibrations, Jackson saying, 'You've got to hear this *band*, man! They're gonna change your life!' He opened his MacBook, its case garnished with a peeling BJM sticker, clicked on his BJM playlist, and played the song 'Whoever You Are.' He was right. After that bass hit and the song exploded into my ears, I faithfully descended into The Brian Jonestown Massacre's acid-drenched, beautiful, sorrowful, mind-altering world of pain, resistance, and melancholy, and I haven't left since.

'Take Acid Now And Come See The Brian Jonestown Massacre' was actually the theme of one of the band's earliest flyers, and it sparked such a buzz in early 90s San Francisco, where the BJM are from, that it made it onto a primetime news program about drug culture. The reporters bemoaned that the antiauthoritarian spirit of the 60s had reared its ugly head once again. 'We wish we could find out where all this acid is being manufactured,' a local police chief grumbled on the program, 'so we could then, uh, take, uh … *appropriate* action.'

Anton, flanked by an army of teenagers, would put up giant posters featuring the phrase everywhere, and the next week they'd put up flyers with little baggies attached, filled with tiny tabs of colored paper, as a joke, although co-founding member Travis Threlkel tells me that some of the tabs were real. The first time BJM bassist (and later guitarist) Matt Hollywood spotted one of the flyers, he was riding the bus down Haight Street during the holidays, and he thought to himself, *That'd be interesting, to have to explain that to your parents, if that was your band.* Then, when he got closer to the next poster, a few blocks up, he realized that it was, in fact, *his* band.

9

---

* Dr. Leary spoke these famous words at the Human Be-In in San Francisco on January 14, 1967, among other occasions.

The first BJM record I bought was *Give It Back!*, which is the one 'Whoever You Are' is on. It is the first of a couple different albums that *Dig!* documents the making of. After that, I dug for the early records, from *Spacegirl & Other Favorites* to *Thank God For Mental Illness*, and then I got the records after *Give It Back!*, *Strung Out In Heaven* through *And This Is Our Music*. *My Bloody Underground* came out a couple months after that first acid trip, and I was frying every other day by that point, but I listened to all of these records and wondered about how Anton had made each of them. They were all so different, but they held a common thread. Whether it was an obscure noise collage, a ten-minute drone, a stripped-down folk number, or a full-on rocker, they all had this same vibe, this same driving, antiauthoritarian, dark spiritual wholeness that I hadn't found anywhere else, ever. They were like the soundtrack to life and death itself.

One thing that intrigued me was the way that Anton would end many of the albums' liner notes with his full name, followed by the year of his birth, and then a dash followed by the current year, as if to convey the idea that if this were his final work, his last gift of music to the world, that he would want this gift to also be his epitaph, just in case he died.

When I first started writing this book, it didn't take me long to realize that any comprehensive history of the band would at best comprise a slim fraction of the intricate tapestry of Anton's mythos, which is the stuff of legend, though the band's one-time producer and engineer, Mark Dutton, encouraged me to believe the hype. 'There's not a lot of made-up shit in that world,' he told me. 'It *all* happened.'

* * *

The name Brian Jonestown Massacre is a portmanteau of two mysterious, tragic figures of the 1960s: late Rolling Stones guitarist/founder Brian Jones and murderous cult leader Jim Jones. Brian Jones was partly responsible for introducing exotic instrumentation from faraway cultures into Western rock'n'roll. A misunderstood artist and innovator in his time, he ended up a member of the fabled 27 Club,* face down in a swimming pool. Jim Jones, by contrast, was responsible for one of the most catastrophic single-event losses

---

* A proverbial 'club' whose members are mostly famous musicians who died at the age of twenty-seven, among them Jim Morrison, Janis Joplin, Jimi Hendrix, and Kurt Cobain.

of American life until 9/11, having orchestrated the mass suicide of more than nine hundred of his followers in Guyana.

In addition to the BJM logo, images of Brian Jones appear often in album and poster art from the band's early period, thanks in part to a collection of books owned by Joel, who used to make flyers with Anton at their local Kinko's in San Francisco, where Dave D. worked for a while. Joel also named the song 'The Ballad Of Jim Jones,' from 1996's *Thank God For Mental Illness*—the last of three BJM records released that year—figuring there were plenty of references to Brian Jones in the catalogue, but not enough of Jim.

While Brian Jones and his Rolling Stones were without doubt influential on the BJM sound, Anton wasn't trying to emanate their music so much as he was taking after their founder. He thought it would be interesting to have the same approach as Brian Jones within the context of a band. 'I'm into the whole 60s sound and those intense feelings musically in that pop format, those classic pop structures,' he said in 1998. 'I'm really into folk music [and] that's what I consider my project to be: a folk-rock project.'

Anton defines 'folk music' as music of the people, for the people. 'I'm interested in creating cultures that replicate themselves,' he later said. 'You create an environment that you can function in.'

The environment in which Anton functions is definitely not for everybody. When asked if he's ever gotten any negative reactions to the band's name, he's said that it has been an issue since the beginning. People who were upset by it would confront him, but he felt their energy was misdirected. All he has done, as far as he is concerned, is acknowledge that the words themselves existed. So, if people get upset by what he calls his band or names his songs, it has to do more with their own worldview than it does Anton's aesthetic.

The name can also be read as a play on the dangers of fame and celebrity as they appear in our cultural narrative—something Anton claims he's been aware of since childhood. It was never his intent to cause harm to the victims of the 1978 Jonestown Massacre or their families by naming his band and music project in part after it. 'There was the interesting correlation between the way people treated rock stars and the whole cult nature of the thing,' he explained in 2014, 'like the way Jim Jones conducted himself … in front of his congregation.'

KEEP MUSIC EVIL

Though Anton is intrigued by the intersection of rock stars and cults, his goal as an artist was to be neither. He has always pointed out the bullshit in the music industry, and the sick social and corporate evils it fosters. Against this backdrop, he has said he views his work as '99 percent … dealing with love on a spiritual level,' and as such he's chosen 'to wrap the project in certain abrasive iconography,' such as the name, 'as a means of self-preservation.' Aware of the business's tendency to turn beautiful songs into adverts, he wanted his band to be 'too hot to handle,' even 'dangerous,' and he has compared his music to an 'exotic fruit with spines.' In other words, maneuver your way past the shell, the thorns, and maybe the first layer of meat, and you'll get to the good stuff.

Another way to say this is: *keep music evil.*

* * *

One thing that *Dig!* captures perfectly is Anton's antagonistic, ever-evolving relationship with the music industry. This is an artist who got his start in the 1980s Orange County punk scene, and who later was so broke when he got to San Francisco that he had to busk down Haight Street for cigarette money. He couldn't afford to record at studios, much less pay his own rent, so did his best with what he could to make the best records he could. To be someone like that and attract a strong following anyway, and to get to where he is today—movie or not—is a testament to his enduring talent and dedication. For Anton, staying power comes down to what an artist can add to an already vast popular lexicon, though he feels in his heart he's made a solid contribution. 'The music business tends to play up record sales, but there is a higher level of success, and that is being able to inspire others to study the arts,' he told the *Jerusalem Post* in 2012. I couldn't agree more, because, as you'll see, whether you make it or not, as long as you don't quit, you can really accomplish something.

This was also Ondi's stated intention with *Dig!*, though she is aware that most people who watch the film are primarily occupied with the band's chaos and violence, rather than their ideas. 'My whole purpose of making the film in the first place was to inspire people to be creative,' she says. The *Guardian* likened the film to an indie-rock *This Is Spinal Tap*, and Anton has acknowledged that the band's notorious image has always been a part of their charm. '[We've] always had that goofy side. I never wanted to play with people who were too good musicians. I taught my friends to play and it was a problem,' he said. 'Some of the most charming people I played with had serious drug problems, and I'd end up involved with them. There's the tragicomic aspect right there.'

Anton may say he's neither rock star nor cult leader, but upon first hearing his words in the opening scene of the movie—'I'm here to destroy this fucked-up system. I said use my hands, I will use our strength. Let's fuckin' burn it to the ground'—I was hooked like he was one, and from there the obsession grew far beyond my humble record collection, such was the potency of his charisma.

* * *

For the next BJM show I saw, I had to drive all the way to Denver, because they weren't coming through Phoenix. Inspired by a brief encounter with Anton earlier that day outside the venue, where I gave him my first manuscript, I poured myself into this idea of writing this book—to interview anyone and everyone who would talk to me, and tell their stories, though Anton would say only *he* knows the true stories. But, see, memory is a strange thing, and often, within any group of people, there are three or four different versions of the same events. Who knows where some of the stuff in between comes from. You think you remember places and people exactly as they were, but time has an interesting effect on things.

Once that next tour was over, I followed up with Anton, in search of advice, a direction. He wasn't having it. *It isn't my job to write your book*, he told me. *Find the story, steal it, or invent it.* So here it is, from the beginning. As it was told to me.

13

PARTONE

NOTES FROM TEPID PEPPERMINT WONDERLAND

GODSPELL

Born during the Summer of Love on August 29, 1967, in Newport Beach, California, Anton Newcombe grew up in an epicenter of the psychedelic culture with which he would later grow so fascinated, but his interests extended beyond the clichés of Vox guitars and paisley shirts and scarves to the true meaning of the word 'psychedelic'—expansion of the mind. It didn't go too far past the 60s at first, though. 'I listened to Jimi Hendrix, The Beatles' *Rubber Soul* and *Revolver*, Simon & Garfunkel … I liked every kind of music,' he once said.

Anton's mom, Patsy Latscha, loved music, and she would take Anton to record shops with her when he was a kid. On one such outing, when he was five, she handed him some money and told him to get something he thought he would like, so he went home with an Isaac Hayes LP (either *The Isaac Hayes Movement* or *Shaft*, depending on the telling). By age nine he was composing, and by age eleven he was detuning and taking apart guitars.

Among the string of Anton's creative and musical projects throughout the 80s, as he entered his teens, was a band called Electric Cool-Aide. They practiced in Anton's garage space sometimes, cranking it up until his neighbors complained about the noise. His next-door neighbor—who did not complain—became aware of Anton's passion for music and gave him his 60s vinyl collection after he'd 'outgrown' it.

Anton also found inspiration in contemporary groups like The Church, The Smiths, Cocteau Twins, Joy Division, and the production work of Joe Foster. Foster was a member of Television Personalities and went on to produce The Jesus & Mary Chain's first single ('Upside Down'), sign My Bloody Valentine, and start Creation records with Alan McGee and Dick

Green. McGee credits Foster with defining what came to be known as the Creation Sound.*

I've heard that Newport Beach could be a drag back then. Be out at night past ten o'clock or get caught without an ID and the police might harass you, maybe even throw you in jail for the night because they didn't like the way you looked. But cops weren't the only ones teenagers had to worry about. Bullies chased Anton and his friends down the street, too. The stigma of bullying, combined with Anton's lifelong individualist attitude, led him to Southern California's late-70s/early 80s punk scene. He even dressed the part, wearing earrings made from dead pigeons' feet lacquered by his old buddy and like-minded troublemaker Nick Sjobeck, whom he met in junior high (and who would go on to lead Electric Cool-Aide). Witnessing the punk scene up close led Anton to realize that a lot of people who went to these shows were glorifying destruction for its own sake, when what had appealed to him about punk was the idea of destroying the need for validation, and, where that might have concerned his music, a wall had been torn down for him.

From punk, Anton learned that it wasn't necessary to follow this commonly held notion that artists must follow a process of getting discovered, then having a label or a producer develop their talent, and then receive promotion and marketing and so forth, in order to make things happen for their work or their career. *To hell with all that*, he thought. He would do the whole thing himself.

Anton's former girlfriend and one-time muse, Dawn Thomas, believes that while he struggled with his relationships with his parents, he did enjoy great relationships with his grandparents and his sisters. 'I believe his family had some money at one point. It's hard to tell from the stories,' she says, 'but I've met them, and they're all very sweet people, especially John, his grandpa.'

Anton's grandparents lived in an unincorporated area near Newport Beach's Upper Back Bay, and he remembers his childhood days spent there fondly, fishing and playing on the beach. Anton lived with his mom and sisters in a cluttered, one-story cottage in Costa Mesa's gritty, working-class west side. It was here that he grew up, largely without his father, Robert Newcombe, who left the family when Anton was very young.

---

* '[Joe] developed his own Spector-like technique on a low budget,' McGee explained in the *Guardian* in 2008. 'That sound … was heavy reverb, heavy treble, and a melding of punk and psychedelia.' The influence of the Creation Sound can be heard in Anton's work right back to the very first BJM recordings, long before bands like Crystal Stilts, Wavves, or Vivian Girls took cues from it.

'That was my fault, being an alcoholic,' Robert says in *Dig!* 'I left the family when [Anton] was about a year, year and a half old … I had shown symptoms of schizophrenia … I drank every day. I'd hate to see him repeat his life like myself, two divorces and not getting a chance to raise your kids. [Anton] feels starved for affection, I think, [and] love. As a father, I probably failed immensely, and I feel guilty about that. If he has abandonment issues they're as much my responsibility as they are his. I noticed the album he gave me was *Thank God For Mental Illness.*'

'He always treated me like a Catholic saint, regardless of how old I was,' Anton later said of his father. 'He'd be praising me and asking my forgiveness. It'd be like, *I love you so much—please forgive me.* I can remember going, *You're just not making any sense.*'

Anton's relationship with his mother was also strained from early on, though in different ways. When Ondi interviewed Patsy for *Dig!*, she would not acknowledge her son's music as a respectable line of work. 'She had no clue what her son was about,' The Dandy Warhols' Zia McCabe later said of Patsy, 'but he seems to have come to terms with that.'

'My mom kind of disconnected from me emotionally when I was around six, because of her own head trip,' Anton later said. 'She was never there. She worked nights.'

In second grade, Anton befriended fellow bullying target Jamie Reidling, who, like Nick, knew Anton as 'Tony,' as do some of his other friends from back then. 'He was the weird kid that'd always bring little animals to school in his Boy Scout uniform,' Jamie recalled. 'There were all these little hippie kids who are probably in prison now that'd beat us up. I got my ass kicked and so did Tony. It was tough. If you were a punk kid like us you didn't have too many places to hang out, so we just hung out in his garage getting drunk.'

Even then, his old friends remember, Anton displayed a knack for bluster that would prove key to his success later with the BJM, but beyond that or experimenting with drugs and music, Anton's intellectual interests also blossomed. As a teenager, he grew fascinated with tales of Nazi mind control, Charles Manson, CIA conspiracy theories, the occult, and so on—interests that would expand exponentially later, and would carry over into his music. He once speculated that his fascination with these and other subjects began with esoteric-themed television shows such as Leonard Nemoy's *In Search*

17

Of. Not one for the cheap thrills, he found himself more drawn to reading, particularly works of nonfiction. While all his buddies were headed down to the arcade, he'd have his nose in a book.

When he wasn't reading, Anton could be found at the old upright parlor piano his mom kept among the heaps of newspaper and trash in their place. He taught himself to play it and eventually started writing songs. Another friend, Nate Shaw, later remembered Anton coming over to his house to play his 'terrible' compositions, but gave him credit for being 'tenacious as hell.'

Two decades later, when journalist, author, and Elephant Stone Records founder Ben Vendetta compared Anton's earliest work with the BJM to Spiritualized, Anton responded, 'I've got video tapes of me playing that style of music in 1981, before there was even Spacemen 3. I'm into one-note minimalism with continuous drone notes going through. That's the criteria in my composition. All my songs have a continuous note, whether it's cranked in the mix or totally buried.'

In the early 80s, Anton joined local punk group Kronic Disorder as vocalist. Nick Sjobeck's brother, Michael, says that it was around then that the intensity with which Anton was beginning to approach music became apparent. Anton and Michael's friendship spans over thirty years. The two of them went to gigs and often on road trips together, during which Anton would walk into an obscure café and perform his songs without the slightest warning or permission. Michael has many other stories of hanging out with Anton at his old house in Costa Mesa, crashing house parties in Orange County, running with the Communist Party's San Francisco chapter in the dead of night, plastering the town with 'Yankee Go Home!' propaganda, and then Anton being interviewed on a local LA news station after a punk show circa 1983, a tape of which still exists.

On a more recent occasion, Michael just happened to be back down in Orange County, a thousand miles from where he now lives in Portland, when suddenly he came across Anton, fifty miles from where he was supposed to be. Michael did not even know that his old friend was in the States, and yet there he was, glowing on the side of the road while being hassled and questioned by the Newport Beach police like they were teenagers again. 'All the while giving me this look like, *Don't even stop. Keep walking, Michael.* And I didn't! Although it'd been a good year or so since I'd seen him last.'

* * *

After Kronic Disorder broke up, Anton's grandparents bought him his own keyboard. When his mom wouldn't allow him to practice at home, Anton took the instrument to the Sjobecks' garage, where he played for hours on end. This eventually led to the formation of Electric Cool-Aide. Nate Shaw came in on guitar, Nick Sjobeck was on bass; Paulie Medina started out on drums, and then Jamie Reidling took over at the end of 1985. There was a William 'Scooby' Coholon on lead vocals, with Anton was on keys and co-lead vocals.

When they could manage it, ECA practiced in Anton's garage, where they could get properly fucked up, steal a keg or a nitrous tank, and work on songs or posters. Soon enough, they were booking gigs all over the Back Bay. Nick, who has recently reformed ECA, says Anton was in the group for about nine months. 'Tony insisted we kick Scooby out of the band 'cause he *danced too much* onstage, which he did,' he recalls, 'but Tony wanted Scooby out because Scooby could really sing well, and at that point Tony could not sing well at all. In fact, for Christmas 1985, Tony got a Boss Digital Delay pedal from his grandparents, and he would plug his microphone into the delay pedal to mask his voice. At that point, his real talent was in the visual arts, promotion, and songwriting … then, once we kicked Scooby out of the band, Tony moved to lead vocals.'

After dropping out of high school in 1985, Anton worked with Nick doing maintenance at the Newport Channel Inn. The job only lasted a few weeks, as Anton instead invested nearly all of his time and energy into promoting ECA. He spent hours on end at the local Kinko's, making flyers for shows that didn't exist. One of the posters he made had these pictures of psychiatric patients beneath the band's name, alongside the words, 'Paid for by the happy people who make your dreams come true.' He also worked briefly as a plumber's apprentice.

Anton increasingly pressured his bandmates, who were either still in school or had jobs or both, to dedicate more time and effort to the band. As a result, he'd alienate audiences at shows before they'd had a chance to play. 'We have more ideas in our pinkie finger than in the entire Capitol Records building! You don't even know!' he'd say. 'We're going to start a revolution and light the world on fire, and you're going to go down in history as being one of the people that didn't get it!'

'It was always the same diatribe, and if you didn't believe it, there'd be some kind of punitive outcome,' Nate recalled. 'He had all of these large-scale conceptual ideas that nobody paid attention to.' Anton later repeated a version of this speech while looking down, in self-avowed triumph, at the Capitol Records building from Runyon Canyon in Los Angeles, dressed completely in white (as captured in *Dig!*).

'The costume doesn't matter,' he once said. 'It is all about you anyways. What makes you feel good.'

One night in April 1986, Anton was kicked out of ECA following a scuffle at band practice. Anton, who was in one of his moods, violently shoved Nate; Nick stepped in and knocked Anton out with a punch to the face. Mark McGrath, later of Grammy-winning pop group Sugar Ray, was set to become Electric Cool-Aide's next singer after Anton, but the Sjobecks' mother thought him too much of a pretty boy, so the group booted him out. Instead, for the final configuration of ECA, which lasted from '89 to '90, they brought in Tony Scalzo, who was introduced to Anton during this time. 'He was already doing interesting, psych-based stuff by then,' he says.

Scalzo's move into the band proved fruitful. 'ECA with Nate, Nick, and Jamie was where I started writing my own songs to sing,' he adds, 'but by summer '93 I was gone to Texas, where I started Fastball.' A few years later, after Fastball had some hits on the radio, Tony saw Anton at a BJM after-party in San Francisco, during the time when the BJM were signed to TVT. 'We had a nice chat, but our paths have crossed little since the Costa Mesa days,' Tony recalls. 'I've always admired his aesthetic and his drive to follow his own muse. He's one of kind.'

Concerning his being kicked out of ECA, Michael says that Anton was upset with all of them, 'but he's always had strained relationships with most of his closest friends. Even so, he's never lashed out at me in any way, after all these years. I was fiercely introspective as a teenager, and maybe he identified with that, but in spite of all the sensationalism or seemingly staged antics of the early BJM, there has always been a truly heroic side of Anton that suits me well, whether it's him against the world, or him wanting to disrupt the music industry.

'He has his heart in the right place, and he cares about his friends and loved ones much more than anyone would suspect. My sister thought he would become schizophrenic … I thought he was just hypersensitive and extremely energetic from a creative standpoint. Sadly, it looks like her premonition is beginning to come true.'

Twenty-five years after he visited Michael in the mental hospital, Anton was admitted to the psych ward at St. Joseph's in Berlin after suffering a mental breakdown, though his history of mental illness dates back to at least age twelve—maybe earlier. Dawn Thomas says Anton's mom diagnosed him as bipolar at a very young age, adding that he was prescribed Ritalin, which he resented.

'I never wanted permission from anybody or validation to do anything,' he later said. 'My mom is a psychologist so she was like, *You're going to fucking end up in a mental hospital or prison, because you are so belligerent.*' Anton's music might be his escape from that struggle, as well as his means of fighting it, so it's always just poured out of him. Michael says he once possessed miles of cassette tape of Anton recording on the fly into a four-track in the 80s and early 90s. Much of it was lost in storage, but a few tapes still exist.

21

* * *

In 1987, Anton joined a group called Homeland, playing keyboards and vocals alongside Greg Derfer on guitar, Mike Kubisty on bass, and Brad Wilson on drums.* 'After Tony left ECA, we got hooked up with him,' Greg recalls. 'I could talk your ear off about Anton and some good and bad times we had as bandmates and friends.'†

Kubisty, who first met Anton around 1985 in Costa Mesa, later visited him in San Francisco and recorded 'Hide And Seek' with him when he was just starting the BJM, playing bass, acoustic guitar, and doing backing vocals. 'One day he stopped by and said, Why you don't come up and work on at least one song, like the one your messing around with right now?' he recalls. 'So he takes me to this studio that was pretty nice but very cold and somewhere in the ghetto … he worked his magic on the idea and I chimed back in, and *voilà*! I'm pretty proud of Anton in general. He had the guts to

---

* At the time of writing, all of Homeland's songs can be heard online via YouTube.
† Their last contact came in 1995, when Anton came to see Greg play drums with The Lemmings at a club called Mogul's in Hollywood.

tough out a lot stuff to get to where he is.' A live version of the song appears on 2004's *Tepid Peppermint Wonderland* compilation, released to capitalize on the attention that came to the band after the release of *Dig!* 'His bit was really a Smiths song,' Anton writes of Mike's contributions in the album's liner notes. 'I forced "Hide And Seek" out of that.' Milo Warner-Martin, who later played drums for the group briefly, is also credited on the track.

Mike spoke with Ondi for *Dig!* but declined to be in the film, while Greg didn't want to be interviewed for it at all. 'Anton has developed very well as an artist. It was his life back then, as it is now,' he says. 'We all knew he would end up where he is. He always had this huge energy, whereas music was just a hobby for us.'

For Greg, Anton's recent interest in and focus on theme and incidental music, as displayed on more recent BJM records, is no mystery. After band practice with Homeland, he recalls, Anton would toy in the studio until dawn or later, putting in more hours on their Fostex four-track recorder than they did—he jokes that Anton still owes them for repair charges. 'Anton is successful not because he's a genius,' he adds, 'but because he is talented and works extremely hard at being talented.' Some years later, Anton wrote in an email to Greg, 'I've been in the studio for three days and can't come up with anything. I guess I'm normal after all.'

In 1989, Homeland recorded a demo at Pyramid Productions on Newport Boulevard in Costa Mesa; not long after that, the band dissolved. 'They played my wedding in February 1989, so they were playing till then, at least,' Nick says. Soon after that, with a vision stirring in his mind, Anton left Orange County to start a revolution, deciding where to go by flipping a coin. Heads he'd go to Heidelberg, Germany. Tails he'd go to Northern California. He landed in the Haight.

1**2**345

THE WAY IT WAS

More commonly known to 60s enthusiasts as the Haight-Ashbury District that acted as the center of San Francisco's psychedelic rock'n'roll renaissance, locals typically refer to it as simply 'The Haight.' Now overrun with novelty shops, the Haight that gave the world the Grateful Dead, Jefferson Airplane, Quicksilver Messenger Service and other pioneers is no more. The Brian Jonestown Massacre were the Haight's last real psychedelic export before Silicon Valley choked the life out of it.

The Lower Haight, or everything below Divisadero Street, is where the early BJM story takes place. 'That's where the cafés were, plus the [rent] was still cheap,' says Mara Keagle, who is best known for providing the lead vocal on 'Anemone.' 'Before the dot-com boom and the first wave of techies gentrified the city.'

Anton would agree. 'They fucking destroyed San Francisco, didn't they?' he once lamented. 'San Francisco is the exact opposite of a diversified city now.' Back then, he paid $250 a month to live at 359 Haight Street. Today, that isn't even enough to cover Home Owners' Association dues. Rent in the Haight has increased to nearly $5,000 per month since 1990—a 1,000 percent jump. 'San Francisco was great back then,' says Jeff Davies. 'I remember when I first moved there, thinking, *Oh my god, it's so expensive here*, because you would pay $300 for a room in a big Victorian house that has a big front room, bay windows, and a fireplace—and I thought that was so expensive. It's nothing compared to now.'

Matt Hollywood used to work at the Haight location of Escape From New York Pizza, and Joel Gion worked at Reckless Records, just down the block. Some of the band's first gigs were at clubs in the Haight, and their first seven-inch single, 'She Made Me' / 'Evergreen,' was recorded at 734 Shrader, a 1,461-square-foot, two-bathroom condo now worth over a million dollars. Anton lived in the basement there with Travis Threlkel, who started the band with him alongside Ricky, Matt, and a few different drummers before Brian Glaze and then later Jeff and Joel joined.

Nate did his best to keep in touch with Anton, but to no avail, so he drove up to the Bay Area to track him down. 'Sure enough, Tony would ride up on some bicycle with no tires,' he later recalled. 'And once again he'd be telling you, *Dude, you don't even know how fucking lame you guys are. We're starting a revolution here, and it's gonna make Andy Warhol look like a picnic.* And we'd go to whatever house he was staying at and there'd be all these weird instruments, and he had 116 songs that all sounded the same.'

Anton convinced Michael to come up from Orange County and stay with him and his girlfriend for a while. Michael ended up sleeping in their bed, along with four or five others, while incense burned around the clock and sitars lay readily within arm's reach. Caught up momentarily in the bohemian vibe of the time, Michael sat down with Anton for hours over guitars and went through every chord progression he knew, as well as some droning chords in the vein of The Chameleons or Ride, two of their favorite bands. After a few months, however, the communal lifestyle grew wearing, and Michael left town.

By the time Michael left, Anton was better at the instrument than he was, and had written a good deal of songs. One of these, 'Stars,' which wouldn't appear on record until *Thank God For Mental Illness*, was the first song Anton wrote on guitar. A year or so later, Michael came back to San Francisco and found Anton gigging all over town. 'He was playing viciously,' Michael recalls. 'I saw half a dozen shows in the next few years. Every other one was brilliant, and the ones that weren't were chaos.'

Anton told Michael that he'd run into Mark Gardener, the lead singer of Ride, in the Upper Haight and given him a top-secret demo. Ride were another big influence on the BJM and their scene. They broke up in 1996, but a decade later, Anton had a hand in instigating their reunion, after which Mark would collaborate with him on *My Bloody Underground*. (More recently, Joel joined Ride onstage during their 2015 tour.)

Michael wasn't the only one who resisted Anton's nomadic spirit. His bouncing from couch to couch, without paying rent or working a regular job beyond his music, led to a long-held misconception that he was homeless, though he hasn't done much to argue that. 'I was homeless at this time ... kind of,' he later wrote. 'I slept in the studios or with girls.'

Anton never had a place of his own in San Francisco. At best, he paid rent; at worst, he was out on the street, looking for somewhere to crash. Daniel Knop, an old friend of the band, has seen for himself Anton out on the streets. 'He was sitting out in front of a coffee shop with all these homeless people,' he recalls, 'so I gave him five bucks.' When another one of the homeless guys asked Daniel why he had given money to Anton, Anton overheard and shouted at him, 'Because we're both going to be famous one day!' to which Daniel shouted back, 'Yep!'

Dawn likewise downplays Anton's nomadism, noting that there were, more often than not, people he could stay with. 'Anton wasn't really homeless,' she told me. 'I know because he lived with me from 1993 to 1995.' During that time, she adds, 'he acquired a lot of music and recording equipment just by expressing a desire for it, or an appreciation for it, and folks would either lend it to him or just give it to him.'

Anton later stayed with Dawn at her place on McAllister, a half-dozen blocks north of Haight, and then at 1010 Alabama, further south in the Mission, with Dawn's friend Nellie Dorn. Dave Deresinski also housed Anton from time to time, as did one Naut Humon (pronounced 'not human'), who owned a studio Anton later honed his recording skills at, the Compound. 'Naut also bought him things, like an organ, I believe,' Dawn recalls. 'Anton was good at finding magical instruments, and he knew who would be just as excited as him about having them around. He was also good at finding friends to live with, temporarily ... he could offer them the cachet of being in his band or entourage, and a lot of folks were really into that.'

Dawn had met Anton through a circle of friends that she'd moved in with in the Lower Haight in 1993, when Anton asked her then-boyfriend, Joshua Ong, to play music with him. Anton played in their back room and asked Dawn if she would like to join them. She was learning the accordion at the time but also played guitar, bass, and flute. Dawn obliged him, and sparks flew. He would go on to write many songs inspired by her, and she still has an old cassette of Anton, Jeff, and herself jamming and working out 'Straight Up And Down.'

Dawn continued playing music with Anton, and eventually left Josh for him.

25

'I handled it badly, and I regret how it all happened, as [Josh] was a wonderful person, and still is, and did not deserve for me to leave him the way I did.'

Josh's brother, Tim Ong, was the leader of a prominent local band called The Rosemarys, and best friend of Anton's roommate around the time he formed the BJM, Sean Curran. He was also the best man at Sean's wedding. 'The Rosemarys are an important part of this story,' says Paola Simmonds, another friend of the band's from the early days. 'The story *behind* the story.' The way I've heard it, Josh caught Anton and Dawn in bed together and threw all of Dawn's stuff out into the street, and then, later on, Sean kicked Anton out and hooked Josh up with one of Anton's exes, Diana James. 'Anton wasn't paying rent,' Sean notes. 'He mostly lived in the rehearsal spaces after I kicked him out.' Sean's last real interaction with the BJM was when he recorded a never-released session by them at his studio in mid-1994; he says he sold the eight-track reels on eBay a couple of years ago.

Anton lived with Dawn here and there for the next few years, though sometimes he lived with other friends, or at rehearsal studios that Dave or others rented. 'He was good at getting other people to invest in his musical career, myself included,' Dawn recalls. 'We all believed in him and loved him.' For Dawn, the years she spent with Anton were memorable, and theirs was a profound relationship. 'He was driven to realize his musical dreams, and I helped him, enjoyed him, and supported him. I played with him, recorded with him, and believed from the start in his musical genius. I was fascinated by his use of people and his ability to get them to do almost anything for him.'

During the next couple of years, Anton wrote numerous songs inspired by their relationship, as featured on *Take It From The Man!*, *Their Satanic Majesties' Second Request*, and *Thank God For Mental Illness*. If they weren't all about her, they sure do fit. There's 'Vacuum Boots,' and '(David Bowie I Love You) Since I Was Six,' on which Dawn plays accordion. The latter, which echoes the style of Bowie's own 'Space Oddity,' seems to capture the raw emotion Anton felt for her, as does the aptly named 'Dawn,' recorded first for *Take It From The Man!* and later again for *Strung Out In Heaven*.

According to Anton, 'Dawn' marks 'one of the few times I was actually thinking of a real girl that I actually was with and wrote a song about it.' This was also the case with 'Fucker,' while another that might be rooted in this same theme is 'The Be Song.' 'Joel was living with some girls, and Matt and

I were hanging out with this girl Jocelyn,' Anton later wrote. 'She asked me why no one writes like Syd Barrett. This song and "My Man Syd" were my response at once, with a firm, *Oh, but they do … .*'

Dawn also inspired fan favorites 'Cold To The Touch' and 'Free And Easy, Take 2.' Anton would later claim that he was inspired to write the latter song, which appears on *Thank God For Mental Illness*, one Christmas, when Dawn kicked him out of her house during a rainstorm. 'Most Christmases were spent at my parents,' says Dawn, 'and Anton did, in fact, come to a few Christmases, so he must be talking about one where he did not come. But whether or not he was actually kicked out, or whether I just left, I honestly don't know.'

To some, Dawn's presence in the group seemed to mark the beginning of a decades-long trend of bringing attractive female singers in and out of the BJM, though according to Tommy Dietrick, who was barely a teenager when he first started hanging with the guys, gender and sex appeal were the least of Anton's concerns. 'Anton lured people into his mystique with ease,' he recalls. 'It didn't matter if you were a girl with musical ambition or a guy who wanted to strum along on guitar. You always felt that you were doing something important when you played with Anton, and he always made you feel that way because you knew, as did he, that there was no Plan B. The only problem is that there was no Plan A, either. You knew he would never be able to hold down a regular job serving coffee or waiting tables. You just *knew* that. He simply was not and is not capable of any other kind of life, and in his relationship to his music he has never wavered. The ship could sink, but then he would just build a new ship. That ship could sink and he would build another. He would just stand back up and carry on.'

Dawn emphasizes that it was always important to Anton, and to his muse, that he be a martyr—that much of his songwriting is melancholy at its center, and that the deepest kind of sadness that fuels his songs. It was this sadness at leaving Dawn that inspired 'Free And Easy, Take 2,' whether or not the events transpired as the song suggests they did, although Anton insists the story is true. 'Listen to the words,' he later wrote. 'The story is all there.'

Dawn, whose birthday is on Christmas Eve, does remember one Christmas when the two of them argued about Anton's unwillingness to seek regular employment, even part-time, and how the bulk of his shelter and food was provided by her or others, when he wasn't living in some obscure practice space. Anton told Dawn that making music was his job, for better or for worse, though he did have jobs here and there. Around 1992 or 1993, Tommy's brother, Alexander Mann, got him a telemarketing gig with the Silicon Valley Toxics Coalition, whose objective was to raise money and awareness for environmental concerns of Northern California, but the job only lasted a couple of months. He also took a job at a Comedy Traffic School a couple blocks South of Market, off 11th and Folsom, where he'd answer the phone to customers with the words, 'Comedy school's a blast! It takes less cash! This is Tony speaking. How can I help you?'

Daniel Knop was the assistant manager there, and had hired Anton, who'd ride his bike to work from the Haight with a four-track in his backpack. 'He was playing me all of these four-track recordings of his first couple of records,' Daniel recalls. 'All the stuff with the sitars and African drums, he did all that by himself. He played everything on it. It was amazing. With his first paycheck he bought a 60s leather jacket and leather pants.'

When he wasn't answering phones, Anton spent his shifts reading. 'He would read a whole book in one day,' Daniel adds. 'He would always be reading. He was always enlightening himself.'

Daniel and Anton set up the band in the basement after-hours one weekend and threw a party in there. The show was packed. 'I had to leave because I had something going on, so I gave the keys to Anton,' Daniel recalls. 'I totally trusted him, and, I swear to God, everybody and their mother was in that office watching them play. Anton *spit-shined* that office, and it looked exactly how it looked before I left. Even the garbage cans were empty. There was no sign of anything. I mean, it smelled a little bit like beer, but we burned some incense and it was cool. I was blown away by his responsibility.'

Once Anton found out management was calling in to check on the workers' customer service skills, though, he didn't last much longer. 'He started thinking everyone was the secret caller, so he started attacking people on the phone,' Dave says. Anton was let go once he started telling customers that he 'was onto them'—that he knew they were 'working for *the man*.' Daniel was fired too around the same time, but for doing too much speed. It was time to build another ship.

'Oftentimes, Anton would perceive that people did not like him or were doing things to him, reshaping his memories as they happen to protect himself as a defense mechanism,' Dawn recalls. 'He is actually very sensitive, and has created many defenses to protect himself. In all fairness, I do this as well, of course. As do we all.'

When he was first getting settled into town, Anton started networking among the community of artists and musicians who lived in the Haight. Among them was a fellow talented musician of a similar age named Aaron 'Arrow' Motter, whom Ricky Maymi says looked like a member of Sisters Of Mercy and acted like a character out of a John Hughes film, with his shoulder-length black hair and goth vibe. Arrow had a skeleton pirate marionette named Dante who came with his own pirate-ship stage, which Jeff remembers being made out of papier-mâché, and he performed puppet shows to an original soundtrack of his own making down at Fisherman's Wharf.

Arrow played guitar and piano beautifully, and Anton started jamming with him. Arrow also jammed sometimes with Ricky, whom he had met through their mutual friend Peter Booth Lee, who took tons of pictures of the BJM early on. One photo he took of Anton and Ricky was used often in promo materials, including the *Brian Jonestown Blotter* tabloid spoof that came with the now out-of-print release *Tangible Box*, and was also on their first tour poster.

Arrow suggested that Anton and Ricky should play together, since they were into the same kinds of music, so they arranged a get-together at the Café International on Haight and Fillmore. The two of them hit it off immediately over a game of chess that marked the start of a friendship and musical relationship that has endured for nearly thirty years.

Ricky soon introduced Anton to his best friend, Travis Threlkel. Ricky and Travis had known each other since grade school, and all three had been into similar music in their teens. Ricky was the virtuoso instrumentalist, Travis the budding songwriter. Both were younger than Anton, who embedded himself in their group and eventually came to dominate it.

Travis wanted to be in a band, despite not having quite come into his own as a musician yet, and Anton found that appealing. He's always been as drawn to inexperienced players as he is to experienced ones, because he understands the spectrum of people's abilities and styles and applies them to his projects liberally. Oftentimes in the BJM back catalogue there are songs where parts are performed by people who'd never been in a studio or recorded a song before, much less written one.

Travis learned fast, and, according to Ricky, he and Anton almost immediately embarked on a healthy songwriting competition. Just days after meeting, they recorded a 'top-secret demo' on Sean Curran's Tascam 424 four-track at his place in the Lower Haight, which is where Anton and his girlfriend at the time, Sally Farmen, were living. Sally came from a family of Oregon farmers and had organic meats stocked up in the freezer, so the ritual became to go to their place in the afternoon to learn and record a new song, then Anton would make dinner for everyone and they'd eat and smoke a little pot and hang out. Like Matt Hollywood, Sean was from Santa Barbara, and he wanted to make music like Ride and The Cure with his band, Nebtwister, who would appear alongside the BJM in the *Tangible Box* set.

Sean, who also worked for about a month at the Horseshoe Café—another coffee shop that had recently opened and now no longer exists—remembers those days well. '[Anton] wanted me to start a band with him,' he says. 'They were playing my tape over the sound system. Anton liked it, and he came over … he moved in two weeks later.' It was there, in April 1990, at 674 Haight Street, apartment 2—a white building with green trim, which at the time of writing sits between Sushi Raw and Danny Coyle's—that The Brian Jonestown Massacre was born.

When Anton had finished recording these first four tracks, he mixed them down to two on his flatmate's stereo and added more tracks using Sean's Alesis HR-16 drum machine, as well as his SM58 mics and his Microverb and Midiverb II effects units. He mostly used his own Kay Airline—a 50s/60s guitar later popularized by Jack White—for the guitars, but made heavy use of Sean's Big Muff and MXR yellow distortion pedals, performing the basslines on the Kay as well.

'He recorded hundreds of songs on my four-track in our apartment on Haight Street,' Sean recalls. According to Ricky, 'In all of those early demos, it was just all Anton freestyling over [the] Alesis drum machine when everyone was convinced that it was some drummer with a groovy feel. Anton was literally writing a song or two or four a day, every day, for weeks, and before we even started to play shows we were just conceptualizing this band in a sort of young, silly, acid way.'

One day, Anton had been in a deep sleep on the top bunk of the bed at Sean's when he rolled over the side of the bed, fell out, and broke his arm, but it didn't stop him from working on the demo. 'I remember him struggling with the cast to strum,' says Travis. Sean was there when the accident happened. 'I heard Anton moaning, so I went to check on him and he was all fucked up laying on the floor,' he recalls. 'Probably fell seven feet. He had to have pins put in his arm.'

Anton has attributed this specific event to the beginnings of his subsequent opioid abuse. 'I was in hospital for two weeks on morphine and Demerol,' he told the *Guardian*'s Paul Lester in 2014, 'and what that does to your brain is, it sets you up, because there's nothing in the world that's quite like that. So eventually I tried opiates, whether hydrocodone or whatever it was that led to the opiate addiction, which ended up being heroin.'

Once Anton had recovered from the fracture, he and Travis played their finished demo for Ricky, who was so impressed by it that he saw right away why Arrow thought they should play music together. 'Travis and Anton would take turns writing songs, but Anton was always there with more ideas, and sometimes different versions of the same idea,' he recalls, 'while Travis came up with the strange chords, like on "Swallowtail" and "Carousel."' Sean remembers the three of them having band practice in the living room; they didn't have a name yet, so Anton temporarily borrowed 'Electric Kool Aid' from his old band.*

Michael claims to have witnessed firsthand the creation of the name Anton ultimately chose for his lifelong project. He says it came from a street flutist named Brian, outside an Upper Haight café. One time, Anton jokingly called him 'Brian Jones,' to which Brian the flutist replied, 'Town Massacre.' Some sources suggest that 'Brian Jonestown Massacre' flyers were plastered all over town the next day, though Ricky disputes this telling. 'We were just taking acid a lot then and coming up with these dumb ideas, making up these dumb imaginary band names, and Brian Jonestown Massacre stuck,' he later said.

Another longtime friend of the band, Del Beaudry, speculates that Travis designed the logo, as Travis did a lot of the art and design work for the BJM in the early days, including *Tangible Box*. Travis worked downtown as a

---

* There is some confusion surrounding the spelling of this band's name. Often, the band from Newport Beach is referred to as Electric Cool-Aide, but the band that Anton later named Electric Cool-Aide has also been referred to as Electric Kool Aid. For the purposes of this book, the Newport Beach band is referred to in this text as Electric Cool-Aide, while the San Francisco group that evolved into the BJM is referred to as Electric Kool Aid.

professional graphic designer, creating computer-altered graphics on a top-of-the-line Mac. Travis confirms he was responsible for creating the iconic logo—a circle and star with the words 'The Brian Jonestown Massacre' going around it—but says Anton chose the image of Brian Jones that ultimately evolved into what it is today, using a photocopier to project the image onto Travis's black star design. (Travis continues his visual creative pursuits today with his San Francisco–based tech design firm, Obscura Digital.)

Del met Anton one day after Ricky told him that he and Travis had been playing in a band with 'a guy from LA' that he wanted Del to meet. Ricky then brought Anton to Del's flat on Fillmore, where Anton, armed with a cheap acoustic guitar, said to Del, 'I want to play you a song.' The song he played was 'Monster,' as later recorded for *Take It From The Man!* Del wasn't all that impressed, but when he saw the band play live as Electric Kool Aid, he changed his mind.

One of the band's first shows was at a transgender bar called the Black Rose in the Tenderloin district. 'I was waving my freak flag high in those days,' Jeff remembers. 'I was high, and I was in a great town—a town that inspired you to great heights or art—there was a sense of great history there, from the pirates to the beatniks to the hippies to the punk rockers, straight through to the BJM. The Black Rose was a gay/trans bar, and they started having rock'n'roll shows, so we played a show there.'

* * *

Jeff Davies was born five months after Anton, on December 29, 1967, in Washington, DC, and grew up at his grandma's house in Falls Church, Virginia. His parents had him when they were very young. His mom turned sixteen two weeks before he was born, and had left him and his dad before Jeff turned one. The summer after he finished sixth grade, Jeff and his dad moved out to Albuquerque, and by the time Jeff himself turned sixteen, he was out on his own, having moved into a warehouse space in 1985 or '86.

In the summer of '87, Jeff met a guy named Darren who'd come to Albuquerque with his girlfriend to get away from the city. The couple ended up breaking up, so Jeff hopped on Darren's motorcycle, and the two of them spent two months making their way back across the West. When they finally got back to San Francisco, Jeff had maybe twenty or thirty bucks to his name.

'Darren knows people,' he recalls. 'I don't know anyone. The first night we get into town, he says, You can stay at this girl Evelyn's house. I spent all my money the first night taking her out to dinner, and after a week I ended up sleeping with her. One night she was at work and I got out of there, slept a couple days in the park, then I went into this bar on 16th Street, the Firehouse, and I met this girl Fiona. She was a bartender there. Went home with her. That went on for a week or two, and I ended up living with her for the next two years, somewhere around '89, and then I was living in the Lower Haight when I met Anton in about '90.'

Anton had found his way to a gig Jeff was playing at the Peacock Lounge—a club right next to the church where the Reverend Jim Jones once held the People's Temple, before taking the congregation to Guyana—with a band called Planet Of The Hairdo Apes that featured Jeff and his friend and later ex-girlfriend Roxanne, whom he taught how to play guitar. Their band was inspired by a performance art band called Imperial Butt Wizards, whom Jeff had played with in Los Angeles. When the show was over, Anton snatched up Jeff's hollowbody guitar while no one was looking and walked about a mile down the street before he caught him with it. 'After the show he was talking to people and I stole his guitar,' Anton later recalled. 'I walked to my house with it but turned around because I don't steal.'

According to sometime BJM member, roadie, friend, excellent storyteller, and impeccable dresser Christof Certik, Anton never actually got that far, as Jeff caught up to him. 'Oh, I thought I'd help out and carry this for you,' he says Anton told him. Jeff, who knew Christof from his job at the Record Vault and from parties around town, confirms this account. 'After the show I'm looking for my guitar. *Where's my guitar? Fuck! Where's my guitar?* It's a big room, there's lots of people there, and my guitar case is gone. I go outside, and when you walk down the door, it's Haight Street, and out the door one way is gonna be Fillmore, and the other way is gonna be Steiner. Halfway down the block, almost to Fillmore, is someone walking real fast with my guitar case. I run up. *Hey, what the fuck are you doing? That's my guitar!* and it was Anton, and he said to me, Oh, I just wanted to help you guys load out. He was walking off with my guitar. Never met the guy before.'

Anton was wearing overalls with no shirt and had a bowl cut like Mo from The Three Stooges, with the sides shaved underneath. Jeff was in a loincloth and fur diaper, as earlier that day he'd found a fur coat and repurposed it for the show. 'In the next couple weeks I ran into him again, and eventually we ended up playing music together,' he continues. 'Very shortly after that, he ended up living just a couple doors from Matt's, with Sally and Sean.'

Jeff, impressed by Anton's brashness, was suitably charmed, and he subsequently joined the band. 'Next time we were playing, Jeff just walked up onstage and started playing with us in the middle of a song,' Anton said. 'I did not even ask him.'*

At the time, Jeff wore braces on his teeth, and he would joke that he wanted to put rhinestones in them, which he later did. 'I got them put on right before I moved out of living with my dad from Albuquerque,' he recalls, 'and I had them for years, but I'd only gone to the orthodontist once or twice, so my teeth never got straightened. The wires popped out, and I ended up putting some rhinestones in them for a while, so for like a year I had these on my top teeth, these brace settings with purple, green, and red little rhinestones in them.' Years later, Jeff still had the brackets on after removing the braces, because he couldn't afford to have them taken off.

Jeff wasn't in the first incarnation of The Brian Jonestown Massacre, however. Most reports say that this band consisted of Anton, Matt, Travis, and Ricky, with one Patrick Straczek on drums, but Daniel Knop says Ricky was on drums at the first show. There was also a Greg Helton on drums around this time—until he was busted for dope possession—and Brant Graff also played drums for the group.

At one of the band's early gigs as Electric Kool Aid—maybe at the Black Rose—Del remembers Anton declaring to the crowd that he was putting together another band, and that this other band, he announced, 'It's going to be called The Brian Jonestown Massacre. Isn't that a great name?' This, says Del, 'would be what Anton said to everybody, anytime he was hanging out. *The Brian Jonestown Massacre! Isn't that a great name?*'

---

* Jeff can be heard on almost every BJM record, from *Spacegirl* and *Methodrone* to *Bravery Repetition And Noise*. More recently, he contributed guitar to Joel's album *Apple Bonkers*. One time, on the way to a Nick Cave show, with his hair up in his signature bouffant—which Joel calls his 'Alice from *Brady Bunch*' pompadour—and wearing frosty pink makeup, Jeff spotted a polyester, zip-up beige-and-brown jumpsuit lying in the street. He snatched it up, put it on over his clothes, and wore it to the show. 'I remember the jumpsuit,' he says. 'It was sleeveless. It was a weird chef-like pantsuit. Super-tight.'

James Mervine, who until recently had been playing bass in a band called Enrique, picked up the sticks for Anton's new EKA for about six months during the first half of 1992. Anton intended this band to be more of a 60s garage-rock act in contrast with the more heavy, shoegaze vibe he was developing with the BJM. James did about ten gigs with Anton's EKA, and says, 'They were all quite good. I was at a loose end and just wanted to be in a band where I didn't have to do anything but show up to practice and play gigs. It was perfect.'

James's path to joining the band was similarly straightforward. His girlfriend (and now wife) Helen had a friend named Luella, who had told him she knew someone looking for a drummer; James had a chat with Anton, and, just like that, he was in. 'I had no ego issues with Anton, so we got along fine,' he recalls. 'Plus, I had a few good connections with nightclubs in town, so I got us a few gigs, or at least one at the Paradise Lounge. Anton really saw [BJM and EKA] as two separate styles, though I must admit I couldn't see much difference. To him, there was a real, distinct difference, though I know that eventually he did incorporate some EKA songs into the BJM set.'

Most agree that as the styles of both projects began to blend, the group started using the Electric Kool Aid name interchangeably with The Brian Jonestown Massacre. 'I think it may have been Electric Kool Aid for a couple of gigs, and the Jonestown name hadn't been used yet,' says Jeff. 'And for a minute it was thought of as two separate projects, but then it kind of just became the Jonestown.'

Del Beaudry worked with them from that point forward in something of a managerial role, until Anton holed himself up at the Compound to finish the BJM's first full-length album, *Methodrone*, by which point Dave Deresinski was officially managing the band. Dave knew everyone and had been around in the scene from the very beginning. As Sean puts it, Dave was 'as much a member of BJM as anyone—the *fifth Beatle*, so to speak.'

'Dave was always kind of their manager,' says Daniel, who attended the first BJM show, worked with a couple of the band members, and also sang backup vocals on 'All Around You (Intro)' for *Their Satanic Majesties' Second Request*. Daniel was another staple of the San Francisco goth scene, and had likewise had been friends with some of the guys for years. 'I knew them because of Ricky, because we all hung out at the new-wave goth clubs,' he says.

Across the street from Anton in the Lower Haight was a record store

35

specializing in experimental music owned by a guy named Alan Herrick that Anton went to often. Prior to making the first BJM tape, Anton had given Alan a tape called *Psalm 93—Child Of 60 Bitches*, which Alan really liked. During his visits to the store, Anton would often tell Alan about 'the best band he could ever put together,' Alan later recalled. 'It would be *way* out there, bigger than anything—not the manufactured slick British "babyfood" but something supremely psychedelic and broad but accessible and dangerous.'

Alan didn't doubt him. 'One afternoon I sat on my stool behind the counter of the record store, and Anton came in a serious flurry … dark circles under his eyes, arms moving about like windmills, a single cassette tape in his hand,' he continued. '*This is it—it's big. We have it now and I have the name. All of it came all at once … check it out … Brian Jonestown Massacre.* I smile and laugh—it is a beautiful name, so perfect for where we are at the time, in the world, with music, for everything. He grabs a pen off the counter and scribbles *THE BRIAN JONESTOWNE MASACRE ANTON 861-8683* on the front and back label of the cassette and hands it to me to put on the stereo. As the first track starts up he says, That's it—I am *so* down with this now and I need to sleep soon. He disappears out the door.'

The first Brian Jonestown Massacre demo tape, with no other information accompanying it, other than Anton's ph one number, plays itself out and joins the collection of demo tapes on the shelf. It is 1990, three years before any Brian Jonestown Massacre album is released, and quite possibly one of the only recordings of the original lineup.

According to Travis, they made as many copies of the tape as they could and handed them out to anyone who would take them. Among the recipients were The Dandy Warhols, who would later come down from Portland to play some house parties—neither band knowing then the adventures they were about to undertake, or where their respective paths would lead them.

The tape in question is, to the best of my knowledge, the one now known as *Pol Pot's Pleasure Penthouse*, as officially released by Burger Records in 2012, thanks to Joel, and on vinyl by Anton for Record Store Day 2017 (for which he was declared one of event's five 'champions' by its organizers in the UK). 'It's a demo tape. That's why it never came out,' Anton noted in a YouTube comment in 2012. 'I should know. I wrote, recorded, and played it all.' Along with *The Diane Perry Tape*, 2011's *Singles Collection*, *Tepid*

Peppermint Wonderland, and *Spacegirl & Other Favorites*, it is among the best recordings to sift through to get the clearest picture of the early BJM sound.

One of the songs from those times, 'Fingertips,' was recently re-recorded by Anton and the band at Anton's studio in Berlin with new protege Tess Parks, and then another of his collaborators, Friederike Beinart, did the vocals in French for a different mix. It amazes me how little is different between the old version and the two new versions, despite their being over twenty-five years apart. I love Friederike's and Tess's vocal takes equally. So did Iggy Pop, who spun both sides of the 2016 single version on his BBC Radio 6 show, starting with the French version. 'I've always liked what Anton Newcombe does,' Iggy told his listeners. 'I mean, that sounds like proper, sophisticated, smooth, subversive pop music to me, and it's done in his own studio in Berlin, and I know he's been around here and there, bounced around, and I'll bet he's enjoying the freedom you can find in that sort of big and comfortable city where everybody isn't always poking their nose into your stuff.'

This seemed to be the case during the old Haight days as well, because what is equally significant about these early recordings is how they echo Anton's more recent work since 2008, most of which has been recorded in Berlin. A lot of the records from this period are swirling, droning songs with heavy reverb guitars and ethereal keys over groovy drumbeats. According to Brant Graff, another fan of the *Psalm 93* tape, 'Anton worked then just like he does now, writing and recording all the time, always bubbling over with ideas, everything a work in progress, little to no second guessing. It was just like you see him work in his Berlin studio now, except back then he did it on a four-track.'

After leaving San Francisco for Victoria, British Columbia, Brant was passing through the city on his way down to Orange County when he spotted Anton on Haight and pulled over. 'I went inside his flat and met some guy with a big pompadour and heavy makeup, wearing a thrift store cardigan, and playing guitar on an empress couch in front of a bay window,' he continued. 'That was Jeff Davies.' Anton walked Brant back to his car and handed him a TDK Type 1 cassette tape. He'd written 'The Brian Jonestown Massacer' on one side and 'Untitled—1991' on the other.*

---

* Sean claims that Anton eventually asked for his help to correct the spelling of 'massacre.'

'He crammed as much music as would fit on a ninety-minute cassette,' Brant recalled. 'The second the music fades out, the tape ends. I played it hundreds of times on my crappy car stereo … then the tape sat in a shoebox for fifteen years, moving with me from place to place until 2006, when I had the cassette transferred to digital at Mr. Toads in San Francisco.'

'E To G' is a jangly number on the demo, with a tick-tock beat, though according to Brant, Anton had said the title was actually 'Rotary 8.' 'The Phone Song' shows Anton's early interest in capturing different sounds, like cars, radio broadcasts, answering machine messages, and ringing telephones, to incorporate into his music. Songs like these two, 'The Phone Song,' 'Chameleons,' 'Space,' 'Psychedelic Sunday,' and others on that tape give us our earliest window into understanding Anton's knack for rhythm, and how his ascensions through layers of melodic drones work both together and against each other in those ways.

After 'The Phone Song' comes 'Thoughts Of You Too,' which sounds like an early version of what turned out to be 'Thoughts Of You,' which was later recorded under the name Acid for *Tangible Box* and also appears on *The Singles Collection*. After that is 'Chameleons,' and then the first recorded version of 'Evergreen.' The latter song would be recorded one more time with vocalist and Haight local eufloria* before Elizabeth Dye sang on it for *Methodrone*, which is the best-known version, as it also appears on *Tepid Peppermint Wonderland*. There's also 'The Quiet Song.'

* * *

As they handed tapes out to anyone who would take them, Anton, Travis, and Ricky started recruiting more people for the group. Daniel says that the BJM was Ricky's first band, but Ricky says he didn't exactly join right away, as he had been playing in another band with Jeff called The Tulips.* It was around this time that Jeff went down to LA to play with Imperial Butt Wizards, before he eventually made his way into The Brian Jonestown Massacre.

Joel Gion was hanging around back then, too, but he wouldn't join the band for a couple more years. Before moving to the Haight, he'd grown up in a redneck town. As a teenager, he rebelled against the conservative social

---

* The Tulips formed after Jeff and Fiona broke up, and included one Burt Blodgette (whom everyone called 'Burt Bloodgut') and a drummer named Cujo.

norms that came with life in rural America. That anti-establishment attitude made him a perfect fit for the Jonestown. 'I remember when I first met Joel,' Jeff says. 'He was such a skinny, sweet little kid.'

Joel was actually Travis's friend first. He met Anton mere days after meeting Ricky, who insisted he try out for the band on guitar, even though he'd only been playing a couple months. 'I failed big time,' he recalls, 'but Anton was nice and showed me some guitar tricks. And then they found Jeff soon after, so that's still a happy ending.'

How Matt Hollywood got in was that Anton and Travis spotted him through a window, playing bass at his home on Haight Street, a couple of doors down from Sean's place. They figured out which apartment the window belonged to, and went up and knocked on the door. Matt ended up quitting art school to join the band in time for their very first gig at a frat party in Berkeley late 1991, opening for The Winona Ryders. Among the first songs they wrote together as a group were 'Wisdom' and 'Whoever You Are.'

Longtime fan and friend of the band Crystal Apel went to her first EKA/BJM show when she was seventeen. She met Matt at the Horseshoe Café, which was right by the Peacock Lounge, a few months later. They'd sit there swigging coffee, chain smoking, and playing cards. Back then, Matt had a short cropped bowl cut, dyed black; Anton was his stylist, and, according to Crystal, he had used an actual bowl. The night ended with Matt drawing a mural on Crystal's back with colored markers. 'For many years you couldn't go anywhere without seeing a BJM stencil on the sidewalk or a sticker plastered somewhere,' she recalls. Another time she was at a twenty-four-hour burrito joint in the Mission at three in the morning with Dave and an old friend of his, Metallica guitarist Kirk Hammett, when suddenly Anton walked in barefoot, strumming his guitar down the aisle.

Having recruited such a group of talented players, Anton's project outgrew four-tracks and pre-programmed beats, and it came time for him to take his band into the studio. Del Beaudry claims to have paid for the first 'official' BJM recording session with Ricky's uncle Ed at a studio south of Market. Working with limited studio time and budget, Anton clashed with Del over how the songs should be recorded. He wanted to lay everything down as you would in a typical studio setting: drums first, maybe with scratch tracks, then bass, guitars, vocals, and so on, but Del pushed for the band to record live and overdub later, if necessary. Anton refused, and not much was produced from the session.

Del learned pretty quickly that almost any situation involving the Jonestown could fall apart on a whim. For the band's first paying gig at the Peacock Lounge, he says, he rented the venue, promoted the show, and ran the door. 'You could rent it for 100 bucks,' Daniel notes. 'It wasn't open all the time, it was just for rentals.' (Daniel was at this show, too, as well as the one in Berkeley with The Winona Ryders.)

Ricky played drums at the first Peacock Lounge show. 'The kick drum's spikes came out, so it was moving like a foot or two,' Daniel recalls. 'There was no stage. I just went up to where they were playing and I sat there and held Ricky's kick drum through the whole set, so it wouldn't keep moving. I couldn't hear for, like, two days.'

Del wanted to charge five dollars for entry, but Anton thought that was a rip-off. 'Go two or three dollars,' he said. The date of the gig was February 28, 1992. Sean's friend Tom Kayser, whom he'd known since 1979 and grown up with in Santa Barbara, had earlier told Anton that it would've been Brian Jones's fiftieth birthday. It could have been no other way. 'Anton, lots of people are going to come in here,' Del argued. 'They're just going to wander by from the bars not knowing what's going on and come in.'

Del eventually told Anton he'd put 'five dollars' on the flyer, but that if anyone came to the door and said they couldn't afford five or were friends of Anton's, he'd let them in for two or three. Del kept to his word, but that wasn't the last of his troubles that night. He'd put the BJM second on the bill after another local band, Marzipan, but Anton insisted the BJM close the show. So as not to complicate things, Marzipan were promptly paid the $100 Del had guaranteed them following their set, but by the time the BJM finished their own set it was well past two in the morning. Anton approached Del to collect. Tired and brain-fogged, Del gave him his cut out of what was left, expecting he'd divvy it out to the rest of the band accordingly, but Anton disappeared into the night. Once he realized what had happened, Matt quit on the spot. He'd been guaranteed $20, but Del wasn't going to follow Anton around arguing about that kind of sum. And that was the BJM's first show.

12345

WHO PUT THE BOMP?

When they weren't on the verge of almost breaking up, the band discussed which record labels they wanted to send demos to. Foremost among them was legendary garage-rock label Bomp!, founded by Greg Shaw. They sent a tape his way and hadn't heard back until the day after the Peacock Lounge show. 'It took Shaw over a year to track us down after we sent him that tape,' Anton later noted. Once he got the letter back from Greg, he crashed a party at Travis's place to deliver the news. The letter read as follows:

The Brian Jonestown Massacre
c/o Tangible Records
674 Haight St
San Francisco, CA
94117

Hi,

Thanks so much for sending your tape. It's by far the best tape I've received in a long time.

I only wish you'd included some info, as I have no idea who you people are or what this is all about. Is there something you could send? Any press stuff, photo, history, anything?

Irrespective of that, I'm very interested in the band and would love to see you play. Do you ever play? Would you like to play here in LA? We put on big underground parties roughly every month here, and I think you'd fit in quite well in the sort of physiodelic multimedia satyrconceptual sensorium we aim to create. If interested, to let me know. Recording possibilities can be discussed once we've met and I've seen your show.

All the best,

Greg Shaw*

'Anton showed up with the letter, and said, *Come on, guys. We have to keep doing this*,' Matt recalls in *Dig!* 'Me and Travis were both high on acid. We thought Anton was the devil at first, but we ended up deciding to keep playing with him.'

By now, Greg Shaw was already a legend in the underground rock'n'roll world. A native of San Francisco, he had grown up listening to the old 78s collected by his dad, who had played in jazz bands in the 40s. When Elvis came out, Shaw Sr. bemoaned to his young son how 'fake' the singer was, and how he wasn't 'the real thing.'

In 1966, at age seventeen, Greg founded *Mojo Navigator Rock 'n' Roll News*, a precursor to *Rolling Stone* magazine, which he later contributed to. *Mojo Navigator* was printed on six pages of hand-cranked mimeograph paper, which he stapled together. That project eventually fell apart because it grew too big for him to finance, but that same year he went to his first concert at the Fillmore, and he was later was present at The Rolling Stones' disastrous Altamont concert at which four people died. An omen, perhaps?

Greg started *Bomp!*, first as a magazine, in January 1970. 'I got a straight job for a couple of years, and then I just couldn't stand being away from music, so I started up another magazine, this time calling it *The BOMP!*, and sent it out to the old [*Mojo Navigator*] subscribers, and just started doing it for my own enjoyment. There was only about ten people reading it. And gradually it grew and became like a real magazine, and then it got national circulation, and then it got so big I couldn't print it anymore. The only way to

---

* After years of trying to track this letter down, Anton included a facsimile of it with the Record Store Day 2017 release of *Pol Pot's Pleasure Penthouse*.

put out a magazine is to pay the printer in advance, but you don't get paid by distributors until like a year later.'

Greg's 'straight job' was working at United Artists in LA for $120 a week, which he did while putting out *Bomp!* and writing as a freelance for the bigger rock magazines. At UA, he wrote bios and print ads for bands like ELO, The Move, and Hawkwind; became friends with some of his childhood heroes, like Bobby Vee and Del Shannon and The Ventures; and hung out with the likes of Led Zeppelin. Four years later, *Bomp!* evolved into a record label that has since released over 250 albums and singles in the decades, putting out records by Iggy & The Stooges, Devo, The Romantics, Spacemen 3, The Germs, and countless others. As Matt notes in *Dig!*, 'People wouldn't know about 60s garage music if it wasn't for Greg Shaw. You wouldn't know about bands like The White Stripes if it wasn't for him turning people onto 60s music.'

And not just 60s music. Greg was one of the first people to promote punk rock. In the mid-70s, he went to New York to hang with Andy Warhol and gave The New York Dolls access to the media. When Iggy Pop was in LA doing his record *Kill City*, long before he ever heard 'Fingertips,' Greg would run into him at parties. 'I was dating this girl whose sister he was dating,' Greg later recalled. 'He was going to marry her so he was always over at their parents house. The parents were these Nazis, swastikas on the wall, totally surreal. I would be there for a barbecue or something and [Iggy] would show up.'

In one version of this story, Anton and Travis had sought out Greg and Bomp! themselves, but their correspondence was eventually returned because they'd provided an outdated address. However, Chelsea Starr, who worked with Greg for many years, disputes this. 'You heard wrong,' she told me. 'Anton told me that he had no idea who Greg was when he met him.' Either way, Greg was eventually able to find the band and get that letter to Anton after his former partner Victoria Byers discovered a bad review of a BJM show in the back of a local rock zine called *Ben Is Dead* a couple of months later, in April 1992:

THE BRIAN JONESTOWN MASSACRE
If We Get Any Worse We'll Get Invited To The New Music Seminar This Year For Sure!

'That which is far off, and exceeding deep, who can find it out?' —
Eccles. 7:24

Somewhere in this mountain of noise there are some singers, I
just know. The credits list four of them. Buried somewhere in the
molasses of all those processed guitars and junkie drum patterns
there were hints of some singing going on. I detected a sigh
here and there in the best Jesus & Mary Chain tradition, but the
perpetrator(s) stopped short of forming actual words or couplets.
Lots of bad drugs in the Haight, that's for sure.

'What attracted me to The Brian Jonestown Massacre at first was the quality
of their demo. It had absolutely no professional quality at all,' Shaw later
said. 'It was smeared and smudgy and it had the wrong return address on
it, but the music was brilliant … it became my personal quest to find them.'
Elsewhere, he noted of the demo, 'It sounded like it was coming from a far
away place through a purple haze of weird drugs. I thought, *These guys have
got something going for them, I have to track them down!*'

44

Shaw remained The Brian Jonestown Massacre's most faithful champion
until his death in 2004. Anton was his anti-Elvis, in a way. The real deal.
'Greg loved Anton, and was also a terribly sweet person,' Dawn Thomas says
of the garage-rock guru. 'He gave him the freedom to do what he wanted with
his music, and [then] he put it out.'

Tommy Dietrick's band, Your Precious You, did a few shows with the
Jonestown and ended up playing in Santa Barbara and also in LA's Chinatown.
Greg came to both shows, Tommy says. In Santa Barbara, they played at a
student hall that held at least five hundred people, but there were only about
ten people there, so Tommy and Matt hopped in a car and scoured the city
for anyone else who might come out to the gig. The next night, they arrived
in LA to play the Hong Kong Café, and Greg's squeeze Victoria was the
opening act for the show. 'She was a kind of hippie, psychedelic guru who
was performing an Aphrodite ritual which involved lots of candles, ceramic
dildos, and vaginas,' Tommy recalls. An underage friend of his who lived in
Northridge had been granted permission to come to the show that night, so
she came with her dad and left shortly after the dildos and vaginas. While

they were there, Jeff asked them if they had any pot—only to discover that the girl's dad was a cop.

Despite the lack of crowds, Shaw knew he had something with the BJM. Del Beaudry has in his possession a fax of the original agreement signed by Greg and Anton, and says Greg gave Anton the resources he needed to do what he wanted: 'Access to his house, use of all of his computers, a place to sleep, recording time … but that wasn't a real record deal. What they got for the first single was copies of the single to sell.'

A similar situation ensued with *Methodrone*. 'Greg was famous for ripping everybody off,' Del continues. 'I said not to sign with him, and Ricky was against it as well, as I recall, because of Greg's reputation.' Anton, however, now knew a lot more about Greg and his history, and his involvement in the emergent garage-rock revival, and thus wanted to be on the Bomp! imprint. For Anton, the relationship would prove fruitful. 'There was some money from Greg when *Take It From The Man!* and *Satanic Majesties* came out,' Del says. 'I'm not sure how it was distributed, but someone got some money from that.'

'Greg was always involved, trying to get you to sign one of their shitty deals,' says Tommy's brother, Alexander Mann, a member of the band Silent Pictures. 'He always hung around with prostitutes on LSD. In general, a nice-enough man, but without Anton there wouldn't have been that same market for all of that raw blues-rock. Anton has had a [much bigger] effect on the later resurgence of garage rock than people are willing to give him credit for.'

Alex also played with Tommy in Your Precious You, whose named was given to them by Travis. 'Anton was smart, driven, charismatic, even charming then,' Tommy says. 'I never would've guessed the impact The Brian Jonestown Massacre would have on indie music culture—on my own life even—or that they would still be relevant twenty-five years later.'

Tommy first met Anton back in 1991, when he was still in high school. A lot of people hanging around the BJM back then were teenagers, including the band members themselves, and with Anton already well into his twenties, he naturally assumed a leadership position among them, just as he had in the Haight. Before the gigs in Santa Barbara and Los Angeles, Tommy played his very first show, with Your Precious You opening for the BJM at a gig held in a defunct, worn-out warehouse building and filmed by MTV Brazil.

Warehouse shows like these became customary in between gigs at places

45

like the Boomerang, Brave New World, Bottom Of The Hill, The Peacock Lounge, and the Nite Break. They also served as party spots for the able youth. In a good mood and equipped with a backpack full of the 'She Made Me' / 'Evergreen' seven-inch singles, Anton showed up to one of the parties Tommy was at and handed everybody a free single.

Before long, the Dietrick brothers had become good friends with Ricky, Jeff, and Travis, and spent many nights together staying up late with the girls in the scene, smoking joints, listening to records, and usually passing out on a couch somewhere. Despite living in San Jose, Tommy managed to sneak away once or twice a week to play shows and see bands with his newfound mentors. By now, they were in the midst of a thriving indie/shoegazing scene in the Bay Area that included the BJM, Your Precious You, Nebtwister, Orange, Heavy Into Jeff, Galaga, The Rosemarys, Marzipan, and a bunch of other bands, but because he was underage, Tommy ran into some difficulty getting into the clubs to play. Thankfully, Dave Deresinski was often able to sneak him in.

Alex also spent many late nights partying with Anton, and he remembers vividly one of the first times they hung out, at the MTV Brazil warehouse gig. Anton, with a stark but completely serious look on his face, said to him, 'You will *see*, man. This will be huge. I am creating this scene. We're going to take everything that is big over there and make it here. Make it bigger.' *Over there* meant the UK. 'Of course, at seventeen, this sounded great,' Alex recalls, 'but now, seeing the influence Anton has had on so many bands and continues to today, I can appreciate what at the time seemed like maniacal intensity. I am very proud of Anton.'

Another person of note from this formative time is eufloria*, who met Anton at the Horseshoe Café around 1991, when she was nineteen. She had blonde dreads, sold herbal cigarettes (which she rolled herself), and made her own jewelry. Jeff thinks she might've lived with Arrow at one time. She and Anton spent a lot of time together, she says, exploring meditation and other forms of consciousness, listening to sitar music, and smoking ganja. It wasn't long before she'd started gigging with the band, too. She played two packed shows with them at the Peacock Lounge wearing a long pink satin dress that was decorated with huge beaded starfish. There were 16mm projectors running films that fit the psychedelic vibe of the space, as lights sporadically colored the walls of a front room bar and an entryway that led to a back room as you made your way all the way to the tiny stage at the back.

The band and eufloria* then went down to Los Angeles to play the shows that took place not long after relations with Greg Shaw and Bomp! first picked up. According to Victoria, the band showed up insisting they be paid $5,000. They were denied the fee but still all partied together in what inevitably ended up as an all-night binge of hedonistic, hallucinogenic debauchery.

Chris Dupre also began playing in the band around this time, and says a girl—perhaps eufloria*—had driven them down to LA to Greg and Victoria's apartment, and that he had brought with him a huge bag of 'shrooms. 'It was the first time Anton did a completely improvised show, [so] he was nervous about it,' Chris recalls. '[We] turned the fog machine up full blast, and it was complete free jazz noise for about forty minutes. The next night we played the Anti-Club on the bad end of Melrose, [and] the girl who [came] with us randomly tuned a boom-box radio while we did the noise. The *only* people in attendance were the three people who worked there. Absolutely no one came.'

* * *

According to eufloria*, she and Anton wrote the lyrics to the bridge for 'Wisdom' together at his place on Shrader. 'That was my shout-out to the flower posse or whatever,' she says, 'but really I just considered myself an interchangeable girl singer unit.'

Interchangeable girl singer units are a BJM staple. Before eufloria* there were at least three others: Vanessa, whom Anton good-naturedly called 'Singer' on one demo; another girl named Samsara; and a stripper named Karen, whom Sean says Anton was teaching how to play guitar, although she never played a show with them, and died of a drug overdose a year or two later. 'Death by misadventure, let's say,' says Jeff. 'Karen was a girl that I was dating. She was a great girl, something of a pro snowboarder. She just came over to the apartment with me a couple of times, but she was never really in the band. That was before we were really playing.' Anton called her 'Skaren,' which caught on.

A few other notable *interchangeable girl singer units*, including eufloria*, feature on *Methodrone,* which grew out of the same sessions for *Spacegirl,* though the latter's title track was written with one spacegirl in particular, Elizabeth Dye, in mind. 'She used to work at an ice cream shop in the Upper Haight,' Anton later explained. 'I wrote ["Spacegirl"] one day while looking at her eyes through the window of her work from outside.' Elizabeth was completely unaware that she was the inspiration for the song until years later, when a friend showed her the album's liner notes. 'I had a shirt Anton liked, a kind of *Speed Racer*–looking thing with red, white, and blue vertical stripes,' she remembers now, 'and Anton asked to borrow it for a gig he was playing with Jason Spaceman.'

Elizabeth moved to San Francisco in 1992 to go to art school, and she became friends with The Rosemarys through a classmate, Omar Perez, who did projections for their shows. She got to know a big, loose gang of musicians there, many of whom lived in the Lower Haight. 'I had a job at the Ben & Jerry's at the corner of Haight and Ashbury and lived down the street at Haight and Pierce,' she recalls. 'It was a crazy, gritty, amazing time there, and I had a total blast, living very cheaply and going to shows.'

Elizabeth's apartment building burned down one Thanksgiving weekend when a meth lab exploded in the basement of an adjoining building. She got a modest sum of insurance money from the fire, but instead of replacing anything she bought an old used car and her first guitar, a Fender telecaster. The guitarist in the Rosemarys, Ian Parks, asked her to record vocals on a side project he was working on—'sort of a shoegaze-y/wispy female vocals thing,' she says. 'He played some of it for Anton, and Anton asked him if I might want to sing for BJM.' She asked Ian if he thought she should take him up on the offer. 'There will come a time when you've had enough, but you won't regret doing it,' he told her.

'Good advice,' she says now, in retrospect. 'I was about nineteen, and a *young* nineteen, and a lot of things went over my head. I took being in the band quite seriously, and having to go onstage to do a song we'd only practiced four or five times was totally nerve-wracking for me. I didn't fully get at the time that the improvisational chaos of the band was the whole point.'

Anton always treated her with gentleness and respect. 'He was quite sweet—he made me a ton of mixtapes with titles like *It's Just A Game, But It's Deadly Serious*, and I guess he had sort of a crush on me, but it was pretty innocent,' she recalls. 'At least from my perspective. In my eyes, the attention Anton paid me had more to do with songwriting and the *girl in the band* idea that any real romantic interest.'

Elizabeth sang co-lead with Anton on 'Evergreen,' which eufloria* then sang on for the 'She Made Me' / 'Evergreen' single. 'Wisdom,' the second song on *Methodrone*, is missing eufloria*'s vocal, but that role would be picked up later by Miranda Lee Richards when it was re-recorded for *Strung Out In Heaven*. 'I remember not totally liking the female vocal part on "Wisdom" but thinking Anton must know what he's doing,' Elizabeth recalls. 'I was kind of in awe of him—pop hooks came out of his head totally fully formed, and he could just spool out lyrics. There was obvious brilliance. I was there to follow instructions and look cute.'

The string of blonde, wispy interchangeable girl singer units marked the final transition from Electric Kool Aid and everything else Anton was doing to The Brian Jonestown Massacre. 'There was a striking visual difference,' Del Beaudry says of eufloria*. 'Gorgeous and sunny, yet foreboding. She was an authentic chanteuse. She was supposed to be our Nico.' This is the job that was later ultimately taken up and redefined by Joel, though a sharp blonde makes her way in there every now and again.*

* * *

San Francisco is translucent at night. Thousands moving through shadow and darkness. The smell and breeze of the ocean breathes across every concrete pillar. Every pane of glass. Crystal Apel had gone on such a night to visit her friend Beth Johnson when she found a large crowd of people gathering outside Beth's apartment on Steiner in the Lower Haight, a droning wall of sound filling the street with kaleidoscopic glow, Beth having let the BJM set up to play a set on the roof.

'That show would have been on top of Spaghetti Western,' Jeff recalls.† 'That was one of the first shows. I remember dragging the amps out the window.' Several people filmed the show from their windows across the street, while the crowd grew so large that when the cops arrived to see what the commotion was about, they couldn't make it through to stop the music.

Beth had taken a lot of LSD and was hiding in the closet to avoid her

---

* eufloria* now works and lives in Maui as an 'artist, yogini, and world traveler'; Elizabeth Dye now works in Portland, Oregon, as a clothing designer, specializing in handmade dresses and wedding gowns. For more, see their respective websites, eufloria.com and elizabethdye.com.
† The Spaghetti Western was, until 2000, a popular breakfast spot located at 576 Haight Street that was said to serve some of the best biscuits and gravy in town. The building is now home to Memphis Minnie's BBQ Joint.

landlord, who was trying to find her to shut the show down because no one was allowed to set foot on that roof, much less allow non-residents up there. In the meantime, there was the crowd, and the cops trying to get through, and the landlord trying to get in. It was one Luella Jane Wright from London, a subtenant of the building who'd hooked James up with playing in the band and was dating Ricky at this time, who helped them secure the rooftop by hauling their gear through Beth's window. Luella wasn't at the show though, for some reason.

Barry Simons, who would later become Anton's lawyer, was among those watching the band from the street below. This was actually his second BJM show; his first was an after-hours party that was raided by the police, so when the cops showed up this time, Barry figured that they must do so every time the BJM played a show. 'They were going to need me there just to talk for them,' he later observed.

The band quickly amassed a reputation around the Haight that then spread across town. Josephine Tavares, a longtime friend of the group, had been walking on the Lower Haight with some friends when they spotted the band playing on top of the roof. She had not yet heard of The Brian Jonestown Massacre, but she soon found out that they were scheduled to play the following weekend at the Crash Palace on Divisadero, which was owned at that time by this guy she was dating, now called the Independent.* Before that next show, Josephine ran into Jeff and told him about this 'great band' she'd seen playing on a roof, and how she was going to see them that night. 'That's *my* band!' Jeff shouted enthusiastically. 'And *we're* playing tonight!'

Later, during the show, Jeff, sporting a Boy Scout shirt, nodded out onstage. Anton yelled at him for falling asleep in front of everybody, as he was apt to do often when he showed up to gigs smacked out. Del, though, has fond memories of the former guitarist, despite his hang-ups. 'Jeff was a junkie all the way through, and that's all there was to it, but he was a nice guy,' he recalls. 'Nobody had a problem with having Jeff in their house. Jeff didn't steal or rip people off. He was a sweetheart. He had a problem making it to things. Being places on time. Shit like that. But, *goddammit*, he was a good guitar player.'

---

* Located at 628 Divisadero Street, the Crash Palace was also known as the Justice League and is now called the Independent.

23456

THE COMPOUND

As things started rolling with Bomp!, on November 4, 1992, a peculiar man dressed in black approached the BJM after they opened for Spectrum* at the Kennel Club and made them an offer. His name was Naut Humon, and he wanted to hook the BJM up with a manager—namely record producer and music executive Wally Brill. 'They tried to put this *50 percent of everything I ever made* contract over my head, and I just looked at these two guys and I said, *Fuck you*,' Anton later recalled. He did, however, see in Naut's offer an opportunity to learn how to work in a studio. 'I wanted to learn how to record and engineer because I had already been in the studio before with these teenage bands I was in and just saw the engineers butcher our sounds.'

One story goes that Naut, an industrial-goth guru and civil-war buff who survived on a diet of plain yogurt and black olives and dyed his hair jet black, and was possibly a former child star of some sort, met the band through Travis Threlkel's then-girlfriend, Kim Stringfellow. Travis confirms this, adding that he and Kim met Naut at a My Bloody Valentine gig. Naut says that Anton actively sought him out the same way he'd sought out Greg, in that the band would simply park in front of his studio until he let them in.

Del Beaudry says he knew Naut separately through the Record Finder, another old record store just off of Market on Noe Street, which held out as long as it could, until Amoeba ended up crushing its business. Naut and his ex-wife, Mitzi Johnson, shopped there often, and Del claims that *he* was the one who hyped the BJM to Naut, 'which is why he got to that show [with Spectrum] early ... [that was] the first time he saw them.'

Naut's studio was the Compound, a massive, darkly lit warehouse on the

---

* Fellow Bomp! act Spectrum were led by Peter 'Sonic Boom' Kember, formerly of Spacemen 3.

outskirts of Hunter's Point ('back when it was fucking scary,' according to former BJM drummer Brian Glaze). This is where Mike Kubisty eventually came to record 'Hide And Seek.' One time, Daniel Knop says, Brian was headed to the studio to record when people on the bus began lighting matches and throwing them at him. The studio was within earshot of Candlestick Park, too, the surrounding areas strewn with abandoned cars and dumped-off toxic waste barrels.

'Getting out to that area was intimidating for some,' *Methodrone* engineer Adrienne Gulyassy recalls. 'This was a predominantly black neighborhood [and] a high crime area, and this was still the crack cocaine era. So, yes, some felt out of place and intimidated.'

According to Tommy Dietrick, by the 90s the surrounding homes of that neighborhood had come to resemble a 1930s German-Jewish ghetto, but inside, the Compound was filled with every kind of recording gear imaginable, like some kind of post-apocalyptic treasure trove. That said, there was nothing fancy about the place. There were little amp and drum recording rooms, and the control room was cramped full of analogue equipment, much of it financed by Mitzi, whose family made their fortune inventing the reflective speed bumps that can be seen today on the freeways across the USA.

Before Naut inherited the building, it had been the site of a witches' coven, which is fitting, as Naut was so secretive about the location of the studio that people were literally blindfolded before being taken there. 'The Compound is where Anton honed his thing more than anywhere else,' says Joel, who still wasn't quite in the band yet but was hanging around. 'Naut used to let him have the studio in the night hours while he wasn't there doing business.'

According to Dave Deresinski, Anton wasn't allowed in the Compound without him until he began recording *Their Satanic Majesties' Second Request.* Having recorded on mostly Tascam 424 and Fostex four-track machines for the past decade or so, Anton was unfamiliar with the high-tech, state-of-the-art equipment Naut used at the Compound. At one point, he accidentally broke an expensive microphone that Dave ended up having to pay for, in installments, over the next few years.

'Naut let me have the place to myself every night from midnight until about 10am the next day,' Anton later recalled of his time there, sculpting sonic daydreams nightly, recording all the parts himself in the control booth in time to hand Naut a rough mix of the night's work the following morning. 'Every day he would come in and ask, Did you finish that track? and I would say, No, but check this new song out! And he'd be like, *Oh, that's interesting*, and every day he would take a mix of it home to work on, and so I got hundreds of songs that way with him.'

Tim Digula of the band Tipsy was often around the studio, tinkering for Naut, making experimental recordings involving multiple speakers, sampling, and strange playback configurations using what might be described as a primitive form of surround sound.* In addition to Tim, Naut held at his beck and call a team of engineers who were skeptical of Anton at first but eventually warmed to him.

After the 'She Made Me' / 'Evergreen' single, Bomp!'s next BJM release formed part of the *Tangible Box* set of six seven-inch singles, which featured 'Convertible' b/w 'Their Satanic Majesties' Second Request (Enrique's Dream)' as the B-side, plus an additional BJM single, credited to Acid, featuring 'Never, Ever' and 'Thoughts Of You.' The other bands included in the set were Nebtwister, Orange, Hollowbody, and Reverb; some of them were pseudonyms for Anton.

'Convertible' is one of Ricky's favorites from this period. 'When I listen to it, it's like time travel, but it was like that even then,' he says. 'That recording is just Anton, Travis, and myself at the Compound late one night. Best time of the band, in my opinion—before anyone knew who we were, apart from a handful of friends. We would go from Poolside, working on what became *Methodrone*, to the Compound, to work on what became *Spacegirl*. "Convertible" was a part of that. We really should take another stab at it. I've been bugging Anton about it forever, which I'm sure is how 'Our Time' came about.'†

A hilarious BJM 'origin story' that summarizes this time in the band's history up until that point through the metaphor of an alien invasion is recounted in a promo item Greg wrote called *The Brian Jonestown Blotter*, which was included in the *Tangible Box* and featured photos by Peter Booth Lee.

Around the same time as *Tangible Box*, one Mike Toi told Dave that

---

* Tim later played—and now again plays—in a band with Ricky and Travis called The Imajinary Friends.
† 'Our Time' is a reworking of 'Convertible' that appears on *Who Killed Sgt. Pepper?*

he was interested in releasing an album of BJM music on his label Candy Floss, so Mike talked Naut, Dave, and Anton into letting him use Anton's rough demos for what then became *Spacegirl & Other Favorites*. Anton, however, has said that Greg put out *Spacegirl* shortly after finding the *Ben Is Dead* review. He's since dismissed the record as 'the studio trash of my early years,' insisting that that the band's first 'real' album is *Take It From The Man!* The 'Hide And Seek' single Mike Kubisty plays on was also released on Candy Floss, with a B-side of 'Methodrone'—the song that shares its name with the band's next full-length record—recorded live at the Compound in January 1994.

Spacegirl, though largely underappreciated in the BJM canon, is significant for the way it showcases Anton's work as it evolved into *Methodrone* and everything after. If *Spacegirl* lacks the makings of a solid BJM record, it does provide insight into Anton's sonic vision. When 'Crushed' kicks in, the intro noise lasts for well over a minute. It fades in, out of feedback, amid swells in the amps that start to sound like Indian flutes, and then it half collapses, half crescendos into the riff.

'That Girl Suicide' is on both *Spacegirl* and *Methodrone*, and is one of the best songs from this early period, along with 'She's Gone.' 'I wrote that in Diana James's room,' Anton has said of 'That Girl.' 'We bought matching hollowbodies, a guitar and a bass. I wrote the bassline to teach her to play, then I went to practice and showed the band one riff at a time, pretending we all wrote it together. They still think they wrote it, but I know. See, I tricked them, because they wanted to be a band but had no real ideas, apart from Matt, and he lacked the this-is-what-it-takes thing, so it had to be done.'

'Deep In The Devil's Eye & You' returns again to the noise swell, and has this weird electronic beat, but then 'Kid's Garden' takes a step in the 60s-revivalist direction *Their Satanic Majesties' Second Request* would embrace fully. After that, Anton's guitar playing on 'When I Was Yesterday' reminds me of what I would describe as the classic Brian Jonestown sound, with bluesy, reverberating leads over the fuzz note playing over and over. The song's deep, echoing drones sound like a gigantic, fuzzy horn section all playing the same note, like a mantra. If you can find your way to get lost in it, it almost doesn't feel like it's twelve minutes long, even with the longest fadeout ever before it swells once more and finishes. The instrumental

'Spacegirl Revisited' is indicative of this style as well. Things then again shift to post-punk à la 'That Girl Suicide' on 'After The Fall,' which echoes 'Food For Clouds' from 2014's *Revelation.*

Spacegirl was originally released exclusively on LP in a limited run of five hundred copies pressed at Greg Lee Processing. The first two songs, 'Crushed' and 'That Girl Suicide,' also appear on *Methodrone*, but with their drum tracks replaced by live playing by Swervedriver's Graham Bonnar. The others—'Deep In The Devil's Eye & You,' 'Kid's Garden,' 'When I Was Yesterday,' 'Spacegirl,' and 'Spacegirl (Revisited)'—are exclusive to this release, with the exception of 'Kid's Garden,' which appears as part of the *Thank God For Mental Illness* track 'Sound Of Confusion.'

A decade later, the CD reissue added six more tracks, of which 'Fire Song' is also included in 'Sound Of Confusion.' A demo of 'Hide And Seek' appears as another of the additional tracks on the reissue, alongside 'Never, Ever!' which was included on the Acid single, with 'Feelers' as the B-side, in *Tangible Box*. The other additional tracks are 'After The Fall,' 'Thoughts Of You,' and the noisy 'Ashtray,' which Anton reportedly recorded with Matt on his birthday. The record's cover features a profile photograph of a child, purportedly Dawn Thomas, her hair soaped up into a large point like an antennae.

JUST BENEATH THE FLOOR

Methodrone is really what *Spacegirl* should have been, but Anton was trying for something way beyond what the album turned into. He spent a whole winter practically living at the Compound, recording whenever studio time was available, paying for it by sampling synthesizers and keyboards for an early incarnation of Pro Tools. 'At some point I just moved on and … [it] was remixed … by other people,' he later said of the record, for which he says he came up with the title after the first time he met Bomp! labelmate Peter Kember. 'Now there is a designer drug named [Methodrone] in Scandinavia, but I in fact invented it to describe Peter the first time he met me at the studio. I was shocked to learn he was a registered methadone user and brought a jar on tour … you know, his *drone* band.'

When he wasn't playing gigs or sneaking into clubs, Tommy would skateboard down the Haight, occasionally stopping for a slice at Escape From New York Pizza, where fellow skater Matt worked. Having befriended the guys and played shows with them, Tommy had a unique experience as a fly on the wall for many BJM sessions at the Compound. A decent amount, though not all, of the material featured on the early BJM albums was recorded during this 1991–94 period, he says.

By now, Tommy and Alex were good friends with Travis and Ricky, who sometimes drove them out to the Compound. 'We all used to go down there and hang out while Anton and the band worked on ADAT [digital audio tape], tape, or whatever, as things progressed,' Alex recalls. 'The studio was amazing, and it seemed like Dave and Anton had Naut convinced to let them record there for free whenever they wanted.'

However, the first four songs on *Methodrone* were recorded at a studio called Poolside, which had been in operation since '85. They are, says Del, 'the only real studio recordings with Anton and Travis really going at it.'

David Nelson, who owned the studio, remembers the BJM recording there. 'Eric Holland, my assistant at the time, did the engineering,' he recalls. 'We used a [Neumann] U67 [condenser mic] as a mono overhead on the drums, probably 16 track with a 1" tape.' According to Graham Bonnar, who was brought in to add live drumming to some of the tracks, 'Crushed,' the third song on the album, 'was recorded at Poolside with the full band playing. The main thing was getting drums that me and Anton were happy with, then overdubs at Poolside and the Compound.'

Anton was supposed to finish the recordings he had started at Poolside, since Naut had financed the sessions, but that arrangement fell through. 'Anton would get in these situations … and he'd tell us, *We're doing this free recording*, and then it would be obvious that the other side was thinking something else,' Jeff recalls. 'I don't know if he truly was aware of other people's point of view, or if out of his force of will he would make it be so. Poolside, and the thing at [Ricky's uncle] Ed [Dorn]'s—I think that wasn't completely done. People couldn't work with [Anton], and then he would blame them. It was always, *They don't know what they're doing. I need to do it all myself.*'

'Everyone Says' was co-written by Anton and one Paola Simmonds, who'd been around since the band were calling themselves Electric Kool Aid, and is one of the songs that's exclusive to *Methodrone*. Paola says she wrote it and that Anton slowed it down for the recording; originally it was played at twice the speed, she says, but I love it when her double tracked vocals kick in, because she's harmonizing with herself, and one voice is mixed just slightly lower than the other, so there's also this slight natural chorus effect, which you can do more effectively if you reduce vibrato in your singing voice.

Paola lived near the Haight in a huge house on Page and Divisadero that was once an operating bordello. The band crashed with her sometimes after shows, and Travis says he and Graham later rented the attic. 'It was just like the *Monkees* TV show!' Paola remembers fondly. When Tommy tagged along, he'd get so stoned he'd pass out on her couch.

Paola remembers seeing Ricky at all the in-store gigs for the touring bands that she loved. At one gig in particular, Anton had come along, too, and she

57

noticed Ricky was wearing a Church T-shirt. To Paola, The Church were the greatest band that ever was; and, back then, it was extremely rare to run into a fellow Church fan.

After her first BJM show, Paola approached Anton and Ricky on the street outside of the club and asked them if they had any tapes for sale. Momentarily out of copies, they shyly told her no, but then Paola told Ricky that she'd noticed he played a red Vox hollowbody bass, just like The Church's Steve Kilbey.

'You know about Steve Kilbey?' Ricky shouted back excitedly.*

Ricky had been playing guitar in the BJM up until this point, but when Matt left the band in the summer of '92 to move back to Santa Barbara, Ricky took up bass duties in his place, and would stay in that role for the remainder of his first go in the Jonestown. Matt, meanwhile, wasn't digging life in San Francisco and often clashed with Anton, so there was no suggestion of him returning at the time, but he did do so around the end of '93 or the start of '94.

Things went quiet for a while until one day, when Paola and some friends were hanging out at one of the many cafés they frequented in the Haight, Anton appeared out of nowhere, kidnapped Paola, and brought her to the Compound. The session was a controversial one in the then-small BJM community, since the band were already working with one of their standard female singers, though it's unclear which one it was. Whatever the jive was at the time, Paola and Anton knocked out the song that day. Anton liked the way it turned out, and he didn't want to try it again. 'Everyone Says' quickly became popular among the group, their friends, and their fans.

A lot of people were of the opinion that Paola was sleeping with Anton or other members of the band, but she insists that she was only ever friends with the guys and had no romantic or sexual interest in any of them whatsoever— the first of a few women to have made such a claim to me unsolicited. Paola says her lyrics for 'Everyone Says' were inspired by a secret crush she had on The Rosemarys' Tim Ong, and that the BJM laughed when she told them who the song was about. 'I never want to fall in love that way again,' she says now of the experience. 'It hurt so much that I felt physical pain, and I never even got to *touch* him.'

---

*Ricky had actually met Steve at a gig in San Francisco in October 1991, when he was eighteen or nineteen. He later went on to make a record with his hero, 2011's *David Neil—The Wilderness Years*.

Paola's best friend in those days was a fellow Church super-fan by the name of Diane Perry. The two of them were really into shoegaze, and they went to as many local shows they could. They started following The Rosemarys, which is how they came to see the BJM open for them one time, back when they were Electric Kool Aide. Paola had already met the band by then, so this was Diane's first BJM show, but after that the two of them became bigger fans of the BJM than The Rosemarys.

Diane lived with Paola there in that Victorian flat on Divisidero. Paola and Diane stayed on the third floor, and above them was a full-sized attic where the band sometimes practiced. Diane would live there for two more years before moving into another Victorian flat about five or six blocks away. 'Anton was usually borderline homeless, and if he was between girlfriends, which he often was, he would come stay with me and sleep on my couch,' she says. 'We used to watch documentaries, and he liked to cook. He was really good company then.'

* * *

In some ways, *Methodrone* is a document of the band's shifting membership during the early-to-mid 90s. Ricky plays bass on four tracks: 'Evergreen,' 'Wisdom,' 'Short Wave,' and 'She Made Me.' Matt plays bass on 'That Girl Suicide,' 'Wasted,' and 'Hyperventilation,' which are also the only tracks Brian Glaze appears on. (Despite playing on only those three tracks, Brian is featured on the album's cover alongside Matt, Anton, and new member Dean Taylor, who joined closer to the end of the sessions.) Anton's joined by Graham Bonnar on 'Crushed,' 'Everyone Says,' and 'She's Gone,' but he plays everything himself on 'Records,' 'End Of The Day,' and 'Outback.'

'Hyperventilation' was originally titled 'Iggy Pop Sonic Boom,' and you can definitely hear the influence of The Stooges on the song. It's like something off that first Stooges record—like '1969' but at half the speed. (Around 1995–96, Peter Kember did a new mix of the song with Anton and Dave at the Compound, but they didn't like it, and it was never released.)

'Records' serves as one of two interludes on the record, along with 'Outback.' It starts out much like 'Crushed,' with the weird swells and feedback and whatever other things are going on. It gets weirder and more intense as it goes, and then kicks into 'I Love You,' which to my ears is a

Velvet Underground homage. The xylophone recalls 'Sunday Morning,' and the drums are very 'All Tomorrow's Parties,' but not in that same Jesus & Mary Chain way. Anton makes it his own.

The best song on the record, by far, is 'She's Gone.' For me, that song is the moment where this record becomes *The Jonestown*. It grooves. It shakes. It trips and expands. If you let it, it can take you places you've never been. 'The actual lead sound is all of my strings tuned to *A*, and I'm playing no effects,' Anton has said of 'She's Gone.' 'Three fingers at once, then doubled up with a pipe organ and flute Mellotron. I recorded the drums last, and I use my own rhythms as a click track.' (He further explained that the track was recorded using a D&R board from the Netherlands using six Tascam DA-38 digital audio recorders SMPTE time-locked into an Otari eight-track, with Dolby Spectral Recording noise reduction and 3m/Ampex 356 tape.)

As well as the various band members, *Methodrone*'s list a number of different recording engineers, alongside Dave and Anton, who handled some of the sessions themselves. John Karr, who had originally been brought in to help Naut Humon with his live Sound Traffic Control productions, engineered 'End Of The Day.' Eric Holland is listed in the liner notes for 'Evergreen,' 'Wisdom,' 'Short Wave,' 'She Made Me,' and 'I Love You.' The only other engineer with as many credits is Adrienne Gulyassy, who is credited with helping on 'Evergreen,' 'Crushed,' 'That Girl Suicide,' 'Wasted,' 'Everyone Says,' and 'Hyperventilation.'

Adrienne was introduced to Naut and Mitzi in 1993 by producer Wally Brill (referred to more recently, by Anton, as Wally George.) Fresh out of audio engineering school, she worked at the Compound as an intern. At the time, Naut's production company was called Informusik. Recalling her first meeting with Anton, she says, 'I walked into The Compound control room one morning and here was this guy, shirtless, disheveled, unshaven, definitely unshowered, but physically attractive, nonetheless, in that mischievous, boyish kind of way. There was no formal introduction. It went more like, *Adrienne, Anton—Anton, Adrienne*. Skipping a handshake or even a nod, Anton launched into this wide-eyed and maniacal explanation of what he'd been working on, no doubt all night. That's how our relationship began, and really how it remained.'

Adrienne says the *Methodrone* sessions were not 'sessions' in the

60

traditional sense. What Anton was doing were more like random jam sessions, followed by countless hours of overdubbing, sound editing, embellishments, and postproduction tweaks. Drums came last, which is opposite to standard studio protocol, but seems more efficient if all the music is already in time.*

Adrienne remembers most vividly the sessions for 'She's Gone' and 'In India You.' If you think of that song as the bridge between Anton's shoegaze sound and his more 60s-garage sound, there is one thing consistent in all of it—the drone. Adrienne says that one of Anton's ideas was to run a prerecorded guitar track out to one of the other rooms through an old tube amp, distort the signal, then record it back using a vintage ribbon microphone. 'He loved to mix and break the rules along the way,' she says.

Another engineer who started at the Compound around the same time as Adrienne and did much of the same work—mostly file editing and cataloguing—was Jessica Grace Wing. She also helped with 'Evergreen,' though Adrienne says she can't remember the exact details of Jessica's involvement. 'I do know we did some sound embellishing in Jessica's bedroom,' Adrienne recalls. 'She had keyboards, effects processors, and even sound-editing software.'

61

'Jessica was lovely,' Graham recalls. 'She used to pick me up in the morning to go to the studio. We would have coffee and muffins.'†

Graham also played in a British shoegaze band called Swervedriver, and proved a great fit for the songs he plays on here. Shortly after the San

---

* A good way to teach yourself how to record, particularly if you're in a band, is to play along to a metronome or click track. First you layer all the other parts, then, for the drummer, it's like they're playing to a band instead of to the click. If you want to be a recording artist, first you have to learn an instrument. Doesn't have to be perfect, just good enough to be able to go from one chord to another. Then you write some songs. Get a laptop and some cheap recording software, usually an interface that you'd pick up through a site like sweetwater.com or reverb.com. Teach yourself the basics of microphones and recording with them, then record your songs. Mix them, bounce them to MP3s or wavs, burn them on a CD, then play them in a car or your home system. If you play keyboard or piano, get a MIDI synthesizer and play around with the different sounds your software or interface might provide. This is, for me, the best way to make demos nowadays. The more instruments you learn, the more you'll be able to create, and at the end, the drummer—or you, if you're the drummer—does their part last. It is like Anton says: you are the informed but submissive listener. Also, to better understand the recording process, it is not a bad idea to study the history behind some of your favorite records. However, I recommend this only if the information is easily available through online, print, or archival material. Otherwise, you may end up writing a book.

† Jessica passed away from cancer in 2003, at the age of thirty-one. After her time at the Compound she played in punk and electronica rock bands, studied film at Columbia, and later became an important part of the New York theatre scene.

Francisco stop on Swervedriver's 1993 US tour, Ricky ran into him at a concert by Th' Faith Healers and recognized him instantly. Graham ditched his band at the Canadian border, in the middle of their tour, and moved to San Francisco, where Ricky invited him to come jam with the BJM at the Compound. Within a week, Anton had asked him to play drums on *Methodrone* at Poolside.

Though those sessions proved productive, during the recording of 'Wisdom,' Graham declared that shoegaze, which he thought the song exemplified, was dead and over. He did not stick around for long, but he left on good terms, and still maintains friendships with those he knew in the group. Anton has since claimed that Graham convinced Ricky and Travis during this part of the *Methodrone* sessions that he was bossing them around, walking all over them, and stopping them from having fun. Others say Anton's full of shit: that they'd actually been ready to quit for a while; that Anton and Ricky fought all the time, anyway; and that it was actually Travis and Ricky who'd made friends with Peter Kember, who then, in turn, encouraged them to go to Reading, in England, for a month.

This would've been around June 1993; Ricky says he left the BJM in August of that year. 'When Travis and I went to England, it was mainly so I could see Luella again,' he says. Another uncle of his, Vince Welnick from The Grateful Dead and The Tubes, paid for the trip. 'We hooked up with Creation Records' Joe Foster to see what was possible, but that label wasn't interested in BJM, which kind of helped us to make up our minds about leaving the band,' he continues. 'We already wanted out, and when Creation showed no excitement over our demo, which turned out to be the *Methodrone* tracks that we play on, it was pretty easy to walk away. Mind you, this was before [Creation] signed Oasis, so perhaps money was an issue.'

Anton maintains that his account of events is true, subsequently claiming, 'We almost were signed to Creation, but my two guitar players took the tickets and split. Didn't even go to the meetings.' Whatever the truth of the matter, Ricky and Travis flew over to Europe for a month and a half, and, upon returning, formed The Imajinary Friends with Graham, Matt (now back from Santa Barbara), and Tim Digula. Greg put out their record *Lunchtime In Infinity* on Bomp! around the same time Candyfloss put out *Spacegirl & Other Favorites*. According to Travis, however, there was more to his and

Ricky's exit than wanting to do a different band. 'The reason I left was, I thought I wanted to do other music, but mainly Anton was losing his mind and lashing out at people, abusing people that would play with us,' he says. 'It was uncomfortable to be around.'

With Ricky and Travis gone, Anton was left to finish *Methodrone* by himself, and he went through a four-month period with fluctuating members before re-establishing things with Matt and Jeff and then bringing in Joel and Dean Taylor, with Brian on drums. Before Brian came back, there was another drummer, Milo Warner Martin, who is on 'Hide And Seek' and also claims to have played on 'Evergreen,' from *Methodrone*. Though he is not credited on the song, he says, 'Everyone knows that is me. I'm not sure why Anton didn't credit me on that, because we were on good terms … I moved to LA shortly thereafter and saw the new band in the postmodern 60s-psychedelic phase and almost didn't recognize them.'

* * *

At some point in 1994, the BJM played a gig at Bottom Of The Hill. The lineup was Chris Dupre on bass; Ian Sefchick from Creeper Lagoon on rhythm guitar; Jeff on lead guitar, with his super-long hair up in a 60s girl-group bun with tons of bobby pins; and Milo on drums. Anton was on hollowbody and vocals, and that night was wearing an unseasonably warm, full-on parka with fur around the hood, big earphones, and a laurel of fake leaves spray-painted gold around his derelict, cherubic head. Before heading to the gig, Ian and Milo were at Milo's flat in the Lower Haight, greasing up, drinking, and smoking joints. Ian didn't like the pants he was wearing, so he borrowed Milo's thin black Adidas sweat pants, leaving the zippers undone at the ankles.

Chris Dupre's other band, Torn Memory, opened this show, so Chris played two sets that night. They were just getting into a really good, loud sonic groove when Anton approached the mic, in the middle of 'Evergreen,' and spun off it like he'd been shot. He then approached it again and was shocked even more powerfully. He collapsed onto his knees and then fell backward, his shoulders touching the stage, arms outstretched to either side.

The band all looked at each other and continued to play. Anton pulled himself up as the band carried the groove, playing it off like nothing happened. 'But of course we knew it happened,' Milo recalls. 'Something always happens at a BJM show—another stick in the cosmic spokes, leaving a heavy negative pull on a show that was otherwise going swimmingly.'

The band finally ended the song and eyed each other, shrugging, as Anton struggled to pull himself back up. A hush fell over the crowd. The soundman rushed the stage to rectify the situation, and he and the band all came over to attend to Anton. It took him a few minutes to come back to an upright state, but they were able to finish the show. 'Lord only knows how well it went,' says Milo. 'That was over twenty years ago, but, *shit*, it seems like a car accident I saw just last week.'

Eventually, Milo and Chris were phased out of the group. 'Anton fired everyone except me after [a] Halloween gig at Boz Scaggs's joint, Slim's, in San Francisco, opening for Romeo Void,' Milo adds. According to Chris, 'The reason I was kicked out was that I had a hard time playing simplistic drone two/three-chord songs, as I thought I was hot shit and wanted to play jazz. One time we played the main stage at the Paradise Lounge and Dave came up to me while I was going off and yelled into my ear, *Please don't do that!*'

That Halloween night at Slim's, Chris was high on dope and started jumping around the stage, trying to get under Anton's skin. He'd been antagonizing him for the past couple of weeks, in part because of Anton's 'total control' over the band's aesthetic, but also because they weren't getting paid much.

Milo had his drum kit at the front of stage left, facing sideways. Chris came up to Milo, put his foot on the kick, and flashed the 'devil horns' hand signal. 'We're all laughing, high as shit, and I remember we actually pulled out the Stones' *whoo-hoo* outro bridge part from "Sympathy For The Devil," over and over again,' Milo recalls. 'Chris and the boys were being all heavy metal.' (That *whoo-hoo* bit had been incorporated into the BJM's 'Straight Up And Down.')

Catching on to Chris's irreverent spirit, everyone in the band but Anton started following his lead, posing, kicking, and making smooch-y faces like they were members of KISS or something. 'We get a great reception, big applause, leave the stage,' Milo continues, 'and as soon as we get backstage, Anton announces the whole band is fired.'

Anton kept Jeff on and gradually reformed the band. Jeff says this was around the time he was really starting to contribute to the group, and that he was helping pull the band in a different direction. 'As time goes by, history is rewritten,' he says. 'Anton is the man. No doubt. Very prolific. Couldn't happen without him. But I was there, and I did influence style and the type of music. I think I brought it from Anton's sensibilities from a very sad, English, kind of shoegazer type thing into more of a psychedelic, Americana sound.'

My guess is that this was also around the time Matt came back, because this is when he really started contributing songs to the group and taking on a collaborative role—however conflicted things might have been at times over the next few years. Diane Perry claims to have been responsible for Matt getting back into the band this first time, after he quit in '92 and moved back to Santa Barbara. 'Nobody who played bass after Matt did it as well as Matt,' she says, 'so I did some detective work and I got Matt's number, and after a couple of phone calls I was able to talk him into coming back.'

It was also around this time that Joel first came into the band. Joel was Travis's friend, and had met Anton through him. 'Joel dressed really fucking sharp, owned a Rickenbacker guitar,' Travis recalls. 'Had a nice apartment in the Upper Haight.'

By the time *Methodrone* was almost ready for release in 1995, the band found they needed an additional guitar player, so they got Dean Taylor. Dean was working as a cook in town, and, one night after work, he went for a beer at the Cat's Grill & Alley Club, near 8th and Folsom, as was his routine. The Brian Jonestown Massacre were playing in the next room to a small crowd. Dean, intrigued by what he heard, stepped in to listen more closely, and he was blown away immediately. He'd never heard anything like it.

Among the handful of people in the crowd was Diane, who befriended Dean and introduced him to the band after the show. 'I saw Dean sitting at the bar, and I thought, *Man, he has the look. If that guy can play guitar, I'm going to get him to audition with Anton,*' she recalls. 'He had the Beatle boots and the shaggy haircut, and this cool-ass jacket from the 60s.'

Diane arranged for Dean to go out to a rehearsal. Shortly after that meeting, Anton called asking him to try out for the band, so he did, and that was that. 'We all did more drinking and hanging out than practicing, which made the shows a bit loose, to say the least,' Dean recalls. 'But I thought the looseness, space, and spontaneity in those jams were what made our shows cool.'

Dean joined the band around the time Anton was finishing up *Methodrone* and says he might have even tracked some acoustic guitar for a few songs. 'Can't remember for sure,' he says. 'I was in the studio with Anton several times, but, of course, my memory is a little hazy due to certain substances and things.' He is on the cover, though, at least.

Diane stayed around for the band's first couple of years before moving to Sacramento. She came to every BJM show during the early 90s and recorded the band's sets on a tape recorder. Most importantly, she had a car, and she had money from her steady job as a legal secretary, so naturally she became something of a steward to the band as things started taking off. 'Those guys didn't have a car, they didn't have money, so if they needed to go somewhere I would end up driving them,' she says. 'Dave would call me and say, Hey, we got a gig coming up, we need to get the band together to practice. I would track them down, pick them up, then take them out to their rehearsal space past Potrero Hill. I would feed them when they didn't have enough to eat … I was so in love with the band that I just wanted to do everything possible to help so they could be more successful.'*

A confirmed Anglophile, Diane was into shoegaze, the Creation label, Madchester, and English pop, so, to her, the BJM was the natural place to be. The title of 'That Girl Suicide' was actually inspired by her. It was originally called 'Fat Girl Suicide' on account of her reportedly using speed to stay thin, and started out as a rework of Gary Numan's 'Cars,' though the music got harder and trashier some time after it was written. 'Diane was doing loads of speed to be thin and fit in with the rock people,' Joel explains, 'but [the title] was also mean, and a footnote that went away.' Diane confirms this. 'I lost a lot of weight doing meth,' she says. 'Too much weight—maybe thirty pounds—so I was really thin for a while, but I thought I looked great.'

The band also named a bootleg after her. Recorded before Dean joined the band, *The Diane Perry Tape* features solid versions of 'That Girl Suicide,' 'Straight Up And Down,' and 'The Devil May Care,' among others. Some

---

* According to Del Beaudry, Diane having a car 'was a big deal in San Francisco at the time, because nobody drove. It cost a fucking fortune to have a car in San Francisco.' Dave Deresinski also drove the band around, and Del ended up selling him his '82 Dodge van, which would later become the band's first touring van. 'Dave was our manager, and had been for quite a while, when I joined,' Dean recalls. 'He booked shows for us and tried, often unsuccessfully, to schedule practice times and places for us. He put up lots of money for recording, practice, food, and so on. He basically got no respect from anybody, but we all liked him.'

of the songs reportedly originated from a radio broadcast that Diane taped, while others were recorded in the Haight. There is also an early version of 'Telegram,' which wouldn't appear on an official release until 2001's *Bravery Repetition And Noise*.*

The Diane Perry Tape is significant among the various, often-apocryphal BJM bootleg collections because it highlights Anton's musical evolution from the heavy shoegaze and space-rock vibe of the band's earliest recordings to the psych-drenched 60s revisionism of the next four records. The drones and reverberations are there, intact, but Anton's songwriting eventually transcends the otherworldliness of his soundscapes. A solid balance between the two is the key to some of his best work in the BJM catalogue, from 'Wisdom' to 'Memory Camp.' This is the sound that so many people have cited as informing the work of bands like Black Rebel Motorcycle Club and The Black Angels. The most important aspect of this particular bootleg, I think, is that it captures the band live at the time when they were recording at the Compound.

Running Bomp! with Greg Shaw at this point were his ex-wife Suzy, one Patrick Boissel (before he founded his own label Alive! in 1993), and Chelsea Starr. Greg handled everything except promo, which he delegated to Chelsea, who then coordinated with him, Dave, and Anton on various projects.†

Chelsea was in Greg's apartment as he tried various different Photoshop effects on *Methodrone*'s cover. It was his first time using the software, and he was quite proud of it, but his design originally and intentionally had no words, and he wasn't the only one who had input into the cover. 'If I remember correctly, Travis did the design for *Methodrone*,' Matt later said, in a Q&A session on the Committee To Keep Music Evil forum. 'I could be wrong, but it is really similar to his work on the *Tangible Box*. He played on and co-wrote several songs on that album, and *Spacegirl* as well.' Whoever came up with it, Suzy thought the choice of artwork ridiculous, arguing that they couldn't sell a CD without the band's name on the cover. Greg gave in, and Chris Barrus, another hired hand, came in to help tweak the color of the band's name to a bright white.

---

* While not an official release, *The Diane Perry Tape* can be found online.
† I tried to get in touch with Suzy, but she told me in an email that she has a legal agreement with Anton that bars them from discussing one another.

Chris managed the computers at Greg's house and at the Bomp! offices, and he put together a Bomp! website that included the first BJM webpage and a single page of promotional material written by Chelsea, which was then filled in by Chris with a few shots of the band, along with some screenshots from *Gumby* creator Art Clokey's film *Mandala*.*

When *Methodrone* was finally ready for release, Chelsea stuffed the first pressings into plastic sleeves for shipping before the official CDs were done up, ignoring Suzy's objections; she did so secretly at Greg's house because Suzy—the more practical and responsible Shaw—had told Greg that plastic sleeves were too expensive, and that they couldn't afford to use them. They did so anyway.

As for whether shoegaze was dead and over, Anton ended up on the right side of history. *Pitchfork* recently declared *Methodrone* to be the thirty-third greatest shoegaze album of all time, in an article for which Peter Kember provided commentary alongside each of the selections. 'In reality, what begat shoegaze doesn't matter a fraction as much as the records made in that period,' he wrote. 'Some of these bands went on to considerable success— the Mercury Revs, My Bloody Valentines, and Brian Jonestowns … stellar recordings that'll be enjoyed for eons, bands who made records people have never stopped pulling from the racks.'

---

* Some time later, Chris learned Anton had grown up in Newport Beach. Chris was also from Orange County, but from Laguna Beach, and was quite sure that he saw the old Electric Cool-Aide at least once. He definitely also went to Mod Night at the Balboa Theater, where they showed a double feature of *The Kids Are Alright* and *Quadrophenia*, which he says Anton also attended.

45**6**78

BAG OF TRICKS

'We gigged around San Francisco a bunch, and then I left town for a couple months to try and find my brain again,' Joel recalls. 'I was kind of a shit and didn't tell the guys.' He'd vanished without a trace. The band worried about him, but during his absence they recruited Mara Keagle, who worked out 'Anemone' with Anton at his apartment.

Mara has a different take on Joel's disappearance. 'Joel left town,' she says. 'Him and Anton had a big ol' not-so-pretty fight at that same apartment Anton had where we made "Anemone." I was there, Matt was there … that was all right around the time when the Dandys were first coming down to San Francisco.'

Mara went to San Francisco School of the Arts (SOTA) with Miranda Lee Richards, and through her and a couple other people met Dave D., and she already knew Jeff, Ricky, and Travis from the café scene. The first time she met Jeff, they were at this one coffee shop called Ground Zero, just up the street from the Horseshoe. Mara was trying to light a cigarette and Jeff kept blowing her match out, telling her smoking was bad for her.*

Mara, like Miranda and a lot of others, was still in her teens when she got involved with the band. Her focus at SOTA was on music, while Miranda's was visual arts. Eventually, she met Anton, who proposed doing a song together at his apartment with Dawn Thomas. 'We were talking,' she recalls, 'and he knew that I played music, and he was like, *I want to hear you sing, let's do something.* And I was like, *OK, but I don't really write songs.* And he was like, *That's okay, I can show you how to write songs.* So [then we] wrote "Anemone." [We] wrote the lyrics in the back of a Holy Bible with a green

---

* This was likely sometime after Ricky and Travis left the band.

crayon, because that's all we had, and then we recorded it on a little four-track, and that was that song. That's how that song came to be.'

Mara was living south of Market back then, and the band were set to play a gig at Slim's. She wasn't feeling well, but then in popped Joel, who begged her to come sing the song. Mara got dressed, and they walked the two blocks to the venue. 'Dawn was there, giving me moral support and just being totally sweet, and Joel of course,' Mara says. 'Prior to that, I just assumed it was a silly little four-track recording me and Anton did one night.' The song is now among the BJM tracks most beloved by fans.

'Shortly after that [is when] Joel and Anton had [that] big falling out and Joel left town,' Mara continues. 'Anton convinced me to stay in the group and play tambourine, sing, and play keyboards, so I did that until Joel returned.'

For the first live performance of 'Anemone,' Anton, Matt, Joel, Dean, and Brian were all in the group, but Jeff was not present. 'Jeff was not in the group when I was playing with them,' Mara says. 'Anton was trying to get him more in the group, but it was challenging at the time. The dynamic was very difficult, because nobody had a firm grounding.'

Mara toured with the group on the West Coast, starting in San Francisco before heading north, just before Anton assembled the band to help him finish *Satanic Majesties*. Mara was dating Anton's old roommate, Sean Curran, and living with him in an apartment in North Beach. Sean was not keen on her touring with Anton and the guys, however. 'Sean and Anton mixed like oil and water,' Mara says. 'Sean was very jealous, and he really did not like the idea of me getting in a van with all of them and going on a tour, even though we all knew each other, but that's what I was doing.'

Anton and Matt kept calling her. 'We're leaving!' they'd say. 'We're going to shows in Los Angeles! You need to be there! It's important!' Mara finally gave in. 'It caused some problems for me on a personal level,' she says, 'but those problems would have been there if the band was there or not.' Even so, she stayed with Sean for the next five years.

* * *

Their Satanic Majesties' Second Request has long stood as one of The Brian Jonestown Massacre's best-loved albums. The pictures in the record's sleeve are credited to Dave, who is also listed as an executive producer for the record, along with Naut Humon. There's Jeff, with this pompadour, playing what looks like a red Fender Jaguar or Jazzmaster. Dawn playing her accordion. Matt with this bright red 60s shag haircut. Joel being his ultra-cool self. Mara onstage and in the studio with Anton. Pictures of Anton with a crown of flowers around his head, of the band live onstage and recording, and the obligatory shot of Brian Jones playing sitar. The front cover image is a scan from a spread on Mount Rainier taken from the July 1966 issue of *National Geographic*.*

Engineer Larry Thrasher is thanked in the liner notes to *Satanics*, though he was more involved in *Take It From The Man!* It is easy to confuse the two records because they were recorded so close together, soon after *Methodrone* was finished. 'I recorded *Satanic Majesties*' at the same time as *Take It From The Man*,' Anton has said. 'It's more atmospheric. Lots of textural stuff on it. It's mostly just me, but Matt Hollywood contributed some great tracks, too … I am very proud of it, as a whole.'

Matt says of *Satanic Majesties*' opening track, 'All Around You (Intro),' that the album 'needed an opening theme à la "Sgt. Pepper's Lonely Hearts Club Band" or the Stones' "Sing This All Together." Anton and I put the lyrics together as we recorded them, trying to sound as transcendental as possible.' The Merry Clayton–style gospel vocals in the background are by Daniel Knop. According to Anton, the song features 'me, Matt, and Mara— and this song scared the shit out of Mara. Danny sang the fake black part in drag. I brought a van full of people on drugs to sing the backups.'

Daniel's roommates at the time were three goth girls named Carrie, Anna, and Jen. One day they were all having a party at their flat, at 813 Oak Street, and Daniel was in full goth makeup, DJing. 'All of the sudden there's a knock on the door,' he recalls, 'and it's the entire band in Dave's van, and they're like, *Come on, you're coming to sing on our record.* And I'm like, *OK!* So I left the turntable playing, and they took me down to Hunter's Point and we recorded all day. They basically kidnapped me and made me sing on their record. It was cool. It was great!'

Daniel was playing in a salsa band at the time and had a collection of

---

* This wasn't the only time Anton used an image from an old issue of *Nat Geo* for BJM art. Later, he based some of the 'Not If You Were The Last Dandy On Earth' single art on an old Special K cereal ad found in the back of the magazine's February 1967 issue.

tambourines, maracas, bells, shakers, and a bunch of percussion instruments he kept in a suitcase he called the Bag Of Tricks. 'I said to Anton, Hey, you guys are going to need this for your recordings!' he laughs. 'So we played it on that recording, and I never got it any of it back!' Greg tagged along for the session as well. 'There was one little couch area, a mixing board, and then a microphone,' Daniel adds. 'There wasn't any booths or anything. There wasn't anything isolated.'

Following 'All Around You (Intro)' on the record is 'Cold To The Touch,' a Stones-influenced, psych-bluesy sex romp (a style explored more thoroughly on *Take It From The Man!*). It's one of the songs Anton wrote about Dawn, as their relationship began to sour. 'That song is not so much about Dawn as it is about my belief that she is evil and possessed by the devil,' Anton later said, though Dawn was hurting in that relationship as well. The vocal is abrasive. It sounds like there's some kind of fuzz filter on it, as if Anton is talking over a portable radio.

'Donovan Said' and 'In India You' are more characteristic of his orchestral aesthetic. On 'Donovan Said,' the relationship between Daniel's Bag Of Tricks percussion and the drums is striking, and then the tambourine comes in during the breakdowns, but listen to the way the bass follows the blues scale, and then how the synth follows Anton's established drone patterns. In recent years, Anton has often favored the kind of music-making he employs on this track, with the different instruments almost circling each other geometrically. 'I Want To Hold Your Other Hand' from *Aufheben* and much of *My Bloody Underground* aesthetically echo back to Anton's work on *Satanic Majesties* in this way. According to Anton, 'Donovan Said' was written and recorded under the influence of LSD. 'We knew the acid chemists at this time,' he later noted. 'Ricky's uncle [Vince] was in The Grateful Dead, though we never dealt anything.' Anton's favorite song by Donovan is 'Guinevere.'

According to Adrienne, 'In India You' might have been the first song tracked for *Satanic Majesties*, and it operates in the same way, musically, as 'Donovan Said.' Meanwhile, Matt, emboldened by his own songwriting progress, began to move to a more centralized role in the band—enough, at least, to land some of his own songs on a few BJM records. We first hear him on 'No Come Down.' At first listen, I remember thinking he sounded almost like Anton, but on closer inspection it's very much Matt. Anton hovers between baritone and second tenor, while Matt hovers between second and first tenor. And where Anton has his faux-British accent, Matt has a nasally raspiness. Their voices on record are distinct but complementary.

Satanics was the first of four BJM records to feature Matt's songs. Often, they're thematically similar, combining sexual angst and religious imagery with the effects (or after-effects) of various substances, but his charged sexual energy plays well against Anton's esoteric melancholia. Matt's songs were so well received by the group and their fans, in fact, that Miranda says (in *Dig!*) that for a little while there Anton grew jealous of Matt. Matt, though, has consistently dismissed arguments over who is the better songwriter of the two, maintaining that Anton's talent and vision is why he chose to join the band in the first place. '[Anton would] sit in front of a four-track tape machine and plunk two strings on the guitar for five minutes, and you'd be goin', *What the hell does that have to do with music?*' Matt recalls. 'And then you'd hear him play the tambourine beat every couple seconds for five minutes, and then hear him play a little piano part that was repetitive, and you had no idea where it fit into anything, and then he would play back the tape and it would be a symphony.'

73

On 'No Come Down,' Matt's voice is wrought with torment as he sings about a trip gone horribly wrong. Anton compliments his tune and themes with a church organ instrumental in between this song and his own devotional hymn of repentance, 'Jesus,' which is more guitar-based. Whenever a BJM song starts with guitar, you just know it's going to *slay* with the live band, and what is so significant about this track is the lead. Pay close attention to those bending, midrange notes; that Buffalo Springfield–type bending. There's barely anything on it. Maybe a quarter inch of reverb, but that lead is all over the BJM records. Before, it was on 'Wisdom.' That's the sound. As the song closes, there's an organ part that had to have been a first take. At the end, you can hear where the line drags a little. It's like, once he found the tone, Anton went for it; once he got a good take, he said, 'That's it. Let's move on.'

Following 'Jesus' is another instrumental, 'Before You,' a Far Eastern–drenched drone that's recalled later, in *My Bloody Underground*, on the song 'Who's Fucking Pissed In My Well?' in that there's a very similar Middle-Eastern or Indian type of beat, and you can hear a very deep chant or mantra being uttered but can't make out the words. It is very much in the same vein as

'Donovan Said' or 'In India You.' Then comes another one of Matt's songs. He counts it off again, just as he did with 'No Come Down,' but 'Miss June '75' reveals another side to Matt's songwriting: that of the self-doubting romantic. His vocals are a lot clearer here than on 'No Come Down,' but the song has the same lead guitar sound as can be heard on 'Jesus.'

'Miss June '75' turns from romance to fantasy in the last verse, accentuated by Matt's repeated, sexually charged '*I'm almost there!*' as the song builds and fades. In the liner notes, the word 'cheeky' is written in parentheses next to the song's name. My first guess was that the song referred to Zia McCabe, who was born on June 2, 1975, since The Dandy Warhols had become part of the BJM scene by this time, and Zia herself has speculated the same. 'I've often wondered if there was any chance "Miss June '75" was about me,' she says, 'but I never asked.'* Crystal Apel disputes this, however, suggesting that the song is about Matt's girlfriend at the time. 'She played it for her parents before listening to the words,' Crystal adds. I can imagine that must have been awkward.

Next is 'Anemone.' Mara's voice is like mercury crawling down the tip of a ballistic missile on this song; the way the snare hits right when she sings 'you should be pickin me up' is one of the best moments on any record. It's Brian Glaze's favorite BJM song, too. 'It was unbelievable to play live,' he recalls, 'the way Jeff got his guitar so dirty and high-end. Every time we played that song it just flew.' Anton originally wanted Miranda Lee Richards to sing it, but the song was in too low a key for her. Mara's smoky delivery brings a dark sensuality to the piece that is unmatched by any female collaborator, before or since, and it's still best when she sings it live, in my opinion.

After 'Anemone' is another instrumental interlude, the calming 'Baby (Prepraise),' which mimics the music of a later song on the record, though not 'Bad Baby,' which taps into that same droning beat that defines the record over the otherwise bluesy/Stonesy tones of the other tracks. More of the Bag Of Tricks. Then, a sample of a woman speaking Korean can be heard directly before Anton goes into 'Feelers,' a daydream piece in the same musical vein as 'Donovan Said,' 'In India You,' and 'Bad Baby.'

Then there's another Matt count-off, but this time it's for one of Anton's

---

* It wouldn't be the only song Matt's written about the Dandys. And I mean, *really*. Yowza. There are not too many rock'n'roll chicas of that caliber.

songs. ''Cause I Lover' (re-released and re-named 'Cause I Love Her' on *Thank God For Mental Illness*) is possibly another song about Dawn; the versions on *Satanic Majesties* and *Thank God* are nearly identical, although they're probably not the same recording, just an indication of the consistency of Anton's performance of the song, which speaks to its American folk character. Then there's '(Baby) Love Of My Life,' another instrumental, the ending of which is almost exactly like that of 'Bad Baby.' References such as these recur over and over again, so that the sonic narrative of the record is cyclical, circling between different musical themes while simultaneously tying them together.

'Slowdown (Fuck Tomorrow)' drones through sitars at times, but then is accented periodically by a *Sgt. Pepper's*–esque big-band romp, with keyboards substituting for the horns. It's one of the most musically difficult tracks on the record, as though trying to break itself apart. In some ways, it's the record's true finale, but the album does round itself off better with 'Here It Comes' (which would reappear nearly a decade later on *And This Is Our Music*), which is spliced right off of 'Slowdown' before a return to 'All Around You (Outro),' but without any vocal accompaniment. With that, the most fabulous journey inside your head comes to a close.

In his review for allmusic.com, Jason Ankeny writes that the record '[copped] not only Mick and Keith's leering bad-boy attitude but also their their rock-and-roll-circus spirit … the Stones themselves haven't made a record this strong or entertaining in years.' With its consistent musical and lyrical themes of love, sex, religion, and drugs, *Their Satanic Majesties' Second Request* could be the closest Anton ever got to a 'concept' album, perhaps along with *Musique De Film Imaginé*. Often regarded as one of the best Brian Jonestown Massacre records, it set the foundation for everything that was to come after it.

Sometime after its release, Daniel Knop caught up with Anton walking down the Lower Haight. Anton slipped him *Satanic Majesties* and told him it was a 'secret record.' 'I was like, *a secret record?*' Daniel chuckles. 'He always had everything planned out. You know how he is.'

* * *

As was the case *Spacegirl* and *Methodrone*, making *Satanic Majesties* was

75

not without its difficulties. 'Anton has a tendency to alienate people in the studio,' says Mara Keagle. 'He tends to do a lot of the work on his own, plays a lot of the instruments, and that's what *Satanic Majesties* really was.'

Mara temporarily shared a flat with Anton around this time while a place was opening up for her and Sean in North Beach. They would go to the Indian Bazaar together on Valencia Street, and Anton would stock up on cassette tapes. 'He was getting really into the sitar sound and the chord structures, and teaching them on guitars so that the band had that sound,' she says. 'When he started recording *Satanic Majesties* at the Compound, it was pretty much just him. I was there for some of it, but it was all just him, doing all of those interludes in between songs—he did a bunch of those while I was there, and then we recorded "Anemone."'

Take It From The Man! was also being recorded around the same time, but elsewhere. 'I actually tracked "Anemone" for *Take It From The Man!* as well,' says Mara, 'but the sound didn't fit with that album. The recording style was different. *Satanics* was part tape, part digital … and then *Take It From The Man!* was all on two-inch tape, and that was a big deal. At the time, it was analog vs. digital. Of course, five years later, it was completely different.'

Naut Humon was also around for some of the *Satanics* sessions, and was present for the recording of 'Anemone.' 'We went out there on the off hours, so we were out there from ten o'clock on,' Mara remembers. 'Naut was there while I was tracking my vocals. I remember thinking, *Anton, you're torturing me. I don't want anybody to hear this!*'

When Joel returned from wherever he went after the scuffle, he hooked back up with Anton, who played the finished *Satanics* for him. 'Everything I'd always hoped he would do musically with the band flowed into my ears and out the giant smile on my face,' he says. 'It has always been my favorite album. When you make a record, you have to listen to every stage of the recordings over and over again until you get sick of it, but in this case I got to listen to it like a fan, so it still has that special glow.'

Greg Shaw, too, has said it was his favorite BJM record, but the chances of a follow-on faded when Naut and Anton had their own falling out. Instead, Anton hooked up with Genesis P-Orridge and Larry Thrasher and made *Take It From The Man!*

STRAIGHT UP AND DOWN

'Fuck the man!' Joel used to shout from the stage, not long after he first joined the band. One time, he said to Tommy, 'Nine out of ten times, if God is doing his job, man, I'm up there. I'm up *there*, man,' referring to snorting certain substances of choice. As Tommy puts it, 'Joel seemed destined by an act of an all-knowing God of Cool to be put on this earth to smash tambourines and groove out with the BJM. Over twenty years later, it's still proving to be true.'

Joel and Anton had been casual acquaintances for about six months when Anton asked him to play maracas at a gig in Joel's apartment cellar for his roommate's birthday. At some point during the show, Joel lit the maracas on fire. 'The power kept going out and coming back on, so intermittently all guitars, vocals, and lights would cut and you'd just hear drums and maracas and only see the maraca flame,' he recalls. 'We must've been tripping the circuit breaker with all the amps, and then someone would reset the breaker. So the power would go out and then kick back in after a minute or so, and everyone would come blasting out still in perfect time. This happened four or five times, and I've never seen anything like it before or since.'

Dave D. taped the show. After Anton saw the footage, he invited Joel back for the next gig. And, after that, he just kept showing up. At the time, it was uncommon for a rock band to showcase a tambourine or a maraca player as their front man. 'I can't tell you how hard a lot of people were scratching their heads trying to figure out why I was there,' Joel says.

Joel swiftly emerged as the life-as-party muse for the group, too. He walked it, talked it, drank it, popped it, and everything else but slept on it. 'I was really, *really* into being fucked up back then,' he says. 'No one around could touch me on the party level, and they would tell you the same.' The party level was constant. 'Everybody was off the charts,' Mara Keagle adds. 'We were all having a lot of fun in the 90s.'

'It's hard to remember the timeline, 'cause in those days there was no time,' Joel continues, and Jeff agrees. 'We were all young, and it wasn't just being high or anything. It was egos and aloofness ... when you're young, shorter periods of time are a longer part of your life, especially if you're twenty-one or twenty-two, and this kind of part of your life is only two or three years, so that makes months much bigger than you would think a month would be now. A month when you're twenty is like eighteen or nineteen hours every day hanging out with your pals, and you may not do that in two or three [more] years.'

Joel's favorite bands were mid-60s Stones and The Small Faces, and, like Jeff, he feels his enthusiasm for 60s music helped nail the signpost in the ground for the BJM to go in that direction. 'When I joined the band it quickly became apparent where we were taking it, and I knew it was on, and it was quite a feeling,' he once said.

Anton was still tracking new sounds at the Compound—which had at some point around this time become known as the Bloody Angle*—but had all but abandoned the BJM's earlier shoegazing aesthetic in favor of resurrecting 1967's mythical Summer Of Love, whereby he subsequently rechristened Joel 'The Spokesman For The Revolution.' Joel played the role to perfection.

One night, when they were playing the Troubadour in Los Angeles, Joel did one of his high-flying tambourine tosses, but it got stuck in the rafters and never came back. 'I was looking up in the air, checking my pretend watch and looking back up again, but it was gone for good, to who knows where,' he later recalled. 'Two weeks later, I ran into the Troubadour's soundman, and he told me that some local hair-metal band was just playing, and the guitar player was rockin' a solo so hard that it shook the tambourine loose and it came down and bounced off his head!'

Alex Mann remembers meeting Joel back when he lived in a tiny, pass-through space that he painted all black, upstairs in onetime BJM drummer Greg Helton's warehouse. Ricky took Alex there to meet him. 'I loved his character instantly,' Alex says. 'He was out-of-this-world hilarious.' Ricky asked Alex if he wanted to play a gig with him and Anton at Club 181 in

---

* Civil-war buff Naut Humon took the new name from an area in the Gettysburg Battlefield, where fifteen hundred Confederate soldiers broke through the Union line on Cemetery Ridge.

the Tenderloin—an old dance club with 70s pimp decor and a strip-joint aesthetic—but when they got there, the only ones onstage were Anton and Joel. So, to an audience of three or four, Ricky, Alex, and Anton played acoustic guitars as Joel worked the vibe. Alex's acoustic was a shambles by the end of the performance. He'd broken every string but two.

Meanwhile, Anton was forming a new record at Bloody Angle. *Their Satanic Majesties' Second Request* was a significant departure from *Methodrone*, and the first of a few occasions where Anton has hit the proverbial 'reset' button on his project's creative direction. He started carrying around a tin hand drum that he would pull out at parties. At one such outing, someone noticed his leather sandals.

'Ohhh, Mr. Natural!' the guy chuckled.

'That's *super*natural to you,' Anton shot back.

Miranda Lee Richards also came into the picture around this point. She grew up in San Francisco, the daughter of underground comic artists Ted and Teresa Richards; when she was a kid, her mom created a character for her called Suzy Skates for *Roller Skating* magazine—a punk-rock antihero who used her powers to fight corporate greed, pollution, and challenge social norms. 'Suzy was based on what my mother wanted me to become,' Miranda said, 'a strong, beautiful, independent, kick-ass chick.' She later took up modeling and moved to Paris to pursue it full-time after graduating from SOTA in San Francisco, before moving back and returning to college.

Miranda had actually known Dave Deresinski since before she was old enough to drive through her friend Sarah Flicker, who happened to be dating Metallica's Kirk Hammett. Miranda wanted to learn how to make music, so she took guitar lessons from Kirk, who got her started by teaching her Mazzy Star songs. She made a demo of them in his basement, and the tape made its way to Anton through Dave. Anton spotted her walking down Haight one day and shouted her down, then ran across the street and asked her to sing in his band. She said yes. 'Of course, being so young, I was just so excited to start on any project,' she recalls. 'I was really into Mazzy Star at the time, and I thought, *This is my Dave Roback!*'

* * *

On September 26, 1994, during the week *Definitely Maybe* was released in the USA, The Brian Jonestown Massacre opened for Oasis at the San Francisco stop on the Manchester group's first American tour. Before the show, Live 105 DJ Aaron Axelsen tricked Blur and Oasis, who were both in town playing shows—and whose 'Battle of Britpop' rivalry was already well underway—into doing an interview at the same time. Blur had played the Fillmore with Pulp opening the previous day, while Oasis were to play the Bottom Of The Hill that night with the BJM.* It was an exciting time, and after the interview, Aaron took Blur and picked up Jarvis Cocker of Pulp at his hotel, then drove over to Bottom Of The Hill to watch Oasis and the BJM play to a capacity crowd. 'To this day, I still have no idea how everyone fit into my piece-of-crap 1988 broken-down Jetta,' he later said.

Earlier the same day, Anton had bumped into journalist Bill Crandall on a Haight Street bus and pleaded with him to come see the show that night. 'We're playing with Oasis!' Anton told him. 'They're going to be huge!'

In an article Bill later wrote for *BAM* magazine featuring what Joel once said was the band's first photo shoot, Anton recalled the sting he experienced when he actually met the Gallagher brothers face-to-face. 'I met them and they go, Fuck you, asshole! Who are you? And I go, Wait a minute. I've been telling everybody in the world about your band, and *I'm not an asshole.*'

'They wouldn't even come downstairs to watch us play because they were too busy fuckin' snorting coke upstairs,' says Matt, while Jeff adds, 'They were real rude to us. After we got offstage, the Gallagher brothers were just standing there as we walked by, talking shit about us and our set like we weren't there.'

Joel knocked on the door of Oasis's tour bus earlier that day, and when Noel Gallagher answered, Joel offered him some of the best speed in town. According to Joel, Noel told him, 'No thanks, we only do cocaine,' and shut the door, but it turned out only Noel did cocaine, so Joel sold the speed to the rest of Oasis instead, and it ended up nearly breaking up their band.

Oasis weren't the only ones who were fucked up that night. Dave asked Diane to go pick up Jeff and bring him to soundcheck, so Diane went to Jeff's house in the Lower Haight and found him tearing his place apart in search of some heroin he'd hidden somewhere, only he couldn't remember where.

---

* Some commentators feels that for a while there, The Brian Jonestown Massacre were vying to compete with Oasis in the same way that Oasis had waged a war against Blur. However, as Oasis exploded around the planet, my personal view is that energy was then divested toward The Dandy Warhols, who were likewise moving up in the industry, but were more accessible.

tangible records & Soundgasm present

MASSACRE THE BRIAN JONESTOWN

PRESS THE FUCK!

Bless These Things

the brian jonestown massacre

with
Orange
also
Your Precious You

*Take Acid Now.

THURS.
NOV. 11
@9:30**

@ the Bottom of the Hill

CLUB 1840 HAIGHT ST

Boomerang

friday 11/20

DIESEL
HARMONICS

SLANT 6
MOSHEEN

9:PM $3

saturday 11/21

THE
BRIAN
JONESTOWN
MASSACRE

THE
LIVING
END

LOVE NIX
:: M $3

NIE WIEDER
FASCHISMUS

TOP Anton Newcombe, Jeff Davies,
and Ricky Maymi perform as The Brian
Jonestown Massacre in the early 90s.
ABOVE Early BJM flyers were often
provocative, featuring profanity or
politically charged imagery.

ABOVE Anton and Matt Hollywood perform with the BJM at the Black Rose. **BELOW** The earliest known BJM tape over time evolved into *Pol Pot's Pleasure Penthouse*. **RIGHT** Travis Threlkel, Anton, Ricky Maymi, and Matt perform at the Peacock Lounge in the early 90s.

STEREOPHONIC
TAKE ACID NOW
and come see

LIVE 105 WELCOMES

MASSACRE THE BRIAN JONESTOWN

soundgasm
SPIN RAMA

SUN. OCT. 31

ALL AGES WELCOME
SHOWS AT 9 PM
Slim's
333 ELEVENTH STREET
BETWEEN FOLSOM AND HARRISON · SAN FRANCISCO
FOR FURTHER INFORMATION CALL 415 / 621-3330

LEFT The 'Take Acid Now And Come See The Brian Jonestown Massacre' flyer was everywhere in San Francisco during the early 90s. **BELOW LEFT** Anton c.1992–93. **BELOW RIGHT** Anton with Helen Gardner and Luella Jane Wright. **BOTTOM LEFT** Travis Threlkel (*far left*) with Luella Jane Wright and James Mervine. **BOTTOM RIGHT** A packed crowd at the Black Rose.

the brian jonestown massacre

TORN MEMORY | **Your PRECIOUS YOU**

PEACOCK LOUNGE 552 HAIGHT | **FRIDAY EVENING** **NOV. 19TH**

the brian jonestown massacre
benjiman kitestring
mockingbirds
definitely come

saturday july 9
9 pm

$4

peacock lounge
540 haight

now dig this

the brian jonestown massacre

+special guest

Tue. May 31st

11 p.m. $3

Full Bar W/I.D.

dna

11th & Harison soma

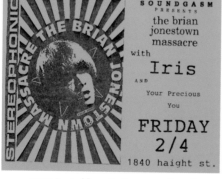

STEREOPHONIC THE BRIAN JONESTOWN MASSACRE

SOUNDGASM
PRESENTS

the brian jonestown massacre

with

Iris

AND

Your Precious You

FRIDAY 2/4

1840 haight st.

ABOVE A set of flyers for Jonestown shows in San Francisco c.1993–94. Tommy Dietrick was just a teenager when his band Your Precious You performed with the BJM in the Haight. He would later take up bass duties in the band prior to the release of *Dig!*

TOP Matt Hollywood, Brian Glaze, and Dawn Thomas perform with the BJM in the mid-90s. **ABOVE** Anton and Dawn. **RIGHT** A moody portrait of Anton c.1994.

A set of photographs of Anton and friends in the mid-90s. **CLOCKWISE FROM TOP LEFT** Anton and Laura Watts; Anton and Dawn Thomas; Dawn; Mara Keagle, who wrote the words to 'Anemone' in the back of a bible with Anton in green crayon, and later sang with Smallstone; Anton.

TOP Anton performing in 1997. **ABOVE** Flyers advertising BJM shows with The Beggars and E.A.R./Sonic Boom in 1994. The latter's founder, Peter Kember, was Anton's labelmate on Bomp! and did a remix of 'Hyperventilation' that was never released.

'It took me like forty-five minutes to convince him that we needed to go to Bottom Of The Hill [for] soundcheck,' Diane says. 'I called Dave and I said, Jeff isn't listening to me—you have to come pick him up.' Dave then came and talked some sense into Jeff, and Diane followed them back to Bottom Of The Hill, but by then the rest of the band had already soundchecked without him.

Still fiending for a fix, Jeff took off, and by the time the BJM's set began he was nowhere to be found. Anton, infuriated, started rubbing his microphone all over his body and putting it down his pants. Then, at the last moment, Jeff and Dave came back. 'Jeff comes in and he gets on stage right in the middle of the set, and he played the most amazing guitar solo ever, because he was *so* high,' Diane recalls.

Joel remembers Jeff ripping the gnarliest, most heroin-fueled solo ever for 'Straight Up And Down' before spending the rest of the show trying to untangle his guitar chord. 'Jeff was a hopeless mess,' says Josephine Tavares, who was in the audience that night. 'He never did get it untangled, the haze he was in. It was awful, and Anton threw a fit. Stopped the music several times. Yelled and threatened his bandmates.'

Oasis closed the show with their traditional cover of The Beatles' 'I Am The Walrus,' As Liam Gallagher sneered into the microphone, Anton turned to Joel and said, 'See that microphone? The one he's got his top lip on? I just rubbed that all over my pubes!'

'That was a great show—one of the best shows they ever played,' Diane recalls. 'We hung out with Oasis after, and then we drove up to Sacramento the next day and we saw them play in this little bar, Malarkey's, that holds, like, three hundred people, and that was amazing.'

'The next night, Anton's like, *I got us on the bill. We're opening for them again!*' Jeff recalls. 'And we drove down ... we get to the place ... we go in, but we're not on the bill, and after the first band soundchecked, before anyone has started playing, Anton goes, *We're on. We're just going to use the first band's equipment.* So we went onstage. No one's asking anyone. The soundman didn't realize ... Anton tried to pull a fast one on everyone, and didn't want us to hear him bullshitting. It was soon apparent we weren't on the bill, and this was just a fucking escapade, but after the fact you have to applaud it!'

81

'Oasis was actually really impressed with them, and I know it takes a lot to impress Oasis,' says Diane, who maintains that in fact *she* sold the speed to the Manchester band, and that she and Joel had gone over to his friend's to get it early, on the morning of the Sacramento show at Malarkey's.*

The Jonestown's next gig was at the Foothill Club in Signal Hill, on the outskirts of Los Angeles, and then the gig after that was at the Trocadero Transfer in San Francisco. It was the first of many shows they'd play with The Dandy Warhols, and also one of Dean's first gigs. That night, the band met performance artist Genesis P-Orridge, who had come to watch the gig high on acid and wearing an extravagant white fur coat, sporting a previously-owned-by-Brian-Jones pinstripe suit, complete with a silver bob and silver-capped teeth.

'I know who you are,' Anton said to him.

'I know who *you* are,' Genesis parroted back, then began to rave about their music. 'Do you know where I got this coat that I'm wearing?' he asked. 'Brian Jones's estate sale!'†

82

* * *

Chris Arvan engineered one of the earliest known recordings of the song 'Straight Up And Down,' back in 1994 or 1995.‡ Chris was a musician of around the same age as Anton who had moved into a place called Rocker Rehearsal Studios at 2950 3rd Street around the time Anton formed the BJM. The space was about five miles from the Haight. No windows. Showers

---

* Oasis stayed wide-awake after their adventures with the BJM through San Francisco and Sacramento and then played a disastrous show at their next stop, at the Whisky A Go-Go in Los Angeles. The band members started playing different songs throughout the set, and Liam kept disappearing behind the amps to do more lines. Noel got on the mic and said something about it, to which Liam responded by whacking him with his tambourine. Noel chased him offstage into the dressing room, and then flew back to San Francisco that night with the band's stash—without telling anyone—to hang out with a girl called Melissa Lim, who he'd met at the show with the BJM. While he was there, he wrote the Oasis classic 'Talk Tonight,' which is all about the trip, while Melissa reportedly also inspired Noel's song 'Don't Look Back In Anger.' Finally, the tour manager located Noel and got him to agree to fly to Las Vegas, where Oasis demoed '(It's Good) To Be Free.' They decided to give the band another go, and the rest is history. And all because Joel and Diane cranked 'em up. (Oasis's side of this story is recounted in the 2016 documentary *Supersonic*, which I highly recommend.)

† More recently, Genesis told *Spin* that the coat was given to him by a Rolling Stones roadie.

‡ There was also another tape made later at Studio D in Sausalito that Miranda Lee Richards says she sang on that might have had versions of some songs that ended up on the record that became *Take It From The Man!*

upstairs. You could easily live there for two hundred bucks a month. Anton lived next door for a time, all by himself. 'He had the BJM stickers with Brian Jones's head right in the middle of it,' Chris recalls. 'He was trying to put together the band. I don't think he had it completely together yet. They'd maybe played one or two shows.'

Chris recorded 'Straight Up And Down' there with Jeff, Matt, Anton, and Brian. Chris maintains that Jeff did most of the guitar work for the demo, and that Anton came in later and did maybe one guitar part. 'It was done all digitally. I had a four-track digital thing, one of the very first versions of Pro Tools … I don't know who wrote it, but the only person on the track was Jeff. Jeff played just about all the guitars, and Matt played bass, and I think Anton just did one part … Anton wasn't even there when we did Jeff's parts.'

Anton has a different take on things. 'We recorded *Take It From The Man!* twice,' he said in 2014. 'First with this producer. He wanted to get on board, and so he recorded the record and he chopped it all up to make it like so perfect, then he wanted like three [percentage] points [of the royalties] and we just laughed in his face. Then he got so pissed and he said he was going to destroy the recording. I was like, *Fuck you dude. I'm gonna kick your ass the minute I see you on the street.* He did end up destroying it, but I let him off the hook, as far as the violence.'*

By now, the BJM had started hanging out more and more with The Dandy Warhols, and Anton has said that he might have even written some of the songs for *Take It From The Man!* during parties at Zia's house up in Portland, after shows. 'I used to really love writing songs in front of people with acoustics or whatever, just to show off with my mates,' he's said. 'It used to make me really happy to be clever.'

One time, the Dandys were playing a warehouse show somewhere in town when Mara got a call at work from Dave. Her roommate had been to the warehouse party and invited all the Dandys back to their place. When Mara got home, all of the Dandys were in her living room; they'd parked their van in her roommate's parking space in the underground parking, but when they pulled in, they took the side door off of their van. 'Scraped it off of the side [backing

---

* Chris didn't destroy the tapes; in fact, he shared with me his mix of 'Straight Up And Down.' There's no solo, vocals, or buildup on the track, which is barely two minutes long and isn't much more than a sketch, but it sounds like it would have been a slicker and heavier version than the one that appears on *Take It From The Man!* It sounds a lot like Oasis, actually.

in], so they were all stranded there at our apartment for like two days,' says Mara. During that time, she adds, the Dandys' front man, Courtney Taylor-Taylor, 'grew completely fascinated by the Jonestown and Anton.' After that, the bands would hang out together every time they were near each other. The Dandys reportedly got hold of one of the BJM demo tapes around the same time they formed their group, and then a year later, around the time as the Oasis gig, they went down to San Francisco to play some parties. According to Dave, it was Travis who got the tape to them—which Travis doesn't deny.

Anton's take on this story similarly lines up. 'I met Courtney, or rather Zia, first,' he's said. 'They were fucking ripping me off because I was sending tapes to Thor [Lindsay] at their label [Tim/Kerr Records] long before he had a band. They just believed the hype.'*

After the Dandys' second time playing with the BJM—on March 3, 1995, at the Paris Theater in Portland, Oregon—Courtney swore he'd never play another show with them because they'd made such a big mess onstage before their set. This turned out not to be the case, however, as they played together two weeks later at the Purple Onion in San Francisco, then two months after that, on May 13, at a place called Starcleaners owned by their longtime friend Jennifer Shagawat.

Jennifer was twenty-two when she moved to San Francisco from New Jersey to start Starcleaners at 18 Sycamore in the Mission. Not long after that, she met a guy called Jason Lee (not the actor) who introduced her to the BJM with a basement gig in the Lower Haight. Jen and Jason later started a band together called NoiseStar, which Dawn then joined; and since Dawn was dating Anton, they hung out with him all the time, too. Of the club, she recalls, 'I read a children's book called *The Starcleaner Reunion*, and this book moved me, and it still does. It's still my favorite kid's book, so that's how I got the name of the space. I put a banner in our window, *Starcleaner*, and the premise for me was that everyone's a star and they need a place to shine, because we were all in bands nobody would book, so we started our own thing, and that was the whole premise.' Not long after she'd set up the space, Anton made his way over, took a look around, and said, 'Oh, fuck yeah, we can do some shit here.'

'The club was totally illegal,' Jen continues. 'We sold an herbal speed

---

* Of interesting note: Thor Lindsay appears in what are possibly the last photographs ever taken of Nirvana singer-songwriter Kurt Cobain before he committed suicide at the age of twenty-seven.

84

tea, and then a downer tea, and that was our trip, and it was free. Donation only. The door was five dollars, and then everybody brought their own booze, so you could imagine it was like everyone literally doing all the drugs and alcohol they wanted, seeing these amazing bands.' Anton soon took charge of booking shows at the warehouse, and the BJM played there throughout 1994.

On April 11, 1995, Genesis P-Orridge was in Los Angeles with Love & Rockets, staying at a house owned by producer Rick Rubin, when a fire broke out and lit the whole place up. Everyone escaped without injury but Genesis, who fell out of a second story window trying to escape and broke his wrist, elbow, and ribs on the concrete stairs below. He spent the next week and a half in ICU, prompting Anton to put together a benefit show for him at Starcleaners.

'I remember playing the show with Genesis,' Dawn recalls. 'He said *nice accordion* to me.' Then he looked at Jennifer, who was playing a bucket, and told her she was a good drummer. 'I probably didn't say a word, I was so nervous,' Jennifer recalls. 'He's a pretty intense person. That show stood out for me because I was just learning the history of Psychic TV and understanding who Genesis was.'

A month later, Anton booked the Dandys. 'I didn't know shit about the Dandys,' Jen continues. 'I had no idea they were huge, or that they were in the process of being signed to Capitol, and that show was a big deal for us because it was a total madhouse—probably the largest show we had.' Dave Grohl, Metallica, and The Flaming Lips were all there. Jen couldn't work the door quick enough. 'This was a showcase. They had come to see who they were paying for on the label. That show was where the Dandys were signed, and I know on the radio they name-dropped Starcleaners a few times, saying it was their start, but it wasn't their start at all. That was Anton making that happen. Anton made them look that cool, because he could see that this was going to seal the deal for the Dandys. Anton never said that to me, but Capitol was there.'

That night, the Dandys stayed with Jen and her brother. 'We took one of their CDs, because anytime a band stayed with us we'd take one of their CDs and put it in the house collection,' she laughs. 'Courtney got up and was totally pissed, and demanded his CD back!'*

---

* Courtney dismisses this. 'We didn't have CDs back then, and I wouldn't have cared, or rather would've been pretty stoked to have our music in their pad if we had something,' he told me in an email. 'Some people like to be the center of drama, whether real or invented.'

KEEP MUSIC EVIL

That was the last time the BJM played Starcleaners. A week and a half after that show, the two bands hit the Paris Theatre up in Portland again, and then the next day they played at Zia's house for her twentieth birthday. That August, the Dandys toured down the West Coast, and Daniel Knop remembers them coming to town the night before Anton's twenty-fifth birthday to play the Great American Music Hall.

Naturally, there was a party, but the BJM's chaotic lineup and living situations meant the Dandys were kept well enough at bay so as to not foster a healthy partnership between them. As such, it could be argued that the seeds of rivalry between the two bands were sewn from the get-go, although Courtney refutes this. 'The Dandy Warhols have never felt any rivalry,' he says. 'Why would we? We thought they were amazing whomever was in the band, and they were so wild we loved being around them.' Whatever the case, the Dandys' release on Tim/Kerr that led to their signing with Capitol, *Dandys Rule Ok?*, was so good that Anton was determined to one-up them with the next BJM record.

* * *

'Larry [Thrasher] was interested, and told us how Genesis had seen our band,' Anton said of Larry's involvement with *Take It From The Man!* The first time Larry heard the BJM was when Genesis gave him a copy of the cassette that had been produced at Studio D. Larry liked it but thought the digital effects and over-compression buried the otherwise magical overtones of psychedelic rock. When he first saw the band live, though, he loved them. All he could think of was the Stones circa 1965. 'That was the sound I proposed to Anton,' he says. 'He was completely on the same page with me.'

Larry grew up in Kentucky but had lived in San Francisco since 1984. He knew piano and guitar, studied baroque guitar music in the 70s, and in the late 80s had studied tabla drums with Swapan Chadhuri.* He also studied Indian folk music in Maharashtra during his initial travels in India and collected rare instruments. Returning to the USA, he played in bands and put out some records before meeting Genesis in 1993, at which point he started playing

---

* A Grammy-nominated and award-winning tabla virtuoso, since 1981 Swapan Chadhuri has served as director of percussion at the Ali Akbar College of Music in San Rafael, and for the past twenty years has also served as department chairperson and senior faculty of the World Music Program at the California Institute of the Arts.

tablas and samplers in Genesis's band, Psychic TV. For *Take It From The Man!*, Larry used the same lo-fi blueprint of tape and vintage effects he used to record the Psychic TV album *Trip Reset* a year earlier. He is still a fan of this approach to recording and uses the same method today for his project Thrasher Qawwal in India, where he now lives.

Genesis and Larry loaned Anton and the band their studio so they could make their record. Given what was happening in BJM-world at the time, Genesis quickly became hip to the Dandys, too. In *Dig!*, he says they were the only two bands he'd made an effort to see in the past three years. Anton has said it was him, Dean, Matt, Dawn, and Brian who showed up the day of recording, and that Jeff was too junked out to come. Jean-Paul Ligon was another guitarist who had played in the band from 1994 to 1996 during this time, and might've tracked some guitar during sessions for *Take It From The Man!* in Jeff's absence.

Brian claims that Jeff was in fact around for those sessions, and that *Take It From The Man!* was largely a collaboration between himself, Matt, and Jeff, but with Anton clearly the leader. 'Anton and Matt wrote the songs—mostly Anton—and Jeff's guitar tone and style absolutely tore ears apart, especially live,' he says. 'We played some amazing shows and really clicked as a band—whatever Larry and Anton were going for, it came out both fresh and distorted. Even so, I pretty much quit after that record.' Brian cites Anton's increasing control over the band and creative differences as primary motives for his departure. (He left about two weeks before Ondi Timoner started filming *Dig!*)

'Glaze has his head up his ass,' Dean counters. 'There was rarely any collaboration on anything with Anton telling everyone what to play. Anton actually sat down on the drums *showing* Brian what to play, so I don't know where he got that. Matt wrote a few songs, but Anton almost always had his input, one way or another, even if it was adding tracks after the recording was finished, and I'm not even sure if Jeff was around for that record.'

Diane remembers Jeff being there, too. She was present for many sessions out at Larry's recording and rehearsal space in a place Brian called *Bumfuck, Emeryville*. 'It was kind of high up in this warehouse, and it had a view,' she says. 'It was magic to sit in on those sessions, because Anton was at the height of his creativity, and Jeff would come over and lay down these tracks that would cause your brain to melt, they were just so beautiful.'

Anton stayed with Larry during their time at the rehearsal studio. He and Joel slept on the studio's concrete floor for a number of nights, eating all their meals from the snack machine in the hall. According to Larry, instead of a pillow, Anton used a copy of Meher Baba's book *God Speaks*, to which Larry had introduced him.

Larry and his friend Nancy Friedberg were longtime Meher Baba devotees.* 'When Anton found out about Baba, he was really interested,' Nancy says. 'He even took a picture of Baba from me.' Nancy she used to bring food over to the studio, and she almost immediately formed a kinship with Anton. Her house became a place Anton could escape to here and there over the next few years. (He crashed at Naut's sometimes, too, until they had their falling out.)

For *Take It From The Man!*, Larry and the BJM used mostly old RCA ribbon mics, vintage tube U47s, and any gear they could muster from the 60s. Likewise, all the amps and guitars and effects were from the 60s. They intentionally stayed away from digital outboard gear, and boasted of this in the liner notes. Larry studied photos of early Stones sessions and tried to do similar things with the BJM's mic placements. 'It was music 24/7, and we spent lots of time with the mic placement to get the best sound—almost a week,' he says. 'Anton focused mostly on the kick mic, and the way the bass drum was tuned way down. We tried to get the most sicko sounds we could.'

'We were there to record about seventeen songs,' Anton later said, 'and when we got there, there were about sixteen microphones set up for the drums, and so I asked [Larry], *What the hell is this? We don't need sixteen mics for the drums. Take all of these away. I'm gonna use three mics for the drums and we're gonna record it live, all at once. We're just gonna put all the guitar amps down the hallway, the drums will be in here, and we'll put on headphones and we'll just play our set.*'

Larry tracked the band live and all in the same room over two or three days to a sixteen-track recorder, which he overdrove to get noticeable saturation. They ran through most of their live set, as well as a few experiments, playing song after song like they were playing a show, and ended up with three or

---

* The fixation must've lasted a while for Anton, too, since Ondi remembers him being 'really into the Meher Baba at the time, because the Meher Baba never touched money' when the filming of *Dig!* began almost a year later.

88

four versions of each. Once they got a good mic-placement formula down, they stuck with it, overdubbing guitar solos and backing vocals later.* 'Anton would continue to use the basic formula on *Thank God For Mental Illness*, and on the records he made after he moved to LA. That vintage sound just works so well with his music,' Larry says. 'I really see these BJM guys as spirits from the 60s returning to claim something left behind. They *needed* that kind of sound.'

Larry left the BJM to themselves while the tape rolled, hoping to capture whatever tension and excitement might occur. 'The band was in their prime period in those days for walking that thin line between complete self-implosion and expressive brilliance,' Larry says. 'The biggest challenge was keeping them from killing each other.' At one point during mixing, he was forced to impose a rule of only one member at a time in the studio, having come in one day to the stench of bourbon, glass shrapnel laying all over his analogue mixing desk. 'They'd smashed a half-full whiskey bottle all over the place and tried to keep me from knowing by doing a pathetic, rushed job of cleanup.'

Larry kicked out everyone except for Anton, and the two of them continued working. Then, as he set up the mix for each member, he'd invite them in to comment on the takes he had chosen. 'Some of the uniqueness of that record came from me making editorial decisions not based on my own taste or opinions, but coming from a completely irrational process determined by inter-band conflicts,' he continues. 'For example, Matt's guitar had to be as loud as Jeff's to keep peace, and likewise there were parts that were out of tune that I normally would've mixed down, but I had to keep them loud in the mix to placate this or that person's dysfunction. So everyone in the band had input into the mixing process that way.'

Larry laid down the drums and bass foundation for the mix. Anton again obsessed over the bass kick—his main focus sonically throughout the project. They mixed each song with charts and set up the mixing desk each time they

---

* That's why that record sounds so cohesive. When you're tracking to tape to make a record, unless you want to make everyone's jobs harder, mic placement is everything. Drummers hit drums differently for different tones, at different speeds, at different measures of strength. If you keep shifting things around you just make more work for yourself. That's why the songs on *Spacegirl* and *Methodrone* sound so different from one another, while *Take It From The Man!* and others from this period have a consistent character.

went back to a song. Nothing was automated, so the mixes evolved over several weeks, until one night a manic Anton stayed up while Larry slept and did run-offs of everything where they had left it. Larry was disgruntled the next morning, but he soon laughed it off. He liked the end result, anyway, as it left an extra layer of raw, unpredictable sheen. For Larry, producing the BJM required, and deserved, total engagement in the spirit of rock'n'roll.

The finished product, then, is a distilled, dragged-through-the-grit, full-on 60s rock'n'roll record. There is something about the energy of *Take It From The Man!* that for me makes it superior to *Their Satanic Majesties' Second Request*. There is something about the atomic energy driving the songs that can really get the blood pumping. You can hear in those guitars an aggressive, post-adolescent angst, a vibe akin to The Stooges on *Raw Power*, or The Beatles' early period—that youthful, hormone-driven energy. The Dandys' first record has a lot of that same vibe: it's loud, abrasive, and teeth-grinding, like speed in your herbal tea.

Matt is twice as present here than he was on *Satanic Majesties*, having contributed the songs 'Oh Lord,' 'B.S.A.,' 'Cabin Fever,' and 'In My Life.' Opening track 'Vacuum Boots' started out as one of his simple, Stones-style riffs but exploded into new dimensions when Anton added his own guitar melodies. 'Live, it sounded more like Joy Division,' says Brian. 'Straight-ahead punk.' The same applies to tracks like 'Who?' 'That was fun,' Brian continues. 'We were just starting to hang out with the Dandys and ripped them off a little bit.' Matt says the song was a blast to play live. 'Who doesn't like to holler into a mic in unison with five other people?' he asks in the liner notes. Anton, meanwhile, lays on the British accent and names various different colors. Yellow. Orange. Green. Blue. (The second song on 2017's *Don't Get Lost*, 'Melody's Actual Echo Chamber,' similarly runs through a list of colors.)

Joel interprets *Take It From The Man!* as largely being a 'December's Children nuts and bolts rhythm & blues sound. We don't purposely go out for that. We just like that music. I think there were higher standards for music during the 60s. You could take Top 40 music from then and check out the quality.'

You can hear that same attitude in 'Oh Lord,' which has been Matt's signature song ever since. It's only E and A, over and over, but there's something about the *sound*. Not just the music but Matt's voice itself. His vocals are more present and confident on this album, but as with 'No Come Down,' the triumvirate themes of sex, religion, and drugs percolate through his songwriting; while not as lyrical, 'Oh Lord' is a tried-and-proven live staple that personifies Matt's rock'n'roll grit. Along with 'Not If You Were The Last Dandy On Earth' and 'Got My Eye On You,' it stands among the greatest songs he's ever written or recorded, though Anton would later contend that Larry Thrasher cut a version of 'Oh Lord' with his vocals that 'sounds like Iggy and Ian McCulloch on acid, and, no offense, but it blows this out of the water. And this was when Brian could still kind of play drums well.' What drives it isn't the guitar, though. It's the high-pitched part of that organ line. The breakdown on the song is proof that the song was recorded live. The stops, slowdowns, and speed-ups are completely natural and in their own organic time signature, like they rehearsed it that way. (It's possible to nail that same kind of thing with a metronome, but really fuckin' hard.)

Matt is at his snarkiest on 'B.S.A.,' which features one of the best guitar solos ever to appear on a BJM record.* The vibe of the song lands somewhere between the Stones and T.Rex, with all that sleazy feedback. His softer side comes out in 'Cabin Fever,' which is in a similar same vein to 'Miss June '75.' 'Matt was living in a utility room with no windows and was sleeping after the session,' Anton later recalled, 'so I tacked on the whole ending with Joel while he was asleep. The drum sound on the ending was a Crimean battle drum, blood-stained and magic. It belonged to Genesis, actually. I was asked not to touch any of the magic stuff. Oh well. That's rock'n'roll, and *real* magic.'

We are given a stronger dose of both sides of Matt's narrative coin on this record. One is aggressive, tough, in-your-face, the other defined by a brooding and self-loathing vulnerability, as on 'Cabin Fever.' In the bridge, however, he employs the same form of rolling, lyrical narrative he used in 'No Come Down.'

Matt had intended for the next song, 'In My Life,' to be sung by Mara, but she was sick during the week it was recorded, so he and Anton doubled the vocals instead. The result was a much tougher rock'n'roll romp. According

---

* 'BSA' is an acronym for the Birmingham Small Arms company, which manufactured motorcycles from the 1930s until the brand ended in the 1970s—the kind you'd expect Marlon Brando or James Dean to ride in one of their films. Hunter S. Thompson rode a BSA A65 Lightning for the year he rode with the Hell's Angels.

to Anton, he plays drums and bass on the song; Dean is on lead, Joel is on tambourine, and Matt plays rhythm. 'Great solo from Dean—one of the few tunes he is actually on.'

Following 'Oh Lord' on the record is the bluesy, blistering 'Caress.' Contradicting his statements elsewhere about which band members were present for the recording, he has since praised the 'great Jeff Davies solo' on the song, so maybe Jeff was there after all. 'Way better than Eric Clapton,' Anton continued. 'Fact. Clapton can't write a song to save his life.'*

'Caress' reminds me of something The Kinks or The Zombies would do, but it also has the quasi–spaghetti western/British Invasion feel that would later be mined more fully on *And This Is Our Music*. The band then goes into '(David Bowie I Love You) Since I Was Six,' with Dawn's accordion on the track setting it apart from everything else in the BJM canon. To me, this song, like the later 'The Devil May Care (Mom And Dad Don't),' is Anton at his most sorrowful. I can see him closing his eyes, listening back, the look on his face the moment he knew the mix was right.

Concerning 'Mary Please,' Brian remembers there being 'a real cheesy sixty-four-track recording of that song floating around.' Engineer Chris Arvan, he says, 'was trying to make the sound Euro-slick, like Oasis, and Anton hated those recordings—I think people would laugh if they heard it.' Anton himself has recalled making 'Mary Please' at practice, adding that it 'sounded a lot tougher live.' 'Monkey Puzzle,' on the other hand, is his rework of The Small Faces' 'You'd Better Believe It,' from their eponymous debut. 'Miranda was supposed to sing on it, but she chickened out,' Anton has said. Next up are 'Fucker' and 'Dawn,' both of which have a jangly acoustic feel—perhaps a nod to what was coming with the next record.

The most famous song on *Take It From The Man!*—and until recently a staple set-closer—is the sweeping 'Straight Up And Down.' The band played the song at a Sunday afternoon lunch show attended by Del, who hadn't heard them in a while, when, after about ten minutes, the band *whoo-hoo*'d into the

---

* It is no secret that Anton is no Clapton fan. He once told *Entertainment Weekly*, around the time *Dig!* came out, 'People talk about Eric Clapton. What has he ever done except throw his baby off a fuckin' ledge and write a song about it?' To his credit, Rob Campanella did his part to do damage control, telling *Stereogum* in 2017, 'I was sitting right next to Anton when he said this—and it's unfair that this quote keeps getting posted like it does. It's completely out of context and gives the entirely wrong impression of what actually went down.'

mics à la the Stones' 'Sympathy For The Devil,' like they had on Halloween at Slim's, before meshing that with the *na na na*s from The Beatles' 'Hey Jude.' The second version of the song on the record takes this form as the music escalates into the latter half of its eleven minutes. 'That song title was Joel's line,' Brian recalls. 'He'd say, Yeah, man, you guys were right on, straight up and down, man. That guy never left his character. He was always like that.'

Anton struck gold over twenty years later when HBO asked if it could license the song for *Boardwalk Empire*. Series creator Terence Winter chose the song himself. 'I wanted unexpected,' he explained. 'I didn't want to do some Charleston, which didn't really kick in until 1924 anyway, and everything I heard from the period had people doing the Charleston. I had been a fan of The Brian Jonestown Massacre, so we tried it, and I said to the editor, That really works for me.' The resulting deal, Anton says, was worth 'two or three or four or five 90s record deals for indie bands. It's like twenty Ariel Pink deals at once.' (He was later given a 'Top Television Series' award for the song by ASCAP in 2011.)

'Straight Up And Down' swings with ballsy swagger right up until it slows down. It's like the band has powered down, but then, just like on 'That Girl Suicide' or 'All Around You,' there is an explosive breakdown following a much softer buildup. Then comes Jeff's guitar, ripping everything to shreds before the song makes its landing.

The album then draws to a close with 'Monster'—another song that features a lot of Jeff—and the bluesy title track, which has Joel singing a lot in the background. Listing to this and then those early White Stripes records, it's hard not to wonder where Jack White might've gotten some of his ideas.

* * *

In late 1995, a publicist at the Bomp! offices rang *Alternative Press* editor Robert Cherry and said she had a brilliant musician he had to know about, then handed the phone over to Anton, who laid out his plan for world domination to Robert (whom he would later thank in the album's liner notes). 'He was obviously working hard to hype his band—I think at the expense of Oasis, an early obsession,' Robert recalls. 'But he was funny and extremely charming, and we had a lot in common musically.'

KEEP MUSIC EVIL

Robert subsequently wrote up a short profile of the BJM for *AP*'s June 1996 issue. Then, that spring, he invited the band to play the magazine's South By Southwest party at a bowling alley. 'I wasn't present for that one, but my wife, who was [*AP*'s] ad director at the time, witnessed the performance,' he says, adding that the show 'collapsed after only a few songs, and may have ended in a fight and/or one of their periodic breakups.'

Diane and Dave had driven the band out to SXSW—their first time playing the festival. 'Dave had a van and I just had my car, and I had like two or three of the band members in my car, and some of their gear in the back,' Diane recalls. 'That was fun, but we did so many drugs that we were all really wasted. Every single one of us was completely wasted. I did meth on that whole trip just to stay awake. It was like a ten-hour drive or something. I didn't get any sleep that whole two or three days that we were there. The band played really badly, they were so out of it. It was one of their worst gigs. When the drugs are all working, everything is fine—if everybody got the balance right, between the uppers and the downers. If the balance was off, there could be a fight onstage and it could all fall apart.'*

94

When the band got back to California, Anton paid a visit to his family and friends in Orange County. Days later, the band were scheduled to play another gig with the Dandys, opening for Love & Rockets, on March 22, 1996, so Anton had Michael Sjobeck drive him to the gig from Laguna Beach in his 1968 Volkswagen SQ-back eighteen hours before he was due to go on. They stopped in Santa Barbara and arrived in San Francisco around four in the morning.

'That particular gig was pivotal for the BJM,' Michael recalls. 'It suddenly appeared they were going places. Anton handed me his guitar two minutes before they took to the stage and said, *Here. Tune this*.'

Anton introduced Michael to Courtney Taylor-Taylor that night, but Michael was immediately put off by the Dandys' front man. 'He gave me a

---

* Diane's BJM adventures wound down after that jaunt. Five years of heavy drug use had taken their toll. She knew she had to get clean, so she separated herself from her drug buddies and sources and moved home with her parents up in Walnut Creek, where she quit cold turkey, before later moving to Sacramento. She left San Francisco for good in May or June of 1997. 'I was getting tired of the whole thing,' she says. 'It was really chaotic, and Anton was more into heroin than ever. He was basically a junkie, and he wasn't a fun junkie. If you were a child on Ritalin, speed will make you mellow, but heroin might make you aggressive, because the Ritalin changes something about your body chemistry.'

how're you gonna help my career? kind of look,' Michael says, 'but I thought the band brilliant, with Zia being extra-generous with the titty-flashing.'*

'BJM were brilliant too that night, with the expected missteps of being unusually tight or possibly restrained with their time limit,' Michael continues. 'And at the after-party Joel was his usual charming, stylish, ultra-animated self. I still have the poster from that show somewhere.'

Michael remembers the show as taking place at the Fillmore, but Joel insists it can't have been there. 'We weren't allowed to play the Fillmore in those days because of our bad rep around town with other venues' he says, 'but they finally let us in there to open up for Primal Scream a few years ago.'

Venues weren't the only thing catching the Jonestown's bad rep. After Anton and Dawn split up, he played a tape for her of a radio interview he did where he was telling the interviewer that she was out of the band, and that she was a witch who was trying to put some sort of curse on him. 'He seemed totally out of his head at the time, and he told me that he had not slept all night, so he had been up, and his voice was just about gone,' Dawn recalls. 'When he got manic like that, his judgment would be impaired, so it was customary for me and my housemates and friends to roll our eyes when Anton was on his soapbox. He could get really preachy. There were a fair amount of drugs and drinking going on, so we figured half the time he was on something. His behavior was annoying but also endearing. He was very loving, but he could be very confrontational as well.'

It grew to be too much for Dawn, and she ended up separating herself completely from Anton and the band and going her own way. Sometime after that is when Anton hooked up with Sophie Guenan and made *Thank God For Mental Illness*.

95

---

* Zia would regularly go topless during gigs back then, but by the time *Dig!* came out, she had pretty much retired the gimmick. As Dave Deresinski notes in the film, 'When Zia went back to England, and she didn't take her top off, the crowd totally did not respond well, because they were all expecting it.' Dave ran deep with the Dandys, too. 'I think I got really high on coke for the first time with Creepy Dave,' Zia says in *Dig!* 'We were totally in love with each other for about seven hours.' (For the record, Dave is not really all that creepy, but was given the nickname because he's so tall. He's also been called 'Yeti,' 'Big Dave,' and 'Dave D.')

678910

A BEER AND THE TAPE

Sophie Guenan appears on the sleeve of *Thank God For Mental Illness*, as well as in *Dig!* Some reports suggest she met Anton in early '95, while she was a student at Mill's College, living with a group of European artists in a big Victorian house on the corner of Laguna and Page, in front of the Zen temple there. One of her roommates was Mallory Margueron, whom Jorge Diaz de Bedoya—known from *Dig!* as George from The Minstrels, or 'Minstrel George'—says helped produce and record *Thank God For Mental Illness*. According to Jorge, portions of *Thank God* were recorded at the house, although Joel says he had not heard of any of it being recorded there until I mentioned it to him.

The special edition DVD of *Dig!* includes a bonus scene where Jorge, Joel, Anton, Sophie, and Barry Simons are all together at the NXNW music conference in Portland. Barry had worked with Anton since the rooftop show and was also the lawyer for The Flamin' Groovies, who had some music out on Bomp!*

Jorge says this was the first time he saw Sophie, in the lobby of the Belmont Hotel. 'She was absolutely sublime. I liked her from the first moment I laid my eyes on her. She was very hip and at the same time had loads of European charm and sophistication, and her accent when she spoke English was extremely sexy.'

Sophie and Jorge soon found they shared a passion for French literature.

---

* 'Anton is probably the easiest client I've ever worked for,' Barry says in the movie. 'Whenever I work with him he is always cordial. Respectful. Intelligent.' He said the same to me years later, when I visited him there at his office in San Francisco, where I spotted a huge box stuffed full of papers labeled 'BJM' on a very high shelf. I pointed at it and told him I'd sure like to get my hands on that what was in there. 'Oh no,' he said, patting my back as he walked me out. 'I'm afraid you wouldn't find anything of interest in there ... '

'She taught us a lot about books and poetry,' he says. 'I was quite superficial until I met Sophie. That woman made a man out of the uptight arrogant little rocker I had been before. To me, she was a revelation.'

Jorge had started The Minstrels when he was in high school in Quebec City. When he was sixteen, he fell in love with a twenty-year-old art student. 'I started the band mainly to impress her, and because I wanted to get out on the road and discover the continent and the world,' he says. 'Playing music was my way to live a great adventure with friends and by all means escape having to ever get a job which to this day I managed to avoid.' Jorge is now a filmmaker and scores his own soundtracks, but back when The Minstrels first crossed paths with the Jonestown, in late 1994, they were a trio: David Lachance, Nic Jodoin, and Jorge. Later, as Sophie and Jorge started to fall in love, she joined the group; by 1997, the lineup also featured Jennifer Stratford on guitar, Doug Lee on organ, David on drums, and Jorge on bass.

The Minstrels first met the Jonestown at a club in the Haight. 'They were amazing-looking kids and had a lot of great ideas and you could talk with them about every subject,' Jorge says. 'Anton was very sweet guy, extremely charming and bright. Nothing like you see in the movie, or what his reputation became as they gained notoriety over the years. They ate little and at very odd hours and almost never slept. Well, in those days, none of us slept that much at all anyways.'

Jorge distinctly remembers the BJM tracking *Thank God For Mental Illness* at Mallory's and having listening parties on the recorder there, a Korg sixteen-track. Some of the photos included inside the sleeve were also shot at that house. Besides Sophie and Mallory, two others lived there: German photographer Erik Pawassar and his girlfriend, Ute Farrar. Living across the street from them were Jeff and Roxanne, but while this alone would seem grounds enough for Anton and Sophie's paths to cross, Jorge purports that Anton and Sophie met in a bar.

Sophie brought into the group the songs and style of Leonard Cohen, Nico's *Chelsea Girl*, French New Wave cinema, Baudelaire, Paul Gaugin, and Serge Gainsbourg and Jane Berkin. In return, Anton turned Sophie on to Hank Williams. 'Anton loved her, and at the very beginning of their romance they had a great time, and they were very close, before hard drugs tore them apart,' Jorge says. 'They were married the following year.'

Jorge remembers listening in on many animated discussions between Sophie and Anton about CIA brainwashing techniques, mind control by the mass media, and similar subjects that were really at the core of Anton's preoccupations at the time, and had been since he first discovered them, along with his interest in secret societies and various other spiritual sub-currents. Sophie's father was an officer of the French air force who had been involved in his country's nuclear tests in the South Pacific. As such, she was very aware of issues involving the exploitation of indigenous populations and psychological warfare, so they clicked on those subjects, too.

'They both were very much aware of the hypocrisy inherent to Western cultural imperialism and capitalism,' says Jorge. 'In one respect, they were looking for ways to exist as artists outside of that system, and use it and extort from it to create dysfunction within its patterns and rules. That's why Anton was so inclined to sabotage certain deals. He adamantly refused the status-quo definitions of success and of achieving the so-called American dream.'

Because so many of the songs on *Satanic Majesties*, *Take It From The Man!*, and *Thank God For Mental Illness* were recorded and released during the same time frame, it can be easy to confuse which songs came from which sessions. Larry Thrasher thinks Anton took songs from the *Take It From The Man!* sessions and put them on *Satanic Majesties*, and that parts of *Satanic Majesties* might have been tracked at Naut's. Anton still had some of Naut's vintage mics and gear that they used on *Take It from the Man!*, so the same gear was definitely used on *Thank God For Mental Illness*, which accounts for some of the closeness in sound. It's also the case that the band's lineup was pretty consistent during this period. Anton was moving between three studios, including Larry's, and eventually bits of these sessions collided in the bipolar creative schizophrenia that is *Thank God For Mental Illness*.

'The title came about because everyone was saying I was insane,' he's since said. 'And I just thought to myself, *Thank God*.' The cover art is a photograph of Joel pulling a comical face with blood smeared around his mouth and teeth. 'I cut my hand and painted my mouth with blood,' he recalls. 'It was my Christopher-Lee-as-Dracula. My eye pupils explain the rest of the situation.' The band as they appear in the booklet for the record is the band we first meet in *Dig!*

Anton has said that he borrowed a cheap eight-track and made *Thank God For Mental Illness* in the time it took for two of his bandmates to go out and score drugs, for a total cost of $17.36. (When asked what he spent the money on, he replied, 'A beer and the tape.') However, Joel insists that the album was recorded over two or three nights at a rehearsal space Anton had access to in the Tenderloin, not at Mallory's.

It was not uncommon to track whole albums in these kinds of rehearsal spaces. 'All of the albums from this period were situations where Anton would make connections with people who could lend him their spaces during the nighttime,' says Joel. No drums were tracked for the record, and in fact no full band was available at that point anyway, so Anton and Joel often gigged as a duo. 'Special time for me, you can imagine!' Joel laughs.

Anton seized the opportunity to perform and refine his acoustic work, though Joel sometimes took time off to pal around with a new gal he'd been seeing. After tracking all of his parts, Anton rang Joel to say, 'If you don't come down here *right now*, you're going to miss it, and you're not going to be on the next record!'

99

Joel ditched the girl and headed for the Tenderloin. As he tells it, when he arrived at the studio, Anton told him how, the night before, he'd heard this voice from inside one of the rehearsal rooms that was perfect for 'Those Memories' and 'Free And Easy, Take 2,' a pair of songs he'd written about Dawn. Anton brought Joel went up to the room, they knocked on the door, and one Kacie Lynn Camble answered. They showed her the songs, and, impressed, Kacie agreed to sing backup, tracking her parts that same night. Later, when the band recruited Bradford Artley to drum in the live lineup, Kacie performed with them for a few shows. Anton saw star potential in Kacie, whereas Joel felt she was vying for his position. 'Some little plain Jane, going for mine?' he recalls. 'It was kind of silly. I don't remember where she ended up going off to, but no hard feelings from me. She did a great job on those songs.'

The next night, Jeff Davies (whose influence on the three records released in 1996 is undeniable) joined Joel and Anton in the Tenderloin to lay down lead guitar. 'It wasn't just me and Anton doing *Illness*, as you know, but I was partying so much at the time that I barely got on it,' Joel continues. 'That's why Sophie was supposed to replace me, but I got my shit back together at the last moment, and it ended up being me and Sophie on dual tambourine duty. She pretty much copied my whole attitude thing, so we were in sync, visual-wise. I was pissed at the time, but it must have looked pretty fucking cool, thinking about it now, and all that *It Girl*, whoo-hoo, and Spanish Bee *Hee-yah!* stuff is Anton, me, and Jeff, as well. Anton plays most everything, I did some percussion, and Jeff, of course, plays the more smokin' guitar stuff.'

One of the best-loved songs on the record, 'Ballad Of Jim Jones,' is Anton at his most Dylan-esque, and set the mark for where he was going to go in the next few records. The song is not actually about Jim Jones but about Anton himself.* The song has a harmonica part, too, which is perhaps what most separates this record from the others.

Joel named the song when he and Anton were at Del Beaudry's house—the only time Joel says he was ever there. During the visit, Del gave Anton a Masonic Bible, one of several Masonic items Anton would acquire over the years. The three of them were listening to the new recordings when Anton asked Joel, out of nowhere, 'What should we name *this* song?' Joel said 'The Ballad Of Jim Jones' without missing a beat. 'I felt there was a lot of Brian Jones references and none about Jim Jones,' he recalls, 'so that was the motivation there—plus it would be an eyebrow raiser.'

Another poignant moment on the record is 'Stars,' the first song Anton ever wrote with words and guitar. 'The joke is, I release old stuff on every record, so every time anyone says, I like the old band, well, it is still that band, because I *am* the band,' Anton has said. 'I did it all unless I say, and what *old sound*? I've tricked you, you see, because I release songs and share them as I see fit.'

Keeping to that form, Anton included within *Illness* an in-album EP titled *Sound Of Confusion*, which was mostly recorded a few years earlier at the Compound, before Ricky and Travis left the band. The EP, he later explained, 'is me and Ricky recording "Thoughts Of You" or "The Fire Song" at the Compound. Matt wrote the bass and words for "The Fire Song," but I ran with the concept when I lived on Shrader in the Haight.' Ricky and Travis

---

* 'Ballad Of Anton Newcombe' might've been too much of an ego trip for anyone to take seriously, although 'The Godspell According To A.A. Newcombe' would come later—a spiritual sequel to 'Ballad' wherein Anton channels the figure of cult leader Jim Jones to relay his own narrative of spiritual cleansing and rebirth.

also play on 'Fuck You For Fucking Me.' By bringing things full circle in this way, Anton was closing the songbook on one era as he geared up for the next, just in time for the band's growth in popularity in the underground.

* * *

On June 17, 1996, the BJM opened for Electrafixion, featuring former Echo & The Bunnymen members Ian McCulloch and Will Sergeant, at Bimbo's 365 Club on Columbus Avenue. One Derek Hoeckel, who'd been playing in the band that year as an extra guitarist, was in the lineup for that gig and helped design a flyer with Joel and a guy named Mike Prosenko, who would later end up doing the graphic design work for *Strung Out In Heaven*, *Bringing It All Back Home—Again*, *Bravery Repetition And Noise*, and later for *Dig!*, as well as records by Black Rebel Motorcycle Club and others. He also helped Miranda Lee Richards with her album *The Herethereafter*.

On August 10 and 11, 1996, the BJM opened for Peter Kember's Experimental Audio Research at the Kilowatt. Longtime fan Chris Reid attended the gig with his girlfriend Elli. California was in the midst of a huge blackout at the time, and traffic was at a standstill, so they walked an hour down Market to the Mission. When they got to the Kilowatt, that side of the block still had power, and it was show time.

101

Chris had heard of the BJM from the Bomp! catalogue, for which he remembers the tag line being something like 'recommended if you like Spacemen 3.' He had the first two seven-inches, and the *Methodrone* and *Spacegirl* LPs, so he was looking forward to an evening of psyched-out space rock and shoegaze. What he got instead was an all-acoustic guitar jamboree. Sophie and a few other girls, maybe including Kacie, were up onstage, along with a semicircle of guys armed with acoustic guitars, Anton at one end, and Joel front and center with his wild hair and tambourines.

Chris has conflicting memories about where he stood in the well-attended crowd. He can picture himself against the east wall on a barstool, watching Anton argue with an audience member, but he can also see himself further to the other side and more toward the front as Joel nonchalantly flicked cigarettes into the crowd and 'accidentally' let his microphone get too close to the monitors, causing them to squeal with feedback, much to Anton's annoyance. After Anton scolded him for this, Joel would slyly smile and do it again.* Chris also remembers Anton having a cymbal that he bowed and sent through a delay, and debating with the soundman about how long the delay should be.

A couple of weeks later, Anton mixed *Thank God For Mental Illness* in one day, starting at seven in the morning and finishing by one in the afternoon. Then, as he says in *Dig!*'s very first scene, 'Found a drummer. Taught him all the tunes.'

'And he did, too,' Joel says.

That night the band—back together and in fighting form—showed up too late to play a gig at the old Popscene at Cat's Alley and were turned away. It was Anton's twenty-ninth birthday. Outside, in the parking lot, Anton met a young, aspiring filmmaker by the name of Ondi Timoner, who'd made arrangements to come and film the show.

---

* 'Joel at the time did have an incredible talent when he was loaded for pushing people's buttons and making them angry,' Matt Hollywood says in *Dig!*, before Courtney Taylor-Taylor adds, 'That was when Joel would like throw chairs and bottles and stuff. He got fun after that.'

PART TWO

DIG! A LITTLE DEEPER

So the movie begins.*

Filmmaker Ondi Timoner had just graduated *cum laude* from Yale. She was on her way to San Francisco from Los Angeles with her brother, David, for their sister's wedding, when they swung in to meet The Brian Jonestown Massacre for a project she was doing for MTV called *The Cut*, about ten bands on the verge of getting signed. Since there was no gig to shoot, she ended up filming the BJM 'after-party' at 210 Waller Street until four in the morning. Dave Deresinski roomed there with Elise Pearson, who would end up being involved with the band for a decade. She'd met them a couple of years earlier, when she was in the agent-training program at William Morris. Elise couldn't represent the band, but she still used her credentials to book gigs, including an upcoming trip to SXSW. She quit that job eventually and moved to SF from LA to live at 210 Waller with Dave D., and the two of them became best friends for a while, at which point she started working more with the band.

When Ondi met Anton, she was immediately struck by his charisma. The first BJM show she shot was at the Viper Room in Hollywood in September 1996—almost two years before the band first met and started playing with The Dandy Warhols. There were representatives from eight labels present to see the band, and Anton spent the bulk of the money Greg Shaw had loaned him for the trip on sitars, leaving the rest of the band without food or cigarette money. Tensions grew quickly.

Nina Ritter, who appears early in the film, around the Viper Room scene,

* Part two of this book loosely follows the narrative of *Dig!*, although to lay out the pieces of the film, shot by shot, and then arrange them in chronological order is no easy task. Perhaps the best thing is to go by Joel's maxim: *'In those days, there was no time.'*

worked in A&R at Virgin until 1990, then moved with her boss, Nancy Jeffries, to Elektra. She was promoted to A&R director there around 1992; she helped bring in Deee-Lite and Feeder, put together a few compilations, and stayed at the label until 2000. She was not at the Viper Room that night. 'I was not involved in the Viper room disaster, nor was I there,' she told me.

After hearing about the band through a mailed-in demo and some indie press around 1993, Nina went out to dinner with them, and they had such a good time that Jeff offered to pick her up the next day to hang out again. That next night, she was waiting in front of her hotel, expecting a car, when Jeff showed up on his bicycle. She hopped on his handlebars and he pedaled them off to meet the rest of the band.

The sequence of images and narrative presented in this part of *Dig!* implies that Nina set up the Viper Room gig as an industry showcase for the band to play soon after scouting them, but Dave disputes that. He says this show has been confused with a different showcase Nina went to, at the Great American Music Hall. 'David is correct,' Nina confirms. 'That was a gorgeous, violence-free show. Later on, I brought Nancy to a private gig, and it was a disaster. No set list. Fifteen-minute gaps between songs. We did not sign them.' (This, again, is contrary to what is stated in the film.)

Jeff was not at the Viper Room either. A guy named Robert Desmond was playing instead. Just before the show, David Landau, a booking agent for the band, told Ondi, 'As long as there's no fighting onstage, I'll be happy.' Famous last words. The film shows Robert and Anton arguing onstage while Joel starts kicking cables around. Anton nearly goes ballistic, and then, when Robert steps in, all hell breaks loose. Anton lunges at Robert, and the two of them fall down in a heap of microphone stands, cables, and guitars. During the scuffle, one of Anton's new sitars slides off the wall it's leaning against and cracks. Once they've pulled the brawl apart, Anton tries to tend to the instrument, but he's whisked out the back door before he can do anything.

The show sabotaged, his sitar and band in shambles, Anton blamed the whole ordeal on Robert. 'Broke my fuckin' sitar, motherfucker,' he says.

'Poor Robert,' Joel says. 'He tried so hard. He was going to come in and help Anton. Be the right hand man and organize everything.'

Robert, who was only in the band long enough to appear in this scene and a photo in a *BAM* magazine spread, claims his brief appearance in the film is a misrepresentation. 'It was oddly portrayed by Ondi, with the implication that I was somehow not down with trying to get the band signed that night at the Viper Room,' he says. 'At this point in my life, I was hoping for nothing more than to finally get with a band that could make it big.'

Ondi dismisses this. 'I don't think I implied that in any way. I don't think he comes off as someone who was against a deal at all,' she says. 'I think he comes off as someone who is trying to play guitar in a band. I don't even know where he gets that from. If anything, I thought I saw Anton self-destructing that night—which was typical for him at that point in his life. That was going to be his big break that night, if he wanted that break. But he didn't want that break, because that's just not Anton. He didn't want that easy road.'*

The next day, at Greg's, Anton invited Ondi to go to Portland with him and Sophie to meet the Dandys, whom he praised as partners in the revolution. 'Forget about those other bands you're filming,' he told her; all she would need was the BJM and the Dandys. That's when he showed her their first record, *Dandys Rule, OK?* Both Anton and Joel have said that it's their favorite Dandys record, and Diane said when she first listened to it with Jeff, they were blown away. But Courtney was far more interested in achieving success with his own group than championing Anton's revolution, which to Ondi he seemed to not have any idea about.

Ondi stayed in LA but kept in touch. Despite being drawn to the BJM and the Dandys, she didn't drop the other bands she'd tapped for *The Cut* right away, though eventually she would be forced to abandon that project altogether, once MTV turned it into an *American Idol*–type game show. It was at that point that her vision for *The Cut* became *Dig!*, as the shock of Anton's antics wore off and she realized that forming a narrative around the two bands would be the best way to make the film.

The *BAM* article came out about two weeks after the Viper Room incident. I bought one of Joel's old copies off of him, and I laughed when I first saw the picture of Kirk Hammett on page ten as I thought about him, Dave, Crystal, and Anton in the burrito joint, and his recording those demos with Miranda Lee Richards, teaching her how to play and record.† There's an advertisement

106

---

* The Dandys' Peter Holmström has said that he almost played that show instead of Robert, adding that had he done so, things might've taken a completely different turn.
† Hammett could not be reached for comment.

in the back for Mr. Toad's, where Brant Graff's copy of the first BJM demo tape was digitized, then an advertisement for Bomp! in the indie label section.

The magazine was published on September 25, 1996, and sometime after that, Anton and Sophie headed north. Anton's plan, once they were in Portland, was to make music with Courtney, but the Dandys had just signed to Capitol, so Court put the kibosh on Anton's revolution pretty quick. 'Anton loved [the Dandys] so much, and he packed up his car to go play music with them, and that's when the relationship went south,' Ondi recalls.

Courtney did offer to let Anton and Sophie stay for a week at his place, but he showed them the door after a couple of days, having realized he couldn't handle them anymore. 'He had taken my spare foam pad for sleepover houseguests and I never saw it again,' he told me. 'What would he have done with it? My foam pad? It even had a fitted sheet.'

Anton had a different take on things. 'Sophie and I were having trouble finding a place to rent, because people are weird in Portland,' he said years later, in a MySpace post. 'So, Courtney said, *Hey move into this place and take over. The person on the lease is a drug addict.* But he sort of set me up, because he knew it was a nightmare. The bass player from Steppenwolf owned the house. I tried to talk him into letting me take the lease, but he was like, *No, these people fucked me over*, so Courtney is kind of a fuckhead for that.'*

Sometime after settling in Portland, Anton phoned Joel to ask him to come join them. Joel promptly hit the Greyhound to live with the newlyweds at a rehearsal space at Suburbia Studios run by Tom Roberts, aka Pig Champion of the band Poison Idea. He describes the place as a 'two-level, practice space, jive-ass fuckin' hole … most people went [there] to practice, but we were *living* in it. Me, Sophie, and Anton. For six months.' (Zia McCabe agrees the place was a dump, calling it 'one of the most depressing places in Portland.') Future Dandy Brent DeBoer (Courtney's cousin) had a space a couple of doors down around the same time, while Tom's space was between the two of theirs. Tom died in 2006.

Ondi and David did eventually make it up to Portland, cameras in hand, to document the despair. They found Anton, Joel, and Sophie all sleeping on the

107

---

* Courtney refutes this account. 'I'm a shit-bag for trying to get him a house in Portland to rent? I've never known anyone from Steppenwolf … who makes this shit up?' Joel, meanwhile, was not in Portland yet—'Anton's apartment hunting was before I got up there,' he says—but he's sure Anton's memory of events 'must be true.'

same mattress—or maybe foam pad—broke and hungry. By now, Anton and Sophie were married. 'They got some hippie dude to marry them,' Elise says.

The marriage, while not a sham, was not all it was cracked up to be, either. 'Sophie was from France,' Joel says. 'She wanted [US] citizenship. They were going out, [but] their marriage had a lot more to do with citizenship than it did as actually being husband and wife. It was kind of a deal they had, but they were also boyfriend and girlfriend at the time.'

Jorge Diaz de Bedoya, who later married Sophie after she and Anton split up, dismisses the claim that Sophie married Anton in order to get a visa. 'In fact,' he says, 'she overstayed her Visa several times and did nothing about it for years. Only after 9/11 did she pay her fines and clear her record so she could travel and make her films.'

One of Joel's criticisms of *Dig!* is that it incorrectly portrays Anton as an overbearing partner to Sophie. 'Anton's not quite as big of a jerk as he looks [in the movie], in my opinion, having lived with him for those months,' he says. '[Sophie] would play little head trips on him, because she'd spent a lot of money on supporting him—and me for a while—but thank God she found Jorge and went on to something really great for her.'

* * *

Michael 'Spike' Keating from local Portland band Swoon 23 (later managed by Dave) befriended Anton and the others during their time in Portland and visited them at the Jive Ass Fuckin' Hole, where he found them growing six-day beards, staring at static on the TV, and surrounded by empty potato chip bags and bottles. Swoon 23 were also good friends with the Dandys and played at Zia's first show with the band along with a bunch of others. Also in that band were Spike, Megan Pickerel, Marty Smith, and Jeff Studebaker. That year they recorded the album *The Legendary Ether Pony* in Memphis, and the next year released it on Tim/Kerr, which had also put out *Dandys Rule OK?*, touring the record with both the BJM and the Dandys. By 1998, Marty had been to so many BJM shows that when they were in need of yet another drummer, he was able to jump on the sticks in NYC and Toronto and play like he'd been with the group for years.

Megan later hooked up Travis Snyder with his gig as the BJM's roadie and tour manager, which he'd hold for two decades. '*He's* Anton's right-hand man,' future guitarist Frankie Emerson told me of Travis. 'Anton fully trusts him to tune his guitar, which is stupid, because Travis didn't even own a tuner. That's how fucked up Travis was, but he finally got it together.'

Travis hung around in the same circles as Swoon 23, the Dandys, and the BJM. Swoon 23 and the BJM ended up doing a fair amount of touring together. 'When they were in town, some or all of them crashed at my house,' says Megan. 'I have a lot of great memories, drunken and hazy as they are!'

Joel got pretty drunken and hazy with the Dandys that New Years Eve at La Luna. Brent was also in attendance. Since first meeting the BJM, the Dandys had played a ton of shows up and down the West Coast, then across the county to NYC and back with Electrafixion and Love & Rockets. From an industry standpoint, the BJM were eating their dust. The Dandys had also made it over to the UK already that July, after signing to Capitol in September, right around when Anton met Ondi and told her about them.

The La Luna New Years Eve party was massive, lasting until well past four in the morning. In *Dig!*, Ondi juxtaposes footage of the party with images of Anton in the lockout space recording 'The Devil May Care (Mom And Dad Don't),' which I've heard more than one person say that it is the most important part of the film, because you actually get to see Anton do what he does best: make beautiful music, completely out of his brain and body all at once. Synthesizer, percussion, guitar, xylophone, vocals, all captured live from the Jive Ass Fuckin' Hole. 'All of those Theremin-type sounds are just from an eight-track,' Anton told author and journalist Ben Vendetta a couple of years later. 'These people who are making [*Dig!*] watched me do everything in forty minutes, rushing right through it. I think it's amazing. The sound of it is nuts. It's like my personal *Pet Sounds* shit.'

As Ondi shows Anton singing lines about his parents, we are given scenes of them offering competing narratives of blame about how Anton, now nearly thirty, has turned out. Anton's mom seems to not take her son seriously, and laments the path he has chosen. His father, on the other hand, blames himself for at least part of Anton's manic behavior. Then, as Anton is shown recording the song in the lockout space, it is revealed that his father took his own life on Anton's 'next birthday.' After the botched narrative of the Viper Room, this is the next of many things about the film that are chronologically incorrect. As the reveal of Bob Newcombe's death occurs simultaneously with the scenes of Anton in the Portland lockup space, presumably on New Years Eve 1996, the viewer might assume that Bob died on Anton's thirtieth birthday, in 1997. However, everybody I have spoken to about this has said that Anton found out about his father's death on the day of a show at the Troubadour, where the band played—with a whole other lineup—on Anton's thirty-first birthday, in 1998.

* * *

After splitting from Portland, Anton, Sophie, and Joel moved in with Elise, who'd relocated to Seattle, and stayed with her for a few months. That next month, in February, they played a gig at the Crocodile Café, followed by an after-party at her place. Ondi filmed just about everyone there, including Megan, Dave, Matt, and Spike, putting some form of liquid down the back of Joel's pants. Everyone but The Dandys was there. Anton pours dish soap down Joel's pants and smacks his ass a couple times for good measure, sending tiny bubbles into the air in every direction of Elise's kitchen.

Among those at the after-party was Brad Artley, who took up the sticks for the band sometime after Brian quit. Despite being on the poster and most promotional materials for the film, however, his name does not appear in the opening credits.

One night, Brad was in a San Francisco club watching his friends' band, The Supernaturals, when Joel walked in, spotted him easily in the crowd, and walked over to ask if he wanted to play drums for the Jonestown. Brad, surprised by the gesture, didn't immediately jump at the thought of it, but he didn't shut the door right away, either. Joel explained the band had some dates booked and beckoned Brad to follow him out of the club. Anton was parked outside, in this little mustard-yellow Subaru station wagon he'd had for a couple years. Brad sat in the front passenger's seat and shook his hand, and the three of them drove off to discuss Brad's recruitment prospects. Eventually, Joel took off into the San Francisco night, leaving Anton and Brad to smoke joints and listen to BJM recordings on the Subaru's tape deck, agreeing that somewhere between the Stones, Syd Barrett, and The Jesus & Mary Chain, they were going to get along.

Like Anton's, Brad's childhood in San Diego was filled with music. His mom played piano and his sisters had guitars, and he got his hands on whatever instrument he could find. As a teenager, all of his friends played guitar in bands. Brad remained on the outside, itching for a piece of the action, so he picked up the sticks. In those years there was a small 60s-garage revival happening in San Diego, centered on bands like The Crawdaddies, The Tell-Tale Hearts, and The Event, who had all consequently released albums through Greg's Bomp! sub-imprint, Voxx Records, alongside The Flamin' Groovies and others. At age seventeen, Brad fit right in there. He had Beatle boots, tight pants, and a Brian Jones–style haircut, which he still wears today and which everyone remembers him for.

Brad's seemingly random encounter with Joel that night at the Supernaturals gig was not his first brush with the BJM. He'd moved to Oakland around 1990, but spent plenty of time checking out the scene in San Francisco, where, a couple of years later, he kept seeing a flyer posted up around town featuring a picture of Brian Jones and the words *Take Acid Now And Come See The Brian Jonestown Massacre*. He even stopped in at a Haight gig during the spring of '93, but he wasn't digging the shoegaze vibe the band had going on then. When he next saw the BJM, a couple of years later, their earlier aesthetic had been replaced with the 60s-garage vibe he'd left behind in San Diego. Excited by the band's new sound and direction, he walked backstage to meet the guys. Joel, Matt, and Dean were immediately keen on him. Not only could he play drums, he had the look to boot, so the four of them pulled a speed-fueled all-nighter at Popscene—a club night at Cat's Alley—and ended up jamming at Brad's practice space until dawn.*

Brad didn't join ranks right away but hung around until Brian officially left, a couple of weeks before the band met Ondi, which is when he was approached by Joel, the rest of the band having talked Anton into giving him an audition. Brad practiced twice and then played his first show at a party in Hollywood with the Dandys. By then, the BJM had been banned from a few different clubs in San Francisco, but the notorious image that followed them enticed Brad. At one club, Jeff emptied a whole bottle of sparkling water into a monitor, frying the circuits. Anton promised to hold a benefit gig to replace the monitor, but it never happened. ('That caused me a lot of hassle,' says Dave.)

Once Anton, Joel, and Sophie moved back to San Francisco, they

---

* Early on in *Dig!*, Eric Shea—one of Popscene's promoters, along with Aaron Axelsen, Omar Perez, and Jeremy Goldstein—calls the BJM 'the band you love to hate and the band you hate to love. [Their] live performances are infamous.'

approached Brad to go on a short tour through the northwest, but it seemed they weren't going to be back before Brad's rent was due. *Fuck it*, he thought, caught up in the rock'n'roll spirit of the moment. *I'm just gonna go along with it and be homeless, too.*

A couple of years later, Joel would boast of the band's nomadism. 'It's not like we all have jobs and go to a practice space twice a week and play,' he said. 'We're living it. We gave up on jobs, lived on the streets, and did whatever it took to make it go down. If you're going to ask for something like being in a successful band, that's a big thing to ask, and you're going to have to pay some serious dues. It's all or nothing. You have to go through the downs to get to the ups.'

After the gigs in the northwest, Brad accompanied the band at shows in Phoenix, Albuquerque, and El Paso. In April, the band played SXSW again, right around the time they moved into LA's Atwater Village neighborhood. Jennifer Brandon was covering SXSW '97 for *Big Brother* magazine and interviewed the BJM on Easter Sunday. Prior to the interview, she and the band watched *The Ten Commandments* with Charlton Heston.

Jennifer had approached Ondi at an earlier show in LA to ask how she could help with the film. Ondi hired her as an intern and gave her the task of logging footage. 'Courtney was staying at [Ondi's] house during that time,' she recalls. 'That was when [the Dandys] had just got signed to Capitol. There was this sense that they were going to become a huge band, and Courtney was a bundle of nerves. Ondi's house operated as the epicenter of the BJM and the Dandys, and it was insane and intoxicating to witness it all. It's like they were in a race to get to the top, but no one knew what the top was … everyone wanted to get there though, hell or high water.'

Jennifer wasn't the only person the BJM were meant to cross paths with at that year's SXSW. Colleen Jetton—Anton's right hand for a time—would fall under his spell there, as would one Scott Pollack of Which? Records. Music lawyer and band manager Dennis Pelowski had been in Austin for the festival for about a week when he caught the band's gig at a tequila club called Touché. Brad was the target of Anton's taunts that night, as Dennis remembers it, and half of the band's forty-minute slot was spent starting and stopping as Anton berated him. 'Brad's face, you could see, was *let me get through this set*. I saw maybe twenty minutes of music.'

As the band closed their set, Dennis approached Dave and asked where they were headed next. Dave told him they were headed back to LA, so Dennis got their number and called them from his place in Minneapolis. 'Most artists don't want to know what the business side is. They're afraid of it,' Dennis says. 'You could tell Anton was already clued in, whether through himself or the people he was around.'

A couple of weeks later, Dave invited Dennis out to see a show in LA, where he ended up partying at the band's new house at 3261 Larga Street in Atwater, commonly remembered and referred to as 'the Larga house.' Picturing the scene, Dennis recalls, 'No furniture really except couches. Beer bottles, whiskey bottles. Boots everywhere. Ashtrays filled with smokes. Those guys were *literally* living communally.' According to Brad, the place was 'a madhouse, but we did really well when we were living there. It really was more like the *Monkees* TV show than what Ondi represented, he adds, echoing Paola Simmonds's sentiment that it was 'more like a big fun party that never stopped.'

Dennis found a window to chat with Anton and told him that he was amazed that the records his band had just put out through Bomp! in such quick succession were so different stylistically from one another. 'This is nothing,' Anton told him. 'I'm sitting on about three thousand other songs. If I could, I would put out an album a day.' Dennis next wanted to know about the band's touring history. He learned that they'd never ventured further than the West Coast, they didn't have a booking agent or a reliable van, and incidents like those at the Viper Room and venues around San Francisco had damaged their reputation with bookers and talent buyers across the country. Anton wanted very badly to tour, if only to kill their bad reputation.

Dennis's wheels were turning by now, and he asked Anton if he had a contract with Bomp! Anton told him that it was just the handshake deal with Greg, but that he owned the masters. Dennis advised him to copyright everything and to license his music out but not give up his rights, adding that when he got back to Minneapolis he would see about throwing a tour together. Nothing big—maybe eight to ten shows. He'd figure something out.

'You want to know something?' Anton told him. 'I've been studying contracts for as long as I've been studying the A chord.'

Right before moving to the Larga house, the band had set up temporary

113

headquarters at Dave's parents' house in Palo Alto. They all lived in little rooms or slept on the couch in the living room, which doubled as their practice space. With plenty of food and booze at their disposal, Dave's dad, Stan, a clinical professor of medicine, helped fund Anton and the band, through Dave, when money was tight. 'Old Man Deresinski is righteous,' Joel says in the film. 'He has done so much for this band.'

One of the cinematographers who ended up working on *Dig!* was Sandy Wilson, whom Ondi met through Billy Pleasant, who at the time was playing in Touchcandy, another of the bands Ondi was looking at for *The Cut*. Sandy crashed on Ondi's couch in exchange for working on the film, having just moved back to LA from NYC in January, and was embedded with the band to film during their time in Palo Alto. That lasted for only a couple of weeks, but it was during this time that Peter Hayes, who would later front Black Rebel Motorcycle Club, auditioned for the group in the Deresinskis' living room— an arrangement set up by Barry Simons. 'It was Anton, Matt, Jeff, Dave, Brad, and myself,' Sandy recalls. 'We were just hanging out there doing fuck all. Watching TV.'

Peter remembers the day of his audition well. 'I'd seen 'em play a few times before, and I heard that they were a looking for a guitar player to go to Los Angeles, so [I was] introduced to Anton at one of their gigs. He said to come on out to Dave Deresinski's parents' house, so I drove out there in my van and tried out. I was set up in the living room, working at a gas station on the graveyard shift, basically just listening to [BJM] tapes and shit like that, trying to learn their songs. As many as I could, you know? I went and tried out, and I'm not sure if they were all particularly that impressed with my guitar playing, but they wanted my van.'

When Peter showed up for his audition, Anton told Sandy not to be 'in his face' with the camera, so Sandy set up in a loft area that overlooked the living room using Ondi's 'spy cam' adapter to film the audition, which was cut from the final version of the film. Peter is introduced playing acoustics with Matt on the porch steps of the Larga house, after Sophie exits the band and marries Jorge.

Though the film's portrayal of Peter seems to jive with Joel's characterization of him as a 'stupid fuckin' hippie,' Jorge remembers Peter's time in the BJM more positively. 'He was playing the acoustic all the time, writing and practicing songs around the house,' Jorge says. 'It was like everybody knew he had it in him from the moment they knew him. Anton had a great talent at recognizing talent.'

Greg got the Larga house soon after that, and Elise moved back to LA to live with the band and Dave there. Greg paid some of the rent; Elise's parents and Dave's parents helped out as well. Everyone was determined to make it work. 'I booked the band,' Elise says, 'and we made our money that way for living expenses. They didn't have much, let me tell you. Joel had no shoes, and Dave would give me money to take Joel shoe shopping. They had tape around their Beatle boots. They were *broke*.'

Josephine Tavares came down with Dave to visit the band that spring. 'The Larga house was dirty. Absolutely disgusting,' she recalls. 'When I walked in, everyone was passed out but Anton, who was sitting there making music with Miranda'—Miranda Lee Richards, one of many from the San Francisco scene to migrate to LA.

One night after a gig, Josephine and the band all went to a party in the hills and came back to the house to continue the debauchery. 'I found a little dry corner to huddle up in,' she continues, 'and woke up the next morning to see a girl come out of one guy's room to go into another's. Brad was hungover on the couch, holding a piece of sandwich bread to his eyes, as if that was going to cure his hangover.' Not wanting to hang around, Josephine split to go get cigarettes with Peter.

* * *

In March, shortly after the band moved into 3261 Larga, Ondi filmed Jeff shooting up. He wasn't the only one using the drug. 'Anton was a raging heroin addict then, and Jeff was a professional heroin addict,' future tour manager Brad Clark later told me. 'That's what ruined *everything*.'

'Heroin makes him evil,' Sophie says in the film, after fighting with Anton, 'but he doesn't know that, because he can't see himself.'*

'That place was insane,' Jeff's ex, Sonia Pacheco, says of the Larga house. Sonia had just met the band and started hanging around at their shows, which

---

* Right after that, Courtney mentions how Sophie fell in love with Jorge and together they moved to Tahiti. In real life, things did not happen so quickly. 'It took her a long time to fall in love with Jorge,' Elise says. 'They lived at my house on Descanso Street for months together before she finally decided she loved him.'

led to relationships with both Jeff and heroin.* Elise's experience of living there was much more peaceful, however. 'There were no junkie types at the house,' she said, 'Anton met them elsewhere and kept a low profile when he did it, although it is true that he was mean when he was on it. It was also very obvious when he was on it.'

Whatever the case, it's clear that heroin wrecked its way through the Jonestown. Dawn Thomas came down from San Francisco to visit and found Anton hadn't changed since the last time she saw him. 'The Larga house was a train wreck,' she says. 'Anton was doing a lot of heroin and surrounding himself with folks to help fuel that. I still loved him a lot at that point, but I knew that he was pretty far gone.' Anton became even more confrontational toward her once Ondi came around. 'I remember being in a club, and Anton telling me, *Don't hassle me, they are making a film about me and I am going to be famous*,' she recalls. 'He had an entourage with him, and [Ondi] was filming him ranting and raving. I left.'

By now, it was no secret that Ondi thrived on Anton's amped-up attitude, and some say she encouraged it—including Dennis, who claims Ondi manipulated and took advantage of Anton. 'I remember sitting at a party, and Ondi was there,' he recalls. 'Never met a bigger snake. She's sitting there, talking to him, saying, *Anton, this film is about your art. This film is about how you're an artist, and the Dandys are not* … it's so edited away from what was really going on.'

* * *

The Jonestown did well in Hollywood in the spring of '97. They were starting to play big shows, often sponsored by a vodka company or a cigarette brand, as with their appearance at SXSW that year. Sometimes, the first half of their

---

* Sonia says that Jeff hated LA, and that Anton used her to get Jeff more involved with the band. 'Jeff always did what Jeff wanted to do,' she continues. 'Anton would take me aside into little corners at clubs, trying to talk to me about Jeff, and he'd say, *So, Jeff listens to you, and I need you to talk to him about this project I want to do with him*, and he'd go on to tell me about how he wanted to do this & and Garfunkel act with Jeff and how he always says no, but if I were to mention it as being cool, Jeff would change his mind. I'd go home with Jeff and be like, *So, Anton wants me to conspire with him to get you to do this Simon & Garfunkel shit* … and he'd be like, *Yeah, he's been talking about that for years. No way.*' Jeff, however, says Sonia egged on the two of them. 'Sonia's a weird one—she would throw more competitiveness in there. She met me when I was in the band, and then she would not want me to go play music with them.'

gigs would feature Indian belly dancers, tablas, and sitars, and the second half would be full-on electric rock. Things were really happening for once, and there was no place to go but up. 'There were movie stars, rock stars, all kinds of girls,' says Brad. 'We got invited to cool parties at Madonna's house or wherever.'

It's at this point in the film's narrative that Ondi lights the spark that set off the BJM's 'feud' with The Dandy Warhols, during a scene centered on a Dandys magazine photo shoot with photographer Marina Chavez at the Larga house. By now, almost a year into her project, Ondi understood the relationship between the two bands better than anyone.

Until now, it wasn't all rivalry and bickering. Courtney had actually tried to help out the BJM earlier in the year, during the Dandys' first trip to the UK, when, between back-to-back gigs in London, he gave a tape of the Jonestown to Sean Worrall, editor of the underground zine *Organ* and later head of ORG Records. 'The "feud" was just Anton's invention, and him trying to get some publicity,' says Sean, who had also heard about the band from other contacts and Organ readers in the States. 'For a time it worked well for him as far as the actual "feud" went, but now and again he'd go too far. He was good at that, going too far.'

The Dandys' new record, *Come Down*, was finally set to come out on Capitol that summer, and in the film Courtney is excited to show Anton the final mix for the first single off the record, 'Not If You Were The Last Junkie On Earth.' Anton appears unimpressed. Some have said that this is because Anton thought the song was about him, but for Joel, this misses the point. 'I think [Anton] just thought [the song] was pure and utter shit,' he says.

Between that, the Dandys' success and Courtney's lack of interest in his revolution, Anton had already started to see his friend less as a comrade and more of a competitor. When the Dandys did their David LaChappelle–directed, $400,000 video for 'Not If You Were The Last Junkie On Earth,' the BJM showed up but left the set thinking their pals had sold out (although not before helping themselves to the catering, of course).

For the Dandys, the 'Last Junkie' shoot was a three-day party with a couple hours' of sleep sprinkled in. During this whirlwind, Ondi convinced Courtney that the Larga house would be ideal place for the Dandys to stage a magazine shoot, giving them the bohemian image they desired but where too

117

hygienic to live with. Courtney says this is when things between the bands and Ondi first took a turn for the worse. '[Ondi] guilt-tripped us into shooting at the BJM house … *C'mon, you're their only friends* and bullshit like that,' he recalls. 'Dave Timoner at one point asks me to tell the camera what we're about to do. I said, *We are going to this fucked household, to shoot photos, cos you want us to.* He replied, Wasn't my idea, it was Ondi's. That sure didn't make it into her movie, just the "fucked household."'*

The Dandys crash the house with Chavez, who can be seen wearing a denim jacket, though she says she never gave Ondi official permission to include her in the film. The director was clearly now centering her project on the band's dysfunctionality, and actively participating in the chaos. The Larga house might have been an ideal place to host a grungy photo shoot, but Elise disputes the idea that the house was trashed. 'Our Larga house was rarely a mess,' she says. 'I personally kept it very clean.' Courtney agrees. 'The house was not a mess as some people have said, but rather tidy,' he says.

The BJM had played a show the night before and hosted an after-party. Among the guests were the actors Harry Dean Stanton and Michael Been, father of Robert Been, who brought Stanton to the show and was Peter's initial gateway into the band. Stanton jammed for a couple hours in Joel's bedroom, and naturally everyone got wasted. Dennis was there as well. 'Brad had a demeanor about him where he was very formal,' he says. 'When Brad heard that Harry was is in the house, he went darting from room to room, kind of peeking and going, *A star is here! A star is here! A real genuine star is here!*'†

When the Dandys arrived back at the Larga house, gacked out and giggly,

---

* 'Nice *documentary*,' Courtney adds. 'The only scene of us that she didn't set up, the only real *documentary* was the [scene with the] French police. Her waking me up after three hours of drunk sleep and handing me the phone with Capitol's radio guy, going to the goofball desert video shoot, you name it, it was all some trick or trap. She doesn't believe she can make a positive film. She only believes in her ability to make ugliness. Every film she does.'

† Zia was at the party too, as was Peter Holmstrom, and you can see the back of her head in the scene with Harry Dean. Years later, in a Facebook post following the actor's death in 2017, she recalled, 'I met Harry, Harry met me rather (that's how the introduction actually went, since we were the talk of the town for a hot minute) we were both on the front porch chatting, smoking probably, I pointed out the comet and said something like, *Hey Harry, there's the Hale-Bopp comet up there, it won't pass by earth for another 4,200 years, isn't that amazing?* He looked up to where I pointed and replied, in his patient voice I'd heard in so many cool movies, *Time. What is time? No one really understands time.* We both stared into the sky quietly for a moment before he turned away and walked back into the party.'

to rouse the hungover BJM that next morning, Zia and Peter's presence the night before was forgotten, and it was like the first shot had been fired at Sumter. 'The first fucking strike,' Joel says in the film, 'when these motherfuckers came over to our house after *our* party, after we invited them and they didn't even fucking come, then they come over the next morning, [to] try and cop our whole scene, *man* ... that was strike one, and then we retaliated with Matt's song.'

Courtney never understood the reasoning behind this. 'We *told* them we were coming over,' he says in the film, though he would later retract that. 'We didn't contact the BJM about coming to shoot because we didn't know anything about it,' he explains. 'Ondi had told our label that she needed us to shoot at their house and that she had gotten the BJM ready. When we showed up, [Matt] Hollywood was alone and wrapping cables ... they had enough stuff for us to do some creative things so at least we pulled off what Ondi had said that she wanted: *to keep the BJM's name in the press in hopes of getting them a label.* My band had no reason to be jealous or contend with them. We had made it, and we tried to help them anyway we could.'

As Joel alluded to above, this was when Matt wrote 'Not If You Were The Last Dandy On Earth'—a playful jab at the Dandys, played in their own style. Brad says it came out of a living room jam with Matt, Joel, and him. In the film, Anton oversees the production. Courtney later threatened to write a song aimed at the BJM called 'You're Not 14 But Your Girlfriends Are.' 'It always amused me how "Not If You Were The Last Dandy" got taken as evidence that Anton was stalking the Dandys,' Matt says, 'since he didn't even write it.' At the time, Anton argued that the song 'was more in response to Courtney calling me up and saying, I ripped off another one of your songs,' while Joel has likened the satirical elements of the tune to 'what Ray Davies of The Kinks would do in the 60s.'

Matt, for one, knew the song was a good PR move. 'This whole, *Oh, the feud was stupid and silly* ... well, every time you read an article about The Dandy Warhols, it mentions The Brian Jonestown Massacre. Every time you read an article about The Brian Jonestown Massacre, it mentions The Dandy Warhols. We kept each other in print. We kept each other in the spotlight, whether it was a small spotlight or a big one.'

Courtney scoffs at this. 'Between 1996 and 2005, we had around a dozen

119

singles get into the Top 40 of music charts around the world. In a busy year, we would do hundreds upon hundreds of interviews, and in a lighter year, only hundreds. Not once were we asked about this unknown band called The Brian Jonestown Massacre. We had to push their music, and we did because it's awesome. All of those BJM records still are.'

With what at least some perceived as a classic rock'n'roll feud bubbling in the press, and their profile gaining traction among A&R reps despite their reputation, 'Not If You Were The Last Dandy On Earth' would be just one of many classic BJM songs the group would write for their greatest album to date, *Give It Back!* Later, during sessions up in Laurel Canyon, Anton would be filmed outside the studio, flashing a grin of satisfaction with the song's progress. 'Move on over, Dandy,' he says snidely. If Courtney wouldn't join him in his revolution, he would become his enemy.

910 1112

I DEDICATE THIS CHORD TO...

Give It Back! started as an offer to make a four-song EP for Interscope, which gave the band three days at a studio called Peer, a gorgeous Spanish rococo mansion in the Park Hill section of Laurel Canyon, about a half-hour drive from the Larga house. Most of the album was cut in a week. Interscope eventually decided against putting it out, but the band still owned the recordings.

A different version of this story goes that the BJM got a $10,000, no-strings-attached 'development deal' from Interscope that came with some studio time, and Anton simply used the time and money to make *Give It Back!* So there was no rejected record; he just got a free record out of the deal, along with some 'snazzy new leather jackets and gear,' as Del Beaudry puts it.

Anton started the record in Portland, where he did 'Devil May Care (Mom And Dad Don't)' and 'Their Satanic Majesties' Second Request (Enrique's Dream).' The latter was recorded much earlier, possibly at the Compound/ Bloody Angle, and features samples of Ricky snoring and an excerpt of a sermon by Jim Jones.

According to Mark 'Muddy' Dutton, who engineered both *Give It Back!* and the follow-up, *Strung Out In Heaven*, the hardest part of working on both records was 'putting together the mishmash of original sources.' Much of *Strung Out* was tracked to DA-88 digital recorders, but a lot of the equipment at Peer was analogue. 'I think I just ended up transferring digital to analogue and then analogue back to digital,' he adds. 'That was rough.'

It was preferable to re-tracking everything, however. 'As a producer, sometimes you can't beat the demo,' Muddy continues. 'Anton has a way like no other of capturing his own insanity on a record, so on some of those songs, both of us, together, we decided it wasn't going to get any better, so we didn't do anything. A lot of the stuff we did at Peer was overdub-type stuff, like vocals, [and] we had a couple of different drummers on that one.'

Muddy, who had been at the Viper Room show, was the in-house engineer at Peer at the time. 'Peer was a pretty magical place,' he says. 'There just aren't companies like that anymore. I got to mix Eartha Kitt and Donovan, and all sorts of two-inch tapes of these great 60s artists' weird unreleased stuff, when I was there. Really fantastic place. Gorgeous black bottom pool. It was a great atmosphere for artists.'

The band had seven days to finish the record. 'They ended up at Peer because everything else was a disaster, and Peer was a big fan,' says Muddy. 'They had enough budget and enough time to do a really quick record, so we pretty much got it done right as they were leaving for tour, and then I finished mixing while they were gone, and just ran stuff by Anton.'

Anton approached *Give It Back!* with the aim of blending the format of their earlier albums together. Opening track 'Super-Sonic' does this gracefully, while also sampling the opening of *The Dandy Warhols Come Down*.

While Anton was tracking in Portland, Courtney had stopped by and heard some of his experiments. 'Courtney went back to his studio and used the [same] technique to start his record,' Anton later told Ben Vendetta. 'When I got the advance copy of [*Come Down*], I freaked.' By now, he was back in LA, at Peer. 'I said out loud, If that's the way it is, then *watch this*. I started my album with his album. It is the same music from their album, and then my record takes off. I sent [it] to Capitol. I knew they would not sue because it would have just given me more press.'

Courtney says he was flattered by the sample. 'He later told me he had sampled classical music before I did, and that he had shown me it. I had composed several chamber pieces in college about eight years earlier and had done it many times with my compositions. Recording classical off the radio is not a very original idea ... I certainly did not do it first, and a decade later neither did Anton. Oh well. Good old Anton.'

Joel says he had to beg Anton to record 'Super-Sonic.' 'He wasn't going to do it, and I begged him and begged him ... and he finally recorded it,' he recalls. 'It's my favorite song on the record.' Anton had trouble with the lyrics, so he asked Joel and Matt to help finish them. They hung around by the pool and wrote, and brought them back when they were done. 'He told us to go home if we didn't finish the words,' Joel adds.

On the Eastern-tinged 'Malela,' Anton tells the tale of a Faustian witch. Lyrically, it is one of his best and most poetic songs. I absolutely love how the sitars sound on this and the song that follows it, 'Salaam,' which would be the last instrumental to appear on a BJM LP until *And This Is Our Music*.

Anton told the band that the acoustic-based '#1 Hit Jam' was a distillation of everything Bob Dylan had ever tried to say with his music into two words: 'Hey you.' Anton, with the group, would within weeks be walking the streets of New York, busking the tune. 'I was busking on Haight Street when I wrote "#1 Hit Jam" and "Satellite,"' he later recalled. 'Joel walked up and heard it and head-butted a window so hard he lost it. There was a cop car right there, and we almost went to jail.'

'Whoever You Are' was written in the earliest days of the band. During practice—maybe the first practice—Anton asked Matt if he had any cool basslines, and this one just came out of him, so they'd been playing it for years already. Meanwhile, 'This Is Why You Love Me' features a rare thing in any Anton-penned BJM song: a bridge.

123

Miranda, who'd been living down in LA for a couple of years by then, appears briefly on 'Super-Sonic' ('I dedicate this chord to …') and 'Sue' ('It's okay'), but more prominently on 'You Better Love Me (Before I Am Gone),' which she co-wrote with Anton. (Later, they'd record one of her original compositions, 'Reign On,' for *Bringing It All Back Home—Again*, with Anton producing and her partner Rick Parker engineering.) 'That song was something I was playing around with on guitar, and then Anton and I finished the lyrics to it,' she says of 'You Better Love Me.' 'There were a few lines I had, and it was definitely written in the style of BJM, so it worked for the band.' Her voice is a perfect fit for the record.*

Jussi Tegelman and Adam Hamilton did most of the drum work on the album. 'I get a call from Muddy at like nine o'clock one night,' Adam recalls, 'and he goes, *Hey, what're you doin'? I need you to grab your sticks and come to the studio, there's a band recording here, and their drummer's in bad*

---

* Miranda's creative relationship with the BJM spanned three albums until she went her own way and released a solo debut, *The Herethereafter*, for Virgin in 2000, having signed to the label the previous year. She recorded much of the album with members of Beachwood Sparks and co-produced it with Parker.

shape.' He was there in ten minutes. He pulled in the parking lot and walked into the studio to find some of the band plugged into their amps, guitars at the ready, while the others were carrying out Brad—who he remembers from his Brian Jones haircut—like he was a casualty of war. 'One guy had his leg, and one guy had his arm, and another guy was on the other side. He was so messed up that he just passed out. I'm like, *Who are these guys?* I'd never heard of them before in my life. They played me the song, and we just started getting first and second takes. It just kind of had a *magic*. We got all these great takes, and I remember finishing that night, maybe two or three songs, and then I never heard from them.'*

On another occasion, Muddy asked Jussi if he could do the drums on 'Not If You Were The Last Dandy On Earth.' 'He said he was producing a demo for some friends of his,' Jussi recalls. 'I walked in one afternoon, saw a bit of analogue gear. Very simple setup. Basic drum kit setup. Bunch of acoustic instruments laying around. Maybe a sitar.' Jussi learned the song in ten minutes—the fastest and easiest session he'd ever done—and then he forgot about it until the record came out, when his dad called him up to say he 'heard that you played on this record by some band called Brian Jonestown Massacre?'

Adam is credited with drums on three of the other songs, 'This Is Why You Love Me,' 'Whoever You Are,' and 'Sue.' 'I was just trying to find the best drummer for Anton's songs,' Muddy says. 'Adam has a very particular feel on drums. I love it. It's like a weird, swing-type thing. Jussi is more technical. I always find the best drummer for the job, because once the drum tracks go down, everything else falls into place, but if the drum tracks aren't great, it's real difficult trying to get a whole track together.'

During one session, Muddy thought he heard feedback through his headphones. Anton ignored it and pressed to move forward, but Muddy wouldn't let it go. 'As an engineer, I couldn't deal with it. I had to figure out what it was. I tore that whole console apart for, like, two hours. Went through every cable, every amplifier. Every tube. I couldn't find anything, and then, sure enough, I walk into a supplemental isolation booth, and Anton had a keyboard with a rock on one of the keys, because he wanted some weird

---

* Brad, meanwhile, cites his ousting from the *Give It Back!* sessions as the primary reason for his decision to leave the band, though he would stick it out for a while longer, and concedes that he 'may have been too drug or drugged to participate' in the recording.

dissonance. At that moment I realized I was dealing with a mad genius, and it changed my whole approach to the record.'

Once the mixes were finished, Muddy called on Mark Chalecki, who worked as a mastering engineer at Capitol from 1989 to 2007. '*Band On The Run*, *Dark Side Of The Moon*, and *Give It Back!*—what do all of these albums have in common?' Mark asks. 'They were all mastered in the same mastering room at Capitol Studios in Hollywood, with most of the same equipment!' *Give It Back!* would be the first of several albums—much of them forming the band's core catalogue—to be mastered by Mark. The others are *Bravery Repetition And Noise*, *And This Is Our Music*, and *Strung Out In Heaven*.

A woman named Raugust is credited with flute on the track 'Servo.' For a while, she played in a band called Sukia who opened for Beck, charted in Japan, got left-end airtime in LA, and were mentioned in *Rolling Stone* as one the top twenty bands of 'The New Millennium Sound.' The article described her voice as 'haunting' but had no idea of her name because she was never credited on the group's only full-length record. The inset artwork simply showed a picture of four tacos with no names.

In late '96 or early '97, Raugust was living in Los Feliz, working as a scenic painter and occasionally DJing at KBLT Silver Lake Pirate Radio. In search of a new roommate, she put calls out to her friends in San Francisco and New York to find someone who might be coming to LA for business. One, Samantha Brennan, knew that the BJM were planning their move to LA at that time and gave Dave her pager number.

Raugust got the beep while at the Onyx cafe and returned the call from a payphone in the back by the bathroom. Dave and Ondi were on the other end, using two extensions of the same phone line to record the call. They'd been scrambling to find accommodation for the band, but Raugust only had one room. Dave decided to check it out anyway and told Raugust he'd get in touch once they got to LA.

By the time Dave made the call, Greg had already found the Larga house, but he invited Raugust over to meet the band anyway, and they gave her copies of everything they had to play on her radio show. She spun the tunes faithfully and was invited to hang out repeatedly thereafter, becoming fast friends with the guys, which then led to her invitation to Peer to play on 'Servo.' When she arrived, Anton wouldn't let her in the room to hear the song until he was ready for her to record her part. Once she was in the booth, she tried working out some flute lines that might work, playing them by ear, with a few chirps from Anton about 'going *way out, crazy* … and I thought I was going to get at least one listen through before recording the part,' she recalls. 'Wrong. That one pass was it, although I'd done nothing that I thought keep-able in that instance.'

Anton was satisfied with the performance. 'Anton has his own ideas about producing—what works and what doesn't work,' Muddy recalls. 'I have to say, easily, in my own career, the guy I've probably learned the most from about being a great producer was Anton. He, by far, was disconnected with any concern of technical consideration. He doesn't care. Anton is fully *right brain*. He's one of the most passionate, music-immersed people I've ever worked with, like Chris Robinson.* Anton is the same, though in a very different way.'

Raugust, meanwhile, had so much anxiety about her part that she couldn't listen to the record for two years after its release, when she was told that Anton had given her her first written credit on an album sleeve. She wondered with horror later how anyone could possibly like her performance, but everyone loved it.

A heat wave descended on Los Angeles the day the band left Laurel Canyon for their first cross-country US tour, literally the day after *Give It Back!* was finished. After seven days in the studio, Muddy needed a break. While the band waited in the van for him to return, Anton, who'd grown an impressive mustache, stripped down and treated himself to the lagoon-style pool. Raugust quickly followed suit. The rest of the group came around after they heard splashing, bashfully dipping their hands and feet in the water. Dave teased the naked Anton and Raugust with his camera until Muddy showed up sometime after that to start mixing. The band took off, their ultimate goal and destination being New York City. Dave was so ready for the trip he vowed to make it a vacation if he had to.

---

* Muddy co-founded The Chris Robinson Brotherhood with the Black Crowes singer, playing with the group until 2016.

TRAGICAL MYSTERY TOUR

After talking to a few different clubs that might host the band in Minneapolis, Dennis Pelowski began curating a tour. He told his friend John Kass from the Prospective Records label about seeing the BJM at Touché in Austin during SXSW, and then at an event staged to commemorate the thirtieth anniversary of Monterey Pop (held on the original event grounds in Monterey County), to which John replied, 'They're fucking great! They're leading the psych wave. They're probably America's best unknown band. If they come to Minneapolis, I guarantee there's enough people here that they'll fill a club.'*

Dennis and John had dates booked for the band in Albuquerque and through the Midwest all the way to NYC. A flyer was distributed via *CMJ* that read:

> *Brian Jonestown Massacre*
> *Record Companies Fear Them—Parents Hate Them!*
> *Kids Expect Nothing Less Of Their Heroes*†

---

* A brief shot of the band at the Monterey Pop anniversary show appears in *Dig!* Not long after that gig, the band played another show in San Francisco, after which Joel went on an blissful, acid-fueled adventure through Golden Gate Park at four in the morning, only to be painfully disrupted by the noise of tens of thousands of runners participating in the 1997 Bay to Breakers marathon. 'With leaves stuck to my back and twigs in my hair I retreated backwards through the brush out of the side of the park onto Fulton Street,' he later wrote. 'I was not only cast out of Eden, but, as it turned out, done with LSD.'

† A young woman named Mary Martley ripped the tour flyer straight out of a *CMJ* right after she was given her first BJM single, 'Feelers.' 'I was lucky enough to see them two weeks later, three times in a row. Little did they know they'd never get rid of me,' she later recalled. This was during May/June 1997; Mary's iconic photos of the band, taken mostly during their Los Angeles years, were later used in the booklet to the *Tepid Peppermint Wonderland* retrospective CD, released in 2004 on Tee Pee.

KEEP MUSIC EVIL

The original plan was for the tour to end in Kansas City, but it didn't happen that way at all. 'We actually played several more shows that were added during the tour,' says Brad Artley, who joined the band for the tour despite not appearing on *Give It Back!* 'It was so disorganized that we looped around the Great Lakes, Northeast, Midwest, and Deep South in circles, just to get to the venues.' *

Once they got to Minneapolis, they joined up with the band Colfax Abbey, who were on John's label; John booked the two bands through the Midwest, starting at the 400 Bar. When they arrived, Dennis asked where Jeff was. 'Had to kick him off,' Anton told him, 'had to teach him a lesson.' Anton had told him Jeff was off the tour after their appearance at the Monterey show. Jeff, angry and devastated, chased Anton around a field on or near the festival grounds. Jeff went off with Sonia for a while after that, which was really when Peter's role in the band came into focus. 'The shows I saw, he was often not even plugged into his amp,' says Dennis. 'Not because he couldn't play, but because I think he was afraid that if he misplayed, Anton would let him have it. So he faked it and got away with until Portland, Maine, when Anton saw the guitar cord lying loose behind Peter's amp.'

While they were in Minneapolis, Dennis had them go down to the KFAI radio station and do an impromptu performance at the Let It Be record store. They had a poster in the store of the band almost half the size of a movie screen. 'Someone from the shop had to have commissioned this thing,' Dennis says. After the in-store, they pulled up to the 400 Bar, loaded in, and then took off for a bit. When they came back, there was a line going into the venue about a block and half long. 'Ten people crammed into a van, you can just imagine the situation they were in, you could just tell,' Dennis recalls. 'But they lit it up—played an amazing set. No disruptions. Nothing. Anton was maybe distracted by it all in a way, but I just think there was this vibe that these guys were enduring. They just went off and fucking *socked it*. Home

---

* During the tour, Anton would constantly cut Brad off by shouting, 'Shut up, Brad!' whenever Brad was midsentence. After a while, the whole band joined in to turn the phrase into a running gag. As soon as Brad would talk, all of them would say, 'Shut up Brad!' in unison to whatever Brad said. One day, the band were sitting in a truck stop restaurant and Brad formally asked them, in a very eloquent manner and tone, to please stop the 'Shut Up, Brad!' game. They all listened quietly and attentively to Brad's speech for about twenty minutes, and as soon as he was finished, there was a short silence among them, and then they all said, in chorus, *'Shut up, Brad!'* Poor Brad exploded and threw the plates of breakfast to the floor.

run.' The audience that night included Dave Pirner of Soul Asylum, Gary Louis of The Jayhawks, and songwriter/producer Ed Ackerson, and afterward there was a party near the University of Minnesota campus.

At the party, Matt Hollywood went up to Dennis and said, 'I don't know anyone here, but there's Winona Ryder's boyfriend,' in reference to Pirner, who had been telling Joel that they should start a band together. 'I'm down,' Joel replied, taking a drag off a cigarette. Earlier, Anton had found himself chatting to Gary Louis at the venue's long, ancient wooden bar. Gary introduced himself as huge fan, then added, 'I'm in The Jayhawks.' After a deadpan pause, Anton replied, 'Oh, yeah. A minor footnote in the long history of rock music.'

The BJM made $1,700 that night from the door and merch sales. Dave was gobsmacked. With a glint in his eye, he told Dennis, 'We'll be all right from here on. Shit, this is a Monday. We're money.'

'Put all of that away,' Dennis replied. 'You're not going to see that again anytime soon.'

By the time the BJM left Minneapolis, it would have been an understatement to say that everyone was happy. They'd come into an unknown setting and left feeling like hometown heroes. 'You don't get to see that enough,' says Dennis. 'When it comes around, you file that in your scheme of things and you see the pathway. If this happens here, it can happen anywhere. Get three or four of those [kinds of shows] on an album cycle, it won't be long before the dots start to take shape. It gives you the one thing that will carry you through the utter hellholes that lay between today and the future: confidence, and the belief this is what *can* happen.'

Colfax Abbey's former bass player, Troy DeGroot, says that the two up-and-coming bands were both hovering in a sort of pre-fame. 'Somebody at our label found out that somebody from Bomp! knew who we were. The next thing I know, the BJM showed up at our house. It was like a circus coming to town.' Troy and Anton quickly became partners in mischief. At a later show in Boston, the two of them took off in Dave's van to go score drugs. When they got back, Dave was livid.*

---

* That show was also the first time journalist-author Ben Vendetta saw the band. He would later become a key figure in covering, and thereby nurturing, the local LA scene through his zine, *Vendetta Mag*.

At the show in Maine, the sound guy was mouthing off, calling the band 'retards' and worse. When the guy went out for a smoke, Anton told Dennis to follow him up to the sound booth, where he proceeded to soak the soundboard with urine. 'That piss has been in me since noon,' he told Dennis, seemingly forever unafraid of electric shock.

* * *

'Who the fuck are *you* guys?'

Anton and the band stood defiantly in the *Alternative Press* offices in Cleveland after their Detroit gig. 'We're The Brian Jonestown Massacre,' Anton declared, 'and we're here to give you one shot at profiling us before we blow up!'

Courtney had flown in to Chicago a couple nights earlier, and rode along with Dennis and one of the guys from Colfax to Detroit; the rest of the BJM were in the van with Dave. 'You could just tell there was turbulence,' Dennis recalls. 'Dave was looking at me, like, *We're only three or four days into this, and I can't take it.*'

After they loaded their gear into the Fox Theatre, Dennis convinced Anton and Courtney to ride along with him on a tour of Detroit. 'I was showin' them John R. Boulevard, where all the automotive tycoons lived in these massive fuckin' mansions for a mile and a half, but they were all abandoned—probably drug dens,' he recalls. 'Anton and Courtney were freaking out, going, *Look at this shit, we could probably buy one of these places and start a music scene!*'

That night, a fight broke out between the band and the audience, as shown in *Dig!* Some local hooligans tried to steal Colfax's van, too, but were thwarted. 'They all left me and Anton to jump into the crowd,' Courtney recalls, 'and there actually wasn't any fight. When we jumped into the crowd, the rednecks disappeared. I remember looking through the people wondering where the hell they went. They were just here. They weren't fighters, I guess. None of them would stand up to us.'

During this scene in the movie, a cowboy-hat-wearing, mustache-bearing Anton busks a song for and about Courtney on the sidewalk. '*Courtney Taylor,*' he sings, '*you're a hell of a guy, don't you know? I met you in the* *van after the show.'** Then Courtney meets Anton in the van, and Anton plays the newly finished 'Not If You Were The Last Dandy On Earth' for him. Courtney feigns flattery and tries giving Anton career advice, but the band's routine of drugs for breakfast, lunch, dinner, and snacks in between would prove too much for him. He left shortly after that for the Dandys' *Come Down* tour, which lasted pretty much all the way from then to Christmas.

Once the BJM made it to the Big Apple, they parked by CBGB and headed for Bleeker Street. Anton took off on his own, so Matt, Joel, and Dean went with Dennis to Washington Square. 'This is when New York was arresting everyone for little nuisance crimes,' Dennis recalls. 'Smoke a joint, go to city jail. So we're in the park, and even though it's New York, we stood out. We're not locals, so we were being watched. You could just tell.'

He told the others, 'Hey, stand by me, and when I light this cigarette, I'm going to pass it, and let's pretend its a joint.' Immediately, two New York City beat cops emerged out of some bushes nearby. 'They had us busted until they saw it was a cigarette,' Dennis continues. 'We cracked up right in their faces. But the point was made. This ain't San Francisco.'

While they were in the city, the band hooked up with TVT's new A&R hotshot, Adam Shore. TVT, owned by one Steve Gottlieb, was one of the largest independent labels in the States at that time. In *Dig!*, Adam says he'd listened to his copy of *Their Satanic Majesties' Second Request* a hundred times, and when he saw in the paper that the BJM were playing three shows in New York he bought tickets to all three. At the third gig, he asked Peter for an introduction to Anton. 'TVT pretty much put their feelers up and told those guys, *We want to sign you*,' Dennis recalls.

Anton also did an interview from a Manhattan rooftop, delivering a mystic vision for his revolution, centered on the idea of opening a 'clear channel of communication' against a backdrop of looming existential dread. This episode was not included in the movie, but it took place after a gig at CBGB that was. At the show, Anton can be seen railing at Dave from the stage, scolding him for not living up to his managerial duties after a drunken attendee hassled Matt during the band's set. Anton thought the man a threat and scolded Dennis for not stepping in, but the guy was actually trying to tell

---

* The melody of this song is the same as that of 'If I Love You,' from *Bravery Repetition And Noise*, though the 'Courtney Taylor' version appears on the 'This Is Why You Love Me' 12-inch.

Matt how much he loved the music. Upset by the whole scene, ten people walked out of the door after Anton called Dave a leech. 'I wouldn't be here without him,' he told the crowd, 'but I *hate* him.'

Anton fired Dave after the show. 'If I could've done it another way, I would've done it,' Anton said from the rooftop. 'I had no control over that shit.' Dave called up Raugust back in LA and convinced her to fly out to New York. When she got there, he told her he'd been axed. That night, Anton walked up to the two of them. 'Did you bring your flute?' he snapped, with not a single word to Dave. 'No,' she shrugged. Anton walked away.

'I really didn't know what was going to go down, now that my connection to the band was fired,' Raugust recalls. 'I had such a loose connection, at best, with Anton. It wasn't until that moment that I realized the invite to NYC was really *from* Anton *through* Dave.'

'I was sad about how Dave was treated in the end of his time with Anton,' says Dawn Thomas, who by now had known the pair for years. 'He put in years of his life supporting Anton.' It's true: Dave had spent tens of thousands of dollars in college funds and loans from his parents to fund BJM records and help with the move to the Larga house. He paid for broken microphones and monitors, handed tapes to Madonna and Neil Young, and pretty much dedicated a whole chunk of his life to doing whatever he could to help the band. But though this might've been the end of Dave as their manager, it wasn't the end of his war with Anton.

* * *

Brad Artley spoke at length about the growing rift between Dave and Anton, which he says had plagued the tour from day one. 'I was caught in the middle,' he recalls, 'but eventually, because I wouldn't side with either of them, they both told me to fuck off. Their fighting went way, *way* beyond. They were always mad at each other. By that time, they'd been doing this for like four or five years, so it was old news for them, whereas I was thrown right into the middle of that. They'd all pick sides and team up, like twos and threes against twos and threes, and I didn't have any allegiances. I was like, *I'll be over here where it's fun, wherever the drugs and the booze are.*'

Anton held a different opinion, telling *SF Weekly* that Dave was a 'flailing businessman' and 'a fucking idiot' who wanted the band to 'live large' like his friend Kirk in Metallica. 'There are a lot of people who live vicariously through the kind of lifestyle I create around me,' he went on, 'but what they really want to do is drink my beer and party with the beautiful blonde women kicking it backstage.'

Dave let the band continue to rent his van for the rest of the tour, on the condition he also ride along, and that he drive. He drew up this contract for Matt and Anton to sign for use of the van from June 9, the date of the show at CBGB, to June 18.

The next day, Anton told Michael Dutcher, the band's agent at Engaged Booking, that he'd fired Dave. Almost immediately, Michael started moving into a managerial position, and scrambled to get together more dates at Anton's behest. The first show he booked was in St. Louis; from there, the band made their way back to Minneapolis.

Dennis met up with them on a rainy night in St. Louis. When they said they'd only been paid twenty bucks for the gig, he offered to take them on a tour around the city to cheer them up. Anton and Dean were game, so off went the three of them in the van, with Anton driving. 'In St. Louis, the streets aren't paved—probably even to this day, right?' Dennis recalls. 'Super-muddy, super-slick, and Anton comes whipping around this corner. I was like, *We're going to die*, because the van just suddenly went into an uncontrolled skid, crashed through the street up over this small curb, we're going so fucking fast, and I was like, *We're going to hit a tree or a pole and that's it for all of us.*'

The van came to a violent stop and everybody got out to find the front end mounted on top of some old foundation bricks at the site of a house that had been razed. 'If the cops come, we're fucked,' Dennis continues. 'If some guy around here comes, we're fucked, but we're *really* fucked because the van is stuck half in, half out of this house foundation. So the three of us, we just lifted, best we could, the back end, grabbed, like, some branches out of a tree, so there'd be traction, and we got the fuck out of there.'

'Don't tell Dave!' Anton hissed.

Once they got to Minneapolis, Dennis booked the band, unannounced, at a venue called Ground Zero. It was a tiny little club with a small stage that in retrospect was not best suited for the size of the band, nor their energy. Bill Sullivan, the owner of the 400 Bar, came to the gig and was amazed with the

133

performance. Dennis wanted them to play Minneapolis a couple more times that week, but the band needed to get to the other dates Dutcher had booked for them. Once Dennis saw where they were playing, and that Dutcher had filled their heads with dreams of decent lodging and catering, he knew they were being sent to the slaughter. He tried to warn Anton, but his mind was made up. 'I have to do this,' Anton told him. 'I've got to finish what we started.'

The BJM got to their show in Raleigh too late and didn't get to play, but some sympathetic hipsters hanging around the parking lot invited them back to their place to play a show at a local rehearsal space, and they spent the next three days 'skinny-dipping at pool parties with the daughters of tobacco blue blood,' according to Jeff Stark's report in *SF Weekly*. One of those daughters was Kate Fuqua, whose brush with the Jonestown would, as with many people over the years, change her life. Kate and her girlfriends were, to the BJM, nymphs of a forgotten era. 'The very first conversation I ever had with Anton, probably topless . . . I told him that I was unable to conceive children—a big fat lie that I was sterile somehow—and he never looked at me with lust in his eyes ever again,' she recalls.

Raugust, who seemed to have a lucky power of disappearing before the fights broke out, was showering and getting ready to crash at Ryan Adams's apartment a couple blocks up from where everyone else was when Dave and Anton got into another fight. Dave had passed out on a couch outside and woke up to Anton spitting on him. 'You're in *my* bed,' Anton told him, still pissed about missing the gig. Per Stark's report, Dave told him to fuck off, so Anton ran inside and grabbed an unloaded .22 rifle off the living room wall. Dave roused himself and blocked the front door shut, so Anton went through the back door, came round the side, and pointed the rifle at Dave.

'Get the hell out of Raleigh or else,' Anton told him.

'Go ahead and shoot me,' Dave scoffed, thinking the rifle was a BB gun, 'and then I'm going to shove that thing up your ass.' It turned out that the gun was an old replica, so it couldn't even shoot. 'It maybe even had a saw cut in the barrel, and there was no bullets for it,' says Kate. 'All he could have really done is hit Dave with it. Of course, Dave did not know that, nor did he know this place or any of these people, so he immediately was like completely paranoid, he's like, *I'm in this house with these Southern rednecks, of course the gun is loaded!*'

Realizing the gun was useless, Anton grabbed Dave's leather jacket off the couch, threw it on the lawn, unzipped his pants, and said, 'Have you ever been at a fucking horserace and listened to a horse piss before? For like, ten minutes? Man, this jacket is wrecked.' Apparently, pissing on things was something of a nuclear option for Anton on that tour.

Dave stood helplessly by as Anton unloaded his full bladder all over his jacket. Later, once Anton was in a deep sleep, Dave quietly unloaded the band's gear onto the lawn and took off in the van on his own, back to New York. 'When Dave left Raleigh, he headed to Virginia to go to Dave Brockie from Gwar's house,' Kate recalls. 'He had Raugust with him, and the van blew up. One way or the other, they weren't going to make it.' Dave gave Raugust two options: she could either stay with him, and he would guarantee getting her home again, or she could risk it by going with Anton. She played it safe that round and left with Dave.

The Jonestown were stranded in Raleigh. 'They ended up out there in this mansion with this pool in the back,' Kate continues. 'One of my friends' rich parents bought a plantation with actual slave quarters on it, and when Anton found that out, we all turned into Southern belles. He was being a complete dick to my friends; I was nineteen or twenty, full of myself, and I looked right at him and I said, Southern hospitality has its limits, and if you're not going to be nice, you can go out on the street and figure out things from there. Basically from then on, Anton was like, *You're the only person in the world I trust*.'

The party continued for the next few days, and hormones raged. 'They were *all* acting totally insane,' Kate recalls. 'I barricaded my girlfriend Margaret and me in our friends' parents' master suite—like, put a piece of furniture in front of the door. The next morning we found them all asleep outside in the yard.'

135

* * *

Eventually, Kate and Margaret drove the band from Raleigh to their gig in Charlotte, then down to Gainesville, Florida, so they could meet back up with Ondi. There, Anton called Dennis Pelowski for help and told him all about the fake gun, pissing on Dave's jacket, Dave taking off, and how he had called Greg Shaw for money but was turned down, reputedly because Greg had given him tons of CDs to sell on the road, but Anton was giving them away instead. ('I *could* sell it to them,' he explained, 'but they'll remember it more if I *give* it to them.')

Then Anton suggested Dennis put out *Give It Back!* on his Diablo Musica label in exchange for giving the band the financial help they needed to get them through the rest of the tour. Dennis agreed to do so, but he wanted to confirm the licensing agreement in writing. He also had some advice for Anton and the others. 'I'll help get you guys through the rest of the tour, but I don't think you should *do* the tour,' he said. 'I'll give you that money to get home, but I'm not going to underwrite a tour, rent a van, get you through the rest of these states, get you guys hotels, 'cause that's what you guys will need. It's going to cost too much, and you're going to be bitter about it later, that you don't have anything to show for it.'

Dennis flew down to North Carolina and told Anton that both he and Greg would have to sign the licensing agreement for *Give It Back!* if he were to do any more work with the band. Barry Simons told Anton not to sign the deal, but Greg and Anton were keen to do so. Thinking he'd just scored a sweet record deal, Dennis rented a van for the band in Atlanta—a one-way rental that needed to be delivered to Norman, Oklahoma, by a certain date. The band's next show was in Athens, at the 40 Watt, so Dennis agreed to meet them halfway, at a hotel in Rock Hill, South Carolina.

Dennis watched on as the band pulled up at the hotel. A couple of them went to check in while the rest of the guys scrambled up the stairs with their gear. 'The owner saw them, and he was telling them he can't have that many people in the hotel,' Dennis recalls. 'And they tell him, Oh, they're just friends—they're here visiting.' After things calmed down, the band stripped off and jumped in the pool. 'The owner comes up and says, I'm calling the cops! I said, You guys, when he says he's calling the cops, that's not bullshit—he's calling the cops! So we scrambled out of there, loaded their gear, and drove to Athens.'

In Athens, Dennis tried in vain once more to convince Anton to end the tour. 'Nope, we're doing the tour,' Anton told him, but again, that night, the band walked away with only twenty bucks.

On their way to the next show, in Asheville, they passed a farmhouse, and right there on the lawn was a van that was perfect for them, so they stopped to check it out. 'Cargo space in the back,' Dennis recalls. 'Great shape. You could tell the owner loved it. I think he wanted $2,700, and we talked him down to $1,800. We were like, *Look, if you want to sell it, this is what we can pay you. We don't have the money.* I was going to wire it to him, but that had me going back to Minneapolis.' The owners couldn't make a decision, so the band carried on to the gig in Asheville, where Joel pleaded with Dennis to stay with them. 'You gotta stick with us,' he remembers Joel telling him. 'You gotta keep trying to convince Anton. We all want to leave. We're starved.'

Dennis tried again to convince Anton to end the tour, but Anton insisted that he wanted to go back to get the van they'd spotted at the farmhouse. Dennis explained that his kindness had run out; he was still willing to help, but from this point forward, if he were to contribute anymore, he'd need Anton to sign the contract.

They went back to Athens to give the van one last look. Dean checked it out, gave it the thumbs up, and Anton signed the contract. Dennis promised to wire the money for the van the next morning, but the farmer told him no, he needed the money now, so Dennis gave him $900 in cash on the spot, then flew back to Minneapolis from Asheville, while the Jonestown stayed in Athens, at the home of one of Colfax Abbey guys' uncle.

Dennis wired the rest of the money the next morning, then things got weird. 'Everything was chill until Anton signed that contract, and then there was suddenly this suspicion,' he recalls. 'I put a clause in there, because Barry was telling him not to sign it, and the clause I put was, *Your attorney was given this agreement two weeks ago, has reviewed it with you, and has instructed you not to sign it. You're acknowledging this, and you're acknowledging that you're ignoring your attorney's advice.* I made him initial that, and after I did that, I just felt like, *Fuck.*'

The band drove their old rental van back to Atlanta, where they had a gig at Smithe's Olde House, and then they went out to pick up the new van. Ondi and David had met up with the band in Atlanta, but they couldn't all fit in one car to go retrieve the van. Moments after they left, the farmer called Dennis. 'Apparently they just ripped up over the guy's lawn,' Dennis recalls. 'The guy said they left like there were cops after them! And I was just like, *Ohh, fuck!*'

That night in Atlanta, the band were transferring their gear to the new van when Anton jammed a finger, blamed Peter, and started pummeling him. Later, at their hotel, Anton, frustrated with their dwindling funds, asked Brad to pitch in. 'Ask someone else,' Brad grumbled, then Anton pulled him off the bed onto the floor. Joel stepped in to break it up.

The next day, as we now see in the movie, the band and filmmakers headed along Highway 85, and then Route 441, where they drove head on into a drug and alcohol checkpoint in Homer, Banks County.

Without thinking to ask Ondi if she was clean, Anton waived his rights and invited the checkpoint officers to search them. Ondi was caught with a quarter hit of acid and some pot and booked for possession, while Anton was issued a ticket and arrested for driving without a license. Barry bailed Anton out, while Ondi had to wait in jail until her brother David could bail her out.

This was the last straw for Dean and Brad, who flew back to California. Matt didn't have the money for a plane ticket, so Joel talked him into staying on the tour, as he was the only one with a license. Dennis flew back to Atlanta again to help Anton pay his ticket, and they all carried on back to Florida.

The next day, sixty miles out of Atlanta, the van they'd just bought off the farmer threw a rod and coasted into a gas station in Butts County. 'For like a day and a half, they had to stay in this truck-stop lot in Butts County,' Dennis recalls. 'Hot as fuck. They were like, *Goddamn Brad and Dean. They were smart. They left*. It was Anton, Matt, Joel, and Peter, and I think that was it. People have seen the film, but this is a period of time when Ondi was in jail. There's no film of *this* shit.'

The band found a nearby salvage yard, where they were offered a few hundred dollars for the van. One last time, Dennis tried to convince Anton to quit the tour, but the band still had dates that Dutcher booked for them, so they hauled over to Birmingham—to the shittiest club Dennis had ever seen. He could see they weren't going to make any money. 'Anton, spend this money wisely,' he said of the cash they'd just got for the van. 'You're going to burn a lot of it getting through these gigs.'

Anton put the money in his pocket, and Dennis returned to Minneapolis. 'We rented a U-Haul, and we were staying in the back of this fucking U-Haul,' Joel later recalled. 'Our next gig was in New Orleans, so we drove there, and there was this lightning storm. First thing we did when we got in town was get drunk, and then we played our show … that night at the hotel we were trying to sleep, but there was this lightning going off, striking across the street, and we couldn't.'

Anton locked the guys in the back of the truck and left the group in front of the Howlin' Wolf Club after the gig before going off in search of women and booze. They got themselves out somehow, when Dave, who was on his way back to California from New York (having fixed the van and turned the trip into a vacation), miraculously spotted the rest of the band waving him down in New Orleans as he drove past the venue at around one in the morning.

Anton woke up the next day alone. The band had quietly loaded the gear out of the U-Haul and into Dave's van as he slept. Anton called Dennis. 'Now *I'm* fucked!' he told him. 'Those guys ditched me!' Dennis called up a friend to find a place for Anton to stay in New Orleans until he could book a flight down. His license suspended, Anton met Dennis at the airport and they drove to Austin. There was a show booked there at Emo's, with the Minneapolis band Like Hell also on the bill, but when 'The Brian Jonestown Massacre' took the stage and it was just Anton, people started booing.

There was another band from Dallas on the bill too, their name now lost to history. 'They were like, *Look, you're gonna get the same shit tomorrow night, and we're playing with you again in Dallas. Why don't you teach us your songs, and we'll back you up?*' Dennis recalls. So off they went to Dallas. Anton hadn't slept for three days, but he sat there trying to teach the band his songs. Of course, when showtime arrived, it was a total disaster.

'That band sucked,' Dennis continues. 'They couldn't play. Anton was losing it. I was like, *That does it, dude. We're done. Whatever dates Dutcher has you playing, you're not. You're going home.*'

Dennis drove Anton to Norman, Oklahoma, so they could turn in the U-Haul. Anton had previously set up a showcase for Colfax Abbey back in Los Angeles at the end of July, so the Colfax guys made a plan to come and pick him up on their way out West.

Somehow, Adam Shore and Steve Gottlieb from TVT had found out where Anton was, and called him at his hotel in Norman. 'Steve's telling Anton, *You're going to be a big star. We have to have you,*' Dennis recalls. 'And I keep hear Anton going, *Hang on a second, someone else is calling. Hello? Warner Bros?* He was pretending he was in an office where there was a bank of phones, carrying on these fake conversations, then he gets back on the phone with TVT: *Gotta go! Someone else jumped in line ahead of you!*'

Anton put down the phone and turned to Dennis. 'It'll ring in five minutes,' he told him. 'You pick it up. When they ask for Anton, you say, *Anton who?*'

If that tour had any single characteristic to it, Dennis says, it was that Anton was collecting data and intelligence to confirm his theories—a sort of research and development. Everyone was telling him he'd done what he needed to, that he should go back to LA and start planning a more organized tour, but he wasn't having any of it. 'I have a lot of people I need to prove wrong,' he told Dennis. 'I'm not going to cancel any shows, I'm finishing this tour.' He kept his word.

'I saw them all fall, in twos and threes, and there he was, driving a U-Haul with no driver's license from New Orleans,' Dennis says. 'His view was that his willpower overcame the circumstances. It was the most superhuman feat I've ever seen. Anton understands people's behavior so well, he can heap abuse on them because he wants them to be better. Every time I saw him criticize someone, he was right.'

Not long after returning home, Dennis says he received a letter from Barry Simons saying he was going to report him to the California State Bar, and alleging that Dennis got Anton doped up on heroin and coerced him into signing the contract.

You fuckers are going to play this game, huh? Dennis thought to himself. As far as he was concerned, Barry was a *putz*. 'He's fucked so many bands, it's not funny,' he says. 'That's what I kept trying to tell Anton: *You can't have these fuckers. They're not respected. You're going to get screwed over and over again.*'

Dennis sent a letter back to Barry's partner, David Stein, threatening to sue all of them for defamation. 'David's a good lawyer,' Dennis continues. 'He's the opposite of Barry. I told him, *You guys have one hour to retract that letter and if you don't, I'm suing you, and I'm suing you today. No room for fucking discussion. Retract that letter right now.*'

David Stein retracted the letter, fired Barry, then called Dennis to apologize.

Next, Dennis called Greg Shaw. 'Why'd you let that happen, Greg?' he snapped. 'That's why I had you sign the contract too!'

Greg explained the way he worked with Anton to Dennis, deflecting in any way he could: *I put his music out, I do everything he says, I pay him money. I'm not doing this to make money. He's got a great vision.*

Though he ultimately lost his bid for *Give It Back!* following his fall out with Barry and Greg, Dennis nevertheless went away impressed with Anton. 'That guy does not know the meaning of the word *surrender*,' he says. 'All this shit, and all the crap I was going through … you're lucky to run into someone like that, and to see it.'

* * *

Once Colfax Abbey arrived in Norman, Troy DeGroot overheard Anton on the phone, promising someone *else* a future album in exchange for money to make it the rest of the way back to LA. That was Scott Pollack, who was making arrangements with Anton for his label, Which? Records, to put out *Bringing It All Back Home—Again*, which is likely the next thing Anton and the band recorded after *Give It Back!*, just before starting *Strung Out In Heaven*. A lot of the songs on that record were written during this tour, and they capture the spirit of the tour perfectly.

When they got to LA, the tragical mystery tour continued with a DMT adventure at Greg Shaw's involving Anton, Troy, Greg, and a crowd of authors and writers. Once they'd arrived at Greg's apartment, Troy noticed Greg's wrecked car parked out in front. He was told that Peter Kember had banged it up while on a hunt for drugs.[*]

That evening, Troy helped Anton assemble the cover art for *Give It Back!* over a bottle of Jack Daniels and some valium; he says Anton that wanted it to echo the style of Colfax Abbey's *Penetrate*, with its three tiered, warped pictures, and the two covers are certainly alike in that respect.

Anton also convinced Colfax Abbey to become 'The Brian Jonestown Massacre' for a few shows, just like the band in Dallas. Chris Strouth, formerly of Twin Tone, recalls that these shows were 'the beginning of the end of that incarnation of the BJM, and had a massive impact on them as individuals.' He describes Anton as something of an indie-rock Rasputin: 'Incredibly charismatic with dark tinges, but it always felt like a bit of fiction—the kind of fiction that you believe for so long that it starts to become true. When he got involved with Colfax, we knew it wasn't going to end well.'

As Chris tells it, Colfax Abbey left for the show with a budding drug

141

---

[*] Greg's partner, Victoria Byers, confirmed this story to me. 'Greg always lent his car to junkies,' she says, 'and several were wrecked.'

problem and came back with a substantial one. Up until then, they'd been an extremely hard-working band on the rise, doing big headline shows throughout the Midwest and getting serious airplay. Their label's intent was to sell them to a major, but after that tour, Chris says, Colfax imploded hard. 'The unspoken part of it was heartbreak,' he says. 'At some point the cost of *success* became too much to pay. In the end, all the members got sober and carried on with their lives except for one, Christian Rangel, who I have no idea about. They're all stronger now and in much better places, but that says something more about them than it does Anton.

'Anton left a very big wake in his path, with some heavy casualties,' Chris continues. 'Everyone we were talking to stopped talking to us about Colfax Abbey once Anton was a part of it.' For Chris, it was like some sort of Hemingway story: send boys to war and they come back damaged men. 'Could Colfax Abbey have gone on and done something big?' he wonders. 'Maybe, maybe not. If you're going to run away with the circus, you can't be all that shocked if you end up the guy smelling like elephant shit, and no one wants to sit next to the guy that smells of pachyderm dung.'

'We did actually become The Brian Jonestown Massacre for many shows after the band broke up that tour,' Troy recalls. 'We played with them at different times during this period as guest musicians … Anton and I became really close for a period of time.' After all was said and done, Anton encouraged Troy to continue music at all costs. 'Anton would say, *When we get older, Troy, we better not stop making music. Don't stop doing this. We're going to get to the top. We'll be there together. I'll be so fuckin' pissed if you stop.* At the time, I was a fuckin' junkie, playing music because I thought I was going to change the world … which we could've done, if we weren't junkies.'*

* * *

Once the members of Colfax Abbey had had their fill of Los Angeles and made preparations to leave town, Anton convinced the *real* BJM to return. On July 22, 1997, they played what would be their last show with The Dandy Warhols for many years to come at the Doll Hut in Anaheim.

A couple of days before the gig, Courtney, who's just a couple months

---

* After a couple more riotous gigs with the Jonestown, Troy quit music and headed back to Minneapolis. He now owns a moving company in Wisconsin.

older than Anton, had broken up with his girlfriend and spent his thirtieth birthday at Ondi's house, depriving Sandy of sleep, as he'd still been crashing on Ondi's couch. 'He proceeds to sit on the couch next to me, even though I'm like, *I want to go to bed*, and he starts talking and chopping lines,' Sandy recalls. 'I never get a word in edgewise when suddenly, the sun came up.'

Heartbroken and frustrated at Capitol for telling him the new Dandys record didn't have any singles, Courtney definitely wasn't in the mood for what transpired that night at the Doll Hut, as captured on film by Ondi: Anton screaming in the Dandys' tour manager's face. Zia trying to calm him. Everyone shouting at everyone else. Joel stepping in, cigarette in hand, and wedging himself between the other two men …

'Our tour manager was not a fight starter,' Courtney recalls. 'The BJM had started some shit with him, and being a martial-arts guy he told them he would fight them if they wanted to. That ended it. They did some other shit when they played, but I don't recall what. They sounded great, and we thought we were all having fun.'

When the BJM hit the stage, the Dandys' tour manager resumes his argument with Anton from the audience. The fight erupts again, and Joel steps in again, this time beer in hand.

'We love you!' Victoria shouts from the audience, while the band tune up. 'So love each other! Because we love you!'

A screech of feedback. A drunken chord. Matt steps to the microphone. 'Oh Lord you know it ain't riiiiight …'

Outside the venue, Christian from Colfax and Ondi explain the entire story of the botched tour, Dave's firing, and his subsequent rescue of the others, to the Dandys in their van. Then, as the Dandys load their gear into their trailer, Anton taunts them from just inside the entrance.

Brad Artley, who'd been out of the band since flying home from Georgia, returned to the stage at the Doll Hut for what would prove to be his last show with the Jonestown.* Anton paid him and Peter ten apiece for the gig and spent the rest of the band's cut on beer. By now, he had metamorphosed so much from the guy everyone knew in the Haight that his bandmates could

---

* A year later, Brad came along for an audition when Anton held tryouts for drummers at the Purple Onion, and Anton agreed to have him join the band again. 'I went down to LA for a couple weeks while they were planning the London and Japan shows,' he recalls, but things fell through soon after that, and he went back to San Francisco and joined The Richmond Sluts instead.

think of no other rational reason for his mood swings than to blame them on his new droopy mustache.

'That *fucking* mustache,' Joel says in the film. 'The mustache that took over his mind.'

'He turned into Hitler when he got that,' Miranda Lee Richards adds.

Anton soon swapped out the mustache for muttonchops, but they didn't change his attitude. If anything, he took it to the next level. He started wearing white all the time and hanging out with Colleen Jetton, aka Tex, who was there at the Doll House gig, having met the band at SXSW back in April at a private rooftop show along with Jennifer Brandon, right before graduating UT Austin with a degree in chemical engineering. She hopped back with the band to LA, invited along by Jennifer, who'd seen the BJM play in LA and asked Ondi about helping log footage.

'Jennifer made her own T-shirt for this aforementioned event that read *The Brian Jonestown Massacre Sucks!*' Colleen laughs. 'Somehow I was responsible for taking both Brad and Courtney back to the Larga house [after the gig], though Anton had already given me a personal invitation and directions to Greg's house. I went to Greg's and was hangin' in the living room, and who comes to the door? Courtney and his fan-club joker entourage, asking to pimp out Greg's hot tub … Greg stopped the Courtney-opportunist party at the door and sent them away to party elsewhere.'

Shortly after the Doll House show, Anton began organizing the now-iconic photo shoot up in Runyon Canyon for *Magnet* magazine. He invited as many people as he could get to come along, including Colleen; Kate, whom he'd likewise convinced to come out from North Carolina; and Miranda, who was living on Fountain Avenue back then, and says Anton and her used to go on hikes up there. In those days, she says, Anton would just show up at her doorstep unannounced. 'Anton went into my bathroom and put a message on my bathroom mirror that just said *YES* like the Yoko Ono exhibit,' she recalls. 'When I came home [my roommate] goes, *Anton was here earlier*, so I went back into the bathroom and was like, *What is this?* He was a little bit out of his mind at that time. He would do stuff like that. He wouldn't call or anything. He'd just come over.'

10 11 **12** 13

WEAR WHITE AND COME WHEN I CALL

Adam Shore had worked in record stores for seven years before getting his first job after college as a publicist for TVT. Then, after four years of that, he did product management and marketing, wrote the copy for TVT's first website, wrote up the label's catalogue, and helped open offices in Canada and the UK. Then he worked A&R for the label, starting out with a few television theme-song compilations, reissues, and soundtracks, and helped negotiate deals with Snoop Dogg and Ice Cube.

Over the next four years, Adam put out over thirty records at TVT, but he really only signed two bands: Guided By Voices and The Brian Jonestown Massacre. The BJM were his first signing. He had convinced the label that they were the best band in the country. 'There was an incredible amount of love for BJM at TVT,' he recalls. 'From the top down. Everyone, from Steve Gottlieb, the owner, to the staff, especially—everybody really felt that this was their band, this was their time. They bought it all. They loved the shows. They loved the music.'

Adam and Barry negotiated a deal between TVT and the band that included a $150,000 recording budget. 'That was a really good deal for a band like them,' Adam continues. 'It was competitive, especially because other labels weren't trying to sign them. We weren't negotiating against anybody. There was no bidding war.' When negotiations began, Anton told Steve his terms. 'I want nine thousand, nine hundred, and ninety-nine dollars and ninety-nine cents. All in.'

From there on, Michael Dutcher stepped in to handle Anton's business negotiations. 'That's how I became his manager,' Dutcher says, adding that he had been responsible for landing the deal in the first place, and that he cashed in a few favors with some friends who were willing to go along with his scheme to plant a column in the press saying they wanted to sign the band, in order to bait TVT. TVT had Nine Inch Nails, but Trent Reznor wanted out of that deal to go to Interscope. So things weren't exactly rosy between TVT's Steve Gottlieb and Interscope's Jimmy Iovine, whom Dutcher knew. As Dutcher tells it, when Steve read the column about Interscope wanting to sign the Jonestown, he called up Jimmy and settled all the bad blood over NIN by having them hand over the BJM to TVT.

TVT might have been at the cutting edge, but the BJM had a lot of influence at Capitol, too, and that was another avenue Dutcher explored. The Dandy Warhols had the ear of the A&R reps, Mark Dutton had been doing all the BJM's mastering there, and Anton had recently befriended one Frankie Emerson, whose girlfriend, Krista Crews, worked for Perry Watts-Russell, who signed the Dandys to Capitol, as well as Everclear and Meredith Brooks.

With all of this in place, Dutcher negotiated a multimillion-dollar deal with Capitol whereby he would run the business end of an imprint label created with the intent to release new BJM music, or whatever kind of artists Anton wanted to put out. A dinner was scheduled with a Capitol A&R rep whom Dutcher was friendly, to begin talking terms. Anton showed up in a fur cap, high, sweating up a storm, and going off about how he was a Mason. In the end, the Capitol rep was so freaked out that in the middle of the dinner, when Anton had excused himself to the bathroom, she took all of the cash out her pocket and put it on the table. 'I'm so, *so* sorry,' she told Dutcher, 'but I've got to get out of here. This is fucking nuts.'

Joel was there, too. 'Anton was in full form,' he says in *Dig!* 'She had said later that she was afraid for her life.'

'Anton *destroyed* that deal,' Dutcher continues, 'and then, three days later, we had to go to New York [to meet TVT].' At the last minute, Dutcher lied to the TVT execs, telling them that Anton had an ear infection and couldn't come to the meeting—so that he wouldn't blow this one, too. But the flight arrangements had already been made, and the tickets were already in Anton's name, so Dutcher showed up at Ondi's one morning to take a Polaroid headshot of Joel and laminate it onto a false ID, so that Joel could pass for Anton. 'The only reason I could pull that off is that there were no pictures of the band,' he says. 'TVT had no idea what they looked like.'

It worked. In this pre-9/11 era, when security standards were incredibly compared to now, Joel breezed past airport security as Anton. At the meeting, when Steve couldn't make up his mind about terms, Dutcher gave him an ultimatum: 'Figure it out by five o'clock the next day, or The Brian Jonestown Massacre will sign to Capitol.' News of the disastrous meeting from earlier that week had not yet circulated among industry reps, so Steve fell for it. 'I had no deal with Capitol,' Dutcher says. 'I had no deal with anyone. I was playing poker with no cards, and we literally signed the deal at 10:05am, on that Friday afternoon, at the end of July or the beginning of August 1997.'

After dining with the TVT execs in New York, Joel called Matt, who'd quit again after the Doll Hut show and was staying somewhere out in Texas, to tell him the news, pleading with him to return to the band, as TVT wanted not just Anton but the two of them as well. Matt reluctantly agreed. Dean also got back in the mix. After flying home with Brad, he'd moved back to San Francisco. Once the deal was signed, Joel went to the restaurant Dean was working at with Daniel Knop in the Haight, the Gold Cane, and talked him into re-joining the band.

Once they got back to Los Angeles, Joel found that Anton had already cashed the TVT check, bought a ton of gear with the money, and U-Hauled it back to their new digs in Echo Park at 2013 Vestal, a big house overlooking the city near Baxter and Alvarado street, where Anton was planning to build 'the ultimate studio.' He had gone to a guitar store off Hollywood Boulevard and left with three twelve-string guitars, billing them to Dutcher, who was not pleased with the bill, although he concedes, 'It's not unusual for musicians that have a deal to go in and say, *I'm going to take these guitars and have my business manager send a check.*'

Muddy joined Anton and the others on a couple occasions to help purchase recording equipment, much of which Dutcher says was bought from Guitar Center after he and Joel returned to LA. Muddy had signed on to produce the band's follow-up to *Give It Back!*, and recalls how Anton bought 'a bunch of really cool old gear, old amplifiers and stuff. Me, being the guy who was sitting behind the console, just kind of supplemented it with whatever I needed. Anton was involved in every detail of everything.'

Anton also bought a giant Hammond B-3 organ, a couple of Vox guitars, some sitars, and a Pearl Ludwig drum kit, but his shopping spree didn't just

147

stop at gear. 'He bought all these white outfits and had this fur hat, and had these two chicks I'd never seen before on his arms like he was Charlie Manson,' Joel later recalled. 'He starts yelling, *I had that* [TVT] *contract destroyed and another one was drawn up and you and Matt aren't on it!* … I knew it wasn't true, but we had to just go along with it because he was so manic, like you see in the movie. It just seemed easier to go along with the fantasy.'

Joel and Matt's end of the deal became rent, groceries, and $20 a week. 'We had no car, and we were stuck way out in Echo Park, so it got pretty depressing, but it obviously wasn't about bread for me, even though I did fly over with his plane ticket to clinch that record deal,' Joel continued. 'I thought my big payday would still come, but alas, I'm still waiting!'

* * *

One of the two women hanging on Anton's arms was Kate Fuqua, from back in Raleigh. Anton had called her from a payphone, back when he was staying in the back of a U-Haul. 'You're the only person in the world I trust,' she remembers him telling her. 'You're the only person who can tell me no.'

Soon after that, Brad called Kate and asked if she wanted to come out to California, telling her that the BJM could use her help. There was something of a romance blossoming, so Kate went out to LA to be with Brad and ended up staying at the Larga House, just as the band started transitioning into the Echo Park house. She started going to business meetings with Anton. 'Really just to keep him from slipping out,' she says 'He was on a lot of drugs. There were a couple times I thought he was going to fly across the table and strangle someone to death.'

The other girl on Anton's arm was Colleen Jetton—the naked girl with the shotgun on the back of the *Love EP*, the band's first TVT release in the lead-up to *Strung Out*. By now, Anton had rechristened her 'Tex' after one of Charles Manson's followers, so Joel's analogy is spot on. Anton's interest in Manson was piquing at the time, and he went so far as to claim that he'd gone to the prison where Manson was held and worked out a new version of Manson's song 'Arkansas' with him.

In *Dig!*, Ondi asks Joel if this is true. 'I don't see how he could've,' he tells her, 'but it was certainly great to have him come down from San Francisco and be like, *Yeah! I recorded with Manson!*' (As Greg Shaw would later note,

Anton 'thought that the Manson thing would be shocking, but he also heard something in Manson that appealed to his own intensity.')

Tex moved with Anton to the new BJM house in Echo Park, having turned down a funded PhD fellowship at UC Berkeley to pursue what she calls a 'spiritual journey' instead. 'I accompanied and lived with Anton [the rest of] that summer while he was signing with TVT, as a stabilizing intermediary between him and Michael Dutcher after the entire band had [fallen apart] from the tour-from-hell,' she says.

Tex and Kate were both present for the all-white photo shoot in Runyon Canyon. 'I basically rode around with Anton and Tex, going to meetings, the screening of *Gummo*, parties in the Hollywood Hills,' she says.* 'When he started to get to a point where he would really lose it, I'd tell him to cut it out, or to shut up or something, because that's literally what he asked me to do.' After about six weeks of that, Kate moved to San Francisco with Brad, and they dated for a while. 'We used to wear the same size clothes, and I really liked that about him,' she recalls. 'His record collection was something that was very nice to live with. He was a very clean man.' Tex moved in with Jennifer Brandon that summer. 'We played music, went to shows, and were as close as sisters,' Jennifer recalls. 'Then she started hanging more and more with Anton and kind of disappeared.'†

The *Love EP* was released in anticipation of *Strung Out In Heaven* and features rough mixes and demo versions of the songs Anton was working on. The master tapes were lost after the original release, but during those early sessions Anton was at his most musically and lyrically focused—or so it seemed. The cover photograph of Tex and Anton was taken by Nancy Friedberg, who had a rental cottage at her place that Anton and the others would periodically crash at over the years, in her backyard on Alcatraz

149

---

* *Gummo* stars Chloë Sevigny, whose friend Tara Subkoff ended up dating Anton not long after the premiere, which was held at the Telluride Film Festival in Colorado on Anton's thirtieth birthday, August 29, 1997. The film's LA premiere, attended by Anton, Kate, and Colleen, was on October 15, 1997. Leonardo DiCaprio, Gwenyth Paltrow, Rose McGowan, Marilyn Manson, and the Dust Brothers were also present.

† Jennifer eventually left the BJM scene and became a band manager at Artists Management Group, then continued at the firm after a buyout. While in that job, she toured all over the world and managed a few artists, trying in vain to recreate the kind of excitement she'd experienced being part of the BJM scene. 'What Anton does is incredibly unique and totally authentic,' she says. 'He's probably the only artist I've ever met who both lives and breathes his art.'

Avenue in Berkeley. Like Larry Thrasher, Nancy was a Meher Baba devotee, and she liked to release tension by blowing up jugs of propane with shotguns. (She was also among the first Burning Man participants but left the tribal-esque gathering once they banned firearms.)

The gun Anton holds on the front cover—in the same image as appears on *Strung Out In Heaven*—is Tex's .38 Smith & Wesson, given to her by her father. Nancy developed the photos by hand. The back cover shows Anton, dressed in white, and Tex, who is naked, and who claims she did not give permission for the photo to be used as album art. 'Unauthorized pimpin' of my tits and bush,' she calls it. Anton had taken her to Nancy's to pick up the prints and some shotgun shells, then the two of them hopped in Nancy's 1989 Mazda B2600 pickup to embark upon what she describes as 'an adventure to Indian stores to pickup Indian soap, Indian tapes, then [he] takes me to Kinko's to Xerox some brightly colored messages that were then used to individually wrap them all up with the shotgun shells and put the Dandys band members' names on them.'

Tex helped Anton copy, wrap, and pack the shotgun package, and then they delivered it to the Dandys, as we see in the movie. The portable white CD player Anton skated around with at CMJ a few weeks after the Doll Hut show was also hers, and was an object so dear to her that she named it Peepo.

Anton explained the whole business of the shotgun shells to Ben Vendetta a couple years later.

> [The Dandys were] set to play San Francisco at the Purple Onion. My loyal servant at the time, Tex, and I were staying in Berkeley. I went and bought some gift-wrapping paper, some Indian stuff like pictures, incense, and swastika brand soap. We grabbed four twelve-gauge shotgun shells from my gun cabinet and drove to Kinko's … I looked in the paper and found a picture of their band. I blew up each member to 8½ x 11. I started to box up my gifts, wrapping them all in photos of the band. It was psychotic, to be sure. I wrapped one shell for each member and wrote their names on it. I closed the box. I picked out the best card with a setting sun on the cover. I wrote something like 'please enjoy your success while you can' and signed it 'Best Wishes BJM.'

We drove to the club in hopes that we could just leave it there for the band. As we turned the corner they were crossing the street. I skidded right up to them. Tex said, 'Hello, faggots,' [and] handed them the box … I said 'Enjoy' and told them I was heading to India. We peeled out. Tex and I went back to LA. When I got back I faxed a picture of Tex and I sitting on a pile of wood. In this photo I am holding a twelve-gauge pump-action riot gun. Tex is naked. Under the picture it read, 'This time next year you'll be choppin' my wood,' implying that no matter what, if he got dropped, he would always have a job. At this time, I was preparing to go to CMJ. I was set to headline over The High Llamas and The Dandy Warhols. My manager received a phone call from the lawyers at Capitol Records. Not only was I being kicked off the show at CMJ, but that I was going to be put in jail for attempted murder. I laughed.

Nancy says that the shotgun shell stunt made the bands' faux-rivalry tangible. 'It had nothing to do with reality. If there was a war, and you needed someone to take care of you … that'd be Anton. He knows exactly when to move.'

Colleen never told me how her days as Tex ended.

* * *

151

The Dandy Warhols toured for practically the whole of 1997, playing with Supergrass, Radiohead, Teenage Fanclub, and The Charlatans, performing all the way across Canada and the United States a couple times before going on to Europe. In March 1998, drummer Eric Hedford quit and was replaced by Courtney's cousin, Brent DeBoer. With all of Ondi's cameras around, Brent was thrust head on into the ever-climaxing BJM vs. Dandys faux-feud. He took it with grace.

The BJM also had a new drummer—or actually a couple of new drummers. After Brad came a guy called Christian Omar Madrigal Izzo, who was brought in by Dean. He'd started hanging with the band in 1995, and then played and toured with them around the time they were working on *Strung Out In Heaven*; he still has a DVD featuring a live video of their show at the Dragonfly in Hollywood, also from 1998, but incorrectly portrayed by Ondi as Matt's last show. (He isn't in *Dig!*, except for a few brief live shots.)

KEEP MUSIC EVIL

Prior to the BJM, Christian played on six or seven records with Rozz Williams of Christian Death, and he claims that TVT paid the band's rent for a year in Echo Park. 'If it was a bigger label, I don't think you'd get that, no matter who you are,' Anton said later. 'They were really down to earth about letting us learn from our mistakes and didn't want to push us to be career driven. They were willing to let us just be ourselves.' Joel agreed. 'They dig the band and let us be totally free,' he said. 'They didn't want us to be something we're not. They liked us the way we are and didn't want us to change for them.'

In the film, Anton wheels around with Tex's Peepo outside of the CMJ showcase he would be banned from a few weeks later, handing out copies of the 'Not If You Were The Last Dandy On Earth' twelve-inch single to passersby, telling people he's 'the Son of God' and demonstrating that he is very bad at roller-skating. Greg stood by helplessly watching. The B-side to the single is a recording of Anton playing records while Joel talks about them as the pair of them smoke Peyote together.

Anton now had a name for his revolution, too. Asked the following summer, 'What is the Committee To Keep Music Evil?' Greg responded, 'I'm afraid that's top secret, but they have quite an agenda.' The 'Last Dandy' single was the first release credited to the Committee. The catalogue number was EVIL-1.

During the weekend of CMJ, after the Doll Hut fiasco, Dutcher, Greg, and Anton all stayed at the Hotel Delmonico on Park Avenue, New York, where The Beatles met Dylan and Andy Warhol introduced The Velvet Underground to the Psychiatry Society. The building was purchased by Donald Trump back in 2001 and converted into luxury condominiums.

As they were checking in, they met up with Adam. 'A&R guys are always trying to get in between the manager and the artist, but that's what they're *supposed* to do,' Dutcher recalls. 'So we're checking in, and Adam gives the clerk the corporate card, and one of the things you can say is, *Incidentals, are they on the card or not?* And I said, *Adam, don't let it be on the card, we'll take care of our incidentals*, and he's like, *No, Anton gets whatever he wants …*'

152

Dutcher had Adam sign a paper stating something to the effect of, *Adam Shore is responsible for all hotel bills here, and they can't be charged back to the band or to our account with the label*. Adam signed it and left. The weekend ensued, and in the middle of the night, before they went back to LA, Anton phoned Dutcher's room, asking for his address. On Sunday morning, Dutcher walked into Anton's room to behold a board crate three and a half feet high, two feet wide, and four feet long. Anton had bought all the wine in the cellar and charged it to the label.

The following day, after they'd flown it back to LA, Steve called Dutcher and screamed at him down the phone. 'I *told* Adam not to do it,' Dutcher told him. I've heard the damage ended up being between $3,000 and $6,000.

Elise was working at Dutcher's home office when the wine was delivered. 'Anton is an idiot and a fool,' Dutcher laughed, popping open a bottle as he turned to her. 'The ink wasn't even dry on the TVT deal when he ordered all of these. Here, you want one, Elise? He wouldn't know good wine from bad, and he paid ten times what it's worth!'

Anton trucked most of the wine back over to the house in Echo Park. '[Anton] bragged about how he liberated all this wine from The Man for us, but we never got to drink any of it,' Matt says in *Dig!* 'It was part of the special stash for [the] *Supreme Leader*.'

Anton is shown enjoying some of that Supreme Leader wine in his hotel room during a brief scene in the film, presumably from that same trip, when a tall, stocky man brings up more wine. When they ask the man how he's doing, he replies 'I'm doing *dandy*!' completely unintentionally. After he leaves, Anton brags about the money he's been spending.

That same weekend, Anton visited the TVT offices with Adam and Dutcher to meet the corporate staff, handing out more 'Last Dandy' singles to everyone. With TVT, he'd found a vessel for his revolution to keep music evil, but all he could see then were stars and dollar signs. 'I'm gonna make you a *shitload* of money,' he kept telling people. Among those listening to this tirade was Paul Burgess.

By 1997, Paul had been at TVT for three years. As the company's executive vice president, he was responsible for driving up revenue. 'That meant selling units and making profit so that we could pay our bands, our bills, our staff, and sign more acts,' he recalls. 'I had to make tough decisions on marketing

153

budgets for every project. Even before [*Strung Out In Heaven*] was recorded, I was prepared to support it.'

Previously, Paul had worked at Caroline Records. Before that, he was a club DJ, record-store clerk, and college-radio stooge. 'I knew BJM but only owned one of the albums at that point,' he says. 'Adam brought some CDs in and they quickly went into top rotation in the marketing, PR and sales offices. We *loved* them.'

Unlike many in the BJM fold, Paul holds a favorable opinion of Dutcher. 'I think he tried his best to keep the band together,' he adds. 'TVT was always a more commercial label than their indie peers ... we wanted every act to reach their full artistic and sales potential. That included BJM.'

Jason Consoli, who worked PR for the label, remembers Anton's first visit to TVT. 'We sat together in the reception area talking for like an hour. It was pretty surreal ... [Anton] had some kind of Freemason's bible on him that he was going on about, and that it was something he wasn't supposed to be in possession of, so he asked me to *please not tell anyone about it* or people would come after him. I could tell right there that he was someone who was just bursting with ideas and energy, even if it was a deranged kind of energy.'

Anton had also recently acquired a Masonic ring, which he purposefully displayed whenever he talked business. 'That scene in the movie, where Anton has the Mason ring?' Dutcher scoffs. 'I bought him that ring from a Salvation Army store on Hollywood Boulevard.'

Masonic artifacts aside, TVT dumped tons of funds into marketing the band. They even gave away signed BJM tambourines with some copies of *Strung Out In Heaven*. (You can see Dean signing some in one of the extra features on the *Dig!* DVD.)

'To many of us, BJM was our opportunity to show that we can find great, credible, and cool acts and drive them into the charts,' Paul recalls. This was just the kind of team Anton needed to get behind what he called his 'most important record yet.'

Robert Cherry visited the band in Echo Park to interview them for an *Alternative Press* piece that would came out around the time *Strung Out In Heaven* was released. He was impressed by their progress in the short couple of years he had known them. 'The house in Echo Park seemed like a step up for them,' he recalls. 'By then, they had the label money and a manager;

they had the studio up and running, beautiful vintage guitars hung on the walls. Anton also had a Dreamachine in his bedroom* and a Masonic Bible he was using to support some conspiracy theory he had at the time.' Robert interviewed each band member during his visit. 'Matt Hollywood's interview was memorable for that fact that he wanted to be interviewed while reclining in bed—fortunately fully clothed,' he adds. 'Apparently it was a long-held goal of his.'

* * *

And then the shitload turned to shit.

Three months or so had passed since Anton signed to TVT, and Dutcher was starting to sweat. As Anton's success increased, so did his heroin use. As Dutcher recalls, 'He couldn't get [the record] done, [so] we had to enlist the help of Muddy.'

The resulting album sounds like a completely different band when you hold it up against *Spacegirl* or *Methodrone*. 'Anton had an idea of the order of the songs,' says Muddy. 'The whole record was a story to him. Any good record is like watching a season of TV. It starts in one place and it ends up in another place. That's what Anton did with the record, and that's kind of a lost art. People don't really do that anymore, unfortunately.'

During the sessions, right above a picture of the controversial Indian guru Sathya Sai Baba, a sign was posted on the door of the house that said:

STOP! DO NOT KNOCK!!
If you hear music—do not enter or knock
We are working—please wait or GO AWAY!!

---

* An experimental strobe-like spinning lamp invented in 1959 by Brion Gysin and Ian Sommerville, later championed by the likes of William Burroughs, Dr Timothy Leary, and others for its creative properties. According to the Dreamachine website, the device 'has been reputed to create multilayered geometric and organic shapes and symbols, swirling in a rhythmic pulse of holographic imagery, giving a feeling of being surrounded by colors. The flicker corresponds to Alpha Waves, which are normally present in the human brain while being both alert and relaxed where mental imagery is more easily created and visualization techniques are more effective. Aldous Huxley remarked, The Dreamachine is an aid to visionary experience.' For more on Dreamachines, see John Geiger's *Chapel Of Extreme Experience: A Short History Of Stroboscopic Light And The Dream Machine* (Soft Skull Press, 2004). The device can be seen briefly in *Dig!*, though if you're an artistic person who could use an Alpha Wave boost in your creativity, I'd recommend investing in Transcendental Meditation instead.

After knocking out *Give It Back!* in a week, Muddy struggled with *Strung Out In Heaven*, which took a lot longer. 'Anton had a desperate schedule and idea of what he wanted in his head,' he says, 'and if it didn't go that way it was really difficult for him. Often, in art, the voice in our head paints a picture of what we want … in reality, achieving that, it's almost always, or maybe always, impossible. It's a series of compromises, and, in my opinion, Anton was not a man who liked to compromise. A compromise to him was sacrilege—something that made the music not as good, and he's here to make music. That's what he's on the planet for.'

So deep went Muddy's involvement that as time went on, he ended up scrapping parts that weren't working and overdubbing them himself. In that sense, Muddy and Anton's working relationship for *Strung Out* was more dynamic than before. However, *Dig!* shows Anton angrily kicking Muddy out of a session, and then Matt lamenting Anton's disastrous behavior, particularly his heroin habit, and the ways Dutcher had been enabling it, which in the narrative of the film leads to Anton's kicking Muddy out.

Session drummer Adam Hamilton says the struggle between Muddy and Anton was almost a daily battle, but Muddy downplays this. 'I saw Anton go ballistic on a lot of people during those times,' he says, 'but the minute Anton and I started working together he was always really respectful of me. I think he knew I had his best interests in mind, and I always tried to respect what he wanted, because he has such a strong musical vision.'

Just like with the rock on the keyboard, Muddy had to learn to say *fuck it*. 'We would be recording a track, and I had to use headphones because I was just sitting in the room with everybody,' he recalls, 'and I'd hit STOP and there'd be a sound, like a crackling sound, and I'd go, What the fuck is that? I'd walk around, and somebody would be frying bacon in the kitchen, just in the room while we were recording. It got to the point where it was like, *You know what? All of that is going to have to be on there.* I learned to just let it go and just move on as best as we could.'

As before, several session drummers were brought in for *Strung Out*, among them Johnny Haro. 'Very technical drummer,' Muddy says. 'Very solid. Very straightforward.' There was also Norm Block, whom Muddy describes as 'a force of nature.'

Perhaps fittingly, pride was a strong theme for Anton on both *Strung Out* and *Bringing It All Back Home—Again*, which followed it. 'Wasting Away' is a perfect example of this, and is notable if only because Anton, doing his best Dylan, addresses societal ills directly in his lyrics. A working title for the tune was 'Kids Today.' 'It's an observation on this whole TV baby culture we live in,' Joel observed, 'where the media force-feed people, what they know and how they experience things comes through other peoples' media'—an idea that is truer today, twenty years later. 'No one is going out and discovering things for themselves and doing things their own way just to be different. It's all this categorizing and labeling, which is limiting growth. The individual is a dying breed in today's world.' *CMJ*'s January 1999 issue included it as one of the month's top singles.

Anton wears the same cap on 'Nothing To Lose,' which, like 'Wasting Away,' reflects his own inner reservations about himself, projected through characters he's created for the song. Miranda's vocal part gives it a sheen reminiscent of The Mamas & The Papas and all that great Laurel Canyon folk-rock that went on into the early 70s, while her and Anton's singing on 'Wisdom' sounds like an evil version of that idea.

'Let's Pretend That It's Summer' has a more British feel—the kind of *Rubber Soul* sound The Byrds picked up on, though it has a 'Benefit Of Mr. Kite' swing to it, with the synthesized flute solos, and is kind of Kinks-esque, too. Jonathan Sachs—a fellow junkie who'd known the band since the early San Francisco days and moved to LA ahead of them—claims that he wrote and recorded the music to the song at the Echo Park house in a heroin-fueled daze, and that Anton added the lyrics and other layers later. (Sachs was also at the Genesis P-Orridge benefit show at Starcleaners in 1995.)

Whatever was going on musically, all of the breakthroughs Anton made artistically had been dampened by his heroin use. Had he been in a better state of mind and body at that time, the record might have turned out ten times bigger, but as his abuse worsened, so did the record's, and the band's, potential. I've heard several people say that without Matt and Dean, *Strung Out In Heaven* never would have been completed, so one can only speculate as to what it *could* have been, had Anton's circumstances been more favorable.

'Me and Dean, when Dean was there at that point, recorded all of the rhythm and most of the lead guitar tracks,' Matt says. Most of Anton and Jeff's guitar tracks were reportedly canned by Muddy, who carried on engineering the record until Anton kicked him out, as the film shows. 'I did a lot of that, to be honest,' Muddy says. 'On *Strung Out*, I actually played drums on a track. Something happened where I couldn't get the drum track to work, and everybody was gone, so I just re-tracked the drums.'

Muddy worked a lot with Matt, and says that when the chips were down, Matt stuck it out. 'Matt was especially helpful in getting that record done. When everybody else was crazy, and everybody was gone, fighting, or passed out, Matt was there to work, and he did it. Matt took it very seriously and it was very hard on him, because he totally doesn't receive the credit he's due, and people were just there to get in Anton's way, in his head a lot of times. He had a schedule nobody could keep up with. If you weren't there for it, he moved on from you. That's just the way Anton is.'

Matt's songs carry a third of the record, including 'Maybe Tomorrow,' 'Spun,' and 'Got My Eye On You,' and they shine. His other jams are great, but 'Maybe Tomorrow' alone blows everything he did before it out of the water. According to Dean, they wrote the song together. 'We had trouble with drummers playing it,' he says. 'We had to hire someone to play on this one song. For some reason it was difficult for the other guys.'

'Got My Eye On You' had been a live staple for a long time, along with 'Jennifer' and 'Going To Hell,' the opening and arguably best track, which would appear the following year in the raunchy teen comedy *American Pie*. The film features a cameo by Anton's new girlfriend, Tara Subkoff, whom he was with for a while after splitting with Colleen/Tex in the haze of the summer of '97. 'She was a good influence on him,' Dutcher's old assistant, Amine Ramer, says of Tara, and a few others have echoed that sentiment.

Asked in 2012 about the difference between his and Matt's approach to song-craft, Anton replied, 'It's difficult to record or write with me, because I tend to come up with complete symphonic ideas all at once, even if rough, and Matt tends to be thoughtful and refines his words and parts. The strong point is that we truly learned to teach each other how to play music so there is a connection on a certain level, where we know where an idea is headed from its genesis. That can be powerful when the communication is working.'

'Got My Eye On You' features lead vocals by Matt with choruses improvised by Joel—the only BJM song where Joel's vocals really get their moment. It's a gritty, tough song, later leased by TVT to Target for use in a commercials, long after the BJM had left the label. 'Neither Anton nor I made a cent off that commercial,' Matt later lamented. 'TVT didn't even file the proper paperwork with BMI or ASCAP, so we didn't get royalties from it.'*

Despite its difficult gestation, the album was eventually delivered to TVT in the spring, and things finally started to take off. The overall reaction to the record was very strong. 'We loved it,' says Paul. 'It was the band's most solid work, their most fully realized album yet. We knew it would be their bestseller. At the same time, it was clear that there would be challenges with the album and the band.'

Steve Gottlieb liked the record as it was but pushed Adam to work on the mixes more, to make it as marketable as possible. Rob Jacobs, an LA-based engineer and musician who'd recently worked on records by Weezer, Sheryl Crow, and Patti Smith, was brought in to help.

Meanwhile, Steve was also intrigued by Ondi's film project. 'He helped fund it and connected her with many of his film people,' Paul says. 'He believed that it could be a major promotional vehicle for the band, and he loved the concept. Of course, at this time it was not *Dig!* We didn't know what it would become.'

Paul says he loves *Strung Out In Heaven* and still plays it all the time. 'It was their best album, and I was prepared to do everything I could do to support it. However, I also felt it was not a *hit* album. It lacked the revved-up energy, attitude, and big rock sound of the crossover acts of the time. Compared to the Dandys … it lacks that shine and power. It also was missing some of the pure artistic riskiness of the earlier releases. It felt more focused and carefully planned. This might present challenges from the core critics. Again, I love the album. I listen to it often. It is still their most consistent album, [and] the staff *loved* the album.'

* * *

Dennis Pelowski was at SXSW 1998—the band's third or fourth time playing the festival—and spotted Matt, Dean, and Joel at the Green Mesquite. They told him about the $150,000 deal Anton had just landed with TVT, and how

---

* 'He shouldn't feel special,' says Adam Shore. 'TVT went bankrupt and owed money to, I think, four hundred people and businesses … didn't pay tons of bands, lots of publishers, record stores, record-pressing plants, mechanical royalties. They left a trail of debt and walked away.'

159

he'd spent it all on building the studio in the band's new Echo Park house. 'Yeah, and he owes me fifteen fucking thousand and a record,' Dennis grunted, and walked off.

In early April, once the record was finished, the BJM played a gig in Minneapolis at the 400 Bar, as part of the big push before the release, before heading to the UK for the first time. Dennis had become good friends with the venue's owner, Bill Sullivan, after the band's last time playing there, so he caught word that Anton was in town.

At the Minneapolis airport the next day, he served Anton a lawsuit for backing out of the deal that would have given Dennis the licensing rights to *Give It Back!* 'Oh, just like Burger King,' Anton said with a smile as he accepted the papers. 'Have it your way!' Then off they flew to England.

A lawyer from TVT soon called Dennis. 'We were waiting for something like this to happen,' the lawyer told him. 'What do we have to do to make this right?' Later that year, when he learned that TVT had resolved the issue with Dennis, Anton called Dennis to let him know he'd had that lawyer fired.

* * *

In *Dig!*, Jeff, now back in the band, is shown scanning the houses in London from one side of his bus window to the other, never blinking, taking it all in. The next morning, Anton, who must've felt Jeff had learned his lesson by the time they hopped across the pond, wakes up and rolls over in his bed. 'Today, I'm in London,' he mumbles sleepily, with the biggest smile on his face.

On April 7, 1998, the band played their first show in the UK at the Garage in Highbury, London. James Mervine from the old Haight days was now living in London with his wife, Helen, and came to check out the gig. The band's second UK show was at the Monarch in nearby Camden on April 9, which was an even smaller venue. 'Before they went onstage, Anton disappeared,' Amine Ramer recalls. 'I was running around trying to find him. I think I found him in the parking lot somewhere. I assumed it was stage fright, but who knows? It could have been something else, looking back now.' Anton claimed that he was late because the cops had been holding him at gunpoint—until Sean Worall, who'd been helping the BJM get some buzz in the UK with press and radio play through his Organ PR company and ORG record label, pointed out that the British police do not carry guns.

TOP Peter Hayes (*left*) and David Timoner listen as Ondi Timoner and Anton discuss *Dig!* **ABOVE** Jeff Davies played off and on with the BJM from their earliest years until March 2002. **LEFT** Drummer Brad Artley, 1998.

ABOVE 'We have more ideas in our pinkie finger than in the entire Capitol Records building!' Anton told Nate Shaw. He later repeated a version of this speech while looking down in self-avowed triumph at the Capitol Records building from Runyon Canyon in Los Angeles, dressed completely in white, as captured in *Dig!*

★ THE BRIAN ★ JONESTOWN MASSACRE

Swoon 23 ★ Melody Unit
Tuesday, May 5th
THE CROCODILE

FISHERHEAD PRESENTS THE SHADOWY INNERWORLD OF THE

BRIAN JONESTOWN
MASSACRE
SWOON 23
NUTRAJET

SAPPHIRE SUPPER CLUB
SUNDAY MARCH 29, 1998
ALL AGES $5.00 ATD
DOORS AT 8:00PM
SHOW AT 9:00PM
INFO: (407)246-1419

NEW SONG
WHO
SERVO
THAT GIRL SUICIDE
SATTELITE
WHO EVER U R
BSA
CARESS
MONSTER
THIS IS WHY U ♡ M
OH LORD
YEAH YEAH

TOP Swoon 23 played often with the BJM in the mid-90s.
LEFT Charles Mehling, Dean Taylor, and Anton, 1998.
ABOVE A setlist from the band's first US tour.

ABOVE While The Brian Jonestown Massacre's 'feud' with The Dandy Warhols has continued to rear its head in the press since *Dig!* first debuted in 2004, the Dandys actually helped the BJM make headway in the UK around the time the latter group were first in talks with TVT, not long after the Dandys signed to Capitol.

LEFT Charles Mehling, whose arrival on the scene in the late 90s signaled another change in lineup for the BJM. **BELOW LEFT** Charles and Anton. **BELOW RIGHT** Adam Le Blanc, who joined the band around the same time as Charles.

ABOVE Anton, Collin Hegna, and Frankie Emerson performing in the mid-2000s. **RIGHT** Many of the shows the band played around the time of *Dig!* were with Guided By Voices, who like BJM were signed to TVT by Adam Shore.

OPPOSITE, PAGE CLOCKWISE FROM TOP LEFT Dan Allaire; Anton; Ricky Maymi; Dan tuning his drums; Frankie; Collin.

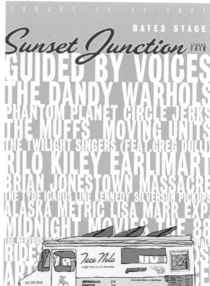

As news of *Dig!* circulated around the world, the BJM and the Dandys buried the hatchet and played numerous shows together, including Lollapalooza, which would signal Matt Hollywood's eventual return to the band.

Prior to the band's arrival in the country, Sean had distributed a press release to get the word out about the band, their gigs, and most importantly their legend, which read:

> *If someone offered you a ticket to see a band who had started riots, broken each others' bones on stage, hired and fired management from the stage, sent personalised loaded shotgun cartridges to rivals, fist-fought with Iggy Pop's drummer, been banned from venues and adored by fans, what would you say? ... So who is it that can cause such mayhem while producing the finest inspirational rock'n'roll? Sex Pistols? Jesus & Mary Chain? Oasis? Forget it, you're not even close. The Brian Jonestown Massacre is the answer, and with a name like that, you know it's going to be a great trip ... [the band] are on their way to the UK, and warn The Dandy Warhols if you see them.*

A second promo item distributed by ORG was a one-page document titled 'The Wisdom Of Dr. Anton A. Newcombe,' featuring quotes taken from Anton's BJM liner notes. *Time Out* magazine ran a one-line preview of the band in its gig listings section ahead of the Garage gig. In *Dig!*, there is a clip of Dutcher reading it aloud to Anton: 'Screwy US indie rock from the headliners churning out a pleasingly skewed blast of drolly assured *Nuggets*-styled US garage fare. There's also a lot of hypnotic droning and a big hippie-grunge sensibility in their whacked-out supersonic mix, too.'

Hot Tickets ran a preview for the Monarch gig that read, 'Hard-living neo-rockers whose recent spat with US frat-pack band The Dandy Warhols is something of an ongoing feud in Stateside gossip columns.' *Music Week* ran a nice feature introducing the band on April 25, with *Spin* having already run a feature on the Dandy/BJM rivalry the previous December. So Matt was right: it did help—at least on the BJM's end. The Dandys, on the other hand, were already pretty big news in the UK by now.

According to the official press release, the BJM's lineup for the UK tour was Anton, Jeff, Dean, Matt, Joel, and one A.J. Morris on drums. TVT handed out lots of glossy postcards and stickers ahead of the gigs, and *Strung Out* was finally released in June. After finishing the record, Anton tried to get

Adam Hamilton to join the band full-time, but Adam had his own band, Joe 90, and they were just about to start doing their own record. 'As much as I loved Anton and those guys,' he says, 'I knew it was probably not a good idea for me to bail out of my band, which had a record deal, to join them. I felt like [they] could fall apart at any second.' Toward the end of the *Strung Out* sessions, Adam brought in his buddy A.J. to play live drums instead.

'He was not a good fit for them,' Miranda Morton-Yap, another one of Dutcher's assistants, says of A.J. 'Cut from a completely different mold.' Miranda had begun working with Dutcher back in 1996, when he was still just a booking agent. Later on, he'd hired Amine, initially because he needed someone to take the band shopping, though her duties expanded over the next couple of years. She'd get phone calls from Anton at three in the morning, and then, when Ondi wanted to shoot footage, there'd be calls every day. By now, Anton would say yes or no, depending on whether or not he wanted Ondi and her crew following him around. That's when Ondi's focus started to shift more toward the the Dandys.

Strung Out In Heaven wasn't getting as much attention in the press as the supposed feud between the two bands, so in July, Sean put out a three-track 'single' with seventeen extra tracks in a limited pressing of one thousand copies. 'This Is Why You Love Me,' 'The Lantern,' and 'Malela' were the only songs listed on the CD—and 'Malela' was actually misspelled as 'Maleka' on the back. Besides 'I Love You,' which is from *Methodrone*, nearly everything else included on the comp was lifted from *Give It Back!*, the three albums released in 1996, and a couple from *Strung Out*. The compilation CD did so well that later in the year it led to the BJM's first radio play in the country, courtesy of John Peel, a big supporter of ORG, and when Peel played anything on his show, people paid attention.

TVT was hoping ORG could open some doors to licensing *Strung Out* in Europe. 'That's why all the hidden tracks were put on there—as a kind of introduction/best of the back catalogue,' Sean says of the compilation. 'It was a strictly limited-edition release, and the very first UK release for the BJM. Most of them sold via mail order to US and Japanese fans, from what I remember, but it did cause the band to get a lot of interest over here in terms of radio play and press in the *NME* and such. First thing I did was take a copy over to John Peel, and he started playing tracks straight away.'

According to Paul, Japan was next on the list after the UK. The band would make it over there the following year, despite the record's lack of momentum. 'Both tours were challenging from a business standpoint,' he says. 'The band was not well known in either market. The touring band was fairly large and there was significant tour support required for the band to execute the tour. TVT stepped up with the cash as we believed in the act. We felt strongly that UK press buzz could spark the press in the US, which was mostly silent on the band up to that point. Of course the Japanese have always loved anything American-60s, and we knew the band would go over very well, despite the minimal potential for album sales.'

High on their triumph in the UK, Anton and Joel spoke to *In Music We Trust* a few weeks after getting back to LA, touting their 'great relationship' with TVT and doing their best to downplay the feud with the Dandys. Anton raved about England. 'London was great … you see it on TV and read magazines about it, but that doesn't prepare you,' he said. 'Joel and I walked into a pub and they were playing the Sex Pistols and The Jam … to just walk in and hear it, and not have to play it on the jukebox or anything—to just hear it out in the open was really a new experience for me.'

As Sean hustled the comp, in the July 1998 issue of *CMJ*, sandwiched between articles on Los Amigos Invisibles and Slayer, was a spread on the BJM by one Kurt B. Reighley, a friend of Adam Shore and Jason Consoli. The photos in the spread reveal a naked Anton, white pants around his ankles, beckoning seductively to the camera to come toward him as Joel, forever in character, sits next to him on a chair in a room at the Echo Park house. There are also individual portraits of Dean and Matt, and another smaller picture of Anton with his genitals tucked between his legs. If you've seen *Dig!*, you'll recognize the band from the Runyon Canyon shoot—everyone in white, with Anton wearing vermillion shades and his fur skin hat. The article offered a small but informative portrait into the band at the time *Strung Out* was being made, their living room strewn with musical instruments as band members, TVT employees, and dazed devotees wandered about.

Despite everyone's efforts, the press did little to boost sales. 'We shipped more records to stores than they could sell,' Paul recalls. 'We overspent on the marketing. We put our asses on the line for the band.' The record, by all definitions, bombed. 'We shipped more than 25,000 copies,' Paul continues.

163

'I believe [the] Soundscan after several years was only around 15,000.'

Dutcher blames the record's failure on the pressures Anton was under to deliver. 'Everyone who is involved with Anton loved Anton when Anton couldn't love himself,' he says. 'Greg, Adam … they were people who really gave a shit about him. Everyone saw this light in Anton, and everyone really wanted to make it happen, and what ended up happening is the best chance he ever had of making the record of his lifetime and probably our generation with *Strung Out In Heaven*, and he got crushed by the pressure. That is the truth.'

Adam Shore remembers the outcome more positively. 'I think we had a bit of success with the record, but it was the moment of alternative rock, and there definitely was no crossover in anyway,' he notes, although Amine remembers Adam being disappointed enough to hand Anton a Dave Matthews Band CD and say, 'Here, maybe you should sound more like this.'

* * *

164

Not long after *Strung Out In Heaven* was completed and released, Matt's tenure in the band came to an end once again. As he tells it, they'd all gone out to a club and came back drunk. Then, while frying up a pan of chorizo, Anton started talking shit, yelling at Matt, calling him an alcoholic, saying that he couldn't handle his drink. Matt started yelling back, and eventually the argument got so out of hand that Anton picked up the pan of hot chorizo grease and attempted to dump it on Matt's head. Matt reached for a hammer and a dull knife on the counter. 'We kinda just ran into each other and started rolling on the ground, beating each other's head against the floor, and he bit me, and I think I probably scratched him or whatever, and then I ended up walking down the street into Echo Park and calling Ondi, and spent the night at her house, and that was pretty much the end,' he later recalled.

'He was not a very nice boy that day,' Anton later said of the fight. 'Luckily, I'm quite agile.' According to Nancy Friedberg, Matt stabbed Anton in the leg. The next day, Ondi filmed Matt leaving Adam Shore a message complaining about the bump on his head and how Anton had bitten him, which effectively marks Matt's exit from the band.

Paul acknowledges Matt's historical importance to the band. 'There was tension between Matt and Anton from when we first met them,' he says. 'It was clear that BJM was Anton's band. It was also clear that Matt had great talent and could make contributions to the songwriting, direction and the live show.' Dutcher agrees that without Matt, the band would have been worse off. '*Strung Out In Heaven* would have never ever been finished without Matt. That record would never have happened.'

Matt and the others did not hold such a high opinion of Dutcher, whom they saw as empowering Anton to become a full-blown heroin addict unmonitored. To this day, I have not met one current or former member of The Brian Jonestown Massacre who has had something positive to say about Michael Dutcher. According to Matt, 'You had someone who claimed he was going to crack down on the excesses, while at the same time enabling it. He'd tell us, *Don't worry, I'm going to make Anton quit dope, I'm gonna put him in rehab*. And then, when we left the room, he'd hand Anton another hundred bucks and let him go do whatever he wanted with it. He just wanted the band to function, no matter how dysfunctional it was, as long it was functioning enough to make money for *him*.'

After leaving the BJM, Matt moved to Portland and formed his own band, The Out Crowd. Anton took it personally. '[Matt] thought it was the "me" show or something,' he said at the time. 'I don't think he realized that part of our thing is a phenomena. It's not going to get repeated for anyone else's experience.'

Joel stuck with it a while longer, and Jeff played with the band off and on until breaking clean in November 1998, having joined a new group, Smallstone, which featured Ricky Maymi, Tommy Dietrick, and one James Ambrose.

Charles Mehling, who'd been hanging around the scene, replaced Matt on bass and played his first BJM show at the Knitting Factory in NYC. The first time Charles had seen the band play was at SXSW '96, in the bowling alley, when he was playing in a band called The Indians. He already knew Dave and the guys pretty well by then. As Charles remembers it, Matt had taken off his bass and smashed it over Anton, breaking either his hand or his finger, and they had to stop the show.*

165

---

* Later, Charles met the group more formally when they played in his backyard at the end of one of their tours. Like Naut Humon's old studio, Charles's place was called the Compound, although the two are not connected in any way. The band were late, and Charles came out to meet them when they arrived. They told him Sophie had tried to kill herself, but they still played. It was the last show they ever did with her.

Just before Charles came in, Arik Ohlson joined the band on drums. Courtney had turned them on to Arik, who met them at their next gig in Portland. 'Anton and I hung out with Courtney at the Satyricon one night, and I jammed with most of the band the next day at Spike's house and that was that,' he says. Dutcher called Arik the next day, and he was in. 'I had no clue what I'd gotten myself into,' Arik adds. He says he lived with Anton and the band in Echo Park for a month and then went on tour with them for a little longer. 'Came back to LA and had to give in and give up,' he continues. 'Incredible music and people … it just became way too much for me to take.' Dutcher let him out of his contract, and Arik flew back home to Portland. He remembers hearing that the next drummer after him OD'd on tour.

Next in line to play the drums was Billy Pleasant, who'd been in Touchcandy, one of the bands Ondi had originally selected for *The Cut*. Billy stayed with Anton and the band for almost a year, starting in July 1998, in San Diego, around the same time Charles joined. As he remembers it, his first tour with the BJM went from San Diego to Albuquerque, through the South, and up the coast into Canada. Eight people, plus equipment.

'Anton would set up his little bed in the little three-by-three square area of this trailer, and be back there, and we wouldn't hear a peep from him,' Charles recalls. 'We'd pull up, he'd come onstage to play, then when we were done playing he'd go back, and every once in a while he'd spring up with this furor in his eyes and rail into everyone, and then we wouldn't hear from him for another month or so.'

The band's gig at Coney Island High in New York was a sellout, with a line down the street. It was TVT's big 'coming out' for the band, and girls stood outside the venue with baskets of flowers, handing them out 'like some kind of Manson cult thing,' as Charles puts it. 'They would have amazing shows in the most backward places, and then every time it was an important show it was a real dud.'

Once Charles and Billy came in, it was as if, one by one, the members of the band would fall away and be replaced with an entirely new cast of characters. A new tour manager, Canadian Brad Clark, joined up around then as well. 'When Dutcher came in, he decided that they needed a real tour manager, and Dave [had been] a disaster,' he says. 'He couldn't organize his piss and his shit together, that guy. The next tour manager quit, and that's when I came in. They called me because I guess I seemed responsible.'*

The other, unnamed tour manager who took the job in between Dave and Brad was purportedly a moderately Christian fellow who disliked smoking. He wasn't going to last long. Charles and Brad were friends, so Charles called him one day to come join the rest of them. Brad had just moved to LA, and for five hundred bucks a week, being the BJM's tour manager didn't seem like such a bad gig. Travis Snyder, who'd made his acquaintance with the band by way of Swoon 23's Megan Pickerel, came along around then as well.

According to Amine, 'Dutcher told me Brad ended up doing drugs with them, and obviously became a very bad tour manager.' But Brad defends his time working for the band, and says that he and Anton got along really well and respected one another. 'I could always talk him back onto the stage, when he would flip out and walk off stage after two songs,' he says. 'I never crossed the line with him. I didn't treat him like a child. I didn't treat him like I was the boss. It was a really good working relationship.'

Around this time, the band filmed a segment for a VH1 show narrated and hosted by Jim Gaffigan. 'There was interest to do a television show around the band,' says Dutcher. His idea was have a therapist fly out once a week to do group therapy with them, and the rest of the week would be filled with all the regular bullshit that went on. This never materialized. A friend of Dutcher's had booked a gig for the band at St Mark's Place as part of the pitch, and on the night she told him it was the most filled up she'd ever seen the place. 'All they had to do was not be high and play, and we could've closed the deal,' says Dutcher. 'By the third song there were maybe forty people in the room, including no one from TVT. They *imploded* onstage.'

VH1 still had the BJM undergo a therapy session with one Dr. Cox to try to remedy the members' apparent hostilities, and the network got enough to air at least a small segment, but no more. 'It went so poorly that they canceled the show,' says Brad. 'Whoever the producer was, they had such a horrible experience dealing with Anton in the middle of that.'

'During our exploration of bands in disharmony,' Gaffigan's narration begins, accompanied by a montage of footage Ondi later edited out of *Dig!*,

---

* Dutcher now has only good things to say about Dave. 'Every band needs a Dave,' he notes, 'and he deserves the respect and admiration of anyone who loves this band, because without him there never would've been me or anyone else. To make it something anyone would give a shit about is because Dave put it on the line.'

'we discovered one group on the brink of total emotional meltdown: The Brian Jonestown Massacre.'

As soon as Brad saw the segment, he could tell Anton and the others were high as kites by the end of it. 'If you go back and watch, you can see them being interviewed dope sick,' he says. 'They'd just rolled into New York. They couldn't find any drugs, they're all in a restaurant, I think, and they're all spaced out and not paying attention, and then someone gets them some drugs, which I think they shoot up in [Dr. Cox's] office, and then all the sudden we're out in a park, and like any of us that knew them, we were like, *These fucking guys!* You knew they all went and got high. They're all whacked out of their minds.'

'When you see that interview, [Anton's] very mellow, and then he ordered some [heroin] and had it delivered to the therapist's office,' Charles adds. 'And so everyone's in this therapy [session], talking, and Jeff is expressing himself and all of this stuff. There's a knock at the door and [Anton's] like, *I'll be right back!* [He] goes out of the therapy session, goes away for, like, fifteen minutes, comes back in. They're wrapping up the session, and all the sudden he's full of ideas.'

'You know what I think? Let's go to the park and get ice cream!' Anton says, so they all go to the park and get ice cream. As they're all sitting on a ledge in the park, Jim says, 'I'll tell you something, you guys seem *so different* from at the beginning of the day.' He suddenly stops mid-sentence. Anton takes a bite of his ice cream. 'What do you mean?' he asks. Jim shrugs off the rest of his comment and leaves it. 'Eh, I don't know,' he says.

'We don't need therapy,' Joel later said, when asked about the band's reputation as a gang of violent, mentally unstable drug fiends. 'It's all about the music and turning people on.'

'The Brian Jonestown Massacre is plagued by so many problems,' says Gaffigan at the conclusion of the segment. 'Will they stay together and thrive, or will they explode in one final spasm of onstage madness?'

Greg Shaw never once thought Anton would hang it up when the going got tough. 'Why would they struggle all these years and get to the edge of success and break up?' he said at the time. 'That would make them like every other band.'

12131415

GOING TO HELL

On August 29, 1998, Anton's thirty-first birthday, The Brian Jonestown Massacre were about to play the Troubadour in Hollywood when his sisters, Corinne and Kellie, came to tell him that their father had died. Michael Dutcher forbade them from breaking the news until the show was over. 'Dutcher found out that day Anton's father had jumped off a cliff, but chose not to tell Anton about it until after we did our show,' Joel says in *Dig!* 'Pretty fucked up.'

'We were all there the night we had to tell Anton his dad died,' Dutcher recalls. Miranda Morton-Yap agreed with him that it was a good call to withhold the news from Anton until after the show. 'I knew before the show, but I didn't want to lay it on him before, so I pulled everyone backstage and I told them,' Dutcher says. 'It was sad. It was fuckin' sad. It was hard. They'd just started to build a relationship.'

'If you've ever been to the Troubadour before,' says Brad Clark, 'the room where the bands hang out is upstairs with glass that you can look down on to where the bands play. You can see the stage, you can see everything down below, you can look down at the club. And we all stood there, watching his sister and Michael Dutcher telling him that his dad had died. Through glass, knowing what that conversation was, that they're telling him his father killed himself. Anton had no reaction whatsoever. He came down, packed up his gear, never said a thing to anybody, and went on like he had never been told a thing. After that, he kind of disappeared for a while.'

'Anybody would be really affected by that,' adds Jorge Diaz de Bedoya. 'so I understand Anton and his depression. Also, you have to remember that a lot of people depended on him, and he, as a bandleader, had to carry all that weight under extremely harsh personal circumstances.'

Anton didn't see it coming. His father, he later recalled, had been 'living with his aunt, taking care of her. He expressed to me that he was very stressed about that; her Alzheimer's was freaking him out. I was saying, *Please don't worry*, but ultimately, fuck him, because suicide is a selfish act. I know mental illness factors into it, but not everybody with mental illness kills themselves. Obviously he was a sick bastard because he left a note saying, *Don't tell Anton.*'

Though he should have probably taken some time off from the band, within weeks he was back at work. The band had a string of US dates booked before their return to the UK in October, and he was still under pressure to deliver to TVT.

The night before the tour, everyone was up quite late. Dutcher ordered a limo to pick them up from Charles Mehling's house. They were supposed to go to Nova Scotia for a festival but were late getting to the airport, and then the next plane had to be held so they could detune their guitars before loading them in, otherwise the pressure from the flight would snap the strings off. They had a dozen guitars with them; some of them were twelve-strings and none of them had hard cases.

They finally got onto the plane and passed out, before waking up in Boston. Travis Snyder was waiting for them there, ready for the drive from Massachusetts to Nova Scotia, but a passport issue at the Canadian border meant they were unable to get to the festival, so instead they carried on toward their next gig in Bangor, Maine, on a two-lane road in the middle of the woods, through dead thick fog with maybe a five-foot field of vision.

'I wake up and Travis was driving,' touring guitarist Adam Le Blanc recalls. 'Anton was driving beforehand, totally fast, on these two lanes. We made it up to Maine, and then everybody got sick and had colds. Anton and I were stuck in a hotel room. We shared a room for a week, and it really got cold. Anton smoking unfiltered cigarettes. No windows. That was a weird way to start the tour.'

According to Charles, Adam had been brought in because Dean had been beaten so badly by some random thugs in Grand Rapids that he had to have plastic surgery to repair a broken jaw and eye socket. 'They took him to an ATM machine to get money and beat him up,' Charles recalls. 'They dragged him off into some house and were going to murder him. We played the show, and then everyone's hanging out after, and someone was like, *Where's Dean?* It was like an hour, and he still hadn't shown up. He finally shows up back at the club, and he looked like the Elephant Man. Completely beaten. He had to be sent home because he was so severely hurt.'

'I was lucky to be there,' Adam says. 'Anton asked me to join, and it was organic, because I was already friends with them and hanging out everyday.' He knew everyone from back in San Francisco, having been immersed in the same social circles and music scene. The band used to go to parties at his loft on Potrero Hill, and his first show was in San Diego, at the Casbah.

'We ended up spending three days in Maine, waiting for the next show, then we went back to New York for CMJ,' Charles continues. The original plan was for them to spend four days traveling up to Canada, then tour through Ontario, then go down to New England, then back up to Canada, then over to the Midwest, before flying to London again to do some PR.

'We went to leave on [that] eight-week tour,' Dean says in *Dig!*, 'and Dutcher drives up in a new Mercedes. Two weeks into the tour, we check into a motel and … Brad, our tour manager, comes back to the van and says, There's no reservation. There's no more money left.' When the band complained to Dutcher about their lack of funds, he told them to 'suck it up.'

Once they got to Canada the second time, after fixing the passport issue, Anton ran out of heroin. After playing what Charles calls 'the worst show ever' that night at the El Macombo, TVT put Anton on a plane to California and sent him to rehab. The rest of the guys returned home the following week. 'Anton's doctor was Dr. Drew, before he became really famous,' Brad notes in the film.*

Once Anton checked out of rehab, the band flew to London to record their first live session for the noted BBC radio DJ John Peel. The session took place at the BBC's Maida Vale studios, which was built back in 1909, originally as a roller-skating club that could seat over 2,500 people.

'Sean [Worrall] wanted to put a record out,' Dutcher recalls. 'Also, because I was in a band way back when, I became friendly with John Peel, so I said to John, Do you want to do a Brian Jonestown Massacre Peel Session? And he said, Yeah!'

---

* Dr. Drew Pinsky, a doctor and media personality, had hosted the radio show Loveline since the 80s, before achieving wider fame with the VH1 show *Celebrity Rehab with Dr. Drew*.

'I got to play the piano that John Lennon and Paul Weller played, and the engineer had worked with Paul Weller,' Adam remembers fondly. 'Beautiful studio. High ceilings and concrete.' Charles adds that Anton used a keyboard there that Syd Barrett played on Pink Floyd's debut album, *The Piper At The Gates Of Dawn*.

The Peel session, which was later bootlegged, featured a number of songs that were to appear on the next crop of BJM albums, as well as some that remain officially unreleased. After recording it, the band played upstairs at the Garage again on October 21, and at the Falcon in nearby Camden the next day. 'The last gig was by far their best attended,' Sean recalled. 'There were probably about eighty people there.'

'England was *incendiary*,' Adam Le Blanc adds.

NME ran a positive live review of that gig the following month. 'Back then, support from the music press was vital. Far, far more important than listing magazines or radio,' Sean recalls. 'Everybody read the *NME* and *Melody Maker* back then ... the power was with the music press.'

The band were then slated to fly to Chicago to play another run of shows in Canada, then to Seattle, then out to CMJ to play three shows in a row in New York, then back over to the Pacific Northwest to tour down the West Coast. As long as Anton was clean, things were working out fine, but then again there is Murphy's Law.

When the BJM hit the road, Anton lent Jorge and The Minstrels the Echo Park house to record their album *Psychotropic R&B* with his home studio gear. By now, Sophie was dating Jorge and had become a full-fledged member of The Minstrels, and together they recorded some songs she'd written about Anton, among them one called 'Speed Messiah':

> *You had the world in the palm of your hand*
> *With all your friends as means to your ends ...*
> *You want everyone to keep you maddening pace*
> *Take your place and show your face*
> *You like to play your games with their headspace*
> *You speak of love and spit on its face ...*
> *Maybe after all the things that you'll have seen*
> *You'll realize what you could have been*

You'll remember those to whom you were mean
Their memories will haunt your scene ...
Speed Messiah, in the end you only lose a friend ...

When the BJM played CMJ, Anton came to Paul Burgess's office on 4th and Lafayette wearing a cowboy hat and a suede cowboy suit. He had his acoustic guitar with him, and he looked like a cross between Gram Parson and Charlie Manson. Paul met him in the lobby and brought him to his office, where Anton told him he'd spent the afternoon busking in Times Square. 'He was soaked in sweat,' Paul recalls. 'After he left, I asked my assistant to go down the block and get some incense. We burned it every day for the next week to try to remove the Anton essence.'

It was sometime during a break in touring, before the Peel session, that Anton moved from Echo Park out to Laurel Canyon by himself with all the gear. 'The label paid all his rent and bills, because he had no idea how to do any of that,' says Sandy Wilson. 'The rest of the band were really bitter because none of them got a dime, and Anton got the house on the hill.'

The house in question was up on Lookout Mountain, across from Houdini's place, and was all painted red. Leadbelly had once lived there. Adam Shore was one of many who felt that Anton's time in Laurel Canyon was his darkest hour. 'There wasn't a lot of creativity that was happening there,' he recalls. 'Anton was hitting rock bottom. Then Anton decided he needed some help, so I helped him go to rehab and get that paid for, and he did that twice.'

Rehab wasn't doing the trick. 'He rented that little house up there, after that tour, which just turned into a big crazy party drugged out house,' says Brad. 'There was always a ton of people up there. It was such a perfect Laurel Canyon spot for him, and I remember calling up there and he had an outgoing message for a long time that said, *I can't answer the phone right now because I'm recording with Courtney Taylor-Taylor.* It was on his voicemail for three months! I think it was one time [that Courtney came out there to record], and Anton left that message. I think he was always jealous of Courtney's success—that they took off and got the recognition, when Anton always felt like they were the better band. I know that always hung over his head.' (The Dandys had been back over to England just a little over a week after the Jonestown did their Peel session. They gave interviews to the *NME* and *Melody Maker* while wearing BJM T-shirts, indicating that the two bands had started to patch up their differences.)

Charles had been talking with Anton about writing songs for the next BJM record, and the two started jamming. TVT had bought Anton ProTools—fast becoming the industry standard—and Charles recalls how infatuated he was with the software, working on it constantly in Laurel Canyon. 'It was perfect for him, because he'd set up the drums and do the drums, and then he'd be able to do the bass and each instrument by himself, and then kind of reformulate them. He had this amazing song and he was playing it for me, and then he's trying to show me, all frantic, *I'm going to move this over here and throw this away*, and he accidentally threw away the entire track and emptied the garbage without realizing it, and then spent like an hour trying to figure out how to get it back out. This amazing song, gone forever.'

Anton asked Charles if he had any songs, so Charles played him some things he'd written. Anton didn't like all of his ideas but took a chord progression Charles had been playing and started to make 'Feel So Good' out of it. Charles recorded his part and went home. The next day, Anton showed him what he'd done to the track. 'He'd moved it around, changed it, completely changed the melody,' Charles recalls. 'Completely changed the song. At the time, I was kind of offended, but very quickly I was really happy he had done it, because it was the only way I was going to get credited with having part of a song with this great band.' Miranda later sang on the song, which was originally supposed to appear on *Strung Out*'s intended follow-up for TVT, *Bravery Repetition And Noise*, but in the end it wasn't released until 2004's *Tepid Peppermint Wonderland*. (A version of it also appears on the *Peel Sessions* bootleg.)

174

* * *

By the end of what Adam Shore calls the '187-date tour,' the band had fallen apart completely. They played fewer shows in 1999 than in the years after they first formed in the early 90s, though they did make it to Japan to play a few shows that spring, where their old buddy Christof Certik joined them on keys.

'Japan was the last tour I really was on,' Dean recalls. 'Me and Christof stayed there an extra week. I have a friend who lives there, so we stayed with him, and I was trying to find a job, or find some way to stay there.'

That friend was Alain Bosshart, who appears briefly in *Dig!* in the scene just before the Viper Room show, when the band are out in Ondi's backyard, playing sitars and bongos. The BJM played at the Liquid Room in Shinjuku, Tokyo, on March 4, 1999, opening for Mercury Rev using rented gear. (Back then, the venue was in a building with a bowling alley beneath it; it has since moved to a new location in Ebisu.) The set list was mostly comprised of songs from *Give It Back!* The next night they played a show at Club Quattro in Shibuya, footage of which appears in *Dig!*

'I wanted to stay in Tokyo just to be able to have a way to get away from heroin,' Dean continues. 'I was not having any luck getting off of it, so I thought staying in Japan would force the issue, but I wasn't able to stay. Me and Christof both left at the same time … back home to San Francisco.'*

The end of the road was nearing for Dutcher as well. 'I was so done with Anton on a personal level by Japan that I got everyone their own interpreter, so I could go anywhere I wanted,' he recalls. 'I wanted so little to do with them at that point.'

The band felt the same way. 'We complained about Dave all the time,' Dean says, 'but after we got Dutcher, we thought Dave was the best. Dutcher was the worst thing that ever happened to us.' As far as Dean is concerned, had it not been for Dutcher's obstructionism, mistakes, and selfishness, the BJM could have made it as big with TVT as the Dandys had with Capitol.

Elise grew suspicious of Dutcher early on. She had even printed out the bloated tour budgets he'd sent to TVT as evidence of his mismanagement, but felt the label was drunk on his promises. Checks for thousands of dollars were reportedly being hand-couriered to his doorstep. Then, after what some people have described as an outrageous spending spree on home renovations and a million-dollar wedding in West Hollywood, Dutcher took his new wife, Debbie, on a month-long honeymoon in Europe. Meanwhile, Elise says, she housesat his place, broke, while Anton and Joel busked for food and cigarette money, just like they did back in the Haight days.

---

* That December, Dean went to rehab, where he remained through Christmas and New Years, and from there he went to live at his dad's house in Los Angeles for several months. He's now clean and living a great life.

Dutcher dismisses these claims. 'The house they were talking about, I didn't own,' he says. 'It was a rental, and the construction was repairs [to] the damage caused in the '94 earthquake.' He puts the blame for the mismanagement of funds on Anton. 'When those guys talk about stealing money ... the amount of money that was *left* to be stolen, after all the bullshit and all the shit that Anton bought? They were mad because *he* ended up spending all the money, and no one cared.'

In spite of everything, Dutcher has no regrets about his time with the BJM. 'I'm glad I did it,' he continues. 'I believed in Anton, and I believed in that band. I believed that band could've been the greatest rock'n'roll band of our generation. I also believe that no one really understands what that pressure's like until they're in it. They say a lot of pressure causes diamonds. There was no diamonds going on here.'

Muddy disagrees. 'The only pressure Anton is ever under is his own standard. Anton is the guy where if somebody comes in and goes, Hey, here's a million dollars to make a record, he'll tell them to go fuck off—and I've seen him do it. I've seen him do it to TVT. He didn't give a fuck. No matter what Anton has, he will make the record he wants to make. It doesn't matter if it's a million dollars, it doesn't matter if it's a dollar, because we've all seen him do it. We've seen him make records from the street, from a van. Call it a lack of common sense or whatever. He doesn't give a fuck. He really doesn't.'

The band tried to keep it together for one last show that year at the Troubadour—their first time back at the venue since the night Anton found out about his father's death—but when everyone met up for their final rehearsal, Anton was strung out. '[The show] was the next day, and Anton was berating someone, and he had his guitar on standing there, yelling, and then he just nodded out while standing up,' Charles recalls. 'The whole band was standing around him in a semicircle, dumbstruck. Everyone unplugged their equipment and left. I've never seen anything like it.'

A guy by the name of Tony O'Neill played keyboards with the band for a brief time around then. Tony knew Anton through Muddy, who had produced a demo for his band, Southpaw, whom Dutcher later managed. Charles played bass in Southpaw, too, and brought Tony into the BJM. 'Every morning we'd show up and Anton would pawn stuff, so we had to rustle up some money to get the gear back out of the pawn shop,' Tony recalls. 'There was too many drugs around. It was a madhouse.'

On the day of the show, Anton sent Tony and Billy out for orange juice. They drove down from Laurel Canyon, but when they got to the bottom of the hill, Billy's VW Bug ran out of gas. 'We had to walk, like, forty minutes to the nearest gas station, fill a Gatorade bottle up with, like, seventy cents worth of gasoline, walk it back up to the car, pour that into the engine, and then we went back up the hill to Anton's again,' Tony recalls. 'We'd been gone for hours, and Anton was pissed. Billy told him the whole story of what happened. Anton's listening, and he goes, *All right, so where's my fucking orange juice?*'

Anton chased them out with his Masonic sword. 'He had this Masonic sword he would take out, that he thought had magical powers or something,' Tony continues. 'We jumped in the Bug, and I don't know how, but the Bug got us to Billy's place, and that was it. Then we turned up at the show.'

As we see in the resulting scene—one of the last in the film—Anton was twitchy that night at the Troubadour. According to a couple of reliable accounts, he had brought a gun with him to the show. Muddy claims he is in possession of the exact gun, a Civil War–era replica—perhaps a memento of Raleigh?

177

Anton, in a fit of sweats, begins to play 'Those Memories' while chunks of fruit are thrown at him onto the stage. He picks up a piece and holds it up in the light. The crowd eggs him on. After a rant, the band starts playing again. Anton's freezes mid-song, takes off his guitar, and walks offstage. Jeff, to his immediate left, waits until he clears the stage before he tosses the guitar into the air. It hits an amp as it lands, and then Jeff jumps off into the audience.

Anton returns to the stage. 'Check it out, Jeff,' he begins. 'You threw down my guitar? I'd like to see you get paid, for *that*.'

As Anton heads out the back, Jeff jumps onto the stage and grabs a mic. 'You know what?' he yells. 'I never got paid for all the years I got fucked in the ass by *you*, so why the fuck am I going to get paid now?' He ends his rant by tossing the mic and mic stand about.

As far as the film is concerned, this is the end of Jeff's involvement in the band, although this would only be the case for another year or two.

Everyone else quit the Jonestown that day except Billy. 'I played fucking tambourine and sang back up,' he recalls. 'It was a grim time.' (Miranda Lee Richards also played this show.)

Jeff adds additional insight into what he saw as his role in the band during this final decline. 'In the Jonestown, you never got any money,' he told me. 'When we got signed by TVT and we went on a real tour, people would just get hired to play in the band, like Charles, or whatever drummer, and I found out one night they were getting, like, $1,500 a week. I was getting $150 a week. And when I brought it up, the answer was, *Well you're in it for the long run*. When Anton got some money, and we each got a Gretsch guitar, one day I was taking it out in between tours to play with someone, and he goes, *Where you goin' with that? That's BJM property*. So I had to pay $1,800 for this Gretsch guitar, out of my $150 a week on the road. It was super-petty, so I walked away—and, of course, there was a lot of competition with Anton toward me that got in the way. The money didn't matter. This was my dream, but Anton has a classic big ego, with a lot of insecurities.'

Joel tried living up in Laurel Canyon, but that didn't work out for long, as Anton kept going off the deep end. He ended up living with Charles for about half a year. 'Joel had to bring something to Anton up at the Laurel Canyon house, and they could hear him recording, so they were too afraid to knock, and they were standing outside for a really long time,' Miranda Lee Richards recalls. 'Anton finally answered the door and grabbed Joel, threw him against the wall, and was like, *Why didn't you just knock? The fucking hell is wrong with you?* So then, the next day, they went back and they knocked on the door. Anton answered, pushed Joel against the wall, and said, *What the fuck is wrong with you? You know you're never supposed to knock like that when I'm working!*'

Muddy had helped Anton set up the studio in the Laurel Canyon place and worked on a new record with him for a while, but it wasn't going anywhere, so he brought in former Tom Petty & The Heartbreakers drummer Stan Lynch to help out. Stan was producing Don Henley at the time with Rob Jacobs, who'd mixed *Strung Out In Heaven*. 'The three of us got together and said, *We all love this guy. He's in a little bit of trouble right now. Why don't we make a record with him? Let's do it together*,' Muddy recalls. 'Stan and I wanted to make a record—we were trying to do something together—[so] this was that project.'

Muddy, Stan, and Rob agreed to go to see Anton in Laurel Canyon. Muddy arrived first, then Stan and Rob followed. They walked in to find the French doors open, curtains blowing in the wind, and a record playing on repeat. 'There was this eeriness to it, because it's skipping over and over again, this little ten-second phrase of a record,' Muddy recalls. 'You couldn't have set this scene up in a movie. You couldn't do it. There was a squirrel eating a bowl of Captain Crunch on the counter in the kitchen. Everything's open. The whole place was wrecked, a total mess.'

At the far end of the living room was a giant poster of Anton— wall-sized, like the one back at the Let It Be record store—which he had evidently been shooting with a crossbow. Suddenly, Anton burst out of another room in a manic state. Turning around, Muddy realized that Stan had gone, so he went after him.

'Muddy, I love you, brother, but I don't know if this is the record for me, man,' Stan told him.

'We tried starting another project, but it just got too much,' Muddy continues. 'It was exhausting for me. Anton was my friend by then, and I couldn't watch. I was convinced he was going to die. Every time I went up there, I prepared myself to find a dead body.'

179

121314151

ALL THINGS GREAT AND SMALL

In 1999, The Brian Jonestown Massacre released the *Bringing It All Back Home—Again* EP, which proved to be just another thorn in TVT's side. 'Anton signed to TVT and then told us that he'd already promised an EP to Which? Records,' Adam Shore recalls. 'We let him do that, but boy, TVT was not happy about it.'

'We had a lunch meeting with someone at TVT and they mentioned it,' Which? Records CEO Scott Pollack recalls. Scott had been talking with Anton about putting out the record as far back as the summer of 1997, when they spoke on the phone while Anton was in Norman, Oklahoma, after meeting at SXSW. 'At that point, we really weren't communicating with the band, so, definitely I think they were probably being urged by Michael [Dutcher] and people at TVT,' he adds. 'I think, from TVT's perspective, it was seen as a distraction from their release, and I can totally see that side of it, but at the same time I think it was keeping with the spirit of where the band was at, by putting out records on a frequent basis that were really of a much more lo-fi quality.'

Scott argues that his label was so small that logistically there was no way it would have interfered. 'It was never meant to overshadow that major release,' he says. 'We worked the PR angle, we got a lot of press, this that and the other, but nothing like what they wanted to achieve with *Strung Out In Heaven*.'

Earlier, in 1997, Scott had gone to SXSW to check out bands whose records he might want to try to put out, and the BJM were high on his agenda. 'They were never that MTV band,' he adds. 'You felt like these guys are doing something very different from what everyone else was doing. I was years late to the table to even have heard about them, but I fell for them very hard. The music was incredible.'

Scott approached Anton, Matt, and Brad Artley in Austin, and the four of them shotgunned a few beers together. He spoke on the phone to Anton a couple of weeks later, and then he saw the band at Coney Island High, during the 'evil mustache' days.

Scott stayed with the van while the band were loading out after the show, and told them he'd love to put out one of their records. Luckily for him, they were broke—or so Anton told him—so Scott gave him a couple of hundred bucks. 'That's how I got my EP,' he says, 'by giving Anton money to help them continue their tour. He said he would send me a DAT tape of a record that we could put out, and I followed up a few times and [eventually] received the DAT that had the EP on it. No instructions. No nothing.'

Scott got the DAT long before *Strung Out In Heaven* was released. 'I had no idea what to expect when we received it,' he continues. 'I didn't know if it was going to be a song, or a full length, but in a way that EP was very unique. It sounded a lot different from their other records. It was more acoustic, and it had that really long Manson song at the end. I thought it was very cohesive, where some of their other things weren't as cohesive. It was still very lo-fi, still very crudely recorded in many ways, but the spirit of that record is intact.'

Scott mastered the record with his friend Sam McCall at Sam's apartment in Greenpoint, Brooklyn. 'It was sequenced in the exact order,' he says. 'There's only so much you could do with mastering it anyway, so we just wanted to EQ it a little bit and sort of sweeten it up, but we didn't really do much to it. We received some artwork. We got a few images. The package design was basically done by [Anton] and this guy'—one Mike Prosenko is credited with graphic design on the record—'and we wound up manufacturing it on CD and LP. Five to ten thousand [CDs] and five hundred or a thousand LPs. I remember the LP did not sell well.'

Which? was distributed by Caroline, so the record was able to go far and wide to stores across the country.* 'We signed the licensing arrangement, so I never owned the recordings,' Scott recalls. 'When I look back on running my label, that was one of the high points. I got to put out a record by a band that was on a really unique musical exploration—that we were really proud of.'

One standout track on *Bringing It All Back Home—Again* is Miranda's

---

* Caroline is a part of Capitol Music Group and distributes Motown and Rocnation's records, among other notable partners.

'Reign On,' which she had record an earlier version of with Anton. She says she thinks they made that track in late '97 or '98, which would place it just before *The Love EP* and *Strung Out In Heaven* in the BJM timeline. 'Anton put this organ over it, and it was really beautiful,' she says of the song. 'It was a better take, but Anton didn't own that recording, so he wanted to re-record it. It didn't turn out quite as good in my mind as the other version we had done.'

Though pinpointing exactly when the tracks were cut is tricky, the lack of chronology in the BJM canon is part of its charm, as Muddy Dutton explains. 'Anton recorded all the time, and he'd lose things. He'd have a bunch of master tapes, and they would get lost for a whole month, and then you'd find them in a shoebox or something. He'd bring it out, and release it, and go back again. It wasn't chronological. Even some of the songs on those records were written on the cuff. Some of them were older songs. Some of them were revamped or whatever. He definitely has a collage type of an approach to putting all this stuff together.'

Bringing It All Back Home—Again contains four new originals by Anton as well as a reworking of Charles Manson's 'Arkansas.' Anton has said that he wrote 'Mansion In The Sky' back on tour in Ohio, while teaching Peter Hayes about songwriting, so it could have been tracked during the summer of 1997. 'I made [Peter] play guitar for eight hours each day,' Anton recalled a couple of years later. 'Every day, I made him go to black neighborhoods and play country music on a corner while people walked past. It was just to get him used to singing and playing, whether people liked it or hated it.'

In *Dig!*, Anton can be seen strumming 'Arkansas' during the all-white photo-shoot in Runyon Canyon, and that was for sure that same summer, while the old version of 'Reign On' that Miranda refers to could've been what she and Anton were tracking back at the Larga house, that same morning Josephine split to get cigarettes with Peter, rather than 'You Better Love Me (Before I Am Gone).' Or maybe they did both—or neither—that day.

Another song Anton wrote on tour, 'The Godspell According To A.A. Newcombe,' marks a fitting end to this period of the band, despite having been recorded earlier. Bookend it with 'The Ballad Of Jim Jones' and the story tells itself. The same goes for 'All Things Great And Small.' Troy DeGroot says he still has some of the original lyrics to the song in his possession, and that it was originally titled 'Everything.'

Bringing It All Back Home—Again was the last Brian Jonestown Massacre record to feature Matt Hollywood until *Aufheben*, while for TVT, the thorn became a gash, and the label never released another BJM record.

Sean Worrall, eager for new BJM music to promote, was left hanging back over in England. 'We tried to do more after the single, but TVT wanted them to be on a bigger label over here,' he recalled. 'We left them to get on with it, and we waited for new music … nothing … still nothing … end of the century, lots of disturbing rumors, but still no music. We got more than one message about Anton ODing and being dead on some floor.'

It was some time between the EP's release and the autumn months of 1999 that TVT began to sever its relationship with Anton, not long after Michael Dutcher walked away from the band after Anton left an angry, hour-long message on his answer machine. For Dutcher, that was the end of it, though he says TVT threw him under the bus to make it easier for them to get out of its end of the deal.

'I cut them probably one of the greatest record deals for [an up-and-coming] band ever created, and, honestly, it took a lot of time to get over that whole separation, because I worked really hard for them,' he says. 'I'm not saying I'm without fault, but when we first met, the thing I said to him was, *I will make it so you can do this for the rest of your life, with or without a record label.* But, I said, *You can't ever let anyone get in between you and I. You can tell people I'm a fuckin' asshole, you can tell people that I make you do crazy shit, that you're afraid of me, that you think I'm gonna kill you. I don't give a shit what story you tell them, but the deal is, I will not fuck you, and you cant fuck me.* And, in the end, he let TVT fuck him. Once they got me out of the deal, the deal fell apart. Everything fell apart.'

Paul Burgess felt there were multiple factors in the dissolution of the TVT–BJM relationship. From a business standpoint, he says, continued efforts to push what the label saw as a failing product were not conducive to its future success. 'The band faded out, and there were internal issues. Anton had issues. Band members came and went. There was not a strong direction from their camp. We had put a great deal behind them, with limited success. If we were to do it again, and most of us were ready, we needed to know the band was equally committed, [but] Steve [Gottlieb] did not feel they were. He moved on.'

183

Anton was not ignorant to his role in it all. Around this time, he committed to quitting heroin once and for all. 'I don't feel ashamed about my drug use,' he later said. 'That's what I was doing. I was holed up in my house in Laurel Canyon, shooting up. It was hurting the people I loved. … I didn't quit dope because I was ashamed of doing dope. I quit it because of the effect it was having on my life.'

While TVT, Anton, the band, and Michael Dutcher all played different roles in the collective implosion—which, in *Dig!*, effectively concludes the story of The Brian Jonestown Massacre—to the band and their associates, the consensus appears to be that blame for the record's failure, the band's disintegration, and their sinking relationship with TVT rests mostly with Michael Dutcher. Among other things, he would reportedly deposit Matt's royalty checks into his own account to collect interest on them before paying Matt, who eventually was evicted from his apartment for not being able to make rent.

Adam Le Blanc has a similar grievance, while others have said Dutcher used huge chunks of the band's advance on himself, and that he was enabling Anton's heroin habit. Even so, Adam Shore points out that while he feels Dutcher did help poison the band's relationship with TVT, the band would have still been doing drugs, and things would have gone south anyway. 'He did poison the well a lot, and I did not like his style, and I did not think he was very good for the band, but, when the band was on drugs, they acted like children,' he says. 'They can't take care of themselves, so they don't know where their next meal's coming from, so they ask Dutcher, and Dutcher asks me, and it became this sort of terrible cycle.'

Amine Ramer had acted as a go-between for the band and Dutcher. They'd call her to get money so that they could get to the next hotel; she'd call Dutcher, Dutcher would call Adam Shore, and Adam would call TVT. Sometimes, Amine would call TVT herself, but she says they'd get pushy with her. Looking back, she sees herself as an unwilling, unknowing agent in the series of events that ultimately led to the band's collapse.

Miraculously, Amine had no idea that the band members were on drugs. She just thought Anton was chronically ill. 'The label had convinced Anton that Michael was taking money, but Anton was getting the money directly from the label, and that's when the band imploded, because the other guys

184

couldn't pay their rent,' she says. 'It was then that the drug thing came out. Joel told me, *You know, you should know this: I'm a tweaker and Anton's on heroin*. That's when it all became clear.'

According to Amine, there was actually a clause in Anton's contract with TVT that said if he was caught using drugs, the label could drop him. Once he realized that he'd lost everything to heroin, Anton quit the drug cold turkey. As far as Joel is concerned, it was like flipping a switch, although Adam says he sent Anton to rehab twice, and Dutcher says three times. Obviously, Anton's commitment to changing his life was not without its difficulties, and for his band and label, the effort proved too little, too late.

MAP, the Music Assistance Program, is an organization dedicated to helping musicians with drug and alcohol problems.* Without it, this story might've ended differently. 'They were great to Anton,' Adam recalls. 'They helped him get through rehab. They paid for it and they mentored him.'

Former Crosby Stills & Nash drummer Dallas Taylor, now working in Los Angeles as an interventionist, was a prime mover in helping Anton kick heroin. 'Anton's a good kid that got caught up in the myth, like thousands of us did, that creativity is born through drugs and that we sacrifice ourselves to the art,' he notes. 'I sacrificed everything, as well as a couple organs, and just got lucky, like Anton, and survived.'

185

---

* For more information on this, go to grammy.org/musicares/recovery.

13 14 **15** 16

OPEN HEART SURGERY

Travis Snyder came up to Laurel Canyon to help Anton through detox, and he lived with him there for a while. 'It was sick,' said Michael Sjobeck, who likewise came down to visit his old childhood friend. 'He was terribly ill. Looked emaciated and sickly pale, but he was still creating music and writing beautiful love songs, because his heart was exploding. He was totally clean within three months.'

Michael claims he was present as Anton wrote 'Open Heart Surgery' for his new girlfriend, Tara, during a weeklong stay with Anton back in mid-October 1999. Michael stayed in the guesthouse. 'There was a back storage unit behind it, and the whole damn place was painted red, with *tons* of guitars and amps,' he recalled. 'It was a seriously beautiful place, with a long driveway leading up to the house, shaded with eucalyptus trees.'

Tara appears in only one brief shot in *Dig!*, as Anton leans in to kiss her; she also was out with Anton and Courtney the day they did the 'goofball desert shoot' with Ondi and Kelly White—now Kelly Timoner, having married Ondi's brother, David—which produced the photo that ended up on the cover of *Bringing It All Back Home—Again*. She's also seen briefly in the video for 'Going To Hell.' 'Tara was always hanging around when I was around,' Brad Clark recalls. 'Her friend Chloë Sevigny used to come to the shows all the time.' 'She was very aloof with anyone who wasn't Anton,' says Sandy Wilson. 'She was intrigued with Anton until she got to know him, then she distanced herself.' An actress and fashion designer, Tara played an uncredited role as a college girl in *American Pie*, which came out that year and features 'Going To Hell' in the soundtrack.

In the middle of the night, during an earthquake, Anton came out to the guesthouse while everything was shaking to show Michael his new song, though he didn't have a name for it yet, and he was excited to show it to Tara the next day. She just smiled at him. 'I could tell it was like what happens if somebody says *paint me a picture* and you paint the *Mona Lisa* of them,' Anton later said of her reaction. 'What would they do? Would they be saying, *My nose is not quite right*?' Anton could tell she didn't understand the song, so had to explain to her what it meant to him. 'That's like open heart surgery,' she told him—and Anton had a name for the song.

'He wore Tara out with his heroin addiction,' Michael recalled. 'He was very kind and open about it. He was not scheming or lying or stealing. He was like a very sickly looking Buddha nearing complete physical collapse.'

Bobby Hecksher, whose band The Warlocks had formed the previous year, claims he too was present when Anton recorded the song. They had become friends recently, and Anton had asked Bobby to come up to Laurel Canyon to listen to the song and some other demos.

Bobby first heard the BJM when he was working at Aaron's Record Store in Hollywood. Intrigued by the name, he put one of their singles on and was blown away. He attended BJM gigs faithfully once they started playing Los Angeles, but didn't meet them formally until a show at Al's Bar. There, he told Dave, 'This is the best band I've ever seen. Here's my number, if they need a guitar player or keyboard player or something.' Anton called Bobby a few days later. Though Dave no longer worked for the band, he was still a fan, and he still hung out with them sometimes. He would later manage The Warlocks on the road.

When Bobby went to audition, it was the most depressing time in the band's career. 'It didn't seem like it was a good time for me to play with them,' he says. 'Hard to explain unless you were there. That's when I met Peter, too—he formed Black Rebel Motorcycle Club at the same rehearsal.'

As Adam Shore and a few others have mentioned, Anton had pawned all the gear that he'd acquired through TVT, but he still had the pawn tickets, and Bobby says he helped make sure they got all the gear back—or as much of it as they could. 'Whatever money was leftover, we gave to the band to get by,' he says.*

---

* Adam confirms the selling-off of the gear. 'Their record was called *Strung Out In Heaven* for a reason,' he says.

Anton encouraged Bobby, who'd been primarily a bass player up to that point, to start writing and singing his own songs. Soon after that, he formed The Warlocks with an old friend of Anton's, Jennifer Chiba.* 'Anton was playing drums for us at first,' Bobby says, 'but he admits he's not a very good drummer. He got his band back together, and here we are.'

It should come as no surprise that BRMC and The Warlocks formed around the same time. Without Anton, neither band would have happened. Both bands' early material comes straight out of the BJM playbook, and together, they represent the earliest manifestation of the BJM-influenced sound we hear today, in bands like Moon Duo—that droning, driving, catchy psychedelic rock sound that lands somewhere between folk-rock and shoegaze. That is the sound Anton and the BJM brought with them to LA from the Haight, and crystallized throughout *Give It Back!*, *Bringing It All Back Home—Again*, *Strung Out In Heaven*, and now into the new record he was working on, *Bravery Repetition And Noise*.

It was around this time that Frankie Emerson joined the BJM, though there really was no 'band' at the time. Anton was feeling defeated, having lost the Laurel Canyon place and broken up with Tara, and Frankie encouraged him to pick it up again. 'There was nothing,' Frankie says. 'It was him, fuckin' depressed, at Bobby's house, in that little tiny bedroom.'

Anton showed Frankie some of his new songs, including 'Open Heart Surgery,' which to Frankie sounded like The Cure. 'I don't know where you're going with this,' he told Anton, 'but I'll stick around, man … hopefully we'll get out of this rut.'

Frankie had been raised on Zeppelin and The Doors, but he found his own musical niche as a teenager in punk rock and the 4AD label. Before joining the BJM, he'd played in a band called Spindrift, who shared members with the BJM and a bunch of other LA psych bands. Kirkpatrick Thomas and Dave Koenig played in both bands, and Jason 'Plucky' Anchondo, who lived with Frankie for a time (and played not just in Spindrift and the BJM but also in The Warlocks, and more recently has played in Matt Hollywood's new band, The Bad Feelings.)

---

* Jennifer had previously dated Weezer's Rivers Cuomo, and is said to have inspired what is arguably their best record, *Pinkerton*, which was mixed by Rob Jacobs. She later became involved with Elliott Smith.

A few years earlier, Frankie had moved to Sausalito with his high-school friends Nasser Mopera and Micole Skertic, who had seen the BJM opening for the Dandys in 1995, at the Great American Music Hall, and handed Frankie a copy of *Methodrone*. 'I had to go to work,' she recalls. 'I said, Check out this band, I just saw them, they are awesome! After two listens in a row, Frank called me at work. Shortly after, we attended quite a few BJM shows.' Frankie prophesied that'd he play in the Jonestown one day. 'We had many late nights of partying and listening to *Methodrone* and *Take It From The Man!* and going to the shows,' he told me. 'Seeing the band play at Popscene at the Cat's Grill ... I told my friends, Well, if I'm going to be in any band in the world, it's going to be this band. Of course, they didn't believe me, and then I got what I asked for.'

Frankie first met Anton in 1997, when he ran into him on Franklin Street while he was having Mai Tais with some of the Dandys. He already knew Courtney because they'd just signed to Capitol, and his girlfriend, Krista Crews, was Perry Watts-Russell's assistant. 'One of our first dates was a BJM show, because they were his favorite band,' she says. 'It took moving to LA and me working with the Dandys at Capitol before he and Anton finally connected. Brent and Court were in town, so we went to meet up with them, and Anton happened to walk by as we were sitting outside. He joined us, and the next thing I knew, Frankie was in The Brian Jonestown Massacre.'

'You want to start a Byrds covers band with me?' Anton asked Frankie that day. Frankie wasn't sure how to take it. He didn't actually join the BJM until February 2000, but his recruitment could be considered the beginning of the band that would last until the *Silver Jubilee* tour. Frankie, Bobby, a guy named Jeff Levitz, and a few others came in, though Jeff Levitz had been around in the BJM scene a while, and had played on *Bringing It All Back Home—Again*.

* * *

It's fitting that the next BJM record would be titled *Zero*, because after Anton lost his father, his manager, his band, his gear, and his label, he was back to square one, bouncing from couch to couch, recording wherever he could and playing shows. Even Ondi had gone, repelled by the darkness of Anton's descent. She'd become focused more on the Dandys, who had exploded after

189

their signature song, 'Bohemian Like You,' was used in a Vodafone advert, though she did film Anton and the band here and there, so, to borrow a phrase from Dennis, there's no film of this shit, either.

Reforming the band this time around would prove challenging—as did finding somewhere to live. After moving out of Laurel Canyon, Anton lived for a few months with Elise Pearson and Brian Butler, then with Bobby, and then with Frankie and Krista for a spell. He stayed for a while at the home of a girl called Natasha while she was away, and also with Mara Keagle, who had made the move to LA after finally breaking up with Sean Curran. Mara was now dating James Ambrose, and had joined his group Smallstone, which also featured Jeff Davies, Ricky Maymi, and Tommy Dietrick. 'After I broke up with Sean, I went to India for two months,' she recalls. 'I met James, and Dave introduced me to Smallstone, and then me and James ended up being a couple for a long time, and that's when I moved to LA.'

While at Elise's, Anton got his ducks in a row and finally got his driver's license reinstated. Greg Shaw, forever to the rescue, pitched in to help and even brought Anton groceries now and then. Things were looking up, but Anton's self-medicating didn't stop with kicking heroin. 'I used alcohol to get out of the opium relationship,' he later said. 'Physically, it was very, very difficult. It took a long time, too, and a lot of willpower and fortitude and focus.'

Trading heroin for alcohol didn't help Anton's mental-health situation, and some felt that Anton's real problem was never actually with heroin in the first place. In *Dig!*, Courtney Taylor-Taylor recalls an incident at Mary's Club, the oldest strip joint in Portland, when Anton 'put away probably about a pint glass of Jim Beam, and then he got crazy. 'What if the whole time it wasn't even the dope or the speed or anything, it was just the booze?' he wonders.

Anton has dismissed any argument that he had a drinking problem, but will admit that drinking never helped him reach his goals. 'When you have that kind of notoriety, especially when people are familiar through your records, it's so hard, because what if you show up and you're not good?' he later told Alyson Camus of WFMU. 'I mean, it happens to me all the time. I get to read articles about how well those guys see you—he's arguing with the audience, and then he played this crappy song, but the name is great, and this and this, you know? And it really bugs you. You just have to remember that you're not what you do.'

By the time Anton and Frankie started putting the BJM back together, so many people from the old San Francisco scene had migrated to Los Angeles—Ricky, Mara, Tommy, Miranda—that the band could essentially be thought of as coming from both cities. LA also had its own Laurel Canyon–style folk revival, with bands like Beachwood Sparks and The Tyde coming up, and when the BJM brought their Haight edge to it, the psych scene as we know it today was truly born. All of Anton's Midas touch spinoffs—The Warlocks, BRMC—went on to great things, and then *that* wave caught up with The Black Angels, who brought the same cross-pollinated sound back into the mainstream from Austin (where it had been conceived by The 13th Floor Elevators back in the 60s).

Anton had kept that sound alive in the Haight in the 90s and built a whole scene around it—a scene people were following faithfully, just as Anton had said they would. Now, with the dot-com boom driving up rents in the Bay Area, the Haight had come to Hollywood. And now, even though his own career had gone off track briefly, Anton could fall back on the psychedelic garage-rock scene that had flourished under his banner.

191

'In the last couple of months, an old-school Buffalo Springfield/Love/Byrds Sunset Strip rock scene has sprouted,' Joel said at the time. 'We're big fans of those bands. It's pretty exciting. Beachwood Sparks … they've got the biggest buzz.'*

At the center of the new scene was Al's Bar and a couple of other clubs around town—Café Bleu, Goldfinger's on Yucca Street, Three Clubs—that would became as significant to the band in LA as the Horseshoe Café and the Peacock Lounge had been back in San Francisco. All of these clubs and a few others were within a fifteen-minute drive of each other.

'Café Bleu was a smaller, more underground version of Popscene like in San Francisco,' says Adam Le Blanc. The Dandys played there, as did Mike Kubisty and Greg Derfer's new band, The Lemmings; The Out Crowd came down to play some shows; Tami and Jimi Hey DJed at the club. Joel DJed there sometimes, too, and Anton found a lot of the people who would later join him on his records in these cliques.

Ben Vendetta's wife, Arabella Proffer, was another regular on the scene.

---

* Joel himself would later go against the tide and move back to San Francisco, where he got a job at Amoeba Records in the Haight and started playing with The Dilettantes.

'You really looked forward to that BJM show,' she says. 'It got annoying when minor celebs showed up just to watch Anton lose it.' She recalls the anchors of the scene being the Silverlake Lounge (now called the Fold) and Three Clubs, the latter of which she says picked up after Café Bleu closed down and changed owners. She also remembers the demographic of the shows changing as time went on. 'Like all scenes ... all the women kind of did this Logan's Run thing where, once they got to age twenty-seven, they stopped seeing gigs,' she laughs. (Her pal Charity Baker was married for a while to Hunter Crowley, who was one of several BJM drummers during the period before the band settled on Dan Allaire.)

Three Clubs was an unassuming venue with a sign outside that said 'Bargain Clown Mart.' It got a small name-check in *Swingers* as stars Jon Favreau and Vince Vaughn were regulars, and filmed part of the movie there; Renée Zellweger also worked there for a time. Today, it is an obnoxious-looking façade, and the Clown Mart sign is gone. The venue was never meant for bands. It was a small side room with dark wood and red lighting, and the bands would set up on the floor, so it really couldn't hold a huge capacity. 'That's kind of what made it so great,' Arabella continues. 'It was a vibe of bands playing in your living room. There were no real trendsetters except denim on denim, and whoever was getting written-up in mags—Beachwood Sparks, Elliott Smith. Anton was on the down and out but everyone was obsessed ... he was never someone you saw that, if things didn't work out, he'd get a job at Taco Bell or become an account executive at an ad firm. Just would never happen.'*

'Everybody hung out at Three Clubs because it was a cool bar, and they'd always have bands play on Thursdays,' says Frankie. 'That was the scenester place. We used to play there. We played there on Thanksgiving one time. We played at Slabtown on Thanksgiving, in Portland. Fucking people threw barstools at us, but then they'd throw barstools at us almost at, I'd say, fifty percent of the shows.'

BRMC, who'd recently signed to Virgin Records, didn't hang around at Three Clubs but did play Silverlake Lounge and had a DJ night at Beauty Bar. 'It seemed everyone was bitter [BRMC] had a record deal at the tail end of

---

* A fun note: Ben and Arabella appears as extras in a movie about The Turtles, *My Dinner With Jimi*, alongside one Mick Marsh, Frankie, and Plucky.

Virgin being a real label, besides Miranda Lee Richards,' Arabella continues. 'The people who worked at other labels like Capitol used to call them *Black Rebel Mary Chain*.' (Miranda had signed to Virgin around the time Anton moved out to Laurel Canyon.)

Another regular on the scene was Tim Burgess from the British group The Charlatans, who'd moved to Los Angeles in 1998. According to Arabella, Tim had been was pretty upset when Ben Vendetta put Anton on the cover of his zine instead of him, and demanded to be appear on the cover of the next issue—which Ben obliged. 'The fact that Tim Burgess felt competition [with Anton] over a fanzine cover tells you a lot,' she adds.

Tim recalls his first meeting with the BJM in his memoir, *Tim Book Two*:

> BJM were the first band I saw in LA, days after moving there. I was knocked out. … We chatted about John Peel, travel, drugs, girls, hair, The Monkees, The Monkees' hair … and a mutual love of Elliott Smith. When our paths crossed I found I had a lot in common with Frankie Teardrop and Charles Mehling. Frankie didn't join until 2000, but timelines and the BJM don't follow the rules of the regular universe … there was something about the BJM that was like the perfect leather jacket—a beat-up style that couldn't be faked, and that made everything around them look drab. They were my newfound gang—brilliant for introducing me to new ideas. Not so brilliant was their need, love, appreciation, and craving for narcotics of every prescription. Ah well! You can't have it all, although we often tried to. Every silver lining has some sort of cloud, but we loved ours.*

Anytime Arabella was out with Ben, they would come home with a stack of demos, in part because no one else but him was writing about the scene, but also because he'd just started working for Dionysus Records. Bands would approach him, thinking they'd get a shot at the big time like the BJM, the Dandys, or BRMC had. 'Everyone wanted to get a big label deal, but at the same time still keep that indie cred which was hard to balance,' Arabella

---

* Burgess later collaborated with Anton on some songs, most recently, at time of writing, 'Fact 76a,' from *Don't Get Lost*.

says. 'Everyone wanted a position the Dandys had. When The Warlocks got signed, people made sarcastic remarks about them being a lame version of The Strokes, as far as marketing was going to go, and then would bring up the, *Oh no, look what happened to BJM on TVT. It'll happen to them!*'

The week Ben and Arabella first started going out, Ben interviewed the BJM, BRMC, Smallstone, and others for his zine. That was July 2000. A year later, he and Arabella were married at Arabella's parents' house in Dana Point, not far from where Anton grew up, in Costa Mesa and Newport Beach. During the reception, Arabella's mom's friends kept asking Anton what he did.

'I've put out nine albums.'

'Oh, how *nice*, but what else do you do?'

'I put out albums.'

'But is that all?'

'I put out a lot of albums, that's what I do.'

* * *

In 2000, Tommy Dietrick—now all grown up and playing with Smallstone— moved with his girlfriend, Melody, into an apartment on Fairfax and Pico. The I-10 roared a mile down the road. Back when Anton was still living in Laurel Canyon, he had taken Tommy for a drive through the city's back roads and alleys in a friend's white BMW. They made their way off the beaten path up to the house. Anton pulled up a few songs that he'd been working on and obliged Tommy to lay down some bass tracks.

'Anton was working on songs for *Bravery Repetition And Noise*,' Tommy recalls. 'I laid down some parts, but none of the songs I recorded on ever made it to the album. He'd just quit heroin, and he was pretty humble then. He knew he had blown [it] and was trying to put the pieces back together.'

Often, Tommy would go to James's apartment to plan Smallstone's takeover of the world over cheap beer and Parliament Lights. James, who was afflicted with asthma, had to pull out his inhaler once they'd finished their cigarettes. Occasionally, Anton would show up, and Tommy couldn't help but notice the air of defeat looming around him, but he retained his charm. 'Everyone still respected him but didn't hesitate to talk about him behind his back,' he says. 'Not necessarily bad things—mostly opinions of what he should do to get his career back on track.'

James grew up in LA and went to college in Santa Cruz, then moved back to LA and played in a band called Magic Pacer. They played a show with the BJM in 1995, and that's what really opened the door for James to find his style. 'If you had seen them back [then], it was just mind-blowing, especially since the 700-pound alternative gorilla was sitting on everybody at that time,' he told Ben Vendetta.* 'It just meant that you did not have to use fuzz pedals or the like to make really good music.'

James was proud to have several former BJM members in his band, including Mara, who like others had made the move to Los Angeles because of rising rents in San Francisco. When Smallstone finished their record, Anton came in to help mix it and also played some drums and organ on it. Greg Shaw then put it out on Bomp!

With his head straight and his passion back, Anton went about repairing his relationships and rebuilding bridges. Even Muddy came back to help produce the new BJM record.

For the first half of 2000, the reformed band played shows pretty much exclusively in Los Angeles, mostly at Spaceland and the Troubadour. This is when Rob Campanella came in. 'Rob offered to let Anton set up in his studio at his house in North Hollywood, which was a bigger space than he had, and Rob had a ton of gear as well,' says Tommy. 'Members of The Quarter After basically became the new BJM lineup, with Dave Keonig on bass, Rob on keyboard, and Hunter on drums.† Frankie on guitar. These were the players who worked on *Bravery Repetition And Noise*, as well as a few guests like Mara, Miranda, and James.'

Tommy and Frankie first met at one of Rob's many backyard barbecues. '[Rob] had a house right off the 101 [freeway], on the way to Burbank,' Arabella recalls. 'He had a home studio and everything—he would never lock the doors, and we couldn't believe it! Andy Dick wandered into the house, drunk, some years ago, because he didn't lock the doors, so I heard.

195

---

* The gorilla in question was the music industry, struggling to adjust to the realities of downloading and the internet, putting its weight behind alternative-rock acts like Fastball (featuring Anton's fellow ex-bandmate in Electric Cool-Aide, Tony Scalzo), the Dandys' former Tim/Kerr labelmates Everclear, and groups like Goo Goo Dolls, Hole, Eve 6, Marcy Playground, and Barenaked Ladies.
† The Quarter After were formed in the summer of 2000 by brothers Rob and Dominic Campanella—who first saw the BJM open for Sonic Boom back in '94, in between the Oasis gig and their first show with the Dandys—with Dave Koenig on bass and Nelson Bragg on drums. They describe their music as 'psychedelic music for the twenty-first century. Led by Rob and Dominic.

He fixed himself a vodka in the kitchen and didn't realize he was in the wrong house.'

'That last album that I play on, *Bravery Repetition And Noise*—that's when Rob came into the picture as a solid [member],' Jeff Davies adds. 'His place is the recording studio, and Anton's equipment kind of morphed into his.'

The void left by Anton's old band was subsequently filled by Rob, Dave, Frankie, Hunter, Bobby, James, and Jeff Levitz; Jeff Davies came back in eventually, as Smallstone were absorbed into the BJM. Miranda would step in from time to time—as she had since the late 90s—as did Mara, while another new addition was drummer Dan Allaire, who took the role after Hunter. As the drummer for Pearlene, Dan had played gigs from Detroit to New York, opening for The Detroit Cobras, The Bassholes, and The White Stripes. He even dated Meg White for a time, before The White Stripes' reportedly management made her call it off.*

During the time that he was staying with Elise in LA, Anton would borrow her car to make the trip to Rob's to lay the groundwork for what was originally intended to be the second of four albums for TVT. Those demos would evolve into *Zero*, which was released on Bomp! after relations with TVT fell apart completely. Many of the tracks appear on *Bravery Repetition And Noise*, too, though Frankie says that *Zero* was recorded not at Rob's but at Muddy's.

Muddy confirms this, but adds that he did not play an engineering or producing role. 'Anton moved in with me for a while,' he says. 'He didn't have anywhere to go. He'd spent all the [TVT] money, and I just let him live there. I really wanted him to keep moving forward, [so] he moved whatever gear was left at that point into my living room. I was gone a lot, and I just let him go at it.'

The band had been renting rehearsal studios around Hollywood, which Greg would pay for, while Anton tried to work things out with TVT. Adam Shore says the label wanted another record, and pushed Frankie to take Anton over to Muddy's to make it happen. 'There was still, like, this open-ended deal that if Anton produced a record to TVT things would've been all right,'

---

* 'Great lady,' Anton once said of Meg. 'She's been down with the BJM since Jack was in The Go. Anyways, White Stripe HQ calls management meeting, and orders fucking Meg to not see Dan or be seen around us at our show, as we are bad for business.'

says Frankie. 'They knew Anton needed a car, so they said, *Hey, man, we'll give you two thousand bucks toward a used car*. Anton goes, *Fuck that, I want a brand new Range Rover*, so they were like, *Nope, never mind, just keep doing whatever you're doing*.

'We did the *Zero* EP around that whole same time period right there,' he continues. 'TVT didn't really want anything to do with what we had going on, so Greg picked it up and released it.'

Shore has a slightly different take on this. 'There was an option for TVT to take the next record, but of course the budget was a bit bigger than the last record. TVT didn't want to pay that money, so they wanted to renegotiate the deal, and the band at that point wasn't professional enough to go through that process again, so the whole thing wound up falling apart, and then, after another year, I wound up leaving TVT, so they lost their champion.'

With this, Adam's—and TVT's—relationship with the BJM ended for good. Seeing no future in rock, the label switched to hip-hop; it would eventually file for bankruptcy in 2007.

Back in October 2000, The Brian Jonestown Massacre toured with Smallstone through the South, then up to New England, and then back to California via the Midwest. Jeff Davies was not yet back in the BJM but was playing in Smallstone, so for this tour the BJM was Anton, Frankie, Tommy (doing dual bass duty with Smallstone), and Jeff Levitz, who had been with Anton the first time Frankie met him a couple years back with the Dandys. Joel came back for the tour as well.

'We got a Lincoln town car—me, Joel, Jeff Levitz, and Anton—and we decided to drive straight to Austin,' Frankie recalls. On the way there, he and Joel were pounding beers; Jeff doesn't drink, so they'd have him do most of the driving, and they were hauling ass. 'Anton was sitting right behind Jeff, and Jeff was joking around … he, like, swerves on the interstate, going, *woah, woah woah*, just being kind of a dick, and Anton starts strangling him, choking him from behind, so now Jeff's *all* over the fucking interstate, all over, like, five lanes, and me and Joel are like, *Fuck, man, we are going to fucking die*.'

Finally, Frankie pried Anton's arm from Jeff's neck, and they were able to pull away unscathed. 'Joel was so fucking scared. I was like, *Woah, this is so fucking rock'n'roll*!' Frankie continues. 'Joel just came back for that

197

one [tour]. I didn't even know Joel, so you've got a couple new guys who've never played together, don't know each other whatsoever, and we haven't even played a show yet. We drove straight to Austin from LA. Twenty-four hours straight, just out of our minds.'

After Austin, the band played up through the East Coast to Toronto, then came back down through the Midwest and ended the tour in Minneapolis. Anton was keen to bring Tommy back into the BJM permanently, but Tommy loved playing with Smallstone, so he wasn't about to quit. So, when it became clear that Anton needed a band to start touring again, Tommy decided he would just do both. He learned twenty-five BJM songs in three days, and played just as many cities in thirty for the tour. He managed to get the parts down, but on this and future tours, Anton, who was big on rhythm, emphasized that he wanted the parts to be played *exactly* as they'd been tracked on the records.* For Tommy, this sometimes felt counterintuitive to how he might have otherwise played the songs, but he did it, knowing the songs had to groove the right way and be played with the right feel, or else they weren't going to work.

One night on the road, Tommy and Anton were sitting in a dilapidated Motel 6 with *Late Night With Conan O'Brien* on in the background, when, after a commercial break, The Dandy Warhols came on to perform 'Godless.' As Tommy recalls, 'It summed up the high contrast between the Dandys' impending success—having exploded with their record *Thirteen Tales From Urban Bohemia*—and the BJM's impending failures, which evolved over and over again until 2004 and *Dig!*'

Another enduring memory for Tommy was the time from he and Anton drunkenly shot bottle rockets out of their hotel windows at people and cars passing on the street below.

The band toured again during February and March 2001. It would be their last with Jeff Davies.

---

* One time, during a show at the Mercury Lounge in New York City in 2003, Anton kicked Frankie off the stage for playing too fast. 'Literally into the fucking crowd, and I bashed a girl's fucking forehead open with my headstock from my guitar,' Frankie recalls. 'Anton just came up and kicked me right from behind and I went flying right over the monitor into the crowd.'

TO TEAR YOU APART

'TVT gave me a lot of fucking rope, and I basically tied it around everyone's neck, and we jumped off a cliff,' Anton, now clean, told Robert Cherry following the spring 2001 tour, explaining the red tape holding back the release of *Bravery Repetition And Noise*, the title of which he described as his definition of rock'n'roll. 'Plus I was fucking around with heroin and shit. That was probably not the best idea.'

'There was always people going in and out [for that record],' Frankie recalls. 'Parts were being scratched and added left and right.' Of the old band, only Jeff appears on the album, though Raugust returned to play flute. The album was recorded over the summer of 2001 and features some of Anton's best-known compositions, among them 'Open Heart Surgery' and 'Nevertheless,' as well as another notable cover: 'Sailor,' a reworking of 'The Sailing Ship,' originally performed by The Cryan' Shames. Hunter Crowley plays drums on a few songs, including 'Just For Today,' 'Telegram,' and 'Nevertheless.'

The opening track, 'Just For Today,' was something of an unfinished experiment. The second song, 'Telegram,' had existed in some form or another as far back as the *Methodrone/Spacegirl* era, when it was recorded for *The Diane Perry Tape*. A live bootleg of the song from 1993 exists as well. After the stripped-down 'Stolen' comes 'Open Heart Surgery,' and then 'Nevertheless,' one of Anton's most lyrically poignant songs. A loop of Jeff's amp making a weird noise like a submarine beep plays throughout the song. Jeff had laid his guitar against his amp when the beep happened, and everyone scrambled to record it before it was gone for good. The echo of the beep can be heard right up to the end, as the stutter pedal rings in 'Sailor.'

Frankie learned quickly that Anton preferred to work fast. For 'Nevertheless,' he called Frankie at work and had him track his part in one take during a lunch break. 'You pretty much have to do everything in one take, even if you don't know the song,' Frankie recalls. 'Anton just keeps it that way. He's like, *That's fine*, and you're like, *Well, I'd like to do it one more time*. And he's like, *No, forget it, we're moving on.*'

For 'Sailor,' Frankie recalls, 'Mara sang through a Fender Twin amplifier. That was her microphone. That's how that vocal came about.' Her voice sounds angelic on the track. Frankie wrote the main guitar part for the song that follows, 'You Have Been Disconnected,' to which Anton added the lyrics and flute hook. 'I was having trouble with the song,' Frankie says. 'I couldn't come up with a bridge or a chorus, so Anton just left the same chords repeating over and over. I don't think he could come up with any changes either. It was like, *Fuck it, we'll just leave it.*'

The next song, 'Leave Nothing For Sancho,' has a similar vibe to 'Spanish Bee' from *Thank God For Mental Illness* but features a layering of sounds that's more indicative of Anton's recent work. 'Let Me Stand Next To Your Flower,' for which Frankie says he wrote the main guitar part, kicks off with a brief noise collage of people talking, internet dial-up tones, and what sounds like a string quartet, before Frankie's thumping chord progression brings us into the world of the song. It ends with the same collage that opens it.

There are two versions of the dreamy 'If I Love You,' which closes the record, either side of the only BJM track where Jeff Davies sings lead, '(I Love You) Always.' 'That was already recorded,' Frankie says. 'Travis Snyder recorded that, and that's really how Jeff got back into the band.'

Raymond Richards of The Idaho Falls played pedal steel on the song in exchange for borrowing a Sennheiser 421 dynamic microphone from Rob's home studio. He recalls how he showed up with his pedal steel without having heard the song beforehand and loaded his gear into the studio. As Raymond set up, a shirtless Anton—who had been in the middle of doing an interview on the lawn outside—came in, set up one of his old RCA 44a ribbon mics, explained it was Mickey Mouse's mic from the days of live radio, quickly instructed Raugust on how to record with it, and returned to the interview. Raymond took a few passes at the song, and within a half-hour had a nice arrangement recorded. Anton came back in, listened to the track, and liked it.

The record's cover image is a photo of the film director Jim Jarmusch, taken by one of Anton's girlfriends, the actress Tricia Vessey, who was pregnant with Anton's first son, Hermann, at the time of *Bravery*'s release, though their relationship did not last very long. Some of Jarmusch's films feature BJM music, notably *Broken Flowers*, starring Bill Murray, which features 'Not If You Were The Last Dandy On Earth.' 'He deserves a little praise,' Anton later said, when asked why Jarmusch is on the cover. 'If he got the cover of *Time* magazine, all of those copies would end up in the dump.'

* * *

Bravery Repetition And Noise was also the last Brian Jonestown Massacre album to feature Jeff Davies. According to most versions of this story, Jeff and Anton had at last grown sick of each other, often interrupting each other during interviews and taunting each other—a state of affairs exacerbated by drugs and booze. While Anton was able to kick heroin, Jeff had not been so successful.

Jeff would learn—as others would, too—that this was an entirely different band from the one he had first joined in more ways than just who was playing, and it didn't take long for him and Anton to butt heads. On Anton's birthday the following year, at a show in Detroit, Hunter had to break up a fight between Jeff and Anton. 'It was his birthday, but also the anniversary of his dad's suicide,' Hunter recalls, '[so he was] very drunk and emotional. Jeff said something stupid in the motor home after the show that sent Anton into rage.' As Jeff and Anton rolled around on the floor, Hunter accidentally stepped on Anton's foot, just hard enough to cause a hairline fracture. The White Stripes, who were just taking off and still based in that city, were at that gig; someone later slashed one of the band's trailer tires, and Anton blamed Jack White for it. 'That's him and The Go in *Dig!*, attacking us,' he's said. 'They even slit our van tires.' (Dennis Pelowski doesn't doubt that Jack attended the early BJM shows in Detroit, and suspects he was at least a 'student' of the BJM.)

The next night, at the Rock and Roll Hall of Fame Museum in Cleveland, Anton played the band's set from a wheelchair. Hunter, who wouldn't hang around for much longer after that, would later record Courtney's voiceover for *Dig!* with Ondi at his studio.

Another telling window into Anton and Jeff's deteriorating relationship is a video clip of the band playing the Tequila Lounge in Toronto on February 22, 2002. Outside the show, they were interviewed by local startup Sugarcube Media. In the resulting footage, Jeff, realizing the interview is happening, and that Anton has a bottle of Jim Beam, sits directly in view of the camera and repeatedly tries to take the bottle from Anton. Each time, Anton pulls it closer. Later on in the interview, he kicks back, annoyed, as Jeff drunkenly praises him. Anton waves the cameraman down.

The mayhem continued at the Grog Shop two nights later, in Cleveland, and a week later, at the Hi-Pointe in St. Louis, on March 2. The band had played nonstop through February, and Jeff says things were finally clicking with the new lineup. 'The band never sounded better,' he says. 'After playing every night, you start to hit this psychic thing … we would end the song on a chord, and then everyone would think the same thing, and we'd go into an impromptu verse without planning it or saying anything to anyone. That's how we were playing, and that's one thing I really miss [about] being around Anton. We played together really good … that's the reason why I stayed through all this craziness that went on, because there was magic there. Me and Anton were both already players, but when we got together we really developed, we clicked, we grew and developed our style together.'

In footage from the Grog Shop show, three songs into the band's set, after 'Nevertheless,' Anton turns to Jeff or Frankie and says, 'Tune your guitar, and I'll pay you a hundred dollars.' After a long rant, he turns to the audience and challenges someone—anyone—to fight him. Someone rises to the occasion, so Anton beats his chest, swears, whips a microphone cord, and readies his mic stand as a weapon, but before anything happens, he bids the audience goodnight and leaves the venue. The band play the rest of their set with Scott Vitt—front man for the BJM's support act, The Asteroid #4—taking Anton's part. 'Though Newcombe was hardly Axl Rose at Riverport, he certainly let everyone down,' Jeff Jarrett of the *University News* wrote after the show. 'The Brian Jonestown Massacre is still worth your time and energy, but some serious growing up needs to be done.'

According to what I've been able to put together, Tricia gave birth to Hermann either earlier that day or around that time, so Anton was anxious to get back to Los Angeles. 'Think of Anton at his craziest, and that's how he was,' says Frankie. 'We were like, *We're trying to get back, man, but this is a long drive.* The tension was insane in that RV. Anton was hammered the whole time, and angry, and refused to put any clothes on for a couple days there, man—he was just naked in the RV, bashing the cabin doors and shit. Punching everything. Hitting everyone's little bunks.'

After the show, Anton and Jeff got in yet another fight, which Jeff lost badly. 'He swung me my by my hair and hit me from behind with this sock full of metal and rocks,' he recalls. 'I hit the ground, unconscious, and he picks me up by my hair and swings me, and this probably all happened within the span of two minutes or a minute and a half.'

After that, according to many of the people I've spoken to, the band left Jeff in a dumpster and headed back west. Frankie had fallen asleep in the RV and didn't even know that there had been a fight; when he woke up in New Mexico, he looked around, but Jeff wasn't in his bed. The others told Frankie what happened, and that they didn't know what to do, with Anton acting out the way he was. By the time Jeff could get back to Los Angeles, he'd lost his job, his band, and his girlfriend, who had since fallen in love with Anton.

'Everyone in the band wouldn't talk to me because they felt ashamed, but I didn't know that for years and years,' Jeff says. 'It was never talked about, but when Anton attacked me in the RV, I thought it was just me and Anton in there, but actually everyone else was [there], too, in their beds, cowering and peeking out from underneath the sheets, pretending to be asleep. When I got back to town and I saw all these people who were supposed to be my friends … everyone gave me the cold shoulder.'*

'When you're in my band, you're like a sharecropper until I set you free—or you run for your life,' Anton told Robert Cherry after getting back to LA. 'I'll get drunk, fistfight, carry gear, sleep in the van, and not shower or shave—when I'm young. That's the beauty of youth. But when I'm an old man? I might be too tired or too fed up for this lifestyle. I might just want to hang out and talk to kids, and go, *You know what? You can [make music for a living], too. I did it, and I'm no genius.*'

When, Robert, who'd seen the Grog Shop show, questioned Anton's ability

---

* Jeff and Anton have not spoken since the fight, except for when Anton called Jeff to give his condolences after he heard that Jeff's girlfriend and Planet Of The Hairdo Apes bandmate, Roxanne Rodriguez, died in 2003.

to raise a child, Anton balked at the suggestion. 'When has anyone ever been ready for a kid?' he said. 'If you have a lot of love and patience and time to offer, it'll end up good. If you don't, and you're resentful and you haven't done the things in your life that you wanted to, it's gonna end up bad. I've toured Japan. I think I can handle a kid.'

The last show of that tour was at the Knitting Factory in Los Angeles. Footage of the show captures Anton ranting to the audience about how he is not for sale, and how he wants to go meet his son and buy something nice for him out of the money he makes from the gig. Elise was there; so was Ondi Timoner, camera in hand. Anton brings his new protégée, Sarabeth Tucek, onstage to play 'Something For You,' and introduces her as his 'sister.' Someone in the audience yells, 'Fuck your brother, you rock!'—presumably intended to imply that Anton's music sucks compared to Sarabeth's, but Anton seems to take the insult to imply an incestuous relationship.

'Hey, you're going to get your head kicked in,' he tells the heckler. 'Say it to my face. I don't think that's funny. I'm not into incest or child molestation. Come up here. Be a man.' The man approaches the stage. Anton kicks him in the head. The cops are called. Just before they arrive, Anton tells Ondi, in the Knitting Factory's green room, 'They want me dead. I'm not joking around, Ondi. I know for a fact it's over. I've already won. My son's here ... today is a wonderful day to die.'

'I was at the Knitting Factory show where Anton kicked the guy in the face,' Arabella Proffer recalls. 'But what the documentary didn't show was, the guy got dragged back by me and started going into convulsions. It was scary. We thought he was dying.'

Brad Clark, who no longer worked with the band, was also there. Anton grabbed him and pleaded for his help, but to no avail.

In the film, the cops drive Anton away to jail. Anton has self-destructed, and Ondi was there to see it.

And now the movie is over.

PART THREE
YOUR SIDE OF OUR STORY

PART THREE

TOMORROW'S HEROES TODAY

Following Anton's arrest, Charles Mehling organized a huge fundraiser at his place to raise bail money. Lots of bands played the bash, including Black Rebel Motorcycle Club, Beachwood Sparks, Peaches, and Tim Burgess. 'Newcombe was arrested last week for allegedly attacking a man in a bar fight and was being held on $30,000 bail by the Los Angeles Sheriff's Department at the time the event was planned,' *Billboard* reported, adding that Anton had since been released, and that the event, billed as 'a backyard barbecue party,' would go ahead as scheduled.

Charles, who'd grown close with BRMC's Peter Hayes and was due to head off on tour with the group a couple of weeks later, ended up filming the video for BRMC's 'Spread Your Love' at the event. Ondi Timoner was present on his first day of rehearsals, and told Charles she would give him a camera to take on the road with him. She never actually gave him one, but the thought stuck in his mind. 'When it was time to leave, I thought, *I'm going to get a camera like Ondi*,' he recalls. 'I had *fun* doing that, and then I made a music video.' The 'Spread Your Love' video helped propel BRMC to success in the UK. Charles has been a filmmaker ever since.

Miranda Lee Richards, Christof Certik, Victoria Byers, and a guy named Lenny Pops were all at the barbeque. Lenny was from the band Spectacle, who'd toured with the BJM during Charles's run, and had later played in the group himself briefly, having met Anton at Three Clubs back in '97. That night, Anton sat down at Lenny's table and asked if he played drums. Lenny said he was a guitar player, but he thought he'd give it a go. 'I was pretty drunk by then and jumped onstage, starting to tap the drums,' he recalls. 'The rest of the band jumped up, and I thought they were gonna kick my ass.

I politely left the stage, and then Anton and I became friends.' Lenny went on to play guitar with the Jonestown for a bit in 2000, and then did a one-off gig with them in 2002. Sometime during that period, he and Anton recorded some songs together that have not yet been released.

Ondi was at the fundraiser too, just before she began editing *Dig!* Based on the footage from the 'Spread Your Love' video, it looks like everyone had a pretty good time; Anton can be seen briefly in the clip, giving a defiant smirk. Later in the evening, he played a DJ set of salsa jazz. 'It looked like Altamont all over again as every greasy bedhead and neo-hippie in Hollywood converged at the Compound, a well-known party house on McCadden Place,' *LA Weekly* reported. 'Despite the threat of rain and cops, everything worked out, even when it didn't seem to, like nasty nymph Peaches' short but sweet opening set, which ended when the power blew during her third tune.'

Arabella Proffer remembers the power going out during Peaches' set, and that Anton's publicist, Betsy Palmer from Bomp!, wore a T-shirt that said 'I am the owl.' 'It was like a *Free Anton* statement, which I still don't get,' she adds. 'Anton eclipsed BRMC on their own video shoot.'

The pendulum of Anton's turbulent life seemed to be on an upswing again. Around the time of the Knitting Factory show, *Free Williamsburg* published a glowing review of *Bravery Repetition And Noise* by Robert Landham, who praised the band's 'unpredictably fresh sound' and hailed the album as their best since *Take It From The Man!*

The period leading up to the release of *Dig!* saw the Jonestown hit the touring circuit as hard as they could, playing regular shows in intimate clubs across North America. Anton's drinking worsened during this period, though presumably not beyond the point of function, as during this period the band performed more regularly and more successfully than ever before, even if audiences would sometimes thin out prior to the band finishing what were often three-hour sets.

That summer, the band embarked on a short West Coast tour with Dead Meadow, followed by some shows with Ricky Maymi's new band, Mellow Drunk. More shows with Dead Meadow followed in the fall, starting in LA then up through the Midwest, over to New York, then down the East Coast before ending in Texas at the start of October.

By now, the band had a new manager, Ted Gardner, to fill the void left in the aftermath of Michael Dutcher's departure. Because of that experience and what had happened with Dennis Pelowski, Anton had grown evermore cautious of signing contracts or making any deals, and instead focused on releasing music and performing on his own terms. Sean Worrall, who hadn't heard from Anton in years, was anxious to release new BJM music across the pond on his ORG label. Anton was recording a new album, and had told Sean he was on track to finish it by November, but when that month came and went, Sean started to sweat. 'Black Rebel Motorcycle Club are playing with Primal Scream in December, as well as doing their own show,' he wrote to Elise Pearson, who had remained with Anton after the Dutcher meltdown and its aftermath. 'We'd like to get out street teams flyering those shows. BRMC have name-dropped BJM quite a bit over here, in interviews and such.'

There was a glimmer of hope, as in December Anton told Sean was nearly finished with the new record—but he wanted money up front for it. Sean was keen to help the band get their momentum back in England, so he offered a 50–50 split. 'The band really don't have a profile here to justify [an advance],' he told Elise. 'There's a lot of work to be done to even get the band back to where they were here a couple of years ago. Once a band has fallen away from buzz here, it's tough to get a second crack.'

* * *

In January 2003, the BJM played a Clean Needles Now benefit at the Garage in LA, followed by some gigs in Las Vegas in mid-February, then further shows up and down the California coastline with The Tyde and The Out Crowd. The lineup at this point was Anton, Frankie Emerson, Dave Koenig, Dan Allaire, and Matthew J. Tow of the Australian band The Lovetones.

Around the turn of the year, Anton had been living with Greg Shaw, who had just married a young woman named Phoebe—who wanted Anton out of Greg's guesthouse. 'He said to me, Elise, Greg's new hippie wife is kicking me out to start an astrology shop,' Elise recalls. He spent a week or so living with Frankie and his new girlfriend, Erika Petty, but before long was calling Elise and asking her and Greg to get him out of there.

Next, he moved in with another LA scene regular, Aaron Frankel, whose roommate was a girl named Daniella Meeker. She and Anton soon started dating, and it was not long before he'd invited her to sing on 'Here

It Comes'—a song originally recorded during the *Their Satanic Majesties* period—for the new album.* Elise had given Anton her laptop while he was staying at Greg's, and now he and Daniella set up a website that allowed him to stream the BJM's songs for free. As Courtney Taylor-Taylor notes in *Dig!*, 'He put every song on his website for free to download, and he still lives in a car … he could be making a killing.'

Elise likewise realized Anton was in serious need of cash, so she introduced him to Dale Bookout of the New York–based label Tee Pee Records, named for its founder, Tony Presedo. She had gone out to New York the previous year with a band called Good Time Women, whom Tee Pee was interested in signing. She set up a show for the band there, which Dale attended. 'He tried to impress them,' Elise recalls, 'but Good Time Women thought Tee Pee was too much of a "rock" label.'

Elise felt a good rapport with the label, though, so she decided to introduce Dale to the BJM. Dale in turn told Tony about the band. Like TVT before them, they were ecstatic about the idea of having the BJM on their roster and soon set on the idea of putting out the band's next record. 'I did a conference call from my apartment in New York with Dale and Anton,' Elise recalls. 'I asked for minimum $8,000 and a rental motorhome. They agreed.'

Dale had been a fan of the BJM since he was a teenager, but he hadn't thought they were the kind of band the label would sign, since back then Tee Pee was a small imprint known predominantly for putting out stoner-rock records. Dale was really young when he started at Tee Pee, having previously completed an internship at Matador Records while studying at law school, but by now had worked his way up to the point where Tony led him throw his hat into the ring to start signing a few bands. His role was a lot like Adam Shore's at TVT in that sense. 'I did business development, I did the books,' he says. 'Because I was in contract law, I wrote all the contracts. I did everything.' Of his introduction to the BJM, he recalls, 'They came to town on tour one time and played at Mercury Lounge. They had an RV outside that they were traveling in, and we hung out that night.'

209

---

* Daniella now works as a neuroscientist at USC, where she is both Assistant Professor of Preventive Medicine and Director of Clinical Research Informatics. She has published numerous research papers on everything from diabetes to PTSD. Anton once memorably described her as 'a hamburger, fries, and a shake to a fat person'—a glib yet accurate description of her combination of brains and looks.

KEEP MUSIC EVIL

Tee Pee would prove to be a whole different ballgame from TVT—and a much better fit for Anton. Since the TVT deal ended, he had returned to releasing records the way he had in the early days of Bomp!, mostly through the Committee To Keep Music Evil. 'Anton was very apprehensive to get into any kind of deal,' says Dale. 'I didn't mind putting my money and my work where my mouth was. I was confident after he saw how we did with that record that he'd give us another one, and that's how it worked.'

Dale and Anton met a few more times after that, and eventually Anton agreed to Tee Pee putting out *And This Is Our Music* in the fall of 2003—much to the disappointment and chagrin of Sean Worrall, who felt compelled to explain his side of things in an extensive blog post soon after the album's release. 'The plan was that Tee Pee were going to release the new album in the US once we had done it here in Europe,' he wrote. 'We had the master recordings, we had the agreement, we had the publicity happening, we had people calling asking for copies to play. No artwork! We heard stories about Anton telling the crowd at SXSW that our rejecting of the artwork was holding up the release, [then] suddenly they had a new single and a new set of recordings out with them. … The masters are still here, collecting dust … we gave up on it all—damn fine band, total nightmare of a bandleader. Can't even listen to the music these days. Sold all his old albums one day and went to the pub.'

In the interim, Elise, who had helped foster Anton's relationship with Sean and ORG (as well as the new one with Tee Pee), had grown increasingly frustrated in her attempts to get the new album to Sean. By the time of SXSW in March, when it became clear that ORG would not be getting the record at all, she and Anton had a huge row and then stopped speaking altogether. That summer, after an evening of drinking and repeatedly trying to call Anton, Elise left Anton an awful, profanity-laced voicemail. When *And This Is Our Music* came out that October, it opened with a recording of the message under the title 'The Wrong Way.' Elise sued Tee Pee and was awarded a few thousand dollars in damages, while the message was removed from subsequent pressings of the album.*

---

* The album originally closed with another voicemail message, under the title 'The Right Way,' this one left by Sarah Jane McKinley of The Out Crowd, whom Anton had briefly dated. She had not granted permission for the recording to be used either, and as such it too was removed from later pressings of the album.

* * *

Anton was still living with Aaron when he agreed the deal with Tee Pee. 'I told him that he had to contribute, so he was paying my rent through Tee Pee for like two months,' he recalls. They'd also talked about Aaron playing with the BJM, since the group's latest guitarist, Daniel 'Bowerbird' Koontz, now had other commitments.

Bowerbird's association with the band had begun a couple of years earlier. 'I would play tambourine or maracas every now and then at local LA shows,' he says. Then, in March 2003, Anton called to ask if he'd like to play guitar on a two-week tour of the Midwest and at a festival in Canada. They had three rehearsals to get the whole set down.

'The funny thing about those BJM songs is that, although each song was relatively easy—only two-to-four chords in each song, mostly simple strumming parts—the difficult part was that every song was the same three-to-five chords, but in different orders,' he recalls. 'One song might be E-D-A, another A-E-D, another D-A-E.' On tour, he'd sometimes get the different progressions mixed up, but because there were two other guitarists, he could mime a few chords here and there if he wasn't sure which chord was next. 'About halfway through the tour, Anton started to get wise to my trick,' he continues, 'and I remember, while miming a few bars in a song, Anton yelled to me to *play the fucking chords!* He kicked me on the side of my leg. Good times!'

Bowerbird was just starting a musical project of his own at this point, so there was an understanding that he would probably only do that one tour, but he remained on good terms with Anton and the others afterward. He doesn't play on any BJM recordings, but loaned Anton his harmonium and (possibly a tamboura) for *And This Is Our Music.*

In the event, the band left for their next tour without Bowerbird *or* Aaron, who was moving in new directions of his own. 'Around that time, Anton got me more well acquainted with Ariel Pink, so I started playing with him,' he recalls. 'It's strange how many people are interconnected. It's more than you would expect.'

Another key moment of interconnectedness came when Aaron introduced Anton to his brother, Jesse, who ended up creating the new album's artwork. Jesse first started to see Anton around town shortly after he moved there in

211

1999, and would provide some insight into the period when Anton left Laurel Canyon and returned to the city when we corresponded in 2012. 'I *officially* met Anton when he moved into the house in Echo Park where Aaron was living,' he said. 'At some point, Anton expressed interest in having me design his next album. I was more than happy to be involved. I mean, how can you resist the mere experience?

'Anton kept very busy, as he does,' he continued. 'I remember seeing various occult books lying around. As far as any memorable conversations, we most likely had brief spurts of talk back and forth. One detail I recall is speaking to Anton on a living room couch during one of the parties, where we talked for a bit within a blur of libations and music. It might've had to do with our ability to have intellectual conversations, or it could've been a matter of convenience, or purely a byproduct of substance intake—I don't think I'll ever know for sure.'*

Anton drew his initial idea for the cover onto paper bags with a red crayon while explaining to Jesse that he had built an orchestra for the record. He'd bring people into the studio, show them what he wanted, and then listened to his ideas played through others. The final cover design says 'Tomorrow's Heroes Today.' 'What do you think I meant by those words?' Anton boasted.

'That was [the BJM's] first artwork that was not Anton rushing it,' Aaron notes. 'Most of their covers are half-assed, so it was like, *Let's do something that was really, like, fuck you.* That was the culmination of all his anger that year.'

Anton was working harder than ever to make a great record. 'And he did,' says Tommy Dietrick. 'Anton made a great album with *And This Is Our Music.* I was blown away the first time I heard it.'

Anton knew Tommy was a fan of The Lilys, so had played him 'Tschusse' (an informal German farewell), which features a guest vocal by Lilys front man Kurt Heasley. ('Thank you Kurt for singing this song for me,' Anton writes in the album's liner notes. 'Did you know I cried the whole take?') This song, like the rest of *And This Is Our Music,* is equal parts haunting

---

* Jesse Frankel, a proud CAL ARTS graduate, tragically passed away on November 25, 2013, in Brooklyn, at the young age of thirty-six. At the time, he was pursuing his dream of being a professional graphic artist. His cover art for *And This Is Our Music* stands as one of his best-known pieces.

and dark. Like *Bravery*, it pulls the listener into a world of mystery and melancholy—a confessional where depression and joy overlap. 'It was like The Brian Jonestown Massacre had evolved to a new level,' says Tommy. '*Anton* had evolved to a new level.'

As well as Daniella Meeker, 'Here It Comes' features the British singer-songwriter Ed Harcourt. Ed had been in Los Angeles, taking a few days off and hanging out with some friends at a party, when around two in the morning he was accosted by a wide-eyed maniac in a double-denim suit.

'Hey, you're Ed Harcourt,' the maniac said. 'I'm Anton from The Brian Jonestown Massacre, and I need a British singer on a song I've written, so why don't you come sing on it? Or are you too much of a fucking pussy?'

The next thing Ed knew, he was in a beat-up old van with someone asleep in the back, and Anton and a friend in the front. He felt like he might have been taken hostage—not unlike Paola Simmonds or Daniel Knop must have felt all those years ago when Anton took them to Naut Humon's studio.

When they reached the studio, Anton didn't have the key, so they went in through the bathroom window. He had the track ready, and he pushed Ed to affect a much more 'British' accent during his take. Suddenly it was six in the morning, and Ed and Anton had a brief but heated argument about the song. 'He really wanted me to know what the song was about,' Ed recalls. 'He was so passionate and intense, albeit pretty unhinged.' Anton later wrote that the song was about 'being really bummed out about the way everyone just gives up and accepts this shitty world as is.' While driving back to Ed's hotel, he endearingly ranted about bands he disliked. Ed awoke a few hours later feeling like death and wondering whether the previous night had even happened. Some time later, *Beer Melodies*' John Fortunato asked Anton how he'd hooked up with Ed and Kurt.

'We are a great band,' Anton told him. 'You figure it out.'

* * *

Back in 1997, Matthew J. Tow's band, Drop City, had toured the USA and stayed in Silver Lake with Chris Barrus, who, since the days of *Methodrone*, had founded his own label, No Fi Records, but still maintained his connections with Greg and Bomp! One day, Chris asked Drop City if they'd ever heard the BJM; they hadn't, so Chris put on *Give It Back!*

213

'It was a revelation for me,' Matthew recalls. 'For the first time in a long time, I heard a band that was doing similar stuff to what I was doing. It might seem now like everyone has that sound, but in the 90s it was unusual. You really had to search for this stuff, so I felt an immediate kinship. It was one of the best albums I'd heard in a long time and I was hooked.'

Chris then asked if Drop City would like to meet the BJM, and took them over to the Echo Park house, where they were rehearsing *Strung Out In Heaven*.* Matthew says his first time meeting Anton was like seeing an old friend. Within five minutes they were sat down over a bottle of whiskey, and Anton was playing him some tunes he'd been working on, later insisting that Drop City stay with them so that he could produce some of their material, which turned out to be the title track to their record *A New Situation*.

While in LA, Matthew was fortunate enough to meet and become friends with Greg, too. Anton brought Greg down to see Drop City play at Spaceland, and subsequently Greg put out the first record by Matthew's next band, The Lovetones, *Be What You Want*, on Bomp! 'The tour may have been unsuccessful, but meeting Anton changed everything,' Matthew adds. 'He wanted me to stay and play with the BJM then and there, but I had other commitments.'

They stayed in touch, and in 2003 Matthew traveled back to the USA for an extended period to replace Kirkpatrick Thomas, who was also in a band called Spindrift, in the BJM. Anton sent him a list of songs to learn, and Matthew ended up doing two tours playing rhythm guitar in the band, beginning with the two-week trek in March for which Bowerbird was also in the lineup, followed by SXSW, where Anton got into his row with Elise. After that, the band traveled through the South and up the East Coast for a couple of shows in NYC before heading back through the Midwest. They took a break in April but were back on the road again with The Lovetones in May, this time heading up to Vancouver, gigging with The Tyde and Rick Bain along the way, before ending their run at the Casbah in San Diego in mid-May. They returned to the Casbah again in August, before heading up to Ontario for another short tour.

When they got back to LA, Anton and Matthew went into the studio to

---

* Chelsea Starr disputes this, claiming that it was *she* who arranged for Matthew and Drop City to meet Anton.

finish *And This Is Our Music*. There, Matthew showed Anton what became 'Starcleaner' (its title a nod to Jennifer Shagawat's old space in San Francisco a decade earlier) and recorded a scratch vocal for it, with the intention of re-tracking it later. To his dismay, however, Anton wound up using the scratch take on the album and never let Matthew sing it again. When the record came out, John Fortunato compared it to David Bowie's 'The Man Who Sold The World.'

Another song Matthew wrote that ended up on *And This Is Our Music* was 'A New Low In Getting High,' on which he and Anton sing co-lead. Matthew had written it with Anton in mind—Anton having already agreed to produce some Lovetones material for a new album—and thought it would suit the BJM sound. 'It was really just a simple case of, when I played Anton these two songs, he liked them, and we recorded them for *And This Is Our Music*,' Matthew recalls. For him, songwriting is an endless search for meaning, and he connected with Anton on this level. 'The true success of any great writer is to capture the essence of what it is to be human, and then to convey that to the listener, uncertainties and failures included, and in that respect, it makes Anton a great writer,' he says.

The rest of The Lovetones came over to the USA to open for the BJM for the West Coast leg of Matthew's second BJM tour. Like Tommy on the BJM/Smallstone tour, Matthew was doing two shows a night, opening with The Lovetones and then playing with the BJM. 'It was an eye-opener and a big learning curve for me, but they were truly great times,' he says.

Matthew wanted to keep playing in the BJM but had to return to Australia due to his Visa expiring. He's kept in regular contact with Anton, however, and the two remain good friends. In 2005, The Lovetones signed to Tee Pee for a couple of albums, and in 2006 they opened for the BJM on their first European tour, and then on two subsequent Australian tours.

* * *

The biggest song from *And This Is Our Music* is the ghostly 'When Jokers Attack,' which sounds a little like The Yardbirds' 'Heart Full Of Soul.' Frankie plays the main riff on his twelve-string Rickenbacker, while the background melody is played with a slide on a Vox Ultrasonic. Charles Mehling directed an equally ghostly video, rife with symbolism, for the track, having received

215

a call one day from someone at Tee Pee, asking if he'd be available to do it. He was thrilled. The idea was that Charles and his crew would go party at the new BJM house in Silverlake and film both the party and also Anton playing in his bedroom.

Charles and his friend shot all night long and into the next morning in a variety of different setups. Then the band packed up their guitars, piled into the van, and drove away on tour, leaving Charles and his friend, wasted, back at the house. They eventually left, and Charles drove home and went up to his apartment. When he came down the next day, all the windows were smashed, and all of his cameras and dollies and all of the footage he had just shot for this video were gone.

'I woke up totally hungover at two o'clock in the afternoon, and, *Oh my god*,' Charles recalls. 'They'd already said how painful it was to come up with the three grand they had to pay for it, and they're now on tour, gone. We don't have cameras. We don't have footage. We don't have money. All I could think to do was go back to that house.'

Charles grabbed his PD150 camera and a tripod, called up a different friend, and went back to Silver Lake. He knocked on the door but no one answered. 'There's no reason why anyone would be there,' he continues, 'but then this girl comes out from behind the door, and she's really beautiful. Actually, she looked a lot like Brian Jones. She had, like, a bob haircut. She was super-hungover and wasted, too, and I explained my situation, and that she was the only person left.'

Charles asked the girl if she wanted to be in the video, and she replied that she'd do it in return for an eight ball of coke. Deal done, they went through her wardrobe, found a look, and sat her on a bench. They taught her the words and had her sing through the song a couple times for practice, and then, when they rolled camera, she sang it all the way through. And that was the video.

'The Jonestown couldn't believe when they finally got their video that they weren't in it, and that their roommate, some girl, was in it, singing the whole song,' Charles adds. 'It was just a matter of chance that she was there, and she was perfect for the part.' The girl's identity remains a mystery. 'I would love to know who she was,' Charles says. 'We never spoke again. We went and edited it, and that was it.'

Early in the video, a little ceramic Japanese cat can be spotted. 'That was

the cat that they gave us when we left Japan,' Charles recalls. 'I remember
Anton really loved that cat. They were really kind to us, and they presented
that to Anton. He took it to heart, and he still had it a couple years later, sitting
on his mantelpiece.'

* * *

Raugust returned to the band during 2002–03, and there are two things that
stand out in her memory of the *And This Is Our Music* sessions. The first
is that Anton was practically living at the mixing board, and, like a mad
scientist, would tell her that he had hundreds of songs waiting to be recorded,
some over ten years old, so nobody would be able to say his early works were
better than his newer works, as the 'new' was really 'the old' mixed together
with the new. 'He never told me which was which,' she says, 'but it was all
fun to play, so I was happy to be of service.'

They'd often start recording after a gig at a local bar. They'd have a few
cocktails, collect the people they needed, get them to the studio, and track
until the next day. In Raugust's case, her flute was often the last frosty detail
to be added—if it were needed at all—but she helped Anton man the board
for a minute or two here or there while he moved mics or musically directed
the players; she'd showed up thinking she'd record and be off quickly, but
usually ending up staying longer than she was needed. Three days longer, it
turned out on this occasion, so she slept on the floor.

Near the end, Raugust found herself in need of a bath. 'I became a
stinkball, and so did Anton,' she says. 'So he steps into the bathroom to
shower and says, I am a phoenix and shall rise from my own ashes!' A few
minutes later, he emerged from the bathroom and returned to the studio,
sparkly eyed and wearing all white.

The general consensus within the band—which Raugust thought right,
too—was that they did not want flute on every song, but Anton held his
ground. 'I can write flute parts for everything!' he declared. Raugust loved
him for saying that, but she did eventually leave the band. 'I don't think I was
in the band for more than eight months, but it was one of only three bands
I've been in, and I treasure the experience,' she says.

Another returning figure was Tommy Dietrick. After Tommy's last stint
with the BJM in 2000, for the combined BJM/Smallstone tour, Dave Koenig

had taken over bass duties, but by 2003, Dave had put up with about all he could and quit following the band's Australian tour. Anton invited Tommy back, and Tommy agreed to return, in part because he was excited about the prospects for the new record, which would go on to receive rave reviews.

During a show that May at Pat's Pub in Vancouver, an audience member heckled Anton, who within a few minutes had the crowd to his aid. The mob physically forced the heckler out of the club and onto the street, never to be heard from or seen again. Most nights ended smoothly, but Anton's drinking was worsening further. He'd start the morning with vodka and vitamin water, and by the evening he was no longer able to control his temper or his outbursts. His behavior soon started crossing the line. Tommy threatened to leave if Anton kept on, but the threat seemed not to have any effect. Grabbing breakfast one morning on the way from Chicago to Minneapolis, Anton was in a particularly bad mood, and tour delirium was thick. Everyone was tired and ready to go home. Tommy accidentally—or perhaps purposefully— tossed a food wrapper into the back of the van. The wrapper hit Anton, who retaliated by throwing a scalding hot cup of coffee in Tommy's face.

The moment the band arrived in Minneapolis, Tommy called his girlfriend and told her he would be coming home a few days early. He booked a flight home after that night's gig at Bill Sullivan's 400 Bar. Tommy usually handed Anton his bass toward the end of gigs so that he could jam out the last song of the set, but that night, as the last song faded, Tommy unplugged his bass and walked straight off the stage and out the door. He didn't tell anyone he was leaving except Travis Snyder, whom he had forced to pay up before the show.

Tommy wouldn't play another show with the BJM for five months, and that next show would be his last. Two weeks after he got home from that final gig, an excited Adam Shore called him on his cell phone to tell him *Dig!* had just won the Grand Jury Prize at Sundance, to which Tommy replied, 'That's great. I just quit the band.'*

---

* Tommy went on to form his own band, Sky Parade, and to found the Desert Sun, Desert Stars festival, and the Starry Nights festival.

After Tommy quit, the band headed up to Portland, where they asked Matt Hollywood to stand in on bass. '[That] was fun,' he later said of the impromptu performance, 'to play with Anton again, for just one night.' After that, the band picked up again in Denver, traveled west to California, then zigzagged up and down the coast a few times. Just before Christmas, Matt's band, The Out Crowd, opened for the BJM in Portland.

Ricky Maymi was next to re-join the band—after a decade-long absence— soon after the BJM's performance at the Sunset Junction Street Fair.* The band's former TVT labelmates, Guided By Voices—Adam Shore's second signing—played the Fair that night after the BJM. 'Anton was pretty crazy and funny onstage, saying bunch of non-sequiturs between songs, kind of phonetic,' the band's guitarist, Doug Gillard, recalls. 'He'd shout something like, *Cocaine Unicorn!* That wasn't the name of the song they played, he'd just say it, and they'd go into something.'

Cocaine Unicorn was actually the name of Collin Hegna's band with Ryan Sumner. They'd opened for both the BJM and The Out Crowd, and after Tommy's exit, Ryan recommended Anton bring in Collin on playing bass. (Ryan himself had been playing drums with the band for a bit during a time when Dan wasn't available.) 'Anton and I ended up in LA, and Dan decided he was going to go back to school, so all the sudden we needed a bass player and a drummer,' says Frankie. 'Anton's like, *Remember those guys? Cocaine Unicorn? Let's get them, we can get that little duo* … and that *sucked. Totally* sucked. That's why Ricky played drums on that tour.'

---

* Ricky and Anton had not spoken for years, until they began to rebuild their friendship around the time of the BJM/Smallstone shows.

Collin's first gig was December 27, 2003, opening for Love at the Fonda, a few weeks before *Dig!* premiered at Sundance, on January 18, 2004. At age twelve, Collin had started working for his dad at Rainbow Recording in Portland. He began studying music at the University of Oregon in Eugene in 1996, and would hone his engineering and composing skills while there. After graduating with a BS in music, he moved back to Portland and played in bands around town.

Ryan didn't have the best experience during his time in the BJM. 'Anton would yell at him, so he would just freeze up,' Frankie laughs. 'He was just a young kid, you know, with a great haircut. He'd be, like, *I can't handle this, man!* And I'd be, like, *Dude, you gotta hang in there!*'

Ricky, meanwhile, had made his live return at Spaceland in September, following a couple of weeks of rehearsals with the new lineup. The ensuing tour, he says, was 'brutal, but it broke my back in really well. Everything seemed easy after that.'

One of the first things Ricky did once he was back was to play drums on the band's next single, 'If Love Is The Drug, Then I Want To OD,' which they recorded in Orlando, right after a show there at the Social. Chris Tucker from the band The Situation had helped write the song a few years earlier. 'It was a song we used to just warm up to, to get our sound levels right,' says Frankie. 'There were no lyrics written, but we'd start jamming that song a little bit, then we'd kick into the set. Chris Tucker was like, *Dude, you guys should make that a song! Why isn't that a song?* And then he came into the studio and had some lyrics.'

'BJM had this song with no words that was practically the same chord progression as a song I wrote,' Chris himself notes. 'It was kind of freaky that we both had written the same song without knowing each other. Later, we were staying up all night at Frankie's, passing the guitars around, and I played my song. Anton played his instrumental version, and we worked the two songs into one. A couple years later, he was saying all this shit about the song from the new Dandys record sounding like "If Love Is The Drug," and I thought that was funny—because "If Love Is The Drug" is just a variation on [The Dandy Warhols'] "Minnesoter." Basically, we had all been writing the same song for five years.'

Chris was born in Wyoming but grew up back east, playing in bands in

Delaware before moving to LA in 2000. It was around that time that he met Anton and Frankie and helped write the song, which they recorded for the *Zero* EP, with Mara Keagle on vocals. A year or so later, Chris moved to Philadelphia, to focus on The Situation; The Situation did well, but split up soon after the release of their first and only self-titled album, which was issued in April 2006 on Ben Vendetta and Arabella Proffer's Elephant Stone Records.

For the single version of the tune, the backing vocals were sung by one Josie Fluri, whose recruitment is another typically BJM tale. 'We played a show and Tee Pee wanted us to go into the studio and re-record [the song], so we booked the studio after the Florida show,' Frankie recalls. 'Anton grabbed [Josie] to sing to it, and I did all the crazy fuzz guitar. That was a wild time.'

Josie was living in Orlando and managing the Social when she wasn't playing with her band, New Roman Times. A friend came up to her and passed along the message that Anton was looking for someone to do backing vocals on the single, and that it had to be that night, because it had to delivered to the label the next day. Anton then approached Josie, complimented her work with New Roman Times, asked her to come to the studio around four the next morning, wrote down the directions on a napkin, and made her pinkie swear that she would be there.

Aware of the BJM's reputation, Josie brought a couple of her friends with her to the studio. Once in the foyer of the building, she had to step over the rest of the band—completely passed out—to get through the studio. Then Anton walked in and took her over to the control room, where an engineer was waiting—a heavier-set good ol' boy wearing nothing but basketball shorts, running shoes, and a backward baseball cap—before guiding her back to the vocal booth, handing her a pair of headphones and a microphone, and walking back out.

The music starts playing. Josie stands there, listening. Anton stops the track and re-enters the vocal booth.

'Why aren't you singing?' he asks.

'I've never heard this song,' she tells him. 'I don't know how it goes. What do you want me to sing?'

'In the chorus, if you could just sing, *You're so high, high, highhh*, and then just like, on everything else, just like *High high high* but like *Hiii-iii-iiigh*. Like that.'

'Okay, but where does it go? Can we just listen to this together?'

They listen to about half the song, and then Anton stops the track. 'Okay. You got it? Just, the next time, it's, like, *double* that. That's cool right?'

With that, he walks back into the control room. They start rolling. Josie tries it. Anton has her do it again, over and over and over.

'He's very hands-on in the studio,' Josie recalls. 'The engineer was just sitting there, cueing stuff up. Anton was very particular. Every take I did sounded the same to me, but he kept having me try it again. He wanted it a very certain way.'

Three hours later, the sun is coming up and the track still isn't done, so Josie and her pals try to sneak out, but Anton comes out as they're getting to the car. Josie lies that she's just grabbing a cigarette, so Anton pulls one out and joins her, and then asks her if she would do it one more time. So she does it one more time.

The track stops. 'That was perfect,' he says.

Anton offered to pay Josie for the session but she declined, opting instead for the credit, only for Anton to forget to credit her, though this was remedied on *The Singles Collection*. 'When the single came out it was like, *To everybody who's helped me with all these songs, you know who you are*, or something like that,' Josie laughs. 'I was like, *Oh my god, I'm gonna kill him!*'

Dale Bookout says Anton had him organize the late-night session. 'We had a distributor in England, Cargo Records,' he explains. 'The guy in England agreed to distribute [*And This Is Our Music*] if he could also have an exclusive single, so I got [the single] and pressed that real quick.'

'Two mixes exist,' says violinist Zy Orange Lyn, who also plays on the track. 'One with loud fiddle, one with buried fiddle.' (Zy would also play acoustic guitar and sing backing vocals during his brief time with the group.)

* * *

With Dan Allaire, Frankie Teardrop, Rob Campanella, and now Ricky Maymi back in the band, the group had arrived at the core lineup that would remain in place until 2015—a few minor adjustments aside, that is. 'That tour had a Christmas break, then we toured with Guided By Voices,' says Ricky. 'That's when Collin joined. Then we went to Australia, [but] with Koenig. Can't remember why.'

When Anton heard that Guided By Voices' Bob Pollard had liked the way he had been funny and crazy onstage at Sunset Junction, Anton changed his tone. 'Anton was very not funny,' says Doug Gillard. 'Very serious, very somber. I think he was just being contrarian.' He does however remember Anton as being well behaved on the tour.

In Florida, the GBV fans had started this ritual where they would shake up beer bottles, pop 'em open, and spray beer all over the band, so when GBV and the BJM were playing Tallahassee, Doug, Bob, and the others in GBV all wore rain ponchos and swim goggles, ready for the gag. A woman in the crowd had been spraying Doug with beer, and when they ended their song, she reached up and yelled, 'Cheers, dude!' Doug, irritated, grabbed his bottle and toasted her forcefully. The bottle shattered in his hand and tore the skin on his pinky wide open. The band started playing with Doug bleeding onstage. All over his guitar. All over the floor. He threw the guitar down and walked off, but the band kept playing.

'Anton found some paper towels and some duct tape, and bandaged it up right then, right there, and I was able to go backstage and finish the set,' Doug recalls. 'He was the only one back there who cared, so I'm thankful to him for caring.'

223

Zy, who'd been playing with the BJM since Collin's first show, when they opened for Love, helped Anton patch up Doug's finger, and his memories of the event match up with Doug's. 'Some of our gear was still onstage and got damaged, [but] GBV graciously paid for the repairs,' he later recalled. 'Unfortunately, Bob hurt his back at a show in Dallas, [so our tour with them] was cut short, but it was great while it lasted.'

After Orlando, the BJM went through the South and the Midwest, and then over to the Mid-Atlantic for some more with The High Strung. Once in New York, they recorded some live tracks at WFMU that would later appear on *Tepid Peppermint Wonderland*, including 'Swallowtail' and 'Let Me Stand Next To Your Flower.' After a short break, the band headed over to the UK for a run of shows with BRMC that took up the bulk of November,* before rounding out the month with some Canadian dates with The High Dials, and then some more shows in LA and the Midwest.

---

* That run of sixty-plus shows included a number of dates in the USA, as well as the trip to the UK to support BRMC.

Almost a year would pass before GBV invited the BJM to play with them again, at the last show on their Farewell Tour, once again at the Fonda. One of Jennifer Brandon's old clients, Pete Yorn, was backstage with a friend of his, talking to Bob and Doug. Anton was standing somewhere nearby, glaring at them. When Pete noticed Anton, he said, 'Hey, man! It's Pete! Remember? We were at this Hollywood party together?' Anton didn't smile or say a word. When the set change came, Doug spent around five minutes tuning up, setting up his pedal board, making sure everything is ready. Then he came back down the backstage area, so they could all walk back on together as a band, and someone asked him, 'Hey man, did you see the fight? Anton and some guy were tumbling around the room!'

Pete's buddy had gone down the hallway to use the backstage bathroom, and Anton, who was hiding in a side room, had stuck out his leg and tripped him on his way back. The guy got up, turned around, and Anton charged him. 'They had a rolling, tumbling fistfight, rolling over chairs and shit,' Doug laughs. 'I don't know what the outcome of that was. I don't know if they stayed at the show.'

Collin would play live with the BJM for the next fifteen years. He also co-writes the music for Federale with Carl Werner, and co-founded Revolver Studios with Nalin Silva in Southeast Portland above Kelly's Olympian, where Clint Eastwood's famous, Emmy-nominated *It's Halftime In America* 2012 Super Bowl commercial was recorded, among many other projects.

Cocaine Unicorn eventually dissolved, but Ryan and Collin continued playing music together until 2005, when Ryan passed away at the age of twenty-seven. Collin was on tour with the BJM at time, on the way to Albuquerque from Dallas, when Ryan, who'd lived with a blood condition since birth, suffered a blood clot that traveled to his heart. His mom found him struggling to breathe and rushed him to the hospital, but he later died.

'A film like *Dig!* is probably the biggest commercial tool a band could ever dream up,' Ondi Timoner told the *Guardian* during the summer after the film's release. 'The bands featured in it are selling records everywhere the film plays. When it goes to festivals, the record stores sell out.'

This came as a surprise to everyone, not least the BJM, who by now were used to playing to empty crowds. 'We were on tour with Dead Meadow, and we played in Olympia, Washington, and not one person turned up for the gig,' Frankie recalls. 'The owner was like, *Hey, man, I'll just give you guys a hundred bucks, you don't even have to play.* And Anton's like, *No, we're fucking playing!* We played in front of the bartender in this fucking dump … we were like, *Why are we doing this?* But that was Anton.'

By that time, the film had played at the Sundance, Newport, and Provincetown film festivals; before the year was over, it would play festivals all over Europe. Then in 2005, it played all over the world. 'Nobody thought the movie was going to change a damn thing the way we acted or performed, because we were stuck in loose cannon mode,' Frankie continues. 'It wasn't until we started getting bumped up to bigger venues that we even started soundchecking, because we wouldn't even fucking soundcheck half the time. We'd just load all our own shit and do it.'

Dale Bookout echoes Frankie's thoughts on the film's initial impact. 'We weren't expecting anything to happen from it. We were lucky enough that the timing worked out … the timing of [*And This Is Our Music*] and the documentary sort of went hand in hand, so this small label that we were benefited from the huge amounts of publicity that the band was getting, both positive and negative, all of her efforts, winning the Grand Jury Prize at Sundance, and because of that now they were being asked to play these specialty one-off shows … and it got them up in front of music supervisors' eyes for TV shows and commercials and all these types of things. It afforded them lots of opportunities that they didn't have beforehand.'

The film made a huge splash, with even mainstream media outlets like the BBC reporting on its Sundance win. Not two weeks after the film came out, Anton shared his own thoughts on *Dig!* on the BJM website:

> I care very much about my work, I always have, and hope that that was made clear in the film … I was shocked and let down when I saw the end result. Several years of our hard work was reduced at best to a series of punch-ups and mishaps taken out of context, and at worst bold faced lies and misrepresentation of fact … I accept that people will make up their own minds about this film when they see it.

Jeff Davies has similar grievances about *Dig!* 'After filming for a year or two, she tried to send a little edited version of something to MTV,' he begins. 'They declined it, so she compiled more footage, did a re-edit, until finally she was like, *I'm just going to put it together myself, and put it out myself.* At this point it's been, like, nine years, and so many people have gotten involved, there was probably so much footage at that point, that in the movie there'd be a scene, and it'll be *this*, and then *this* happens, and it equals *this*, but in actuality, the three things have nothing to do with each other, and maybe the last part will be a fight, which she would have started with, and then edited backward to make it seem like it could have happened that way. The first two times I saw it, it was very painful, because it was so untrue—it didn't even talk about what happened to me—and I was calling out Ondi all the time as a troublemaker. She would set up little scenes of fights and be peeking through the window with her camera, you know, while you were fucking or shooting up or whatever, and she'd be talking to you, and then you'd notice, across the room, peeking underneath a hat, was a hidden camera.'

By the time *Dig!* came out, Anton had logged fifteen years in The Brian Jonestown Massacre. After its release, the band's publicist, Betsy Palmer, would grow frustrated at the amount of effort she had to put in to keep journalists focused on the music, rather than Anton's antics. 'As his publicist though five releases, the last years of the filming for the movie *Dig!*, and the chaos, both good and bad, that followed its release, I have been greatly disappointed with journalists who have promised to stay on track, [to] write about the music and his creative process,' she says. 'At the end of the movie it appeared that he had spiraled off the deep end, when in fact he continued to make records and have successful tours and never stopped working.'

Matt Hollywood attended a screening of *Dig!* at the Los Angeles Film Festival in June 2004, and shared his thoughts about the film with the *Sydney Morning Herald* that December, when it was screened at Australia's Resfest. 'I was sitting in the midst of one hundred people, watching my youth unfold on the screen, hearing the crowd gasp or laugh at incidents I was involved in,' he said. 'It was, I would have to say, rather odd … I've witnessed Anton be the most charming, articulate, caring person you could ever meet and then become the nastiest, most vicious person you would never want to meet. The film, to be honest, captures both those sides of him.'

The film will be debated forever, but no one denies that, after it came out, everything exploded. 'It was interesting to see people who suddenly were like, *Whoa! You know them? You were there?*' says Arabella Proffer. 'Gigs outside of LA and SF started getting super-annoying. People who never cared about them before were suddenly showing up for the shit-show. They'd heckle, and still do to this day. Anton gives them what they want, I guess— they want what they saw in the movie.'

A little over a week after Anton posted his rebuttal of the film on the BJM website, the Charles Mehling–directed music video for 'When Jokers Attack' was released. Nobody kept it a secret that the song, its title, and the video were aimed square at The Dandy Warhols, in what was the last real attack launched in the BJM–Dandys 'press war.' Anton didn't even *need* a press war by then, but as anyone with half a brain would, he took advantage of the film and the narrative it presented to increase his group's exposure. 'We set out to change the world,' he said before the band's first Australian show in Sydney that May, offering a subtle dig at the Dandys. 'We're expressing ourselves in different ways. It's not limited to four figurines standing on a stage.'

According to Frankie, the BJM's first tour down under is when Anton *really* lost his shit. Frankie himself had wanted to go out to Australia a

227

week early, before anybody else in the band, to hang out with Matthew Tow before the tour kicked in, but once Anton and Ricky found out about that, they changed their flights to go with him. 'That was hell,' Frankie says. 'We did a radio interview. Me and Anton got fucking hammered in this radio studio, and we're just playing whatever we wanted live on air, and we finally got kicked out of there. They didn't know what to do with us. Anton was drinking, like, a gallon of vodka a day, and he wouldn't *go to sleep*, man. He was just pumped on adrenaline and just wanted to beat the fucking shit out of everybody. Everybody. On the street. The fuckin' cashier. Didn't matter who. And we were going, *How are we going to get through this?* This was supposed to be a peaceful Australian trip.'

The Australian press likewise gorged on Anton's persona in their reviews of the film, the records, and the band's shows. Reviewing the BJM's appearance at the Hi-Far Bar in Melbourne for the *Age*, Craig Mathieson described proceedings as 'more a virulent confrontation between the bitter, obsessive ego of a fallen artist and a fractured audience than a rock concert.' Before their set, Anton had brought a local busker onstage. The audience responded with confusion. 'Respect this man,' Anton commanded, before ranting about the Iraq War and his ill health, at one point coughing phlegm into his hand and showing it to the audience, before using it as hair gel.

'I heard some stories about that tour,' Matt Hollywood later noted. 'You got Anton at his very worst on those shows.'

Meanwhile, back in the USA, the *Dig!* buzz became an avalanche. 'I have footage of myself on the verge of tears because they were such vacuums of humanity,' Ondi told MTV, which praised the young director for capturing 'lightning in a bottle.' 'They would never take responsibility for the way they behaved to each other. They would just get more ornery as the drinks set in.'

Shortly after the film's New York Premiere in March 2004, as part of MoMa and the Film Society of Lincoln Center's 'New Directors/New Films' series, A.O. Scott of the *New York Times* concluded, 'If universities ever start graduate programs in rock stardom, *Dig!* will surely be a cornerstone of the curriculum … as both an instruction manual and a cautionary tale.' As the film opened in theaters across the country, more articles followed.

By October, Ondi and her partner, Vasco Lucas Nunes, had an eleven-month-old son, Joaquim, born just three days after Ondi finished the film.

'He's kept us centered,' Ondi told *Indie Wire*. 'When we won the Grand Jury Prize at Sundance, I had to go home to breastfeed … my feet were firmly planted on the ground, because I was a new mother.'

The acclaim Ondi has received for her work—and her subsequent successes as a filmmaker—are well deserved. Whatever anyone's opinions of *Dig!* may be, mine included, it's hard not to admire her dedication and savvy. Band members and associates may disagree with each other over the *meaning* of *Dig!*, but that's part of the film's staying power. The BJM fan community's endless debating of the film keeps it relevant and alive. Each time I watch it, I see something new. In 2009, *Paste* magazine declared it to be the second greatest rock documentary of all time, just behind *Dont Look Back* but ahead of both *Gimme Shelter* and *The Kids Are Alright*.

Later that October, Ondi was screening *Dig!* in Vienna when she received the news that Greg Shaw had died of heart failure in Los Angeles at the age of fifty-five. Earlier that week, he had developed extremely high blood sugar and was rushed to the hospital. For several days he remained stable and conscious, and his doctors were optimistic that he would recover. Then, out of nowhere, he went into cardiac arrest. They tried to save him, but their efforts proved futile.

Ondi dedicated the screening to Greg's memory. The BJM had been the only new band Greg had really worked with in the decade leading up to his death, in part because of his disinterest in the 90s alternative scene, but also because of his declining health.

A couple of weeks after Greg's death, the band played a Halloween show in Toronto. 'With his head down and back almost turned fully against the crowd, Newcombe and the band barreled through a set that cherry-picked gems from their immense back catalogue,' *Chart Attack* reported. 'With his band furiously pummeling the crowd with wave upon wave of feedback, Newcombe carefully placed his guitar by one of the amps, grabbed his coat from a corner, and calmly sauntered offstage. The band blistered onward for another good few minutes before strolling offstage themselves, but it was obvious what this night was all about: Newcombe was here to play his music, to silence the unbelievers. And with an empty stage and a wall of screech still firing from the speakers of now-abandoned guitars, it's clear that's what he did.'

Others in the press struggled to find the appeal. In his review of the same show for *PopMatters*, David Marchese wrote, 'It's when the music stops that Anton Newcombe seems unsure of who he his, or at least who he's supposed to be.' Suddenly thrust into the spotlight, a new string of challenges arose for the band, and it was up to them to prove everyone wrong once again.

* * *

In the wake of *Dig!*'s release, MTV began associating the BJM with the 'garage-rock revival,' but Anton dismissed the comparison. 'All these people have gotten a lot of notoriety recently with garage stuff—The Strokes, The White Stripes, all these bands—I wanted to do shit that they aren't capable of doing,' he said. 'It's not built into their project.'

Either way, *Dig!* ended up being the biggest boost in publicity the Jonestown had received since TVT had put its muscle behind the band almost a decade earlier. The same was true of countless other bands: even The Out Crowd got some buzz on the now-dying MTV, while of course The Warlocks and BRMC took advantage of the *Dig!* effect where they could.

It was around this time that The Black Angels—a band undoubtedly influenced by the BJM—first formed in Austin, Texas. The Black Angels could be credited with bringing the new 'psych scene' to the forefront of popular culture, leading directly to the founding of the Austin Psych Fest, now called Levitation, which has in turn inspired smaller psychedelic music festivals around the globe since the first APF in 2008. The Black Angels and Spindrift both played the first year of that festival.

The Warlocks, who were at the time enjoying an opening slot with BRMC for their tour in support of *Howl!*, tried in vain to distance themselves from the BJM. 'Is there ever too much made of The Brian Jonestown Massacre connection to The Warlocks?' Michael Christopher asked Bobby, in an interview with *PopMatters*. 'Absolutely,' Bobby replied, before abruptly leaving the room. The Warlocks would have a tougher time breaking out of Anton's shadow than Peter and BRMC.

Around the time the BJM opened for Guided By Voices at the Fonda, MTV announced that Tee Pee would shortly be releasing *Tepid Peppermint Wonderland: A Retrospective*. Those who'd seen the film wondered if a 'greatest hits' compilation marked the end of The Brian Jonestown Massacre for good. But Dale had seen an opportunity in *Dig!*'s continuing exposure, and he convinced Anton to let him put the compilation together so they'd have a product out while the film was still hot.

'He was in the middle of working on *We Are The Radio*, but that wasn't going to be done in time, so I asked him how he felt about it, and he allowed me to do it,' Dale says. 'I was given a very small budget, and I went about picking every song that I loved and deciding how I wanted to put it together and separating them and re-sequencing it until my ears bled.'

Some critics felt the compilation fell short of the group's potential. Anton responded by making it clear that *Tepid Peppermint Wonderland* was not meant as a swan song, but rather as a reminder to everyone of what the BJM were all about. 'We're not finished, not just yet anyway,' he declared. 'We decided that it would be a good idea to exploit any attention that comes our way from the film, Sundance and the DVD. It seemed fair.'

Unlike *Your Side Of Our Story*—a free download of unpolished versions of songs from the back catalogue Anton had made available for free online around the same time—*Tepid Peppermint Wonderland* was to be a proper release. The band toured the States in support of the two-disc release in November, and, after that, Anton got back to work on the *We Are The Radio* mini-album, some of which made it onto the tail end of *Tepid Peppermint Wonderland*.

231

In exchange for bringing *We Are The Radio* to Tee Pee, Dale bought Anton an old Mercedes, which was later christened the *Grey Ghost*. Dale had to go out to LA, where court proceedings had begun over the unauthorized use of Elise Pearson's voice on *And This Is Our Music*. Anton told Dale there was no point in staying in a hotel—he should just stay with him—and picked him up at the airport in the *Grey Ghost* before taking him on a tour of what Dale fondly remembers as '*Anton's* LA, which was one of the greatest experiences I've ever had. He's a really great guy when you get to just see him in his element.'*

As well as the business with Elise, Dale had another issue to deal with: TVT's refusal to allow Tee Pee to include any of Anton or Matt's songs from *Strung Out In Heaven* on *Tepid Peppermint Wonderland*. 'TVT is a machine, very much a business,' Dale notes. 'They weren't about to go in and just give

---

* I'm guessing that the *Grey Ghost* is probably the same car Courtney Taylor-Taylor said Anton was sleeping in for a time. Later, after the car died, Anton left it for good on Silver Lake Boulevard. Frankie's girlfriend, Erika, had an old Mercedes as well, and says she wanted the *Ghost* for parts, but claims Anton wouldn't let her near it.

those songs away.' In place of the studio cuts on *Wonderland* are versions of 'Let Me Stand Next To Your Flower,' 'Hide And Seek,' and 'Swallowtail' pulled from a live radio broadcast on WFMU, recorded on October 23, 2003, and provided to Dale by one of the station's DJs, Pseu Braun.

Pseu saw the band for the first time at the Loop Lounge in Passaic. 'The minute Anton walks onstage, he has this white outfit on and this Peter Tork from The Monkees haircut, and they're calling him Davy Jones because of his haircut, there's all these Jersey yahoos screaming and taunting him,' she recalls. 'He's ignoring them but I'm horrified. So they start playing, people are still taunting him, and Joel nonchalantly flicks his lit cigarette right at this guy's fucking head.' Instead of going after Joel, however, the guy lunges at Anton. A brawl ensues. 'Every time I saw them, I've never seen Anton initiate any conflict. It's always somebody else that initiates it—often, of course, the audience. In this case, all Anton had to do was walk onstage.'

By the time of the 2003 WFMU session, Pseu was in awe of Anton's commitment to his revolution. 'He's completely influenced all this cool stuff, all this rock and roll,' she says. 'He's singlehandedly changed the game, not just for his band but everybody. He posted every single fucking BJM song online for free. This was unprecedented.'*

The following year, Anton returned to WFMU for another interview wherein he revealed his thoughts about *Dig!* as well as his feelings about the recent death of Elliott Smith, with whom he revealed he had developed a close friendship in the years leading up to his death.† He explained that he

---

* The others songs from the WFMU session not included on *Tepid Peppermint Wonderland* can be found online as part of WFMU's extensive Free Music Archive. 'Those tracks were made available right away,' Pseu explains. 'The sessions were recorded at WFMU, engineered at WFMU, and we made a digital recording right there and handed that over, and they signed an artist's release, our project called the free music archive, called fma.org, makes music available for free to whole world. Every band that comes through internationally or domestically, they hopefully sign an FMA agreement, and then whatever live session they have with us goes onto the free music archive. That music is signed away to the FMA so you can go in and like a library look up the music and get all the tracks is some sort of order, so the BJM recordings were made available right away, and we burned a disc for Anton, so he got the source material right away.' Pseu also notes that the WFMU sessions in Jersey City were engineered by a woman named Diane Kamikaze. 'Unfortunately she didn't get mentioned on *Tepid Peppermint Wonderland*, but I just think it was something that was overlooked.'
† Smith died on October 21, 2004, after an argument with his girlfriend, former Warlock and BJM alumnus Jennifer Chiba, at their home in Silver Lake. (Due to questionable evidence, some have accused Jennifer of murdering him.) 'He was among my very best friends,' Anton told *Mojo* around the same time. 'I think of him every day, with every breath I take.'

did not know the details surrounding what has since become of indie rock's greatest mysteries, but discussed his own struggles with suicidal thoughts and how he had tried to get Elliott to talk to Dallas Taylor.

'The last time that I really was like an inch away from killing myself … this amazing thing happened,' Anton told Pseu. 'I scored all this smack … the mood was right, and I said my goodbyes. Perfect environment, and you know what happened? It just dawned on me that, *Wow, I could do this.* This is a done deal. I mean, all I have to do is follow through, and then it was so unimportant. It was like, *Wow, I could do this any time.* And it was super-liberating, and for me it was a non-issue. I never was depressed or somber again.'

Pseu understood. 'He really went on in his way to defend his honor, which he felt was possibly destroyed in those moments on film—all those outbursts, all that kind of behavior. On the one hand, it's part of who he is as a leader—to be able to complete projects and to direct the sound of the band and the players, he needs to be that person at times—but at the same time he was struggling with demons, and that was unfortunately what was captured on film.'

Anton was so impressed with the interview that when *Dig!* later came out on DVD, he agreed that a Best Buy exclusive edition of it would come with a copy of his conversation with Pseu. 'He knew that the movie was valuable to the legacy of the BJM, and worth it all,' she says. 'On one side he kind of stamped his feet about it, but on the other he knew, the way people are reacting to it, responding to it, [he was] getting their attention. Maybe it's not the greatest thing, but this was a moment, for better or worse.'

233

* * *

Tee Pee pushed *Tepid Peppermint Wonderland* with as much energy as TVT had invested in *Strung Out In Heaven*, albeit on a smaller budget, but with the industry changing around them all the time, those efforts proved less and less relevant. 'Independent rock' was now in, and in a big way. As the seven-hundred-pound alternative gorilla had morphed into shock rock and nu-metal toward the turn of the century, a pathway was made for the post-punk and garage-rock revivals. For a retro-futurist outfit like the BJM, *Dig!* came at the perfect time.

'They wound up getting another champion in Tee Pee,' says TVT's Adam Shore, who, in observing the band's hugely expanding fan base, felt vindicated in his original vision for the band. '*Tepid Peppermint Wonderland* is an important document to have, for everybody. It was better for the band to go to Tee Pee than it would have been to do another record on TVT with even higher expectations and probably less of a chance of it being successful.'

The album's liner notes are by Mary Huhn, a music editor for the *New York Post*. Both she and Adam Shore are thanked in the text, as are Greg, Scott Pollack, Pseu, and one Corey Seymore, who edited the notes. 'Mary Huhn had been a big fan of the band for a long time, so she really jumped at the opportunity to write the liner notes,' says Dale. 'And then Mary Martley, the photographer, was so great to hook me up with all those wonderful photos because she had been documenting the band forever.* We put it together and I gave Anton the proof of it, and let him see what I did, and he said it was okay, so we put it out.'

Some of Mary Martley's photos were shot at a show at Mercury Lounge in New York on June 12, 2004, a couple of months before *Tepid Peppermint Wonderland* came out. That night, the BJM shared the bill with Dead Meadow. One of owners of Tee Pee paid the band to fly all the way out from LA, and a promotions company in NYC called Shout! ran the gig. 'Anton said if he was going to come out there … he wanted at least two shows, and for the second show he wanted to make a lot of money,' Dale recalls. 'So one of the label guys had an apartment in a floor above the Tee Pee offices, and he paid the BJM to come up there and play in his living room.'

For the Shout! show, Anton wanted to find an African drum circle, strobe lights, some huge down-feather pillows, and some swords. 'The hardest part was securing the drum circle,' says Dale. 'I talked him out of the swords. That's not a good idea in any situation. I put an ad up on Craigslist. We didn't hardly have any money, so it wasn't like I could just go hire people. Everything I had to do was all by the skin of my teeth.'

The band's last song was 'Hyperventilation.' Anton set up the drum circle and taught them the beat right before soundcheck. 'They were going to go on into this drone like the song goes into, and then Anton was going to take those pillows and rip them open, and then the strobe lights were going to come on, and there'd be feathers flying everywhere,' Dale adds.

234

---

* All the iconic photos in the *Tepid Peppermint Wonderland* collection are by Martley, who'd followed the band since she first saw them on their first US tour in '97.

The drum circle started, but when they turned on the strobe lights they blew a fuse; all the lights went out, but the band's amps were still juiced, so the band carried on playing, in complete darkness, for probably a good five or six minutes while Dale ran around, trying to figure out how to get these strobe lights back on. He managed to get them on just as the song changed, but Anton had already torn open the pillows. Feathers floated out all across the venue. It looked like everything had gone totally to plan, just like Joel's first show in the Haight Street basement—just as Anton had planned it, before he ever stepped foot on the plane. 'There's feathers all in the air, all over the audience, and they just hung in the air forever until they finished the song,' Dale continues. 'Then they walked off the stage. When Dead Meadow came out for their set, the feathers were still in the air, and they thought it was so cool that they took a picture of it. If you notice, Dead Meadow's record that came out after that show is called *Feathers*.'

* * *

With the DVD release of *Dig!* in April of 2005, Anton and the BJM were catapulted into cult status. Fans shared it with their friends, and bands played it in their touring vans.

235

Tres Warren and Elizabeth Hart of Psychic Ills are among those who credit the BJM's influence on the broader psych scene. They'd seen them a few times in the early 2000s, and as Tres notes, 'They'd never finish a set. There'd be a problem with the sound that would lead to an argument with the sound guy or a fight with the crowd. A lot of people would leave … but I got it. That's what happens when you're trying to make something the best it can be and it feels like everything's conspiring against you. When you're putting every ounce of your existence into something and you're obsessed with it all the time, not just for the hour that you're playing a show … it can be a hard thing, but that's what separates the wheat from the chaff.'

Craig Dyer of The Underground Youth credits the BJM as inspiring his work as well. 'I was young and impressionable and they were the coolest band I had ever seen or heard. The style. The music. The attitude. I walked home from the show thinking 'I'm going to start a band,' he says. 'That's an impact they've had from their beginnings to the present day, they've inspired and influenced a whole generation of artists.'

An entire subculture grew out of the film and its impact—one that Anton was not happy about. 'The film tells a story,' he said in 2005. 'That story is not the truth. I was let down. I felt ripped off and cheated. Ultimately, I think they could have done something important. What a waste.'

Ondi understandably reacted negatively to Anton's dismissal of the film in interviews. 'He lashes out at me all the time,' she said around the same time. 'I prefer not to listen to that fake British accent any more.'

Whatever the gripe, it is undeniable that many of Anton's new fans were exposed to his music through *Dig!*, because after it came out, the number of people at the band's concerts multiplied exponentially. Not *all* of them were hecklers, but many a BJM newbie coming to their shows—now selling out on a regular basis—wondered about the absence of Jeff, Matt, and Joel.

Jeff, to his dismay, had been cut from the picture completely. 'These people will talk shit, even in *Dig!*' he says. 'They did a special edition with the second DVD, and they interviewed everyone except me. And they were like, *We can't get a hold of Jeff, he's off high somewhere.* I feel it's just something people repeat, because I've had the same number and lived in the same place for years … so when people say they can't get a hold of me, it's bullshit.'

Matt was still fronting The Out Crowd in Portland and prepping for a month-long national tour with the Dandys that winter. When asked why he'd moved to Oregon in the first place, he said, 'It was the only place I knew people who weren't strung out or dangerously insane.'

Joel was busy finding himself and fronting his own new outfit, The Dilettantes, back in San Francisco, and trying to stay in the game by other means. This included doing a guest role on *Gilmore Girls*, starring as himself in a mock band (alongside Sebastian Bach) called Hep Alien, which falls apart in the show in ways that parody how the BJM collapsed at the Viper Room. (The episode was titled 'He's Slippin' 'Em Bread … Dig?')

Joel had been approached to do the show after his own *Dig!* persona began to resonate throughout pop culture along with Anton's. 'I knew [executive producer] Dan [Palladino] had written some of *Family Guy*, which I'm a fan of, so I thought, *Oh yeah, that'll be fun*,' he told *Entertainment Weekly*, to whom Sebastian Bach recalled, 'I was all excited to recreate the fight from *Dig!* I was like, *I don't need no stuntman, dude!* And I tore a bunch of ligaments in my left knee. It's rock'n'roll. It's okay. I'm on Motrin.'

Joel had also been travelling with Ondi and the film to various festivals, where he'd offer handshakes and commentary. People would ask him what the high point of the film was, to which Joel would reply, 'There was a point where I stayed up for five days. I was pretty high then.'

Joel's promotional duties for the film conveniently ended on the day the DVD came out, April 16, 2005, following a screening at Metreon's Action Theater in San Francisco. Even as he politely mingled with fans, friends and co-workers, he was relieved that in a few hours he would never have to sit through the film again. 'I've had to see this thing thirty times,' he groaned, abruptly ducking backstage after introducing the movie to the gathered audience. He'd turned down the invitation to narrate the film, handing off the task to Courtney Taylor-Taylor instead. 'I wasn't quite ready to be the spokesman for all this jive,' he noted that night. He was also drug-free, working a steady job at Amoeba on Haight and, after years of couch-surfing, living in his own studio apartment in Nob Hill.

Back in 2004, when a girl at Mercury Lounge shouted 'I miss Joel!' Anton had responded, 'Well, why don't you go to fuckin' Amoeba Records and visit him? And, while you're there, buy a record so he doesn't get fired?' Eventually, though, he asked Joel to consider rejoining the band again full-time. Joel accepted the offer, but he nearly suffered a fatal injury during one of his first shows back after stumbling over some gear and falling headfirst off the stage. His leg, tangled in cables, stopped him inches short of breaking his neck.

237

'It's still fun [to play with the BJM],' he explained a few years later, 'but it's different when you're young and making your first charge up that hill, and then you get distracted and start smelling flowers or something stupid and then the old man with the pitchfork comes running out of nowhere and tells you to get the hell off his land and you've blown it.'

'Joel was doing Q&As [and] getting paid to talk about the film,' Frankie notes. 'Everyone was like, *Woah, we could actually come home with a little bit of money. Be able to buy beers for a week.*'

Hard at work, hard at drinking, hard at everything and everyone in his path, Anton railed against the media's misrepresentation of him and his music. In June 2005, he told the *Guardian*, while swigging from a bottle of whiskey, 'It isn't about my fame. I am not the light. I hold the torch so others might see …

I thought that it could serve a greater purpose … I was very much interested in opening a clear channel of communication—with everything, at once, on different levels.'

That same month, as *Empire*, the biggest film magazine in the UK, gave *Dig!* a five-star review, the band tore through London. At the Dirty Water Club, Anton walked offstage several times, knocked chairs over, spilled people's drinks, threatened to assault members of the crowd, argued with the DJs, and gave the audience the finger, before ending the night crashing through the fire exit, scaring people on the street outside, convinced of a conspiracy to sabotage him.

This attitude persisted. 'Anyone want to engage in hand-to-hand combat with me?' he asked the crowd at another gig. 'Please form a queue—single file, no cuts.' At another show, he argued with the doorman and was almost evicted from the venue. And yet in spite of his antics, the BJM's star was on the rise, with the UK dates followed by a date in Paris, a run of sold-out shows in the USA, and a looming appearance at Lollapalooza, for which the band would share a stage for the first time in many years with The Dandy Warhols.

Among the band's high-profile new fans was Iggy Pop, who told *Thrasher* magazine that the BJM were 'a fucking great band! And the way I got into him was I read in my local paper about a documentary and they interviewed the director, and she was saying what a loser [Anton] was and all these terrible things he did. I didn't like how she sounded so much but he sounded cool. So I thought let's just check out his music and I hoped it would be good. There's a new double album out on them, and man, it's good, it's really good.'

Meanwhile, in London, the band were personally invited to appear at that year's Meltdown Festival at Queen Elizabeth Hall by Patti Smith, the curator of that year's lineup. 'This is the greatest accolade we could ever get,' Anton told the audience. 'It makes all the other shit worth it.' Later, he told Dave Depares, who had been following the band around the UK, that playing Meltdown was 'the best day of my life. We're playing on the same bill as fucking Johnny Marr!' When Depares asked if he planned to stay to watch Black Rebel Motorcycle Club's set at Meltdown, though, he replied, 'I *taught* Peter how to play the guitar. Know what I mean? I'm going to the pub to have a *pint*!'

PLAY UNTIL THE DOPE IS GONE

The Brian Jonestown Massacre were one of Lollapalooza 2005's biggest sellers. The festival's organizer, Jane's Addiction front man Perry Ferrell, who was also managed by Ted Gardner, introduced the band to the stage before their hour-and-a-half set. 'Now that I'm mad with power, I wipe my ass with contemporary culture,' Anton told the crowd, before directing insults at another band on the bill, Dashboard Confessional. Clearly, Anton was no fan of the 'emo' scene that had gripped American youth culture, and which he felt was the exact opposite of the punk community he grew up in.

When The Dandy Warhols, who'd enjoyed a similar jolt of press from the film, did their set, they played to one of the biggest crowds of the weekend. After a few songs, Courtney announced that Anton and Matt would be joining them; the duo then came onstage to jam a couple songs before the Dandys closed with a cover of The Smiths' 'What She Said.' In their review of the performance, the *A.V. Club*'s John Modell and Kyle Ryan recognized this event as not only the symbolic end of the BJM's feud with the Dandys but also the closing of the rift between Matt and Anton, though the cameo didn't last long, and Anton remained cool on the idea that *Dig!* had given his career a boost. 'I don't have a career,' he told the *Telegraph* around the time of the festival. 'Korea is a country in Asia.'

In fact, both bands put significant distance between themselves and the film as the press ate it up. 'Anton wasn't happy with it, but he couldn't tell [Ondi] to not put it out,' the Dandys' Peter Holmström noted that summer. 'I wasn't happy with it either. It was a trust thing. I told her some things that were not to be put in, and she did anyway. I was a little unhappy with where she went with the story. It makes Anton out to be pretty one-sided. If he was *that* much of a lunatic we wouldn't have developed that friendship with him and we wouldn't have toured with him.'

'Let's cut the shit right here and get serious for a second,' Anton snapped, in an interview with *Tucson Weekly*. 'This *creature* [Timoner] has been doing interviews all over the commonwealth saying things like, *Before I finished editing the film, they were playing to, like, ten or fifteen people*. What would possess a lesser humunculoidal demon to act like this, to sabotage her own hard work in such a clumsy manner? I've read the works of the greats immortal. This is greed. Plain and simple.'

The 'rivalry' with the Dandys did neither band much good, as critics seemed keen to take a crack at it in more or less every piece on either band. As *Pitchfork*'s review of *Tepid Peppermint Wonderland* put it, 'From a distance, Brian Jonestown Massacre's rivalry with the Dandys has always seemed faintly ridiculous, since choosing between these two wildly erratic, frequently mediocre acts is a little like asking your kid which he'd prefer for dinner: a jar of pimentos or a can of water chestnuts?'

To escape the whirlwind, Anton engrossed himself in the making of what became the first BJM 'mini-album,' *We Are The Radio*, which he recorded with Sarabeth Tucek, who appears right at the end of *Dig!* in the scene where Anton kicks the guy in the head, and she observes, 'Anton is like a shark. He has to keep swimming or he'll die.'

Sarabeth's original intent in coming to Los Angeles was to act. She enjoyed the escapism of the city and had a background in theater, but the business of acting was something she couldn't manage, so she started hanging around musicians, among them Anton, who helped demystify the process of making music for her. After finding her way in, she would never return to acting.

'Sara and I believe this to be the most important work of our lives, and to a greater extent, our time,' Anton wrote of their work together, in a post to the BJM website. 'This is not some namby-pamby pop-culture vomit, regurgitating or emulating something else. These are whispers from the underworld and tears of joy from heaven. These are anthems for all time.'

In his allmusic.com review of the record, which was released on August 23, 2005, Richie Unterberger described it as an uncharacteristically gentle BJM effort. 'The astral jangly feel of several tracks, particularly "Never Become Emotionally Attached To Man, Woman, Beast, Or Child," brings

RIGHT Frankie Emerson helped Anton revitalize the BJM after the lineup we know from *Dig!* fell apart completely, and made significant contributions to *Bravery Repetition And Noise* and *And This Is Our Music*.

RIGHT The BJM played several shows with Primal Scream in March 2009. 'We weren't allowed to play the Fillmore in [the old] days because of our bad rep around town with other venues,' says Joel, 'but they finally let us in there to open up for Primal Scream.' **BELOW** Anton, Frankie Emerson, and Ricky Maymi, 2007.

TOP Collin Hegna, Dan Allaire, and Anton, 2006. **LEFT** Anton tunes a bass. **ABOVE** Anton's 'Crackbook.' He has always utilized technology to get his music to the masses, and in the 2000s released all of his music online for free.

ABOVE Anton, Collin Hegna, Dan Allaire, Matt Hollywood, Joel Gion, and Ricky Maymi onstage in Manchester, England, 2012. **LEFT** Matt, whose return to the group in 2008 coincided with the BJM's most stable lineup.

OPPOSITE PAGE, TOP Anton and Ricky, 2007. **BOTTOM** Anton gives the Dream Machine Festival crowd the finger as Frankie Emerson looks on, 2007.

RIGHT AND BELOW Anton at the Field Day festival in London, 2016. **BOTTOM** Anton, Collin Hegna, Dan Allaire, and Joel Gion onstage at the Fonda Theatre, Los Angeles, 2017.

THIS PAGE Miranda Lee Richards (*left*), Ryan Van Kreidt (*below*), and Mara Keagle and Ricky Maymi (*bottom*) perform with the BJM at the Fonda Theatre, 2017.

FOLLOWING PAGE Joel Gion does one of his high-flying tambourine tosses.

to mind a rather narcotized Byrds … psychedelic folk-rock content to drift along with a cosmic sheen, not so much determined to make an explosive breakthrough to the fifth dimension as much as to hover there.'

Around this time, Anton started pushing the idea that his songs were about God, no matter their true subject matter. Nowhere is this more evident than in the lyrical mysticism of 'God Is My Girlfriend,' but a more accurate sign of things to come was 'Teleflows 5 Vs. Amplification,' an electronic instrumental. When questioned about going in that direction, however, he said he believed most electronic music to be disposable, and questioned the vagueness of the term itself. 'Do you mean Pierre Henry? Delia Derbshire? Or do you mean preset beats and Auto-Tune? I've been playing Minimoogs since 1980, and programing nonstop since then.'

The art for the record was also characteristically different from other BJM records, featuring Polaroids taken by Richard Medina of art by Travis Millard in the hallway of the Little Joy Luck Club in Echo Park. And as Unterberger's review indicates, the record itself is a little softer and a little stranger than *And This Is Our Music*, signaling Anton's readiness to take the band, as a musical project, in a new direction, though what form it would take was not yet clear. There's an abrasive squeal that sounds like microphone feedback, or maybe an already piercing keyboard note mixed in too loud, on the first song, 'Never Become Attached,' which is followed by Sarabeth's song 'Something For You' (as 'Seer') and then 'Time Is Honey (So Cut The Shit).' The songs feature a lot more synthesizer than those on the last record, and the swells and sweeps Anton plays all drone around one or two keys. That juxtaposed against lo-fi folk-rock is very interesting, while the post-digital Krautrock vibe of 'Teleflows Vs. Amplification 5' results in an incredibly imaginative soundscape.

Almost as soon as the record came out, however, Sarabeth broke off from Anton, as against her wishes he'd assigned himself a co-writing credit on 'Something For You' and released it as 'Seer.' Unlike others before her— among them Jonathan Sachs and Charles Mehling—she would seek legal action to redress this.

* * *

A couple of weeks after *We Are The Radio*'s release, the band went out on

241

tour again. Just as they were set to play a high-profile gig at the Bowery Ballroom in Brooklyn on September 18, however, their van, with all of their equipment inside, was stolen. The remaining nine or ten dates on that tour were immediately canceled. The stolen gear, said to be worth over $100,000 altogether, has never been recovered.

The day after the canceled Bowery show, the band went ahead with a previously schedule acoustic show at Pianos on the Lower East Side. Fan reports suggest it went pretty badly, with Anton arguing with The Morning After Girls about who was going on first, yelling at the crowd and complaining about the guitar he'd borrowed for the show, and yelling at the soundman before going up to the booth to set his own levels. Then, after a series of stop-start songs and insults hurled at both the audience and the other bands, he started messing around with The Morning After Girls' instruments before jumping offstage and leaving the venue.

That November, critics were once again writing about the Dandys–BJM feud, as reviews of *Tepid Peppermint Wonderland* were permeated with it. Then Joel's Gilmore Girls episode came out, while in December, the BJM played the Transmusicales de Rennes festival alongside Primal Scream. 'We expected a little more from Brian Jonestown Massacre, made stars of the underground by the documentary *Dig!*,' Vincent Le Deouff wrote in his review of the show. 'Anton Newcombe is unbearable, constantly taking breaks between each song to taunt his musicians, complain about the stage lights, or hurl insults at the audience. It was difficult to appreciate the concert.'*

Meanwhile, on top of the loss of gear, Anton's bank account had been slapped out of shape by the one-two punch of lawsuits from Elise and Sarabeth, but he wasn't about to let them sink him. 'I was sued for the last two albums I did by people who participated,' he later noted. 'They were really frivolous lawsuits, and it cost fifty grand to win both of them.'

They also caused issues with the band's label. 'Tee Pee didn't like that, because they didn't know Anton had ripped Sarabeth off,' Frankie recalls. 'They had to fork over thousands of dollars for that. The whole business thing, everybody in the band is in the dark. We have no idea what Anton's

---

* A few weeks later, The Out Crowd opened for The Dandy Warhols at the Fillmore in San Francisco. 'Good enough for a Jonestown song,' Matt snarled to the audience, before ripping into 'Oh Lord,' as Sarah Jane banged away at the tambourine in front of a screaming crowd.

talking to labels about. We're not going to get a dime in royalties, so fuck it. This can be Anton's headache. We're just there to play music.'

Dale Bookout disputes the idea that the lawsuits had a heavy bearing on the label's relationship, however. 'Both of those lawsuits were nominal,' he says. 'In order for a lawsuit to be material, the amount of earnings from whatever record that they're suing on behalf of has to be substantial, and *And This Is Our Music* didn't sell hardly any copies.' According to Dale, the lawsuits had no impact on Anton's relationship with Tee Pee. But whatever the specifics of what went on, Anton has operated independently of labels ever since.

* * *

Back at Lollapalooza, Anton met a woman named Hannah, who had been invited to attend the festival as a guest of Ricky Maymi, whom she'd been introduced to in 2002 by Marty Willson-Piper of The Church. 'Ricky and I became fast friends despite the fact that he didn't live in New York,' she recalls. 'I would go see him play every time the BJM came through town. I had liked what I heard, but I hadn't collected any records or really followed them at that point. Ricky and I would grab a drink after the gigs, away from the crowd and bandmates.'

Around this time, Frankie was preparing to move to New York City with his then-girlfriend, Krista, and at some point Anton decided he wanted to move out there, too. 'I moved there before Anton,' says Krista, 'but we lived about ten blocks from each other and ran into each other quite a bit.'

Anton, it turned out, had moved in with Hannah, into her two-bedroom on First Avenue and Avenue A, on the border of the East Village and the Lower East Side, and would stay there for pretty much the next three years. In classic Anton fashion, he'd made the decision on a whim. 'I offered to put him up when he told me he pretty much spontaneously arrived with no solid plans,' Hannah recalls. 'He came to New York looking to see if it might be a good fit for him, and to have a greatly needed change of scene. He needed a place to crash while he looked for more permanent living situation, so I thought it would be very short-term. We got along so well, so I let him move in officially after two weeks of being my guest.'

During the time they lived together, Anton would tour off and on with the BJM, playing to packed houses night after night, while Hannah would tour with her own band, The Twenty Twos. When she was away, she recalls, Anton would call her daily to check in, which she says was surprising but welcome. They were both social and busy, so they had plenty of time alone. When Anton was around, he'd support local and touring bands, and he made sure to check out all of his friends' bands, whether he liked the music or not. During the day, he would visit friends at his favorite local spots, or wherever it was they worked. 'He spent a lot of time at the tent on the Bowery, entertaining or entertainingly antagonizing the passers-by,' Hannah recalls. 'Our home became filled with furniture, strange art, and relics from there over the years … he would bring DVDs back from his overseas touring, because a fan gifted him a DVD player that was hacked to play all regions. [British comedy series] *The Mighty Boosh* was our favorite, years before it was introduced in America.'

Hannah and Anton grew very close. 'I'd come home to clever and spontaneous surprises,' she continues. 'I returned home one evening to a flashlight propped up on my dresser, shining across to a note taped on the wall. It was a Smiths quote—*There is a light that never goes out*—it warmed my heart and made me smile.'

When he was home, if he was not listening to the BBC or NPR, Anton was playing music from all different genres, countries, and time periods. 'He ended up with a collection from the Indian takeout, Punjabi, next door to our apartment,' Hannah adds. 'They would say to him, *No remixes! Authentic!*' On occasion, if Hannah slept past noon, she would hear Anton at her door—'Wake up! It's after noon! I made you breakfast!'—and he'd put on a danceable tune and play with her dog, Iggy, encouraging her to jump up on Hannah's bed to help rouse her.

But as Anton's celebrity continued to grow, not even the anonymity of New York City could cloak him. People were even starting to write bizarre fan-fiction about him online. The next couple of years would end up being Anton's last in America, but for Hannah, her time living with him remains a good memory. 'My world opened up, living with Anton,' she says. 'One of the first big parties we had was in the fall of 2005, for The Dandy Warhols, who were in NYC on tour. I'd never hosted so many people in my place before … that was back when all his fans mistakenly thought there was a real rivalry or animosity between the two bands from watching *Dig!*

'Later the same year, I was rehearsing with my band into the late side of the eve. I remember thinking to myself, *I hope Anton is not entertaining anyone tonight; I'm so beat!* But I came home to an even bigger party, hosting The Lovetones … there was a big jam session going on in the kitchen, and after my initial (internal and quiet) disappointment, I immediately resigned myself to joining in.'

Frankie has a different perspective on this period. 'Those times were crazy as fuck, because Anton was really off his rocker in New York City,' he says. When I compared it to John Lennon's 'Lost Weekend,' Frankie replied, 'That was like the lost fuckin' year or two. We had Sune from Raveonettes. He played bass. We had Plucky come out with us. Me, Anton, and Plucky flew to New York for a gig, and Sune didn't know any of the songs, so we're trying to teach him some songs. That was wild.'

While Frankie recalls the wild side of things, Hannah remembers a slightly more domestic, energetic Anton from this time. Like many of his bandmates, friends, and acquaintances, she recalls the great joy he took in cooking and preparing food for people, and the fact that their place was never short of guests to serve food to. 'Anton loved to cook. He cooked vegetarian meals to accommodate me and invited anyone else who wanted to come by … he honestly made the absolute best-of-the-best vegetarian chili and best potato-leek soup and best veggie lasagna out of all the restaurants and home-cooked meals I've experienced—no joke. I've never tasted such delicious zucchini bread baked from scratch. We all know his passion for music, but it carries into everything he does. He was just as passionate in the kitchen. We would even host chili parties … the chili would be started the day before, beans stewed in red wine or dark beer. He timed the addition of all ingredients quite perfectly into the next day.'

245

* * *

It was good while it lasted.

'Would you like to go fuck your boyfriend, or could you serve us some drinks?' said a voice from behind the bar.

Lynn Butta, a friend of Hannah's, was bartending on a typically slow weekday. It was around two in the afternoon, and no one came into the bar she was working at on the Lower East Side, Iggy's—a place that shared the same name as Hannah's dog—until about six, for happy hour, with the exception of a few tourists and bands here and there, breaking from soundcheck at the Mercury Lounge or the Bowery Ballroom.

'Well, I'd like to,' she told the stranger, 'but since you're here, I may as well serve you!'

From that day onward, Anton stopped by Iggy's just about every day for a Campari and soda. Since there were usually few other customers around, Lynn got to know him pretty well. She knew nothing of The Brian Jonestown Massacre or *Dig!*, other than the one BJM song in Iggy's jukebox, 'When Jokers Attack.' Anton usually kept to himself, Lynn recalls. Occasionally, he'd get into it with other customers, and she would have to keep the peace, which she'd usually be able to do, but if either he or the other customers got too drunk, things would escalate. When that happened, Anton would offer to leave, but Lynn never let him.

Months went by until one day Anton came in to tell Lynn he was doing a photo shoot out front, and that she should go to the BJM's show that night at the Bowery Ballroom—that he would put her on the guest list. She served him his usual, but he seemed anxious and a bit disheveled, like he hadn't slept and was still drinking from the night before.

After the photo shoot, Iggy's got more crowded—as it usually did around six—so Lynn told Anton she'd see him later. She didn't get off until nine, however, so she ended up being pretty late to the sold-out gig. She arrived to find the band staring off into the crowd as Anton rambled over them, while the audience chanted, in unison, 'Play some music!'

As she made her way to the front, cheering Anton on, Lynn felt a girl elbow her in the back for getting in front of her. A couple of others shushed her.

At this point, she recalls, Anton starts calling up people in the audience, telling them to get onstage and do whatever they want. One guy starts rapping.

Lynn aggressively raises her hand to get Anton's attention, and then someone lifts her onto the stage.

Anton puts the microphone in front of her.

'What can you do?' he asks her.

'I'm just your bartender,' she says. 'Now it seems everyone here wants to play, so just play some fucking music!'

After that night, Anton didn't come by Iggy's much anymore. Too many fans found out he was hanging out there and started following him around.

'When we went out, I was a bit horrified at some of the "fans" we'd come across,' Hannah notes. 'They would either worship him or mock him, but they always wanted his attention. Many of those would go to bars he frequented just to be able to do that.'

Anton ended up hanging out at another local dive called the Library, which happened to be right around the corner from his place. 'I realized later on that he'd been coming into [Iggy's] as a sort of escape, because no one really knew who he was at the time,' Lynn says. 'He said what was on his mind and respected others who did the same. He always took the time to give me advice about relationships and listened to my problems … he looked out for me, and I will always remember that. Despite what kind of reputation he had, if you really knew him, your perspective of him changed.'

* * *

In one sense, 2006 proved to be something of a cleansing year for the BJM, both as a recording entity and as a live act. For the past six years, they'd toured and played constantly, both before and after *Dig!* At SXSW that year, Anton fronted a jam of 'Feel It' with The Black Angels, and a couple months later, in May, the BJM toured the Midwest on their way to the UK with The High Dials, and then with Icelandic group Singapore Sling that June.

247

On one of the first nights of the latter tour, at the Sugarmill in Stoke-on-Trent, a couple of young hooligans showed up, made their way to a balcony, and began heckling Joel with chants of 'Joel, fuck off!' Joel was able to keep his cool until Frankie got too drunk, passed out onstage, and landed on him. Joel thought Frankie was intentionally pushing him, so he fought back and choked him out. 'He laughed it off, but I think he's still mad,' Joel subsequently told the *Reykjavik Grapevine*'s Bart Cameron, an American journalist who had immigrated to Iceland. 'Kind of a bad way to start the tour.'

The band had come to Iceland and found a devoted following already waiting for them, prompting Anton to invite Bart to come along and document everything. In Manchester, Anton said he planned to join Singapore Sling onstage at an Ian Curtis tribute show, in hopes of getting more people into their set, but the city suffered a power outage just as they arrived and the gig was canceled.

Anton was caught off-guard by fans who would approach him to thank him for the effect he'd had on their lives. 'I'm just a normal guy,' he told Bart. 'I mean, I drink and everything.' He refused to live or act any differently than he had before his new burst of fame, and though it made him miserable sometimes, he still mingled with fans and let them take pictures, just as he always had, prompting Bart to describe him as 'the fans' rock star.'

After their shows in the UK and Iceland, the Jonestown ripped through Europe with The Lovetones. Then, after a two-month break, they were back at it in September, touring the US West Coast and Canada in a run of shows that included one with The Dandys at the Showbox in Seattle.

In October and November, the band returned to Europe with The People's Revolutionary Choir and The Morning After Girls, whose singer, Aimee Nash, would join the BJM for 'Anemone.' Reviewing the band's show at Nottingham Trent University Union on October 25—at which Anton wore the Sherlock Holmes–style cap he'd recently been given by Echo & The Bunnymen's Will Sergeant—Florence Gohard wrote, '*Dig!* or no *Dig!*, tonight the BJM proved they're an entity to their own, and a valuable one at that. You'd be fools not to listen in.'

At Debaser Medis in Stockholm, Sweden, Anton scolded Frankie so much during the gig that the guitarist left the stage at one point. According to Stefan Malmqvist's report for *Svenska Dagbladet*, the only member of the band to escape Anton's wrath that night was Dan Allaire. Around the same time, Anton could be heard talking shit about his band to another Swedish journalist, Quetzala Blanco—a sure sign the tour was ready to end—but a few weeks later, on Joel's birthday, November 21, he was in a much more jovial mood, leading the band and crowd in Southampton in an enthusiastic chorus of 'Happy Birthday' for The Spokesman, alongside a rendition of 'Take Me Back To Dear Old Blighty,' sung in a cadence similar to the version that opens The Smiths' *The Queen Is Dead*.

One of the last dates of that 2006 tour was at Nasa Midvikudag in Reykjavik, again with Singapore Sling. The experience proved to be a crucial turning point in Anton's life. It warmly placed him within an entirely new creative sphere, and opened up to him new realms of artistic possibility and exploration, which he had exhausted for himself in America.

Anton would soon have to choose a new path, but this time no coin tosses were necessary. He would settle in Europe.

On December 5, 2006, The Brian Jonestown Massacre were back in New York, at Webster Hall, for the last show of the year. 'Ever since they stole our gear, we haven't been able to play right,' Anton told the crowd. 'Ever since then, we've sounded shitty. That's okay; I'm not going to let them stop me.'

Though he had grown proud of the band for sticking it through, their new level of fame had brought along with it a heightened reputation, and now, for the first time ever, it seemed he was fighting against that reputation with relative success. 'It was … apparent that Newcombe was a man under siege,' Julia Yepes of *PopMatters* reported. 'The first words out of his mouth were, *I'll fight all of you!* It was clear that [he] felt there were hecklers in the crowd, there only to see him lose control. And he was probably right.'

During their recent tour of the UK, Anton had met the photographer Bev Davies, who shot their shows at the Shepherd's Bush Empire in London and the Ritz in Manchester. She had become a fan of the band after seeing *Dig!*, intrigued by Kelly White's photo of Courtney and Anton out in the desert, in their cowboy hats and sunglasses, and through that connected with other psych bands like The Black Angels and The Warlocks. 'Meeting Anton changed my life,' she says. 'I had been a punk-rock photographer and had quit taking photos, and thought in terms of *that is who I was*, [but] meeting Anton in 2005, I became that person again, a rock'n'roll photographer … by the next year, that was who I was, and I feel Anton saved my life, in a strange and wonderful way.'*

Bev mentioned her encounter with Anton around this time in an interview

---

* A few years later, Anton was inspired to base the artwork for the BJM single 'Iluminomi' on an old poster Bev had in her room.

with *Punk Globe* magazine, but in general, though stories such as this one—or, for example, that of Kevin Junior of The Chamber Strings, a talented musician who, like Anton, had struggled with heroin, and who revealed to the *Chicago Reader* that Anton had tried to help him in the midst of his own battle—circulated online among BJM fans, they rarely received much notice in the press. Instead, the mainstream media's driving narrative was that that Anton was a violent, rambling freak show, his band the same, and that they were stuck in a never-ending battle with The Dandy Warhols, and look at how stupid they all look in *Dig!*[*]

Usually, when critics even bothered to mention the band's records, they would be given a mediocre assessment. It took a long time for anyone to come around to writing a review because they understood or enjoyed the music, rather than because they felt they had formulated an idea of what Anton or his music were about after watching *Dig!* One such writer was Jim Guittard, who in March 2007 described how he had first got into the band in late 1999: 'With the BJM, it's about showing the press or mainstream or others that they are wrong with their close-minded routine thinking. It is a wake up call to society to think more positively and courageously with vision … it's about standing on your own feet. Making your own history … the obvious is, yes, you may have a dysfunctional past but *you can be somebody.*'

In the early months of 2007, Anton spent time helping his ex-girlfriend, Tricia Vessey, who had relocated to New York with their son, Hermann. By now, though, Anton was growing sick of the city—and of America entirely. Which is when he turned his eye to Europe. 'I had a lot going on in the past six years, which is probably why people didn't hear from me much,' he told Melbourne's *Beat Magazine*. 'I was busy raising my son, and I also realized I didn't need to put out a whole bunch of records.'

Hannah sheds some additional light on the matter. 'Anton ended up leaving in 2008 for many reasons, but most of all, New York was wearing him down … his sense of belonging was getting stripped away with all the hangers-on trying to be his best friend but enabling unhealthy ways or suffocating him instead. Another factor instigating his move was the fact

---

[*] Another fleeting exception was a French music magazine's suggestion around this time that Anton had helped drive a revival of the sitar in contemporary psychedelic music, in an article that mentioned only two other Western acts, The Beatles and The Rolling Stones.

that I had been living in an illegal sublet for years, and my time had come; my luck had run out. We were discovered as the very last subletters of the rent-controlled apartment building and got kicked out. I was looking for places for both of us in other parts of the city and Brooklyn, but at that point he was really pretty much over NYC. He needed a change to thrive. We both knew it.'

That need for change would eventually take Anton to Berlin. His then-new squeeze and soon-to-be wife, Katy Lane, recalls, 'We were in New York, and Anton had been talking about moving to Europe for a long time. On a press tour, we met up with a friend of Anton's who lived in Berlin, and they started talking about living together, so we just moved over. We lived with him for the first year or so, which was a lot of fun.'

Katy had grown up in a small town in South Wales and was studying photography when she first met Anton during his 'lost year or two' in NYC in 2006–07. After they fell in love, she bailed on her degree to go on the road with the band, which she has continued to do almost every year since, living what her friend Emma Garland, with whom Katy had shared cigarettes, boyfriends, and a love for Duran Duran growing up, would describe in a 2014 article for *Noisey* as 'every teenager's dream and every parent's nightmare … forever laden with a myriad of film, digital, or instant cameras, she has been scrupulously documenting everything as she goes along—over time, she has built up hundreds of unseen shots which, as well as providing a unique portal into the lives of The Brian Jonestown Massacre beyond the media-gaze, reveal the story of a girl for whom enough was never enough.'*

A musical change was on the horizon, too. On tour in Iceland the previous year, Anton had met Jón Sæmundur Auðarson, with whom he would now collaborate extensively on the first full-length BJM LP in five years, *My Bloody Underground*.

Anton had recorded two songs for the new record at Parr Street Studios

251

---

* In fact, Katy was a Dandys fan first, and had found out about the BJM after reading one of the many articles about both of them after *Dig!* came out. When she gave birth to her and Anton's son Wolfgang, the Dandys sent them a Dandy Warhols onesie and T-shirt as congratulations. Katy showed her photographs in an exhibit titled 'Someplace Else Unknown' at Bold Street Coffee in Liverpool in December 2017. Included were Polaroid portraits of Anton, Wolfgang, The Dandy Warhols, Miranda Lee Richards, Robert Been, Will Carruthers, Tim Burgess, Aimee Nash, SoKo, Birdstriking, and others.

in Liverpool, England, before relocating the sessions to Reykjavik. 'I very much wanted to cleanse my mental palate and improvise over a few days,' he later said of his creative restart on this new record. 'I had to go *some*place, so I went to Iceland.'

After spending the better part of the previous year touring the world, it had come to him all at once, like it'd been waiting to break out of him. He and his new Icelandic collaborators recorded everything within a matter of a few days. 'The neo-classical piece and another track were recorded retrospectively,' he later explained. 'One [was from] 1996 and one [was from] when I was nine, and I just kept them in my head but everything on the record was recorded on the spot, no rehearsal, no writing, just make it up.'

Another collaborator on the album was Mark Gardener of Ride, who co-wrote 'Monkey Powder' with Anton and played on a few other songs. 'I flew Mark to Iceland and recorded some stuff, and I was living in hotels, drinking and going out of my mind and burning through money, so I decided to get a studio,' Anton later said. The two had first met in the Haight during the earliest years of the band—maybe even *before* the band—and Mark had also worked with The Morning After Girls.

252

A month earlier, the BJM had been booked to play Truck Festival in Oxford, but the event was canceled due to flooding. Not willing to let the day go to waste, Anton and Mark got together to save the gig, and an impromptu concert was held at Brookes University instead. During soundcheck, Anton demanded two chairs be moved to the side of the stage. Ride's Andy Bell, who was in Oasis at the time, joined Gardener and played old Ride songs for an hour and a half, and with the Jonestown did an energetic version of Ride's 'Drive Blind.' Gardener and Bell, with the rest of Ride, eventually reunited for a full-blown 2015 tour.

The Reykjavik sessions took place over four days in mid-August, during which Anton and his collaborators made up the music as they went along, while ingesting loads of drugs. (Anton might've kicked heroin, but that didn't mean he was opposed to getting high by other means, and nor had his continued boozing abated.)

Shortly after that, he posted the resulting *My Bloody Underground* online—eight months before it saw a proper release. Right before his birthday, Anton posted the following message online:

Hej!

Having a great time in Iceland, the album is almost complete. Have 12 songs and hope to record more. Waiting to find girls that sing in Icelandic and will do another session on Sunday if all goes well. I plan to post it all online as 'work-in-progress.' I had planned to have a party on the 29th for everyone as it is my birthday but may need to go back to the UK for business. I will update asap.

That's all for now. Much love from the land of the midnight sun.

Anton Alfred Fjordson.
Iceland '07 'get higher than the satellites ...

* * *

At the end of August 2007, just before Anton turned forty, Ricky Maymi and Ryan van Kreidt (who would end up joining the live group later) played with Mark at the Dream Machine Festival in Bradfield, Essex. Among the other bands to perform were Asteroid #4 and The People's Revolutionary Choir. There was also an appearance by Spacemen 3's Will Carruthers.

Around the same time, the BJM embarked on a tour with New Zealand trip-hop band Dimmer, whose drummer, Dino Karlis, would end up playing on various sessions for Anton over the years. Anton, drugging and often drunk, found dealing with angry mobs night after night to be continually mentally and physically exhausting. When a fan threw a bottle at him in Vancouver, a meltdown ensued, and was duly captured for posterity and posted to YouTube.

'Which one of you fuckers wanna die?' Anton asks the crowd. 'Throw a bottle at me and you fuckin' die. Come up here, you pussy. Don't hide, you pussy fuckin' shit. Did you throw it?'

An audience member points to the assailant, and Anton takes notice.

'Somebody saw it,' he says. 'Which one of you fuckers saw the person who threw the bottle at me? You don't do that. You're going to jail tonight. One of you fuckers saw that person. Who wants to fuckin' die?'

Someone else in the crowd claims they threw the bottle. Anton points to them and goes on a tirade. 'You did it? Come up here. Be a man … you go to fuckin' hell, you pussy. If you're a man, come up here and I'll kick your fuckin' ass. That's why they're gonna make you fucking faggots drink from plastic cups … you hide behind girls and throw bottles.'

The crowd cheers. Anton returns to the microphone to continue his rant.

'I know you guys saw the person that did it. I know,' he says. 'That's why we're not going to play anymore. You fucking tell him that he wrecked the rest of the show. You tell him, [but] you don't hurt him. You hear me?'

More cheers. Someone yells, 'Kick his ass!' but Anton ignores him.

'We don't throw bottles, right? We have a problem … I'll kill all of you fucking niggers, do you understand?'*

At this point, Collin, who's been standing near the edge of the stage with Anton, leaves him there and goes off to nurse his beer. You can see in his face that he knows where this is going.

'No, we don't do that,' Anton continues, doing his best to make his tone less abrasive, but his language has sent the crowd into an uproar that will ultimately drown him out. 'Do you understand? Listen! Listen, no I don't give a shit what you think … check this out … we respect each other. We live together, we die together.'

People start yelling.

'Fuck you! You fuckin' asshole!'

The other half of the crowd cheers him on.

A couple of years after the clip was posted to YouTube, Anton would comment, 'Funny how [the video] says a *fan* threw a bottle. Stupid fucker, that's not a fan. It's an attack … the fact is, someone through a bottle at my head. A full bottle. The Germans have a word for people that take pleasure at others' misfortune. *Schadenfreude*.'

The circus continued the following night at Neumo's in Seattle, though this time Anton fought to keep his cool. 'People were throwing things onto

254

---

* The photo that graces the cover of this book was taken by Bev Davies at this show, much to Anton's chagrin, as he railed against both myself and Bev on Twitter. While Anton's remarks during this incident are inarguably shocking and distasteful, his use of homophobic and racial slurs to insult disruptive audience members is nothing new. A decade after this incident, during a June 2018 show in Australia, Anton made a much-publicized rape joke directed at a heckler that led to an online boycott of the band by offended fans, who drafted petitions in hopes of getting the tour canceled.

the stage,' the blogger Straightjacket Fits reported. 'Beer was sprayed at the band and audience in lame attempts to get Anton going. They nearly got it, too … and the set suffered because of it … there was just too much baggage in the room to really enjoy the show.

* * *

Two years had passed since the release of *We Are The Radio*—two years during which Anton had begun to pioneer ways of using YouTube and MySpace to release his music to a wider audience, long before most other bands caught on—and he was anxious to get a new record out so that he could move on to the next thing. Tee Pee was no longer representing the band, and Anton's Committee To Keep Music Evil was only incorporated in the States, so he formed his own A Records imprint, which like Tee Pee would be distributed by Cargo.

My Bloody Underground was the first BJM LP to be released on A Records, and the title of its first track, 'Bring Me The Head Of Paul McCartney On Heather Mills' Wooden Peg (Dropping Bombs On The White House),' would draw a considerable amount of attention. The song itself is a chug-along, lo-fi drone; in the background you can hear a muffled tapping, like the creak of a chair or the clipping of a microphone.

My Bloody Underground is no ordinary BJM record (though of course none of them are). Its abrasive tonality comes off like a calculated reaction to what people might've *expected* a new BJM full-length record to sound like, with *Dig!* well past reaching cult status by then. There hadn't been a full-length since *And This Is Our Music*, and Anton had grown sicker of *Dig!* than he had of New York, the specter of the film followed him so closely that he would drop out of interviews the second it was mentioned.

Now, Anton was taking the music in a wholly new and unexplored direction, making art purely for the art of it. Firstly, there was nothing that sounded remotely like the Dandys, who'd broken from Capitol in 2007 and gone independent themselves. Secondly, the album featured virtually no one from the live band—a trend that would continue for several years. Thirdly, it was highly experimental, with entire songs sung in Icelandic. Many found the record unlistenable—including most of the live band—with the exception of 'Yeah, Yeah,' which had existed for at least a decade.

'Listen! Watch!' Anton says to one of his players before tuning his guitar at the onset of 'Infinite Wisdom Tooth / My Last Night In Bed With You.' Few words are discernible in the mix, but one repeated line is 'Everyone is absurd.' At the end of the song, someone says something in Icelandic. A question, maybe. 'We're done,' Anton replies. You can hear it if you turn it up loud enough.

'Who's Fucking Pissed In My Well?' is reminiscent of the instrumentals on *Their Satanic Majesties' Second Request*, but Anton's creative shift here—and to an extent on the next four albums—was a blend of two distinct techniques, the pastiche and the drone. It's not that he didn't employ them before, but what is different here is that they've become the *means* of songwriting itself—music first, song later, rather than pulling music out of writing. This 'bottom-up' approach is different to that of previous BJM records. Compare the tonality and aesthetic of *My Bloody Underground* to something like *Strung Out In Heaven*, and it sounds like two different bands, but when you consider all of the other records together, the catalogue becomes more cohesive. *My Bloody Underground* is Anton dipping his project slowly back into its original creative well.

Another experimental piece, the shockingly named, neo-romantic 'We Are The Niggers Of The World,' was purportedly the oldest piece of music floating around Anton's head when he tracked it for *My Bloody Underground*. He claims to have come up with it when he was nine, back in Orange County. It isn't a stretch to picture him working the piece out at the Sjobecks', or on the keyboard his grandparents bought him. The video for the song features Anton and collaborator Elsa Maria Blondal taking turns reading a book and playing a keyboard in a graffiti-covered hallway. In the clip, Anton has 'Freija,' the name of the Nordic goddess of fertility, written on his arm. 'I love Elsa,' he later wrote. 'She had just given birth and came to play *let's pretend* with us.'*

Lyrics are again hardly discernible on the cosmic space trip 'Who Cares Why,' but 'Yeah, Yeah' hints at Anton's *carpe diem* vibe during this time, much like 'Someplace Else Unknown' on *Who Killed Sgt. Pepper?*

Frankie was invited to play on *My Bloody Underground* but found he couldn't add anything to it. 'I'd go into the studio and hear these really crappy

---

* Elsa also plays in The Go Go Darkness with Singapore Sling's Henrik Björnsson.

like techno beats and shit,' he recalls. 'I'd be like, *There's nothing I can do with this. I can't even see how I can make this better, because it's already crap.* You can't sugarcoat a turd to make it taste better. I didn't want anything to do with that.' He gave a forthright assessment of the music to Anton: 'This is all you. It should just be your name on them, because it isn't fair that you're dragging the band name through the mud.'

The Reykjavik sessions had taken place at Studio Sýrland. In between sessions, Anton would pop over to the Sirkus bar, a fifteen-minute walk from the studio, where he'd meet up with some friends, among them Jón. Anton told Jón that he had a song that needed vocals, and invited him down to the studio after the bar closed. Anton played Jón 'Golden Frost' and told him that he should try to sing on it.

'We were talking about tax collectors before, at the studio, so I went in and recorded that song in one take,' Jón recalls. 'It was the first song I ever did. There are no backing vocals on it, only me and my lyrics. Typical Icelandic cursing I've used since I was a kid. Cursing the devil with his own words.'

Jón would next become heavily involved in another project, *Book Of Days*, a series of videos that he, Anton, Fiordur Grimsson, and Christian Zaclinsky made for the songs on *My Bloody Underground* and posted to YouTube under the name 'Product Of Iceland.' (There were plans, too, for a DVD release, though this never materialized.) Anton often spent time in Jón's art studio between sessions, and he would bring new songs along with him in the evenings. 'He was full of energy at that time,' Jón says. 'We were recording videos twenty-four hours a day and making art. Some of them were shot here in my studio and others we shot around Reykjavik.' The video for 'Automatic Faggot For The People' shows Anton getting a tattoo under his lips. A delayed scream brings us into the heavy track.

Another track Anton and Jón collaborated on, 'Just Like Kicking Jesus,' was released on an EP after *My Bloody Underground.* An Icelandic version of the song was recorded with Unnar Andrea Einarsdottir on vocals, and Jón made a YouTube video of the song using an old animated clip detailing the tenets of Mormon theology. Elsa Maria Blondal sings on the Icelandic version, while Sigga Boston, the owner of the Circus bar provided vocals for the ambient 'Ljósmyndir.' 'She doesn't make records really,' Anton later noted. 'I just asked her to be on this one because she has such a great voice.'

257

Another track, 'Darkwave Driver/Big Drill Car,' starts out with a minute-long montage of prerecorded news broadcasts. They blend together and become a part of the aural world, which is based around a simple beat and a guitar riff that wouldn't be out of place on a Quentin Tarantino movie. The lo-fi groover 'Monkey Powder' is in much the same vein. The album is rounded off with 'Black Hole Symphony,' which sounds much as its name implies. The iTunes version of the album features 'Amazing Electronic Talking Cave' as the album closer, a track that was originally titled 'The Origin Of Love.'

Critics panned the album. At *Tiny Mix Tapes*, Ajitpaul Mangat summarized the album as 'neither fascinating nor engaging,' while *Pitchfork*'s David Raposa went another notch below the belt. 'The album often sounds like a poorly recorded group of proficient amateurs giving it a go on fourth-hand guitars and some empty paint buckets,' he wrote, 'with the singer warbling through a pillow for good measure.' Raposa barreled down hard on the *Book Of Days* project as well, stating that the videos 'only exacerbate how silly and self-indulgent Anton's attempts at artistic martyrdom are, and have been. The myth of The Brian Jonestown Massacre, a construct that holds weight only with the hopelessly converted, has always superseded and surpassed the actual work of The Brian Jonestown Massacre.'

The worst reviews continued to drum up the old BJM–Dandys feud and *Dig!*, as if either had anything to do with the music. 'Newcombe's genius is palpable throughout the BJM catalogue '93–03,' Alan Ranta wrote at *PopMatters*. 'Several of his early works rank among the finest experiences of rock'n'roll. Hell, the Warhols' Courtney Taylor said he was going to keep buying his records even after receiving his monogrammed bullet ... however, [Anton's] genius is clearly on its deathbed.'

Anton cared not what people thought about the record. He had made it for himself. 'I want to express myself artistically rather than guard my ass commercially, as I've been known to do for the whole length of my career,' he said at the time. 'We set out to do a lot of drugs, basically, and make a really crazy record ... we just did it over four days, with no ideas whatsoever ... it sounds like a post-modern apocalypse to me and it has its own flow.'

A few critics disagreed with the negative press surrounding the record. Katie Knaub was among the first to see that the band's popularity (and that of the movie) had placed them at the center of a new psych scene. Describing the attendees of that year's Pitchfork Music Festival as 'the New Hippies' in a report for *Chicago Innerview*, she cited the BJM, Dead Meadow, BRMC, The Warlocks, and The Black Angels, who had named themselves after The Velvet Underground's 'The Black Angel's Death Song' and used a picture of Nico as their logo (much like how Anton used a picture of Brian Jones for the BJM's).

'It's all a big circle—and a communal feeling still diffuses among a great deal of today's psychedelic scene,' she wrote. 'The aforementioned bands have more of a dark psychedelic rock sound, but definitely bring back a feel of the 60s and morph it into something applicable to the here and the now. Artists like these prove that some rock bands still know how to move their tongues to propose substantial ideas and opinions—and that the movement is still alive and well in select areas of today's musical underground.'

Two days after Knaub's article was published, I took four hits of acid and listened to The Brian Jonestown Massacre for the first time. I had no idea that doing so would lead me on a ten-year odyssey to find the band's story, and that along the way I would learn how to make records, or whip a band into shape, but that's exactly what happened. Life can be strange and wonderful.

259

UNOFFICIALLY UNINVITED TO OUR PARTY

'I'm here to destroy this fucked up system.'

Anton's use of YouTube was revolutionary. Ever since he started posting videos for his newest work—something which started around *Book Of Days*— he's used the form to release his music to his listeners almost immediately after he finishes it, and he engages in the comments section often, laying down facts for the endless stream of new fans who know him solely from *Dig!* or from his misrepresentation in the press. He was among the first artists to do so.

Sometime after the groundbreaking *Book Of Days* video project appeared online, it was announced that *My Bloody Underground* would be officially released on April 15, 2008. In an interview for *Room Thirteen*, Anton enthusiastically discussed what he'd been up to since *We Are The Radio* came out and he left New York—raising Hermann, touring the world, marrying Katy, enjoying the TV show *Cash In The Attic*, helping other bands—and how excited he was about the new record.

When asked why there was so much Icelandic singing on the record, he replied, 'There are only 300,000-odd people on the planet who speak [Icelandic], and a lot of the bands from [Iceland] are singing in English because they want to break out of [that]. I figured I'd go in the opposite direction, just to make a statement.' Having entire songs sung in foreign languages is the most noticeable feature about Anton's records after *We Are The Radio*.

Anton also mentioned that he was working on a French-language record—a project that would eventually become *Musique De Film Imagine*. 'I don't speak French, but I have no worries about it because I understand it, so I'm doing it,' he said. 'I'm just trying to make one piece of relevant art to contribute to the culture.'*

By the end of February, reviews for *My Bloody Underground* were starting to pour in. It was the most-reviewed of any BJM album up to that point, so it's a shame more people didn't understand it, or Anton, by the time it came out.

Sometime in mid-February, *Drowned In Sound*'s Dom Gourlay visited Anton and Katy at London's Columbia Hotel, for what was to be Anton's last promotional interview of the day before he flew back to America to prepare for tour with the rest of the band, who all still lived back in Los Angeles (with the exceptions of Joel, who lived in San Francisco, and Collin, who lived in Portland). Anton scoffed at the comparisons Gourlay made with My Bloody Valentine and The Jesus & Mary Chain, intent on driving home the point that he was not a 'new' artist going retro, no matter what the press said.

It was soon time to hit the road again. In July, the band made headlines—though not the kind they wanted—when an argument erupted backstage following a gig in London, at the Forum. Frankie had gotten drunk and swung and broke a microphone during the show. Anton told him he would have to pay for its replacement. Later, when the band left the stage, Frankie stayed on rambling into another microphone, irritating Anton further. When Joel tried to diffuse the situation by bidding goodnight to the crowd, Frankie ignored him.

'Don't shut front-of-house, man, you fucker,' he announced into the PA. The band returned to play an encore before leaving to a chorus of applause. Things then exploded backstage, and the press had a field day.

The story went that Anton had cut Frankie with a knife or a broken beer bottle in the dressing room during an argument over the busted microphone and his refusal to leave the stage when Anton told him to. Frankie confirms this. 'I ended up in the hospital,' he says, offering no further comment further except that it was 'another good fuckin' night.'

The official police statement said, 'We were called by London ambulance at 11:09 to reports of a man being stabbed at the Forum club in Highgate Road, Kentish Town. A thirty-five-year-old man [Emerson] was taken to hospital suffering from minor stab injuries. A forty-year-old man [Newcombe] was

---

* The *Room Thirteen* interview was just one of many Anton did in early 2008. In fact, he was now doing so many interviews that he had to schedule them in bulk. Sometimes, entire days would be spent speaking to journalists, but as time went on he found he preferred to do interviews by email, so he could keep a record of exactly what had been said.

arrested and later released with no further action because the victim did not want to substantiate any allegation.'

The BJM then released a counter-statement:

1. There was no knife or knives involved in any shape or form in this incident.

2. The cuts to Frankie Emerson were caused by some glass splinters.

3. Frankie Emerson's injuries were superficial to his arm and stomach, he was treated at the Royal Free Hospital in London.

4. These injuries were caused by horseplay by the band in their own changing room after the gig.

5. Anton Newcombe was questioned at Kentish [Town] Police Station to help the police with their enquiries and was released with no charge or caution.

6. Frankie Emerson did not press any charges on Anton Newcombe.

7. Any comments by anyone within or outside the media to the contrary are completely false.

8. The band will continue with their successful European tour.

The band continued on to the Dour Festival in Belgium, the Garden Nef Party in France, and the Benicassim Festival in Spain. 'These things do happen on tour,' a publicist for the band explained, 'when the band are tired and have been away from home too long.' The band then flew back to the USA, ahead of a scheduled appearance on *Late Show With David Letterman* on July 24, but when the show's producers got word of the backstage scuffle the booking was canceled. (Joel in particular had been looking forward to the Letterman gig, boasting earlier in the year that the show would go smoothly 'if we don't scare 'em too much at the pre-show rehearsals!')

The very next day, July 25, the band received word that The Situation's Chris Tucker had died at the age of thirty-six. Early in the morning of July 22, a Philadelphia Police Department vehicle had pulled Chris over for driving the wrong way down a one-way street. Panicked, he ingested multiple bags of narcotics and lost consciousness. He was pronounced dead after a three-day coma. He left behind a five-year-old son, Jackson, and was buried in Wyoming. 'Chris performed with his heart on his sleeve, honestly baring his soul with compassion for himself and others,' Philadelphia native A Girl About Town wrote on her blog three days after his death. That night, the BJM and Singapore Sling played to a packed house at Terminal 5 in New York, one of their only shows in the states that summer. Will Carruthers stood in on bass, and Jón Sæmundur Auðarson joined the band for 'Golden Frost.' They closed with the song Chris had helped write, 'If Love Is The Drug, Then I Want To OD,' before finishing off with 'Prefab Ambulation,' which has yet to appear on record.

Chris's death was not the only one Anton would suffer that year. Sophie Guenan, who had been married to Jorge Diaz de Bedoya from The Minstrels for years, died as a result of what was determined to be medical malpractice that same month. Between the realities and weight of these tragedies, and the opportunities made possible by both his diligence and the momentum provided by the movie, Anton knew things had to change in his own life.

* * *

263

In August 2008, The Brian Jonestown Massacre played a well-reviewed tour of Australia and New Zealand, including some dates with Matt Tow's band The Lovetones, and released the *Just Like Kicking Jesus* EP as a split between Anton's A Records and Iceland's 12 Tonar. The EP included 'Bring Me The Head Of Paul McCartney' as well as two alternate versions of 'Just Like Kicking Jesus,' plus both English and Icelandic versions of 'Amazing Electronic Talking Cave,' the latter featuring Reykjavik artist Unnur Andrea Einarsdottir on vocals.

Offering companion English versions of songs recorded in other languages is something Anton has continued to do in the years since. 'I really want to explore different languages as a way of saying thank you with my actions to cultures that I respect and love or see something of my own spirit in,' he told *Punk Globe* around the time of the EP's release. He even appeared to have made peace with the role *Dig!* continued to play in his and the band's ever-expanding fan base. 'I'm happy that we keep growing in popularity as well as artistically,' he continued. 'We are not a radio or TV band, and that is OK. I don't give a shit about pop—I mean, it's fine, it's business, but at the same time we sell out concerts, make T-shirts and records, and make jobs and travel. I am thankful, and want that to grow for as long as I have energy to create.'

At the turn of the year, Matt Hollywood rejoined the band as a full-time touring member, joining the BJM on the road with The Flavor Crystals and establishing a lineup that would remain settled for the next seven years: Anton, Frankie, Dan, Ricky, Collin, Rob, Joel, and Matt.

In March, the BJM opened for Primal Scream at the Fillmore in San Francisco. Anton introduced Matt to the crowd, who reacted with applause. Three years earlier, when Anton had invited Matt onstage during their set at MusicfestNW, nobody—not even the band—knew that it would pave the way for his eventual return. Now, for fans who just started getting into the band because of *Dig!*, it was like Matt and Joel had never left. The DVD had only been out for a few years, and Matt had been out for almost a decade before he came back, making music with The Out Crowd and also with another project he had called Rebel Drones that Peter Holmström also played in.

Around the time of the Fillmore show, I saw the band at the Clubhouse in Phoenix. A week or so beforehand, I later learned, Anton had quit drinking cold turkey—right before the band's upcoming show at Coachella. He later revealed he'd wished he'd felt more enthusiastic to play the festival, but was too focused on the painful process of detoxing.

'I took an antibiotic and it just blew out my liver,' he recalled to the *Quietus*. 'I couldn't walk. I lived on the fourth floor of this apartment block and I couldn't carry my guitars across the room. I had to put them down and said, That's it! Alcohol was easier to quit than heroin because I was done drinking. It's a matter of taking some pills for three days, to make sure I didn't have a seizure, and then it was done. There was no doubt in my mind that I'd be very quick to die if I didn't do this, and it was never my intention to drink myself to death. As much as I loved being drunk twenty-four hours a day, it was in that 60s cowboy way, or like Sinatra: *A party never stops, let's all drink Martinis forever.* It had very little to do with rock'n'roll.'

As far as Frankie is concerned, however, not much had changed. 'Anton, when he quit drinking—it's not like he became a whole different person, it's just that now he was a *sober* dick,' he says. 'The violence was scaled back. That was definitely a blessing. But still, you're dealing with a person with crazy behavior, whether he was drinking or not. To me, it wasn't that big of a progression, because he still has a lot of fucking issues … whatever he's got going on affects us when we're in the bus together, and he was definitely pissed.'

* * *

After Coachella, Anton returned to Berlin to begin work on *Who Killed Sgt. Pepper?*, which would continue in the same vein as *My Bloody Underground*. With the advent of social media and peer-to-peer file sharing, he started reaching out and connecting with potential new collaborators from all over the world. In this way, social media allowed him to broaden the collaborative aspect of his work. 'I'm more interested in conceptual art than I am in being a singer and I always have been,' he said, adding, 'That's why I'm interested in the recording process … I believe the music lives or dies in the live moment, and then it's gone forever.'

Among those he connected with for *Who Killed Sgt. Pepper?* was the Russian musician Felix Bondarev. Anton offered to fly Felix to Berlin from St. Petersburg to work on a couple of songs. Felix was nineteen or twenty when he and Anton made 'Detka, Detka, Detka!' together. Anton wrote the music, Felix wrote the words, in Russian and English. It's not a stretch to picture two dozen Red Army soldiers doing the *Kozachok* to the bouncy track.

Who Killed Sgt. Pepper? is all about beats, remix culture, and postmodern collage, but when you understand the way Anton has always created music, it's not that different from the tape he made with Ricky and Travis back in the Haight twenty years earlier. The first track on the record, the droning instrumental 'Tempo 116.7,' is a dark but danceable sound-world that would first appear on the *Smoking Acid* EP, which also features a different mix of the track, plus another cut from *Who Killed*, 'Super Fucked,' and English and Icelandic versions of 'The Serious Matter' / 'Í Alvöru Talað.' The only words spoken on 'Tempo 116.7' are *'Unless you don't give a fuck to be free'*; the lyric, BPM, and title are both references to—and possibly a direct sample from—the song 'The Devil Made Me Do It' by Black Nationalist rapper Paris.

The second song on the album is 'Fiungur Hnífur,' adapted in part from Goldfrapp's 'Ooh La La' after it was shown to Anton by an engineer who

265

asked him what he would've done with the beat. The minute Anton heard it, he wanted to make it into a heavy-metal song. 'Let's Go Fucking Mental' is also beat-heavy and features a sample of soccer fans chanting. 'The crowd started singing that at our show at T In The Park,' Anton explained. 'People started getting bouncy and crazy, and I was like, *Holy shit!* I love all these sing-alongs. They're just ridiculous, and I heard that one everywhere.' (The chant sampled on the record is actually by Dutch fans of the team Go Ahead Eagles, from a match a year or two earlier.)

When he came to record 'Let's Go Fucking Mental,' Anton realized he'd left his melodica at the studio during a previous session—something he'd forgotten until he spotted it on the studio windowsill, and thought he'd use it on the track. An Albanian woman was singing in a studio a few doors down. Anton caught her on a coffee break and invited her to sing on it.

Unnur Andrea Einarsdottir had met Anton a couple of years earlier in Iceland, during the making of *My Bloody Underground*, when she sang on 'Amazing Electronic Talking Cave.' Her own artistic vision resonated strongly with Anton's. 'Music is a very physical thing,' she explained in 2008. 'Very often when I hear music, I want it to be even more physical, even so physical that I can touch it or even eat it.' Unnur performed the music and video for track five on the album, 'White Music,' herself, five years before *Who Killed Sgt. Pepper?* was released. In the video, she plays a 'chestharp' while surrounded by albino animals. The song is followed on the album by 'This Is The First Of Your Last Warning,' on which Unnur mostly sings in her native tongue, save for the chorus, which is in English.

Anton had also begun working with Will Carruthers extensively during this time. Best known for his work with Spacemen 3 and Spiritualized, Will would play bass off and on with the BJM for years. For this record, he contributed bass and vocals on 'Let's Go Fucking Mental,' as well as the Joy Division–saturated 'This Is The One Thing We Did Not Want To Have Happen,' among others. Jón Sæmundur Auðarson carried on from *My Bloody Underground* and did videos for the tracks, as well as contributing some guitar. Inspired by his artistic collaboration with Anton, he also started his own musical project, Dead Skeletons, with Henrik Björnsson of Singapore Sling (who also played some guitar on *My Bloody Underground*) and Ryan Van Kriedt.

Anton continues the theme of 'This Is The First Of Your Last Warning' on 'The One,' which was first released on an EP of the same name the previous November, alongside both English and Icelandic versions of 'This Is The First Of Your Last Warning' plus 'Bruttermania,' which features vocals by Felix Bondarev. 'I detuned the guitar, and I think I am using a Telray plug. It's a delay,' Anton later said of 'The One.' Next is 'Someplace Else Unknown,' a droning industrial jam over a thick beat, followed by the bouncy 'Detka!,' the darker 'Super Fucked,' and a dreamy reworking of a much older song, 'Our Time.'

Dino Karlis played drums on portions of *Sgt. Pepper?*, and would continue in that role for the Jonestown's next album, *Aufheben*. His performance on 'Feel It' is epic, to say the least. 'I wish *we* would've recorded that one,' Matt would lament about the song, which features perhaps Anton's most overt lyrical musings on the subject of death over another heavy disco track.

'Felt Tipped-Pen Pictures Of UFOs' is a recording of Anton's friend Nancy from Scotland talking with him about the 'Liverpool experience,' by which he means the nausea-inducing throngs of Beatles tourists in the city. The song begins with a sample of John Lennon speaking to the press in 1966, shortly his infamous 'bigger than Jesus' gaffe caused people to protest The Beatles' music; his phrase '*And now it's all this*' repeats over airy keyboards, like a transmission beaming into space, as Nancy brings us back to reality. 'I've got to say though ... "Imagine"? What a load of bullshit!' she says suddenly, disrupting the mellow vibe before carrying on in her monologue.

While *Who Killed Sgt. Pepper?* was not received quite so negatively as *My Bloody Underground*, it nevertheless baffled critics and struggled to gain ground among new fans accustomed to the sound of the band pre-*Dig!* It was often compared in the press to European house music—an idea Anton loathed. 'How do you know what's a good house track if they all have the same beat?' he scoffed. 'All house music runs at 120bpm.'

Instead, he explained, his focus for this record was to explore the part rhythm plays in the success of mega-selling hit singles. 'I wanted to see what I would do creating on top of those beats and not be grounded by what is popular at the moment,' he said. The best example of this approach is 'This Is The First Of Your Last Warning,' which has the same intro beat as the one featured on Michael Jackson's 1979 #1 hit 'Rock With You.' 'I had the best drummer in Iceland,' Anton continued. 'I said to him, I want you to just play this whole song from beginning to the end, no punch-ins. And then I went in the other room. *I'm* not listening to Michael Jackson. *He* is. Creating a song completely different on top of that. I wanted to see what would happen.'

One of the most noticeable things about the record is how heavy and pounding the kick drum is, which reminded me of something Larry Thrasher had told me about recording *Take It From The Man!*—how Anton was just obsessed with getting that kick right—and here it is, sounding like a hammer in your ears, in all the best ways.

Many of the journalists soliciting interviews with Anton around this time evidently hadn't bothered to listen to the record, as they were still more interested in the onscreen persona he'd come to be known for, which hadn't been helped by his antagonistic relationship with the press.

* * *

A couple of months after coming home from the *Who Killed Sgt. Pepper?* world tour—which saw them play Australia in February and March and Europe and the UK through April and May before finishing in June in the United States—Anton was back to work at Studio East in Berlin, starting recording what would ultimately become *Aufheben*. During the course of these sessions, he would share demos through his UStream internet channel, *Dead-TV*. But then everything came to a screeching halt. Toward the end of the year, Anton was admitted into St. Joseph's psychiatric ward in Berlin, following what some have alleged was a violent schizophrenic episode. Specific details on what went down are hard to come by, but the consensus seems to be that Anton hit his lowest point in a long while.

When Anton returned to public life in 2011, his head was completely shaven. Rumors continued to abound as to what might have happened to land him in there, but whatever it was, the price tag for his two-month stay at St. Joseph's ended up at 15,000 euros, which is part of what prompted the release of *The Singles Collection (1992–2011)*. Another justification for the release was the premiere, in September 2010, of the HBO TV show *Boardwalk Empire*, the ninety-second intro sequence for which was accompanied by a remixed version of 'Straight Up And Down.' The pilot episode was the most expensive television production in history at the time, but fortunately it was a hit, too, reaching more than seven million viewers on its first broadcast. The series was renewed for another four seasons and a total of fifty-six episodes, with 'Straight Up And Down' opening each one, which meant a series of big royalty checks for Anton.

Back in Berlin, Anton returned to work on *Aufheben* and found a mess on his hands. Prior to being admitted to St. Joseph's, he'd busted out three albums worth of material in just as many months. The mixes were then entrusted to Fabien Lessure, as Anton explained in a post on the *Dead-TV* chat room shortly after his release from the hospital. 'I have no idea how to mix any of it now. I ended up in the hospital, so that's the end of that style of creating, when I was doing the rough dumps every day. The board was messed up at this studio. It's all overloaded, so only "Illuminomi" sounds okay. It was a major fuck-up on my part. I was winging everything, so I didn't know the difference. I was really high on MDMA, so Fab is trying to do the mixes now, but I'm afraid of it. It isn't mastered. What I would like to do is keep making things up and present something when I'm ready.'

To my ear, this period marks a clear break between those initial post-*Dig!* records and everything Anton has put out since. *My Bloody Underground*, *Who Killed Sgt. Pepper?*, and the EPs from that period all have a consistent character to them, and the same can be said for everything Anton's done since. Every record since *Aufheben* has a similar energy to the pre-*Dig!* records, although they retain the aesthetic vein he first developed in Iceland.

The rough mixes for *Aufheben* hearken back to the space-rock drones of *Spacegirl* and *Methodrone*, but they also capture the retro-psych vibe of *Satanic* and the airy tech-vibe of *And This Is Our Music*. With *Aufheben*, Anton had at last made the natural progression from his creative restart with *My Bloody Underground* and *Who Killed Sgt. Pepper?* It was a return to form, and a return to stability in his own life.

In May, Anton's distributor, Cargo, put together *The Singles Collection* at its headquarters in London. Alongside a selection of older material—including 'She Made Me,' 'Evergreen,' 'Hide And Seek,' 'Anemone,' 'Not If You Were The Last Dandy On Earth,' and 'When Jokers Attack'—the album includes two tracks from the *Aufheben* sessions that were deemed ready for release at the time, 'Illuminomi' and 'There's A War Going On.' The latter was written and first recorded by one-time 60s folk star Bobby Jameson, for whom Ariel Pink would name one of his albums. Jameson had demoed the song in 1965, but it didn't get a wide release until the 2002 reissue on Joe Foster's Rev-Ola label of Jameson's *Songs Of Protest And Anti-Protest* (for which he was credited as Chris Lucey).

In the intervening years, Jameson had been screwed over by a series of industry suits and fell into a hard life of drugs and booze before sobering up and leaving the music industry in the mid-80s. He spent the next twenty years away from the limelight, until in 2003 he discovered that *Songs Of Protest And Anti-Protest* had been reissued without his knowledge. In 2007, he started a blog detailing his life and struggles to seek royalties for the sale of his earlier recordings. Anton reportedly paid him $2,000 to cover 'There's A War Going On,' which Jameson claimed was the only money he'd ever gotten from songwriting. The cover also brought a surge of support and new listeners to Jameson, who was taken aback by the renewed attention.

* * *

As Anton continued to work on his own health and his newest record in Berlin, *The Singles Collection* came out to general praise in August 2011. Like *Tepid Peppermint Wonderland*, it wasn't an overarching statement. More like a bookmark.

Aufheben was released, at last, on May 1, 2012. The *de facto* release party was held at Crescent Ballroom in Phoenix, Arizona. The record's overriding theme is eschatology—the science of last things. Given the anxiety with which many people greeted the year 2012, one might say that Anton provided the soundtrack to it. The cover art is based on a Carl Sagan graphic included in Voyager Golden Record, which was launched into space by NASA in 1977. 'I thought it would've been funny if a scientist or someone added this one word on this plaque: *Aufheben*, a German word with many meanings simultaneously,' Anton explained. 'To destroy. To lift up. To preserve. All at once. If you think about German culture, the positive parts, and relate it to the history of the last century, society had to destroy it to both save and rebuild it as a means of preservation.'*

---

* In philosophy, the term *Aufhebung* is associated with Hegel, for whom it has the apparently contradictory implications of both preserving and changing, and eventually advancement. The tension between these senses suits Anton well.

Aufheben begins with 'Panic In Babylon,' an instrumental piece that began life as 'Crazy Barn Demo.' The horn of the apocalypse sounds off before the beat kicks in and is layered with various animal noises. The juxtaposition of apocalyptic panic with the notion of a dance party reflects Anton's own sentiments regarding doomsday myths: that is, do not take them too seriously. Listening to it now, I think of Anton showing journalist Sara Scribner his recordings of animal noises back in Laurel Canyon, and how he felt people weren't ready for them yet.

Photographer and graphic designer Eliza Karmasalo collaborated with Anton on the song 'Viholliseni Maala' (aka 'In The Land Of My Enemy'), for which Matt Hollywood wrote the lyrics while in Europe, rehearsing for the 2012 tour. They had at the 8mm Club below Anton's Berlin apartment, while he spun Dead Skeletons' new single, 'Dead Mantra.' They found they shared similar interests and made plans then to record a song in Finnish, Eliza's native language. A year later, they reconvened to make 'Viholliseni Maala.'

Though Eliza had once been the vocalist in a punk band, she was by no means a professional musician, and she struggled at first to come up with lyrics or a vocal melody. Then, one day, the song just happened. 'Like breathing,' she says. 'I wrote lyrics in broken Finnish and sang with little fear. I felt a desire to send out a message and we made it to sound like a forest journey into a strange land. Anton liked that and it fit the tune he was building well. It all came out at once, like a live stream of pure energy. To me the words are like leaves in the wind, forming their own shapes.' Later, she tried a few songs in Bulgarian, and another in Finnish. The second Finnish song sounded darker, and Eliza liked it, but Anton set it aside. She then re-recorded her vocals for 'Viholliseni Maala' in the hope of bringing more power to it, although she says she struggled due to a recent bout of the flu.

The album's third track is 'Gaz Hilarant'—French for 'Laughing Gas.' In July, the *Houston Press* published an article titled 'True Blood: Of Wolf And Anton Newcombe,' in which journalist Jef Rouner mentioned how another HBO show, *True Blood*, had recently made use of the song, which he felt was a bizarre choice for the episode. 'I have a hard time imagining the weres of Louisiana as BJM fans,' he wrote, 'and such folks don't usually peruse the section of the record store where Anton Newcombe is relevant.' I tweeted the

271

link to Anton. 'He misses the point,' he tweeted back. 'The lyrics are *laugh while you can*. Total vampire rock if you ask me.'

Track four, 'Illuminomi,' had been released as ten-inch vinyl single the previous year, with 'There's A War Going On' as the B-side, as well as being included on *The Singles Collection*. 'It isn't lo-fi,' Anton said of the track. 'I just mix it that way. It's art. It isn't meant to be some slick bullshit. The medium is fuzz.' Thibault Pesenti and Friederike Beinert of The RocKandys both appear on the track, providing vocals and flute, respectively.

'I'm being silly,' Anton said of the fifth track, 'I Want To Hold Your Other Hand.' 'Assuming a person has two hands, if John Lennon is holding one hand there would be, in theory, one free for me to hold, too.' Track six, the instrumental 'Face Down On The Moon,' is one of those that was first streamed live on *Dead-TV*. 'The Clouds Are Lies' refines the surrealist elements of the last two records, while 'Stairway To The Best Party' is the track on the record that sounds most like the live band. The riff is a revisionist take on the Stones' 'Paint It Black,' only Anton paints it darker.

The most ambitious track on the record is 'Seven Kinds Of Wonderful,' of which Anton would note, 'It is difficult sonically, but I started to notice some things about the sounds and their effect on the brain. You have to listen to it like a French Lou Reed is in one of the speakers singing in monotones, then a Gregorian message in Old High German is in the other, very high-pitched and distorted with a slow echo, then Morrissey singing magic incantations while pretending to be Grace Slick, and Kevin Shields doing a cut-up on lost Bach and Mozart tablature.'

'Waking Up To Hand Grenades' is the final doomsday cult dance party finale before the world explodes, and the most lyrical track on the record. 'Blue Order / New Monday' closes the album. Its message is simple, but it packs in layers of meaning, offering a commentary on the current socioeconomic and political status of the world. Anton named it in response to Bad Lieutenant, featuring New Order's Bernard Sumner, supposedly ripping off the riff from 'When Jokers Attack' for their single 'Sink Or Swim.' 'It was based on a very unique twelve-string riff,' he said, 'and I was like, *Okay, this is fucking retarded. I'm going to scramble the name of your fucking band so that when people Google your name, mine is going to come up, too, for all eternity.*'

Len Comaratta reviewed *Aufheben* for *Consequence Of Sound* and picked up on the beginning-to-end completeness of the album. 'The sense of belonging and connectivity amongst the songs is self-evident,' he wrote. 'If the track listing is shuffled, that homogeneity might not be so apparent, hinting at the importance of the album's sequence.' *NME* gave the album eight out of ten and included it in its list of 'must-listens' for May, hailing it as the best BJM record since *And This Is Our Music*.

In support of *Aufheben*, the Jonestown toured four continents, opening for The Raveonettes in Australia and playing sold-out gigs all over Europe. Before returning to the United States to finish the tour, they made a stop in Tel Aviv for their first ever performance in Israel. Many of the gigs were also broadcast live on *Dead-TV*. In Berlin, at C-Club, Eliza took to the stage to sing 'Viholliseni Maalla' with the group. In the USA, The Blue Angel Lounge opened for the BJM on the West Coast leg of the tour, while Magic Castles opened on the East Coast.

In December 2012, a few months after the tour ended, Anton and Katy welcomed their son Wolfgang Gottfried Newcombe into the world. By this point, things had calmed down for Anton in a big way. With a grip on both his mental and physical health, he was finally getting to where he'd wanted to be—and strived to be—for twenty years, and it was reflecting positively in his work.

273

In the time between the successful 2012 world tour and the release of *Revelation* in 2014, the members of The Brian Jonestown Massacre explored new horizons. Joel Gion stepped out on his own with his band The Primary Colours. Ricky Maymi lent his knowledge and labor to the emergent Chinese indie rock scene. Collin Hegna's other work garnished widespread acclaim, and his band Federale got their songs into *The Lego Movie*, as well as the Iranian Vampire Western *A Girl Walks Home Alone At Night*.

Some of the period's other developments were not so positive. As Anton began laying down tracks for what would become *Revelation*, Jeff put in motion a fourteen-page lawsuit against Anton's attorney, Barry Simons, demanding his cut of the *Boardwalk Empire* money. He accused Barry of conspiring, with Anton, to defraud him out of royalties due on the songs he'd played on by claiming that Jeff had agreed to give up his rights to 'Straight Up And Down.'

Jeff, who had not achieved the same level of success as some of his former bandmates in the time since *Dig!*, was undoubtedly envious of their success since his departure. 'It was frustrating for me, I must say, that I leave the band, and they just instantly *step it up*,' he says. 'I went to England a couple times, and to Japan, but as soon as I leave the band, they're going to Scandinavia and doing world tours every year.' In 2013, Anton, who was not a party in the lawsuit, asked for a court injunction against Jeff to declare that the guitarist did not hold an interest in the BJM's songs. Jeff filed a counterclaim the following spring, claiming he had co-written six songs with Anton before leaving the band in 2002.

Jeff's suit claimed that in the late 90s, while he was still in the BJM, he had voiced his concerns to Anton about his rights to the songs the pair had written. According to the complaint, Anton had referred Jeff to Barry, whom he alleged had agreed to file copyrights on Jeff's behalf, and to pay him royalties. But Barry, Jeff said, never explained that there were two different copyright registrations that needed to be filed, with respect to song compositions and song recordings. Rather, Jeff was simply assured by Barry that *all* of the proper copyrights would be filed, and that he would receive royalties as they were earned. Jeff went on to claim that he had received a royalty check for $1,000 when 'Straight Up And Down' was used in an episode the TV show *Nash Bridges*, and that he later contacted Barry from time to time to ask if he was owed any royalties, to which Barry always told him that none had been accrued.

Jeff only decided to take serious legal action after he discovered that HBO had licensed 'Straight Up And Down' for the opening credits of *Boardwalk Empire*. Under this license, HBO would be paying tens of thousands of dollars in fees each year. 'Plaintiff is informed and believes that defendant Simons and Newcombe have a history of making false representations to artists to induce them to write compositions and perform on sound recordings in the group The Brian Jonestown Massacre,' the lawsuit claimed.

In August of 2014, a judge threw out Jeff's charges of misappropriation, conversion, and accounting, while also declaring that he had failed to provide enough evidence to support his accusations of fraud, breach of fiduciary duty, and conspiracy. Jeff amended his suit, and by October 14 the case was settled; Jeff would now earn some royalties, but the fight raged on, as both parties filed additional lawsuits against each other. Both cases were dismissed without prejudice on New Year's Eve 2014, with each side ordered to pay their own legal fees. Anton vowed never to play the song live again. Jeff, however, feels avenged. 'All of these people wouldn't help me with the lawsuit, and it was so obvious I was getting fucked over,' he says. 'My name wasn't even filed with the copyright office … supposedly Barry had done fifteen other songs for me, but he lied about them. I wanted my name on stuff, because at that point we were going out of town to play shows, and we had a few albums done, so we went to the office and Barry supposedly did the paperwork. Me and Anton worked out the percentages, and it was really only a handful of songs, but two of the only songs he put

275

through on the form were "Straight Up And Down" and "Monster," and "Straight Up And Down" went on to make more money than everything else put together, so how's that for karma?'

* * *

Anton quickly moved forward. In February 2014, he told *Louder Than War* about the recordings he'd been making in his Berlin studio since *Aufheben*. 'I liked each track on it's own, but I could not see how they all flowed together,' he said. 'But a few of my mates came by for a listen and put it into perspective. They said it was nonstop good songs and that I should lighten up.'

Since Wolfgang had come into his world, lightening up was at the center of Anton's focus. 'I have to look out for him,' he told *Taste In Music*. 'I have to take preventative measures to avoid tripping out on the world, letting my anger turn into something else, or just drinking. I don't drink anymore because I have to think about *his* concerns. He's a baby that has to be protected and looked after. So, as much as I can talk about me flipping my wig or whatever, I'm kinda in a different place.'

Whatever Anton might have lost on his long road to recovery, the revolution inside him was being won, and he'd even found a new word for it. Explaining the title, he said, 'The simple answer is, I love the word. Most of the time I would classify my work [as] *Śruti*, i.e. *what is heard*. Definition of the word revelation.'

Recorded between late 2012 and early 2014, *Revelation* was the first BJM album to be fully recorded and produced at Anton's home studio. Ricky plays guitar on the record, which also features a guest vocal by Joachim Alhund of Les Big Byrd on its opening track, while other guests include Dino Karlis on drums and Ryan Van Kriedt on guitar. Anton plays the rest. The cover was designed by Nina Theda Black.

Alhund sings on the opening track, 'Vad Hande Med Dem?'—Swedish for 'What Ever Happened To Them?' If you turn it up loud enough, you can hear the immediate natural echo of the beat. Speaking of drum tracks, the second song, 'What You Isn't,' is probably the grooviest Jonestown jam in over a decade—if not ever. If the opener is reminiscent of the sounds explored on *Aufheben*, this one hits a sonic vein Anton hadn't explored for years, his aggressive, authoritative sing-speak chugging over a classic BJM riff.

I first heard some of the demos for the album back in 2013. Out of those, I believe only the third song, 'Unknown' (working title: 'That Look In Your Eyes'), and the eleventh, 'Nightbird,' made it onto the record, alongside the previously released 'Fist Full Of Bees' and 'Food For Clouds.'* These four songs are placed evenly throughout the album's sequence, which avoids the overarching narrative style of *Aufheben* in favor of a more viscerally cohesive collection of good songs almost entirely of Anton's sole creation, in his own environment, their audial effects highly potent. That's all that's needed. 'Unknown' and 'Nightbird' are acoustic numbers that are reminiscent of some of Anton's work on *Thank God For Mental Illness* or *Bravery Repetition And Noise*, while 'Fist Full Of Bees' was first tracked around the time of *Aufheben*, and 'Food For Clouds' represents the more complex arrangements inherent on *Revelation*.

Elsewhere, 'Duck And Cover' and 'Second Sighting' are among the strongest instrumentals from (at least) the last four BJM albums, their bright, colorful tones interweaving to create a web of sound, while 'Memory Camp,' 'Days, Weeks And Moths,' 'Goodbye (Butterfly),' and 'Xibalba' capture perfectly what the live band should sound like at their best. All in all, it was The Brian Jonestown Massacre's best album to date, and it remains a favorite among fans. It was also among the band's best-reviewed records at the time of its release, with *Under The Radar*, *Sputnikmusic*, *Q*, *Pop Matters*, and the *Guardian* all publishing glowing reviews.

277

* * *

In January 2015, Dallas Taylor died at the age of sixty-six. Anton offered a heartfelt tribute online, as did others whom Taylor had helped. 'I'm really sad to report my friend Dallas Taylor passed away,' Anton wrote on Twitter. 'I owe him my life as he helped me kick dope.'

The news came just as Anton was gearing up to release *Musique De Film Imagine*, for which he offered the world a taster by first issuing the song 'Philadelphie Story,' which features vocals by the French singer-songwriter, musician, and actress SoKo. He explained the concept of the record in an official statement, writing, 'The album that you are about to hear is a soundtrack, my own creation, a tribute to great directors and filmmakers to

---

* Both songs were included on the 2013 EP *Fist Full Of Bees* alongside 'Everything Fades To White.'

an era that now seems to be behind us. Leaving the smart person to care to imagine that this art could now be in the shadow of its former glory. The interesting thing about this project is that the film does not exist either. Even so, I imagined and I realized its soundtrack. ... Now it's your turn, you are the listener to imagine the film.'

SoKo's appearance on the record came at the suggestion of Anton's wife, Katy. 'I hit her up via Twitter and asked her,' he explained. 'She told me she had never sang in French before. I said, Your culture needs you. I think she absolutely nailed it.' The resulting song is not so much a reference to the 1940s American film but 'ancient Greece and the esoteric,' according to Anton. 'The lyrics have to do with a journey through the underworld [and] resurrection.'

Another guest on the album is the actress, model, and singer Asia Argento, whom Anton invited to work with him after hearing 'Ours,' her collaboration with Tim Burgess. The result of her trip to Berlin, 'La Sacre Du Printemps,' was first released on her *Total Entropy*, but Anton wasn't finished with it yet. 'In the back of my mind, I wanted to see it presented in the proper context,' he said. '[Asia and I] talked about ... making a film together, with her as the director and creative force, and I would focus on the music ... but we need to find funding ... there should be no doubt in anyone's mind that we could pull this off. It's just fucking money.'

'To me,' Asia wrote to me of Anton, 'he is one of the greatest geniuses alive who I am lucky enough to have worked with and shared a moment in life which is very dear to me.'*

Overall, Anton wanted *Musique De Film Imagine* to evoke the mood of something like Jean-Jacques Beineix's film Betty Blue. The album's moody cover image is taken from an old Icelandic postcard, provided by Jón Sæmundur Auðarson, while song titles such as 'Après Le Vin,' 'La Dispute,' and 'L'Ennui' drew comparisons to the works of French masters like Clouzot, Marivaux, Truffaut, Piaf, and Godard.

Most critics praised the album, though *Line Of Best Fit*'s John Platt gave it a not so shiny review. 'I expected definite characters, perhaps using a

---

* It was through Asia that Anton met Anthony Bourdain, whom she dated for a while before his death. Anton appears in an episode of Bourdain's CNN TV show *Parts Unknown*, which first aired just days after the presenter was found dead in a hotel room in France.

leitmotif, but the mostly instrumental tracks offer few,' he wrote. 'I expected definite scenes; drama, bombast among the quieter moments. But each track fades into the last fading into the next and it all goes unnoticed.' Perhaps he missed the part where it was his job to come up with those things himself.

A couple of notable EPs were released during this time as well, namely *Revolution Number Zero* and +/-, which features a lot of the stuff Anton was doing on *Dead-TV* in the lead-up to *Aufheben*. After the announcement of *Musique* came the first in a series of collaborations with the Toronto-based singer Tess Parks, a limited-edition EP on clear ten-inch vinyl containing the songs 'Cocaine Cat' and 'Mama,' released for Record Store Day.

In 2013, at the age of twenty-one, Tess had signed to Creation Records founder Alan McGee's new label, 359 Music, for the release of her first record, *Blood Hot*. She hooked up with Anton soon after, and the two started recording together in Berlin. 'Anton and I were internet friends, and I was always a massive Brian Jonestown Massacre fan,' she said in 2015. 'He heard about my music through our mutual friend Alan … I messaged Anton saying I was coming to Berlin and it'd be great to meet him if he was around. So I went, and we ended up doing two songs together.'

As with most people who work with Anton, Tess found herself learning a lot from him. 'I know so much more about recording and writing from what Anton has taught me,' she told *Stereo Embers*. 'Working with Anton was an education … like getting my masters or something. … He has so many people who care about what he does, and it's so cool that he involves them in the whole creation process.'

A couple of weeks after the record came out, Anton and Tess debuted the music video for 'Cocaine Cat.' Their first record album, *I Declare Nothing*, was released on July 10, 2015, following which Anton and Tess embarked on a series of shows in support of it. That same summer, Philip John, director of *Being Human* and *Downtown Abbey*, began principal photography on his film *Moon Dogs*, for which Anton was tapped to compose the film's entire soundtrack. The film follows two teenage stepbrothers and a girl who comes between them on a road trip across Scotland. It received positive reviews from the *Irish Times*, the *Times*, the *Daily Express*, *Radio Times*, *Screen Daily*, and others, although only the *Radio Times* and *Screen Daily* articles mentioned Anton's 'hooky' and 'catchy' soundtrack.

* * *

The other members of The Brian Jonestown Massacre continued to explore new fields following the release of *Revelation*, and it was during this period that I began to become more closely acquainted with some of them. Getting to that point was a slow crawl. Having started this book in 2009, those first years were dedicated to digging up as much as I could. In the years leading up to *Revelation*, the more I found out, the more interested I became in the recording process and in songwriting craft, and I studied the research I'd done on the band to apply what could seemed relevant and useful to my own musical and artistic projects.

In the early part of 2015, Ricky Maymi could be found DJing in Bejing's Dongchang district and setting up tours for Chinese indie bands like Birdstriking and Chui Wan, among many others. My band, Gorky, was supposed to play a gig with Chui Wan in Phoenix, but there was a Visa issue and they never made it to the States. Later, Anton was so impressed with Birdstriking that he put out a record of theirs on his A Records label.

On May 12, 2015, Joel played at the Solar Culture in Tucson, Arizona, where he and I chatted behind the merch booth about the rave review Fox News TV personality Greg Gutfeld had recently written about Joel's *Apple Bonkers*, among other things. Gutfeld, it turns out, is a surprisingly ardent fan of both psych and the Jonestown; on his website, he described *Apple Bonkers* as a 'psychedelic masterpiece,' and he told me that its quality had led him to think that the BJM 'exists not because of Anton, but in spite of him.'

A year earlier, Gorky had opened for Joel and his band The Primary Colours on their way to Levitation, at the Orpheum in Flagstaff. I'll never forget it. When the stage manager came into the green room to tell me we were up, I looked over at Joel, who was sitting across from me sipping a beer, and he had a sly smirk on his face. He could tell I was nervous but also excited. I'd had with him a blast a couple years before that, too, walking up and down Haight street, where he pointed out all the old BJM spots, but it was this that gig really set me in the mind that music was something I wanted to do full-time.

On the night of the show, Bobby Jameson, who'd grown up partly in Tucson, died, aged seventy, after suffering an aneurysm. 'He was clearheaded to the end,' his brother, Quentin, posted on Facebook. 'He made, I think, a good choice not to opt for a risky surgery, which would, at best, have left him disabled in a nursing home for a few more years. He died true to his own rules of sobriety, honesty, and independence. A warrior's death.'

Bobby's death sent ripples among Anton's closest fans—myself included—although I didn't find out that he had passed until later. When the gig was over, I said goodnight to everyone and headed home, shuffled through the playlists on my phone until I got to *Take Acid Now* and loaded up *Musique De Film Imagine*.

Later that year, on my twenty-ninth birthday, I went to Tommy Dietrick's Desert Stars Festival in Joshua Tree and met Dave D., Frankie Teardrop, Miranda Lee Richards, and The Dandy Warhols for the first time, and made love to a beautiful woman that night at the Sands Motel.*

It was sometime around September 2015 when I heard that Matt Hollywood had, like Joel, formed a new band, The Bad Feelings, and that they would be touring through Arizona. Gorky was set to open for them, too, and once we secured the Rhythm Room as the venue, I designed a flyer based on of my favorite Velvet Underground record, *Loaded*, and hooked Matt up with my friend Troy Farah, who interviewed him for the *Phoenix New Times*.

The week before Anton's forty-eighth birthday, the BJM announced their 25 Years Silver Jubilee tour, beginning in Australia in November, then on to North America and Europe. There would also be another new record, *Mini Album Thingy Wingy*, and another new full-length that would evolve into a double album in 2016.

Days before he spoke to the *Phoenix New Times*, it came to light that Matt had been officially uninvited to join the band on the tour. 'At least *The Donald* has the balls to tell people when they're fired,' Matt tweeted, in reference to then presidential candidate Trump. 'I'll see you some other time, Australia.'

Rumors also began to circulate among the band's innermost circle that Frankie had quit, which Anton then confirmed in an interview with *Drowned In Sound*. He would be replaced by Dead Skeletons' Ryan Van Kreidt. Of Matt's departure, Anton had only a few words. 'Matt Hollywood's doing his own group. We wish him well.' When Troy's *New Times* article came out

---

* We smoked a big fat joint in the bathroom, blowing the smoke out the little window so we wouldn't get busted, the both of us naked except for the cowboy hat I was wearing, but that's a story for another time …

under the title 'Matt Hollywood Doesn't Know Why He Was Fired From Brian Jonestown Massacre,' Anton, who'd refrained from giving an official comment to the newspaper, shared the article on Twitter, alongside the comment, 'Could one reason be he's not so much as written a song with BJM in 20 years? Not one fucking song?'

Matt's departure this time around felt oddly familiar. 'I'll miss hanging out with the other guys in the band, and, you know, going out and giving the fans what they want,' he told Troy. 'It's been years since anyone besides Anton really has been allowed to make any contribution to the music or the albums. It's disappointing to not have even been told that there was a tour in the works, but on the other hand, I can't say I'm really that upset about it. I've got other things going on.'

After Matt's firing and Frankie's quitting, the band that had existed since even before *Dig!* came out—and the band I'd followed closely since 2009—was over. Further changes would follow in 2018: Rob Campanella got the boot, and Dan Allaire and Collin Helga left around the same time. At time of writing, the only original members left in the touring band alongside Anton are Joel Gion and Ricky Maymi.

Frankie lasted in the BJM for fifteen years, and Anton seemed bummed to see him go. 'Frankie had a really nasty accident before the last tour,' he told *Drowned In Sound*. 'He messed up his arm. I mean *really* messed it up, and tried to drink his way out of it, so now he's got his shit together, he's decided to hang up his guns. Which is good, because even though I'll miss my mate I didn't want to watch him die, either … so it's a beautiful thing that way.'

For his part, Frankie has left his future with the BJM open. 'I left voluntarily,' he says. 'I needed some time to recoup and think about shit. I've got stuff going on with myself, you know. I've got a kid, too, and I've got to reel it in … and I need to look out for my health … I was hit by a car, playing with a broken arm, broken collarbone, broken shoulder blade. I was playing with a whole fucking broken right section of my torso. I couldn't handle it. I almost completely ruined my body with that shit. I saw doctors in Sweden, and they're like, *You gotta get off tour*, and I'm like, *No. I'm going to finish this tour*. I was being really stubborn and drinking myself to death. I had no painkillers. Here I am in Europe. Tons of booze. Makes me not feel my arm as much. So, that was hell. Ted [Gardner] was on that tour, and we had little meetings about it. They were like, *We could send you home*, but I didn't want to go home. I wanted to finish it. Big two-month tour all around the world, and then I'll be done. I fulfilled what I wanted to do, even if it was at my body and band's expense. I just wanted to make sure I did it and chilled the fuck out, and that's what I'm doing now. I'm chilling the fuck out.'

Outside of the Rhythm Room, in between sets, Matt and I smoked cigarettes and talked. After his mother had suffered a stroke, he'd been taking care of her in Florida, before moving to Atlanta, once she became more stable, with Reverends' Dandy Lee Strickland, a member of The Bad Feelings who'd played with Matt in the Rebel Drones back in Portland. He mentioned he was thinking about getting together a compilation of his BJM songs. At one point, I asked him about his plans now that he was out of the BJM, and if he was interested in talking to me for the book. He looked away and to the side and took another drag, the dim urban lights affixing a glow to the side of his face. Then he was quiet for a few seconds and sighed. He stayed quiet after that.

Jeff Davies offers some insight into this. 'We all go back so long. Part of it could be that, digging into stuff ... people have to think themselves about specifics. Someone like Matt Hollywood, or me, or Joel, there's specifics where, going back about situations ... you could see it doing some healing. And I have come to terms with some things, especially with that whole lawsuit thing—I really had to think about history and specifics. You have things in your head one way, or you don't think about things, and then when you have to really piece things together or answer questions, it makes you face parts of yourself either you have lied to yourself about or deceived yourself about. [Maybe] that's part of it with Matt.'

283

The gig itself was great. At one point, Matt's guitar broke a string, and Gorky's bass player, Tevin Crabdree, who'd gone to luthier school, jumped up and changed it for him without missing a beat. I watched in awe alongside Ben Holladay, who has drummed in the band ever since I founded it in 2002. The Bad Feelings were missing a guitar, too, so the leads to 'Oh Lord' and 'BSA' and a couple of other classics that night were played on my Epiphone Sheraton.

Not very many people came to the show, but there were a couple of BJM fans who'd come up all the way from Bisbee to see Matt play and left saying they'd had one of the greatest nights of their lives. That's the kind of thing we live for, though—or at least I do—so in the end there were more good feelings than bad.*

A couple of weeks after our show with Matt, The Dandy Warhols played Crescent. Opening the show was Miranda Lee Richards, who was touring in support of her new record, *Echoes Of The Dreamtime*; there was also another band on the bill called The Shelters. In the parking lot after the show, Zia McCabe popped out of the bus and spotted me as I was walking back to my car. 'Hey!' she called out, leaning in my direction out of the bus, and each time I think about this, it's like a scene in a movie I never want to stop watching, she was so luminous. 'Do you have the address to the party?'

'You know what,' I said, checking my pockets, 'I don't!'

Next thing I know, we're shuffling and dancing in a living room a few blocks away to a thumping beat, and there are, like, fifty people at this killer party, an impromptu band jamming in the corner opposite the front door. My best friend Shizuko, who's tagged along on many such adventures, is there with me. I run into Courtney Taylor-Taylor out back, and he tells me about a song he's written for the Dandys' new record, *Distortland*, 'Semper Fidelis,' and how he's used this Sonic Boom–inspired pedal manufactured by the wizards at Acid Fuzz on it, given to him by Anton. 'I'm sure Anton would be horrified to know that that super-rough Powerman 5000, Rob Zombie fucking metal sound came out of his pedal,' he smirks, 'but I love it, man!'†

---

* The same couldn't be said a couple of years later, when Matt followed Jeff's lead and filed an injunction against Anton, disputing his claims of full copyright in some BJM songs. Court documents indicate that Matt's songs—strictly by him and not on *Strung Out In Heaven*—include 'Oh Lord,' 'Cabin Fever,' 'BSA,' 'In My Life,' 'Not If You Were The Last Dandy On Earth,' and 'Miss June '75,' while the Newcombe–Hollywood co-authored songs are listed as 'Vacuum Boots,' 'No Come Down,' 'Ashtray,' 'Fire Song,' 'Sue,' and 'Sound Of Confusion.' Travis Threlkel is also listed as a co-author on 'Sue' and 'Sound Of Confusion.' Court documents also purport that Anton had secretly tried to register some of the co-authored works himself, without informing his former band members, such as 'Straight Up And Down,' and that Matt and the other band members around during *Take It From The Man!* joined Jeff in claiming their partial ownership of the work. Rob Campanella and Dean Taylor have also submitted statements to the proceedings. By October of 2018, Matt was fighting with Anton over rights to twenty-nine different BJM songs, pushing Anton to respond to a list of interrogatories to detail when, where, and with whom much of the old stuff was recorded, to aid with sorting out the disputes. (Perhaps this book could help jog everyone's memories?) At the time of writing, the issue still hasn't been resolved, with a trial date set for April 2019. In the meantime, all of Matt's songs have been removed from the online and streaming versions of the records.

† The following year, Courtney helped me out with mixing ideas for Gorky's single 'Action Pants,' which he told me he wished he'd written himself. That meant the world to me. Since first discovering his band and the BJM through *Dig!*, these people were my musical heroes. My approach to making *Mathemagician* with Gorky wouldn't have worked without what I've learned from them.

The two bands had long since buried the hatchet, of course. In 2014, a few days after our show with Joel in Flagstaff, they united onstage at Levitation for a rendition of 'Oh Lord.'

* * *

In January of 2016, The Brian Jonestown Massacre were announced to play the Field Day festival in London that summer, alongside P.J. Harvey, Deerhunter, Beach House, Yeasayer, and a bunch of other bands. Before that, there was the upcoming North American leg of their own Silver Jubilee tour, starting in Austin, at Levitation, before heading south, then up the East Coast into Canada, then through the west and Midwest, then into Canada again, then down the West Coast, with two shows each in San Francisco and Los Angeles, before ending in Phoenix and San Diego.

I bought tickets to see the band again that June. I'd seen videos of their recent shows, so I knew how good the live band was sounding, even without Matt and Frankie. And I'd been hearing, too, about how they'd been working on a new record, with the live touring band actually playing it. Man, I'd wanted that record for years.* But time sort of froze around then, and my trip began to wind down. Sometimes things go straight up and down, sometimes they begin and end with a wreck, and a wreck was exactly where I thought that June 2016 gig in Phoenix was headed after the guy threw a beer can at Anton.

It started out like the last scene of *Dig!*, when Anton kicks the guy in the head and the cops are talking to Brad Clark outside of the venue with Anton in the backseat of the patrol vehicle—only this time I'm there, at the Crescent Ballroom, and Anton has already stopped the show once to confront the guy with the light shining from his phone. Now he's going off on this other dumbass for endangering the people in front of him, closer to the edge of the stage. I'm expecting a punch, a lunge, or a kick to come at any time, while also hoping it wouldn't.

Anton is all dressed in white, big muttonchops, looking almost exactly like he did in the *Strung Out In Heaven* period. 'Actually, I'd rather go fuckin' to

285

---

* These sessions would eventually be split into two records, *Third World Pyramid* and *Don't Get Lost*. The first would come out in October 2016, around the time the band played their first ever shows in South America; *Don't Get Lost* followed in February 2017, just a few days shy of what would have been Brian Jones's seventy-fifth birthday, and the literal twenty-fifth anniversary of the BJM's first official show at the Peacock Lounge.

a hotel room and watch fuckin' *Deadliest Catch* or some bullshit than play my music for you people,' he tells the crowd, 'because I don't need people to throw trash at me.'

After keeping a few more thoughts to himself, looking down at his guitar, he takes it back. The crowd is shouting for him and the band to keep going, so he introduces their next number, 'Government Beard,' and tells us all about how it's this old CIA disguise thing, but then he changes his mind.

'It's not really about that,' he says. 'It's about me leaving home, because the concept about home when I was growing up as a kid, everything about it … the people I knew and the places I lived, and … California even, right? It doesn't exist.'

He gestures with his hand outward to the audience, in reference to the way everyone has their cellphone out, hanging on his every word.

'See? Nothing is even fucking remotely close to what I knew was a kid.'

The crowd begins to taunt him. They didn't come here to hear his life story. They came to hear music.

'Fuck you!' someone shouts.

'Actually, fuck *you*!' Anton shouts back. 'You know why? Because I said so. You know why? Because if you were fucking smart, you'd be eating health food. Right? Not talking to me. Right? That's true—you'd be eating broccoli or some shit. You wouldn't be standing there in the dark, shouting at me. So, this isn't a fuck *me* situation, it actually is a fuck *you* situation. Peace to you. We're not taking requests. And this also is not descending into chaos. We're gonna play a new song. See? Because *I actually control the situation.* Not you.'

He turns to the band.

'Ready, guys? Round, like an egg, this time.'

Then, he turns to the crowd again, to announce the next number.

'This next song is called "The Lantern,"' he says, his transfigured face shining out across the crowd. The light is white on his body, white on his linens and holy beads. Then, as if to cast a Masonic spell, he points. Directly right at me this time, his eyes all holy fire.

'It's about holding the torch high,' he says, 'so that others might see.'

OUTROESQUE

When I step now and then back into BJM Land, it feels like a dream of life buzzing at its absolute maximum. My interactions with Anton over these years have been few. Besides attending various shows and those few brief moments in Denver, I'd shared a few brief exchanges with him on social media. Maybe one or two brief words in person, but nothing extensive. It wasn't necessary.

For me, for all of his presence across records, film, video clips, written interviews, and after hearing stories about him from hundreds of people and sharing those stories myself, there was enough to piece the puzzle together while keeping the mystery intact, and those people who took time to share their memories of him and their lives in and out of The Brian Jonestown Massacre with me—especially those who have passed on and did not get to see the completion of this project—to them I am forever grateful.

As a musician and recording artist, I was drawn to Anton's creativity and knowledge, though I never thought that would open doors to me sharing the stage with Joel and Matt. Those shows changed my life, because I wanted to learn how to work the way Anton and his band do, to be in that world.

Anton's preference for spontaneity is inspiring. You can slave over a song until you get it right, or you can capture the feeling that pushed you to write it in the first place and move on. Anton taught me the freedom of choosing between the two. You can see both in his work, even in his earliest demos, where you can tell he just wants to hear what he sounds like.

There's a lot of space in those recordings, a lot of room to dream, and a certain dream came true for me when I crossed over into the real world of the band, someplace else unknown, in my quest to learn that rock'n'roll is a valuable and dangerous tradition, and why Anton is one of its greatest progenitors.

For Anton, learning to play and record in San Francisco set the stage for everything after. His project would almost singlehandedly revive the 60s aesthetic for the American underground in ways nobody expected or asked for. Then, thanks to a loving, inspired support network, his band got to the next level, and then another level, one hard step at time.

With the move to Los Angeles came a new aesthetic and mission. A young filmmaker became fascinated by him, and for a few short years went on a wild ride with an unceasingly revolving cast of musicians, record executives, managers, booking agents, hangers-on, hipsters, girls, wannabes, and burn outs. Stifled by drugs, self-sabotage, and violence, the band she filmed imploded, but it was a flash of time.

Anton was left to pick up the pieces, time and time again, for the past twenty-five years, and here we are, still listening, because the music is incredible. At time of writing, the most recent record Anton has put out is *Something Else*, and there's supposed to be another full-length coming soon, simply titled *Brian Jonestown Massacre*. I'm really looking forward to it, and to discovering what the new live lineup is going to sound like with all the new players. I've been working on this book for ten years. Now I just want to enjoy the music.

I anticipate that my BJM saga will fall short for some while exceeding others' expectations, but in my heart I know I have done my best. I am fully aware that my work does not account for every little tidbit of Brian Jonestown Massacre legend, apocrypha, or trivia floating around out there. That's fine. I believe in every word I've written, every word given to me, and I feel I have achieved what I set out to do. It's one thing to say *Keep Music Evil* and another thing to do it. So with that, Dear Reader, it's about time for me to sign off, as I have records to make. I'm finishing one now, Gorky's *Mathemagician*, and I can't wait to share it with the world. I think it's the best music I've ever made, and it's purely in the spirit of rock'n'roll!

I also have films to make. In the summer of 2018, I was accepted into the David Lynch Graduate School of Cinematic Arts at the Maharishi University of Management for its MFA in Screenwriting program. At MUM, they teach you a simple technique called Transcendental Meditation, which the

Maharishi himself taught to The Beatles and others back in 1968, which led to the creation of the *White Album*, which if you ask me is their best one. (It used to be Revolver, but after learning TM and hearing its influence on the *White Album*, that one just takes the cake.)

T.M. is excellent for reducing stress and improving creativity. It resets your nervous system, expands your consciousness, and puts you really 'into the zone.' For me, my first time doing TM was a lot like taking LSD when I heard the BJM for the first time, but with TM, unlike acid, there are no weird side effects. It was the most psychedelic experience I've ever had, and I would recommend every creative person find a qualified teacher and learn it. Only good could come from it.

Filmmaking appeals to me because it requires all of the creative cylinders in the brain to buzz on the same level—the visuals, the writing, the music. You also can't do everything yourself, and the potential for collaboration on such projects is appealing to me. You need a team of people who have your back, just like a band.

Right now, I am working on a fictional, music-based feature called *In The Land Of Good Oaks*, which features a soundtrack of songs that I've written in a retro-country vein, very much unlike the other Gorky records out, and there's a bit of psych folk in there, too. Some of the songs on *Thank God For Mental Illness* and *Bringing It All Back Home—Again* definitely influenced part of the music, though I wouldn't say it sounds like the BJM. The spec screenplay is finished, and I'm in love with it. It's about a fictional outlaw country singer named Rhys Diaz who battles for his soul as he writes the record that will land him the deal of his dreams. That's all I'm going to say about it for now. I'm sure some bits of the BJM saga floated up into the story and the character of Rhys, but there's much more to it. Stay tuned on that front.

289

Still, I can't deny that working on and writing the Brian Jonestown Massacre story has influenced my life profoundly, maybe even changed things for the better. Today is fifteen years to the day of when *Dig!* premiered at Sundance. Everything I've learned from Anton, the BJM, and their friends over the years has guided me immensely in how to approach and execute my creative pursuits, and if you, the reader, consider yourself a creative person, I encourage you to do the same. Make art every day, and don't try to imitate anyone or seek validation through others. Do your own thing, and if people dig it, they dig it. If they don't, they don't. Simple as that. Don't let it stop you, and don't quit. Keep working at it. By being creative, you are making things that others can find meaning in their own lives through, people you don't even know, and that's a beautiful thing.

The BJM story isn't over—and thank God for that—but my time carrying their lantern is. So with that, Dear Reader, I hang up the lantern and leave you with a common adieu shared among a many BJM fans:

Keep the faith, baby!!!

Jesse Valencia
January 18, 2019

ACKNOWLEDGMENTS

This book is dedicated foremost to my best friend Shizuko, my partner in crime who accompanied me on many of my BJM adventures, and has been my #1 supporter through the past decade.

Additional thanks are due to The Brian Jonestown Massacre and their friends and associates, both living and deceased, for sharing their stories with me; also thanks to Ondi Timoner for making *Dig!*, and The Dandy Warhols for their friendship. Thanks to Nigel Osborne, Tom Seabrook, and everyone at Jawbone Press for believing in this project; to Kip Kouri, Leslie Cuc, and everyone Tell All Your Friends PR for all of their support; to my bandmates Ben Holladay, Tevin Crabdree, and Benjamin Turner in GORKY for the wonderful music we make together, and the times we've shared both as friends and brothers (and double that thanks to our fans and supporters!); to Dr. Nicole Walker and all of my professors and fellow students in the Northern Arizona University MFA Creative Writing program for helping me learn how to write this thing (shout out to my MFA crew Kama O'Connor, Stacy Murison, Jesse Sensibar, Eric Susak, Emily Heinrich, Christine Davis, Levi Stallings, Angele Anderfuren, Case Duckworth, Rachel Stevens, Kimberly Kaylene, Katie Johansen, and Tobby Moran); thanks to Greg Gerding, Eve Connell, and Isobel O'Hare at University of Hell Press for the good head start; to Alexandra Tselios and *The Big Smoke* for giving me a platform; and to Lanny Croney, Teddy Croney, Jerry Croney, and all of my friends and associates at WME Theatres.

This book is also dedicated to my close friends and family, whom I love dearly, to my mentors and fellow students at the David Lynch Graduate School of Cinematic Arts at MUM (shout out to my screenwriting group Edie Casille, Jimmy Clabots, Shawn Maus, Jodi Berenger, A.J. Ciccotelli, my mentor Antonia Ellis, and the program leaders, Erika Richards, Amine Kouider, and Dorothy Rompalske); to David Lynch with infinite thanks for his advice and guidance as I go into this exciting new chapter of my life; to everyone else who has helped me along this trying but rewarding journey; and to His Holiness the Maharishi Mahesh Yogi for sharing the gift of Transcendental Meditation with the world, with a special thanks to the David Lynch Foundation for their role in continuing his work.

If there is anyone I did not name here, you are not forgotten, and I thank you for the special role, however big or small, you've had in my life and in this journey. I love you all. Together I hope that we, through the gifts of art and inspiration, may bring greater peace and stability to the world.

Unless otherwise stated, all quotations in this book are taken from the author's interviews.

NOTES AND SOURCES

AUTHOR INTERVIEWS

Aaron Axelsen (email, July 2016)

Aaron Frankel (telephone, August 2016)

Adam Hamilton (telephone, July 2016)

Adam Le Blanc (email, June 2016)

Adam Shore (telephone, June–July 2016)

Adrienne Gulyassy (email, August 2016)

Alain Bosshart (Facebook, December 2016)

Alexander Mann (Facebook, December 2011)

Amine Ramer (telephone, July 2016)

Arabella Proffer (Facebook, May 2016)

Arik Ohlson (Facebook, August 2016)

Asia Argento (email, Aug 2017)

Barry Simons (in person, April 2012)

Bev Davies (Facebook, October 2011– December 2012)

Billy Pleasant (Facebook, May–August 2016)

Brad Artley (telephone, June 2011; Facebook, May 2015–December 2016)

Brad Clark (telephone, July 2016)

Brant Graff (Facebook, May 2011)

Brian Glaze (email, March 2010)

Charles Mehling (telephone, July 2016, January 2017; Facebook, December 2011–May 2016)

Chelsea Starr (Facebook/email, September 2011)

Chris Arvan (telephone, July 2016)

Chris Barrus (Facebook, September 2011)

Chris Dupre (email, May 2016)

Chris Reid (Facebook, July 2012)

Chris Strouth (email, October 2011)

Christian Omar Madrigal Izzo (Facebook, May 2016)

Christof Certik (telephone, summer 2010)

Clay Andrews (Facebook, July 2015)

Colleen Jetton (email, December 2011, August 2012/Facebook, July 2011)

Courtney Taylor-Taylor (telephone, March 2016; email, February 2016–July 2017)

Craig Dyer (email, January 2017)

Crystal Apel (Facebook, May 2016)

Dale Bookout (Telephone, December 2016)

Dallas Taylor (email, July 2011)

Daniel 'Bowerbird' Koontz (email, January 2017)

Daniel Knop (telephone, August 2016)

Dave Deresinski (Facebook/telephone, September 2014)

David Nelson (email, December 2016)

Dawn Thomas (email, June 2010)

Dean Taylor (telephone, September 2016; Facebook, June–July 2011)

Del Beaudry (telephone, October 2010/ Facebook, May 2011–June 2015)

Dennis Pelowski (email, March 2017; telephone, May 2017)

Derek Hoeckel (Facebook, May 2016)

Diane Perry (telephone, January 2017)

Doug Gillard (telephone, February 2017)

Ed Harcourt (email, March 2012)

Elise Pearson (telephone, July 2016; email, July 2012/Facebook, June 2015–April 2016)

Eliza Karmasalo (email, March 2012)

Elizabeth Dye (email, August 2017)

Elizabeth Palmer (Facebook, July 2012)

Erika Petty (Facebook, August–December 2016)

eufloria* (telephone, summer/fall 2010)

Felix Bondarev (Facebook, April 2016)

Frankie Emerson (telephone, September 2016)

Graham Bonnar (Facebook, February 2011–May 2016)

Greg Derfer (Facebook, December 2011–August 2016)

Greg Gutfeld (email, February 2015)

Hannah (Email, September 2016)

Hunter Crowley (Facebook, May 2016)

James Mervine (Facebook, June 2016)

Jason Consoli (email, May 2015)

Jean-Paul Ligion (Facebook, October 2011)

Jeff Davies (telephone, January 2017)

Jennifer Brandon (email, October 2011; telephone, April 2017)

Jennifer Chiba (Facebook, May 2011)

Jennifer Shagawat (telephone, December 2016)

Jesse Frankel (Facebook, January 2012)

Joel Gion (Facebook, April 2011–May 2013; in person, April 2012)

Jón Sæmundur Auðarson (email, July 2010)

Jonathan Sachs (telephone, June 2018)

Jorge Diaz de Bedoya (email, July 2016; Facebook, October 2011)

Josephine Tavares (Facebook, June 2015)

Josie Fluri (telephone, July 2016)

Jussi Tegelman (email, July 2010)

Justine Penklis (Facebook, July 2016)

Kate Fuqua (telephone, December 2016)

Krista Crews (Facebook, September 2016)

Kurt B. Reighley (email, July 2016)

Larry Thrasher (email, March 2010)

Lenny Pops (Facebook, June 2010)

Luella Jane Wright (Facebook, December 2011)

Lynn Butta (Email, October 2016)

Mara Keagle (telephone/Facebook, December 2016)

Marina Chavez (telephone, July 2016)

Mark Chalecki (Facebook, July 2016)

Mark Dutton (telephone, November 2016)

Matt Hollywood (in person, September 2015)

Matthew J. Tow (Facebook, June 2010)

Megan Pickerel (Facebook, May 2016)

Michael Dutcher (telephone, September 2016)

Michael Sjobeck (Facebook, December 2011–December 2012)

Micole Skertic (Facebook, October 2016)

Mike Kubisty (email, September 2016)

Milo Warner Martin (Facebook, May 2016)

Miranda Lee Richards (email, June 2015/ telephone, October 2016)

Miranda Morton-Yap (telephone, August 2016)

Nancy Friedberg (telephone, August 2016)

Naut Humon (telephone, summer–fall 2010)

Nick Sjobeck (email, September 2016)

Nina Ritter (email, September 2017)

Ondi Timoner (telephone, April 2016)

Paola Simmonds (Facebook, November 2010–January 2017)

Paul Burgess (email, August 2016)

Peter Hayes (telephone, September 2010)

Pseu Braun (telephone, December 2016)

Raugust (email, March 2012)

Raymond Richards (email, June 2012)

Rick Maymi (Facebook, February 2013–February 2016)

Robert Cherry (email, April 2016)

Robert Desmond (email, November 2012)

Samuel Knee (Facebook, August 2017)

Sandy Wilson (Facebook, May 2016)

Sarah Jane McKinley (email, March 2012)

Scott Pollack (telephone, October 2016)

Sean Curran (Facebook, May 2015, May 2016)

Sean Worrall (email, June 2016)

Sonia Pacheco (Facebook, May 2016)

Tom Kayser (text message, May 2016)

Tommy Dietrick (email, June–November 2010)

Tony O'Neill (telephone, September 2016)
Tony Scalzo (Facebook, August 2017)
Travis Threlkel (Skype, June 2016)
Tres Warren (Email, February 2017)
Troy DeGroot (telephone, August 2016; Facebook, October 2011)

Victoria Byers (Facebook, February 2011– August 2016)
Zia McCabe (Facebook, February 2016)
Zora-Lux Burden (Facebook, September 2011)
Zy Lyn (Facebook, May 2016)

BOOKS AND LINER NOTES
Tim Burgess, *Tim Book Two: Vinyl Adventures From Istanbul To San Francisco* (Faber, 2017)
Mary Huhn and Brian Glaze, liner notes to *Tepid Peppermint Wonderland* (Tee Pee, 2004)

Harvey Kubernik and Scott Calamar, *Canyon Of Dreams: The Magic & The Music Of Laurel Canyon* (Sterling, 2009)
Anton Newcombe, liner notes to *Spacegirl & Other Favourites* (Candy Floss, 1995)
—, liner notes to *Love* EP (Tangible, 1998)

FILMS AND MUSIC VIDEOS
Black Rebel Motorcycle Club, 'Spread Your Love.' Directed by Charles Mehling, 2001.
Brian Jonestown Massacre, 'Going To Hell.' Directed by Ondi Timoner, 1998.
—, 'When Jokers Attack.' Directed by Charles Mehling, 2003.

Dig! Directed by Ondi Timoner. Palm Pictures, 2005.
My Dinner With Jimi. Directed by Howard Kaylan. Rhino Films/Fallout Entertainment, 2003.
Supersonic. Directed by Mat Whitecross. A24/Entertainment One, 2016.

ONLINE AUDIO/VIDEO
'Anton Newcombe (Excerpt Of A 2003 Interview With WFMU).' Aluson Camus. YouTube.
'Anton Newcombe Interview, NYC Rooftop.' *Dig!* Bonus content. YouTube.
'Anton Newcombe With The Black Angels Part 1.' YouTube.
'BJM Happy Birthday Joel Gion 20.11.06.' YouTube.
'BJM Therapy Session.' YouTube.
'Brian Jonestown Massacre Terminal 5 New York City.' YouTube.
'Brian Jonestown Massacre—1993 Peacock Lounge SF, CA.' SoundCloud.
'Brian Jonestown Massacre—2002 Interview Part 1 and 2.' YouTube.
'Brian Jonestown Massacre—2016-06-01—Phoenix—Audio Only—Full Show.' YouTube.

'Brian Jonestown Massacre—Anton vs. Vancouver!' YouTube.
'Brian Jonestown Massacre. Anton Freaking Out.' YouTube.
'Dandys & BJM—Oh Lord (Austin Psych Fest 7).' YouTube.
'Let's Go Fucking Mental.' YouTube.
'Lorraine Leckie And Her Demons Dirty Old Town.' YouTube.
'Paris—The Devil Made Me Do It.' YouTube.
'The Brian Jonestown Massacre—Live At Liquid Room 1999 (Audio).' YouTube.
'The Brian Jonestown Massacre/Ride—Drive Blind.' YouTube.
'The Libertines, Live @ The North Star Bar in Philadelphia, PA.' YouTube.
'The Out Crowd Live.' YouTube.

PRINT MEDIA

AU Review
BAM
Beat Magazine
Billboard
Chart Attack
Chicago Tribune
CMJ New Music Report
Creative Loafing
Daily Collegian
Daily Telegraph
Entertainment Weekly
Expressen
Free Williamsburg
Gigwise
Guardian
Hear

Independent
International Business Times
Jerusalem Post
Kansas City Pitch
LA Record
LA Weekly
Los Angeles Times
Louder Than War
Magnet
New York
New York Times
Nightshift
NME
OC Weekly
Paste
Phoenix New Times

Reykjavik Grapevine
Rolling Stone
San Francisco Chronicle
SF Weekly
Spin
Stereo Embers
The Stranger
Sydney Morning Herald
Time Out London
Tucson Weekly
Under The Radar
USA Today
Valley Advocate
Vendetta Magazine
Westword
Willamette Week

WEBSITES

alchetron.com
allmusic.com
amoeba.com
avclub.com
bbc.com
beermelodies.com
billboard.com
brooklynvegan.com
consequenceofsound.net
courthousenews.com
ctkme.com
dailyrindblog.com
dandywarhols.com
deirdrecorley.com
der.org
dictionary.com
digitalspy.co.uk
drownedinsound.com
envrak.fr
exclaim.ca

freemusicarchive.org
gorkytheband.com
imdb.com
indiewire.com
inmusicwetrust.co.uk
interpunk.com
iofilm.com
jambands.com
jambase.com
laist.com
law360.com
leftlion.co.uk
lostatsea.net
mtv.com
music-news.com
noisey.vice.com
organart.demon.co.uk
outsideleft.com
pitchfork.com
popmatters.com

portalrockpress.br
prefixmag.com
profiles-sc-ctsi.org
rand.org
reuters.com
robertcherry.com
skiddle.com
slant.com
slate.com
smh.com.au
sputnikmusic.com
stereogum.com
stylusmagazine.com
tascam.com
thebaybridged.com
thequietus.com
thevpme.com
underexposed.org.uk
wfmu.org

295

ENDNOTES

INTROESQUE

'I'm into the whole …' Ben Vendetta, *Vendetta Magazine*, 1998

'I'm interesting in creating …' Kayla Clancy, jambands.com, September 15, 2016

'There was the interesting …' Paul Lester, *Guardian*, May 14, 2014

'99 percent … dealing with love …' David Brinn, *Jerusalem Post*, June 6, 2012

'[We've] always had that …' Paul Lester, *Guardian*, May 14, 2014

CHAPTER 1

'I listened to Jimi …' Kayla Clancy, jambands.com, September 15, 2016

'When you look at …' Kayla Clancy, jambands.com, September 15, 2016

'He always treated me …' Paul Lester, *Guardian*, May 14, 2014

'My mom kind of …' Paul Lester, *Guardian*, May 14, 2014

'He was the weird …' Nick Schou, *OC Weekly*, December 21, 2006

'terrible … tenacious as hell …' Nick Schou, *OC Weekly*, December 21, 2006

'I've got video tapes …' Ben Vendetta, *Vendetta Magazine*, 1998

'It was always the …' Nick Schou, *OC Weekly*, December 21, 2006

'The costume doesn't matter …' Kayla Clancy, jambands.com, September 15, 2016

'I never wanted permission …' Marie Wood, *Drowned In Sound*, January 10, 2017

CHAPTER 2

'They fucking destroyed …' Will Reisman, *Bay Bridged*, May 23, 2016

'Sure enough, Tony would …' Nick Schou, *OC Weekly*, December 21, 2006

'I was homeless …' Anton Newcombe, MySpace blog post, 2009–10

'Joel was living with …' Anton Newcombe, MySpace blog post, 2009–10

'Listen to the words …' Anton Newcombe, *Tepid Peppermint Wonderland* liner notes, 2004

'In all of those …' Gregg Foreman, *Psychic Gloss Magazine*, 2014

'I was in hospital …' Paul Lester, *Guardian*, May 14, 2014

'We were just taking …' Gregg Foreman, *Psychic Gloss Magazine*, 2014

'After the show he …' Anton Newcombe, MySpace blog post, 2009–10

'Next time we were …' Anton Newcombe, MySpace blog post, 2009–10

'One afternoon I sat …' Alan Herrick, internetalbemuth.blogspot.com, January 3, 2011

'It's a demo tape.' Anton Newcombe, YouTube comment, August 19, 2012

'Anton worked then …' Brant Graff, Keep Music Evil forum post, June 30, 2008

CHAPTER 3

'It took Shaw over …' Anton Newcombe, *Spacegirl & Other Favourites* liner notes, 1995

'I got a straight job …' Miranda Morton-Yap, BJM tour documents, July 1998

'I was dating this girl ...' Miranda Morton-Yap, BJM tour documents, July 1998

'Somewhere in this mountain ...' 'I.P. Freely's Anti-Demo Column.' *Ben Is Dead*, March 1, 1992

'What attracted me to ...' Miranda Morton-Yap. BJM tour documents, July 1998

'It sounded like it ...' Greg Shaw, *Vendetta Magazine*, 1998

'She used to work ...' Anton Newcombe, *Spacegirl & Other Favourites* liner notes, 1995

CHAPTER 4

'They tried to put ...' Gregg Foreman, *Psychic Gloss Magazine*, 2014

'Naut let me have ...' Anton Newcombe, *Spacegirl & Other Favourites* liner notes, 1995

'I wrote that in ...' Anton Newcombe, MySpace blog post, 2009–10

CHAPTER 5

'At some point I ...' Anton Newcombe, MySpace blog post, 2009–10

'The actual lead sound ...' Anton Newcombe, MySpace blog post, 2009–10

'When Travis and I ...' Gregg Foreman, *Psychic Gloss Magazine*, 2014

'We almost were signed ...' Richard Bloomer, pmtonline.co.uk, October 8, 2015

'If I remember correctly ...' Matt Hollywood, Keep Music Evil forum post, January 28, 2011

'In reality, what begat ...' Peter Kember, *Pitchfork*, October 24, 2016

CHAPTER 6

'Me, Matt, and Mara ...' Anton Newcombe, MySpace blog post, 2009–10

'That song is not ...' Anton Newcombe, MySpace blog post, 2009–10

'It was unbelievable to ...' Brian Glaze, *Tepid Peppermint Wonderland* liner notes

CHAPTER 7

'When I joined ...' Miss Ess, *Amoeblog*, May 9, 2008

'I was looking up ...' Kelly Osato, *Amoeblog*, May 4, 2011

'Suzy was based on ...' Wayne Hoffman, *Billboard*, July 28, 2001

'To this day, I ...' Leanne Maxwell, *SFist*, August 27, 2010

'We're playing with Oasis!' Bill Crandall, *BAM*, September 20, 1996

'We recorded *Take It* ...' Gregg Foreman, *Psychic Gloss Magazine*, 2014

'I used to love ...' Gregg Foreman, *Psychic Gloss Magazine*, 2014

'I met Courtney ...' Anton Newcombe, MySpace blog post, 2009–10

'Larry [Thrasher] was interested ...' Gregg Foreman, *Psychic Gloss Magazine*, 2014

'Somehow a conversation started ...' Gregg Foreman, *Psychic Gloss Magazine*, 2014

'December's Children nuts and ...' John Fortunado, *Beer Melodies*, May 29, 2009

'Larry Thrasher has a ...' Anton Newcombe, MySpace blog post, 2009–10

'Matt was living in ...' Anton Newcombe, MySpace blog post, 2009–10

'Great solo from Dean ...' Anton Newcombe, MySpace blog post, 2009–10

'Way better than Eric ...' Anton Newcombe, MySpace blog post, 2009–10

'I remember it sounded ...' Anton Newcombe, YouTube comment, October 27, 2010

'I wanted unexpected …' Shirley Halperin and Merle Ginsberg, *Hollywood Reporter*, September 25, 2011

'Two or three or …' Chris Ziegler, *OC Weekly*, May 11, 2012

CHAPTER 8

'A beer and a …' David Mansdorf, *Losing Today*, March 31, 2005

'The title came about …' Chris Toenes, *Indy Week*, August 3, 2005

'The joke is …' Anton Newcombe, MySpace blog post, 2009–10

CHAPTER 9

'Sophie and I were …' Anton Newcombe, MySpace blog post, 2009–10

'It's not like we …' Alex Steininger, *In Music We Trust*, June 1, 1998

'I met Harry …' Zia McCabe, Facebook post, September 16, 2017

'More in response to …' Ben Vendetta, *Vendetta Magazine*, 1998

'What Ray Davies of …' Anton Newcombe, MySpace blog post, 2009–10

CHAPTER 10

'Courtney went back to …' Ben Vendetta, *Vendetta Magazine*, 1998

'I was busking on …' Anton Newcombe, MySpace blog post, 2009–10

CHAPTER 11

'We rented a U-Haul …' Alex Steininger, In Music We Trust, June 1, 1998

CHAPTER 12

'He bought all these …' Bob Ardley, *Daily Rind*, October 23, 2014

'thought that the Manson thing …' Sara Scribner, *Phoenix New Times*, September 9, 1999

'If it were a bigger …' Alex Steininger, *In*

Music We Trust, June 1, 1998

'It's an observation on this …' John Fortunado, *Beer Melodies*, May 29, 2009

'It's difficult to record …' David Brinn, *Jerusalem Post*, June 6, 2012

'Neither Anton nor I made …' Matt Hollywood, *Committee To Keep Music Evil* forum post, January 28, 2010

'He was not a very nice …' Paul Lester, *Guardian*, May 14, 2014

'[Matt] thought it was …' Ben Vendetta, *Vendetta Magazine*, 1998

'We don't need therapy …' Alex Steininger, *In Music We Trust*, June 1, 1998

'Why would they …' Miranda Morton-Yap, BJM tour documents, July 1998

CHAPTER 13

'I was saying, Please …' Paul Lester, *Guardian*, May 14, 2014

CHAPTER 14

'I made [Peter] play …' Robert Cherry, robertcherry.com, 2001

'We tried to do more …' Sean Worrall, organart.demon.co.uk, April 19, 2004

'I don't feel ashamed …' James Montgomery, *MTV News*, September 30, 2005

CHAPTER 15

'It was sick …' Nick Schou, *OC Weekly*, December 21, 2006

'I could tell it was …' Ben Vendetta, *Rock'n'roll Runner*, May 21, 2016

'This is the best …' Tom Murphy, *Westword*, March 8, 2013

'Whatever money was left …' Robert Cherry, robertcherry.com, 2001

'I used alcohol to get …' Louis Pattison, *Wondering Sound*, May 19, 2014

'In the last couple …' John Fortunado, *Beer Melodies*, May 29, 2009

'If you had seen ...' Ben Vendetta, *Rock'n'roll Runner*, May 21, 2016

'San Francisco was already ...' Ben Vendetta, *Rock'n'roll Runner*, May 21, 2016

'Great lady, she's been down ...' Anton Newcombe, MySpace blog post, 2009–10

CHAPTER 16

'TVT gave me a lot ...' Robert Cherry, robertcherry.com, 2001

'That's him and The Go ...' Anton Newcombe, MySpace blog post, 2009–10

'He deserves a little ...' Nolan Gawron, bjmarchives.com, January 22, 2002

'Though Newcombe was hardly ...' Jeff Jarrett, *University News*, March 7, 2002

'We've known Anton and Jeff ...' Derek Phillips, *Glorious Noise*, March 19, 2002

'When you're in my ...' Robert Cherry, robertcherry.com, 2001

CHAPTER 17

'Newcombe was arrested last week ...' John Luerssen, *Billboard*, March 15, 2002

'It looked like Altamont ...' Mary Beth Crain, *LA Weekly*, March 20, 2002

'The band don't really ...' Elise Pearson, email to Sean Worrall, October 30, 2002

'The plan was that ...' Sean Worrall, organart.demon.co.uk, April 19, 2004

'We are a great band ...' John Fortunado, *Beer Melodies*, May 29, 2009

CHAPTER 18

'[That] was fun ...' Craig Mathieson, *Sydney Morning Herald*, December 3, 2004

'Some of our gear ...' Zy Lyn, Facebook post, April 10, 2017

CHAPTER 19

'A film like *Dig!* ...' Alexis Petridis, *Guardian*, July 1, 2004

'I was sitting in ...' Craig Mathieson, *Sydney Morning Herald*, December 3, 2004

'I heard some stories ...' Craig Mathieson, *Sydney Morning Herald*, December 3, 2004

'If universities ever start ...' A.O. Scott, *New York Times*, October 1, 2004

'He's kept us centered ...' Wendy Mitchell, *IndieWire*, October 5, 2004

'It's when the music ...' David Marchese, *PopMatters*, November 16, 2004

'The film tells a story ...' Peter Lindbald, *Lost At Sea*, March 21, 2005

'He lashes out at me ...' Neil Young, *City Life*, March 31, 2005

'It was the only place ...' Craig Mathieson, *Sydney Morning Herald*, December 3, 2004

'I knew Dan ...' Whitney Pastorek, *Entertainment Weekly*, November 25, 2005

'There was a point when ...' Aidin Vaziri, *SF Gate*, April 16, 2005

'I wasn't quite ready...' Aidin Vaziri, *SF Gate*, April 16, 2005

'It's still fun ...' Miss Ess, *Amoeblog*, May 9, 2008

'It isn't about my fame ...' Sylvie Simmons, *Guardian*, June 9, 2005

'A fucking great band!' Pascal Sanchez, *Thrasher*, September 2005

'The best day of my life ...' Dave Depares, davestuff79.blogspot.com, July 4, 2005

CHAPTER 20

'I don't have a career ...' Andrew Perry, *Telegraph*, July 5, 2009

'Anton wasn't happy with it ...' Alex Steinlinger, *In Music We Trust*, August 17, 2005

'Let's cut the shit …' Chris Haire, *Tucson Weekly*, August 11, 2005

'From a distance …' Matthew Murphy, *Pitchfork*, December 8, 2004

'Do you mean Pierre Henry?' Anton Newcombe, psychicgraffiti.blogspot.com, April 20, 2012

'A "fuck you" to …' Anton Newcombe, MySpace blog post, 2009–10

'We expected a little more …' Vincent Le Deouff, *Pop News*, January 2005

'I was sued for …' Jane Rocca, *Beat Magazine*, September 5, 2008

'He laughed it off …' Bart Cameron, Reykjavik Grapevine, July 16, 2006

'I'm just a normal …' Bart Cameron, Reykjavik Grapevine, July 16, 2006

'*Dig!* or no *Dig!* …' Florence Gohard, *LeftLion*, November 10, 2006

CHAPTER 21

'It was … apparent …' Julia Yepes, *PopMatters*, December 19, 2006

'With the BJM …' Jim Guittard, jimguittard.com, March 16, 2007

'I had a lot going on …' Jane Rocca, *Beat Magazine*, September 5, 2008

'We were in New York …' Emma Garland, *Noisey*, April 23, 2014

'I very much wanted …' Frank Valish, *Under The Radar*, September 4, 2012

'The neo-classical piece …' Jo Vallance, *Room Thirteen*, February 16, 2008

'I flew Mark to Iceland …' Alastair Ross, *Cheese On Toast*, October 29, 2015

'People were throwing …' Straightjacket Kiss, finestkiss.wordpress.com, September 9, 2007

'I love Elsa …' Anton Newcombe, YouTube comment, 2008

'She doesn't make records …' Anton Newcombe, YouTube comment, 2010

'On *My Bloody Underground* …' Ajitpaul Mangat, *Tiny Mix Tapes*, May 2008

'The album often sounds …' David Raposa, *Pitchfork*, May 8, 2008

'Newcombe's genius is palpable …' Alan Ranta, *PopMatters*, April 18, 2008

'I want to express …' Yousif Nur, *Rock Feedback*, April 9, 2008

'It's a big circle …' Katie Knaub, *Chicago Innerview*, February 29, 2008

CHAPTER 22

'There are only 300,000 …' Jo Vallance, *Room Thirteen*, February 16, 2008

'These things do happen …' Adam Bychawski, *NME*, July 17, 2008

'if we don't …' Miss Ess, *Amoeblog*, May 9, 2008

'Chris performed with his …' Girl About Town, phillygirlabouttown.com, July 28, 2008

'I really want to explore …' Ozgur Cokyuce, *Punk Globe*, July 2008

'I took an antibiotic …' Julian Marszalek, *Quietus*, February 9, 2010

'Alcohol was easier to qut …' Louis Pattinson, *Wondering Sound*, May 19, 2014

'I'm more interested in …' Wilfred Brandt, *HEAR*, May 9, 2012

'That's why I'm interested …' Bradley Garner, *Skiddle*, March 3, 2016

'The crowd started singing …' Julian Marszalek, *Quietus*, February 9, 2010

'Music is a very physical …' Deirdre Corley, *Swallow Magazine*, 2008

'I detuned the guitar …' Anton Newcombe, YouTube comment, 2010

'How do you know …' Anton Newcombe, Twitter post, June 22, 2015

'I wanted to see …' Julian Marszalek, *Quietus*, February 9, 2010

'I had the best …' Frank Valish, *Under The Radar*, September 4, 2012

'I thought it would've …' Greg Percifield, gregpercifield.com, April 13, 2012

'I have a hard time ...' Jef Rouner, *Houston Press*, July 16, 2012

'It isn't lo-fi ...' Anton Newcombe, YouTube comment, 2010

'I'm being silly ...' Tom Murphy, *Westword*, May 8, 2012

'It is difficult sonically ...' Anton Newcombe, YouTube comment, 2010

'It was based on ...' Paul Lester, *Guardian*, May 14, 2014

'The sense of belonging ...' Len Comaratta, *Consequence Of Sound*, May 3, 2012

CHAPTER 23

'I liked each track ...' Carl Stanley, *Louder Than War*, February 11, 2014

'I have to look out ...' Christopher Hollow, *Taste In Music*, November 12, 2013

'The simplest answer is ...' Michael Cimaomo, *Valley Advocate*, September 23, 2014

'Anton and I were ...' Paul Gleason, *Stereo Embers*, March 16, 2015

'So I hit her up ...' Paul Gleason, *Stereo Embers*, March 16, 2015

'In the back of ...' Paul Gleason, *Stereo Embers*, March 16, 2015

'I expected definite characters ...' John Platt, *Line Of Best Fit*, April 21, 2015

'Matt Hollywood's doing ...' Dom Gourlay, *Drowned In Sound*, September 21, 2015

'I'll miss hanging out ...' Troy Farah, *Phoenix New Times*, September 23, 2015

'Frankie had a really ...' Dom Gourlay, *Drowned In Sound*, September 21, 2015

301

PHOTO CREDITS

The photographs in this book came from the following sources, and we are grateful for their help. If you feel there has been a mistaken attribution, please contact the publishers. **Front cover** Bev Davies. **Back cover** *from top* Dawn Thomas, Charles Mehling, Brad Artley, Tim Herremans. **Author photo** Jim Louvau. **First insert** *early 90s performance, Black Rose, Peacock Lounge (7 images total)*, Helen Gardner; *mid-90s performance, Anton and friends (9)*, Dawn Thomas; *Anton performing 1997* Jennifer Brandon. **Second insert** *Dig!, Jeff Davies*, Jennifer Brandon; *Brad*, Kate Fuqua; *Runyon Canyon, Dandy Warhols*, Bob Berg/Getty Images; *Mehling-era lineup (4)*, Charles Mehling; *mid-2000s lineup (7)*, Erika Petty. **Third insert** *2005–07 lineup (8)*, Bev Davies; *Manchester 2012*, Steve Thorne/Redferns; *Matt*, Marc Broussely/Redferns; *Field Day (2)*, Emma Aylett; *Fonda Theatre (5)*, Tim Herremans. All posters and flyers courtesy of Tim Herremans.

INDEX

306

ALSO AVAILABLE IN PRINT AND EBOOK EDITIONS FROM JAWBONE PRESS